"This book, *Acts for the Everyday Christian*, by Ted Stubbersfield is a must-read book for every Christian who seeks to know more about the origins of Christianity and the teachings of Paul and others at this time. This book explains in readily understood terms how the book of Acts connects the Gospels to the Epistles that form what is called the New Testament in the Bible. I have read a number of religious books by this author, and I find this book to be another well-researched and heartfelt treatise about how special and significant a Christian faith is in today's troubled world."

—RALPH BAILEY,
Architect

"Ted is an excellent writer and his book on Acts hits the mark from so many points of view. His commentary is not bogged down in trivialities but presents the message of acts in a clear easily readable style but without simplifying matters."

—DAN TINGLEY,
Senior Wood Technology/Structural Engineer,
Wood Research and Development

"This very accessible commentary on the Book of Acts is the happy fruit of untiring research, pastoral sensitivity, and entirely trustworthy theology. Ted Stubbersfield hopes to assist us in our study of Acts so that it 'awakens an ache for a similar encounter with the Spirit.' It is the Trinitarian God we keep encountering here, including the risen life of Jesus now active in the mission of his followers, and the sovereignty of God evident in the unrelenting advance of the Gospel."

—STUART PIGGIN,
Conjoint Associate Professor of History, Macquarie University

"Edgar's Acts commentary is hard to put down. It informs and inspires. It brings the book of Acts alive speaking to our contemporary circumstances. It is a must for any individual or group who wants to grow in understanding the mission of the early Christian church empowered by the Holy Spirit. Edgar gives a clear explanation of our risen Lord working through his chosen servants. Edgar provides insightful contextual historical references and relevant Biblical cross references which add understanding. This commentary will inspire and encourage readers in their faith, as they seek to witness to and serve their Lord in the current environment. Many people are open to the new life and hope which is the gift of our risen Lord and Savior Jesus Christ."

—NOEL NOACK,
Bishop Emeritus, Lutheran Church of Australia

"*Acts for the Everyday Christian* is another fascinating book by Ted Stubbersfield. I have been in his home, and he has been in mine, and we together have been out blazing trails in jungle areas of the world. He has been involved in church life, both in the structured sophisticated western world—and also in the unstructured, undeveloped cultures of the world. This book will help us all the part of Acts chapter 29!"

—FREDERICK VANCE KORNIS JR.,
Founder, Heartland International Ministries

"I enjoy reading Edgar's books and it's probably been said many times. His observations of Christians on their journey with God has reflected many of my life experiences. Edgar has a gift of sharing in a way easy to understand—you don't need to be a theologian. *Acts for the Everyday Christian* takes you back to the experiences of the early church and in doing so challenges and encourages the reader. God Bless Edgar."

—TREVOR BURSTOW,
Company Director, T. S. Burstow

Acts for the Everyday Christian

Acts for the Everyday Christian

EDGAR STUBBERSFIELD

WIPF & STOCK · Eugene, Oregon

ACTS FOR THE EVERYDAY CHRISTIAN

Wipf & Stock
An Imprint of Wipf and Stock Publishers
199 W. 8th Ave., Suite 3
Eugene, OR 97401

www.wipfandstock.com

PAPERBACK ISBN: 978-1-6667-8388-9
HARDCOVER ISBN: 978-1-6667-8389-6
EBOOK ISBN: 978-1-6667-8390-2

VERSION NUMBER 02/25/26

Contents

Abbreviations

Ag.	*Agamemnon*
Ag. Ap.	*Against Apion*
Anarch.	*Anacharsis*
ANF	*The Ante-Nicene Fathers*
Ann.	*Annales*
Ant.	*Jewish Antiquities*
Anth. Pal.	*Greek Anthology*
Apol.	*Apologia*
Areop.	*Areopagiticus*
Avid. Cass.	*Avidius Cassius*
B.	Babylonian Gemara
Bacch.	*Bacchae*
BDAG	Walter Bauer, et al. *Greek- English Lexicon of the New Testament and Other Early Christian Literature.* 2nd ed. Chicago: University of Chicago Press, 1979.
CD	Cairo Damascus Document
Chronica.	*The Sacred History of Sulpitius Severus*
Civ.	*The City of God*
De rerum natura.	*On the Nature of Things*
Descr.	*Description of Greece*
Diatr.	*Diatribai (Discourses)*
Ep.	*Epistles*
Ep.	*Moral Letters*

Eum.	*Eumenides*
1 Apol.	*First Apology*
Geogr.	*Geography of Greece*
Haer.	*Against Heresies*
Hist.	*The Histories*
Hist. eccl.	*Ecclesiastical History*
Hist. rom.	*Historiae Romanae*
In Pis.	*Against Lucius Calpurnius Piso*
J. W.	*Jewish Wars*
Ketub.	*Ketubot*
LXX	Septuagint
M.	Mishnah
Mak.	*Makkot*
Mem.	*Memorabilia of Socrates*
Met.	*Metamorphoses*
Mor.	*Moralia*
M. M.	Moulton, J. H. and G. Milligan. *The Vocabulary of the Greek Testament*. London: Hodder and Stoughton, 1929.
Nat.	*Naturales quaestiones*
Nat.	*Naturalia Historia*
Naz.	*Nazir*
Ned	*Nedarim*
NPNF	*The Nicene and Post-Nicene Fathers*
'Ohal.	*'Ohalot*
Orat.	*Orations*
Pax.	*The Roman Oration*
QS	Community Rule/Serekh ha-Yahad
RG.	*Res Gestae Divi Augusti*
Sanh.	*Sanhedrin*
Sat.	*Satires*

Spec. Laws.	*Special Laws*
Tusc.	*Tusculan Disputations*
Ver.	In Verrem

Introduction and Orientation

Acts for the Everyday Christian is just that. This commentary is not written for professionals who relish obscure technical issues. Instead, I have written this for Christians who have not had years of theological training and just want to know what the passage is saying. With this aim, I have tried to simply focus on the core elements, while also explaining terms that other commentaries assume you know. While it is normal to open a commentary with an introduction that discusses the background, authorship, and a wide range of technical questions, I have not done so. These are important, which, after all, is why it is done, but my chapter, "Technical Matters," is found at the end instead. I expect that most of my readers will want to go straight to the comments and immerse themselves in that, rather than trudge through matters that are of less interest. It is your choice whether you read that chapter first or last.

That chapter explains why I believe that Luke, the "beloved physician," wrote his second volume of the history of Christianity, completing it shortly after Paul's two years in captivity in Rome. The wider purpose for writing Acts is debated, e.g., Was it a trial document, or was it for the wider population who may have questioned what this new faith was? What is not debated is its unintended value as a bridge connecting the Gospels to the Epistles.

By and large the incidents that make up this story are told without comment, leaving the reader to assess the events and pass his/her own judgments. The church was born on the day of Pentecost and continued with an experience of the Spirit beyond that of most of us, leading to either a judgment on the book or on ourselves. Some will renounce Acts as little more than a collection of myths and exaggerated memories with little historical value, while, in others, it awakens an ache for a similar encounter with the Spirit. I hope for you it is the latter. The reading of this commentary should not leave you unaffected as you think deeply about how radical our faith is.

As you read through my comments consider the following:

1. How nothing has happened with Jesus that the Father had not permitted and foretold
2. The development of the message of the church from one expressed in terms of forgiveness for sins of ignorance to one of repentance and faith
3. How the message was intended to cross every barrier that people impose
4. The interaction between the church and the Roman empire and their divine rulers
5. Peter and Paul compared as equals but working in different areas.
6. The church's relation to paganism
7. The church's relation to the occult
8. The church's relation to suffering

The Book of Acts covers roughly a thirty-year period, the same as the life of Jesus. His life left followers numbered in the hundreds, but his disciples left a world that was being turned upside down with thousands of believers that stretched from Jerusalem to Rome. Luke's book gives the account of the few that were sent, and in all there are thirty-nine references to the fulfillment of Christ's commission to be witnesses to a risen Christ. But the witnesses were not all apostles; most were everyday Christians like yourself. An imperfect church took this order as applying to all, not the few. Where do you stand on this subject? After an impassioned plea to the Particular Baptists to be active in world missions, John Ryland Sr. is reported to have said to William Carey, "Young man, sit down; when God pleases to convert the heathen, he will do so without your aid or mine." Few would be so foolish to say that now, but to think it, and most definitely to act it, is another matter.

While Luke has much to say about the sent, there is very little written about the senders. Sea passages had to be paid for, likewise accommodation and food. The deeds and memory of the forgotten senders are only known to God. To "go" should only be in response to a clear call, diligent study, and above all, the empowering by the Spirit, but to "send" can be done by all. Reading this book will amount to no more than a "hill of beans" if you are not missional by the end. May the words of Paul to Philemon be true of you:

> I always thank my God as I remember you in my prayers, because I hear about your love for all his holy people and your faith in the Lord Jesus. I pray that your partnership with us in the faith may be effective in deepening your understanding of every good thing we share for the sake of Christ. Your love has given me great joy and encouragement, because you, brother, have refreshed the hearts of the Lord's people. (4–7)

Use this commentary alongside your favorite translation of Acts. Quotations in the comments are taken from the NIV unless otherwise noted. Now, onwards, and upwards.

1

When the Time Was Right

If you are reading this commentary in a "Christianized" country, you should be concerned that large sections of society are determined to be rid of the last vestiges of vital Christianity. If you are asking "How far can our society slide?," then, sadly, the answer is "A long way yet." This chapter deals with the historical setting of the Book of Acts, which was a world very different to our own. It is hard to comprehend how different, cruel, yet at times cultured their world was compared to ours. However, that age was vastly different to the ages that went before it. It was so different that Paul speaks of Christianity being birthed when the time was right, saying, "When the fullness of time came, God sent forth his Son" (Gal 4:4). The timing was so fine-tuned that, had Christianity not appeared in the limited window of time in which it did, the followers of a Jewish carpenter would have had little opportunity for success.

Chaos or control? This can be seen as simply sheer good luck. But the believer is encouraged to look past this turmoil, intrigue, and destruction, and, instead of random chaos, see the depth of God's control of human hearts and the destinies of nations. Present opposition to Christianity in the West pales into insignificance compared to the outright opposition to the Jews and Christians over the preceding centuries, and yet never did nor will our Lord lose control. Acts begins with the promise that Christ will return, which, again, will be in the fullness of time. Quite possibly it will be to a world different to our own, yet a world that has never been out of control.

THE ROMAN PREPARATION

The world had not been at peace from the death of Alexander the Great and the great wars of the Roman Republic. After the assassination of Julius Caesar, Rome was thrown into a long and bitter civil war out of which Augustus was the victor and the Roman empire was formed. This heralded the start of the *Pax Romana*, an unparalleled two-hundred-year period of relative peace. The Romans believed this peace was not held in place primarily by the force of the legions but through maintaining the *pax deorum*, the god's peace.[1] One of Augustus's actions would be to order a census of the world at which time Christianity would enter upon the world. Jesus was born in a stable in a small town in a backwater of the empire during the census. Within a little over three hundred years the emperor would bow his knee to the carpenter. Over the ensuing years, Rome would be the church's greatest foe and at times, as we will see in later chapters of this book, unwittingly, its best ally.

With peace, the empire started to grow and develop. While there were some good roads before the Romans, they developed the best system of roads prior to modern times. These were developed initially for military and administrative purposes (all roads lead to Rome) and were so well constructed that many examples remain today. Not only were the roads that were characterized by their straightness quick and easy to travel on, but Rome had also made them safe, and trade flourished. The seas were also free of pirates, and while shipwrecks were still too common, they also had become relatively safe, regular, and easy. Magnificent, protected ports were built that could cater to ships so large they carried six hundred passengers as well as cargo.[2] Widespread international trade led to complex business relations and methods on one hand and improved knowledge of geography and navigation on the other.[3] Clearly, the ease and speed of communication impacted greatly upon the spread of Christianity but at the same time assisted its enemies such as Gnosticism.[4]

1. Magyar, "Imperial Cult," 386. This is expanded upon in chapter 19, "Technical Matters," under the section "The Immediate Aftermath of Acts."

2. Josephus, *Life*, 3. The average ship at this time could carry between two and three hundred tons of cargo though many were larger. One ship is known to be nineteen hundred tons. Casson, *Ancient Mariners*, 157. The *Isis*, an Alexandrian grain ship, was forty-seven meters long and could carry between twelve and thirteen hundred tons.

3. Casson, *Ancient Mariners*, 157.

4. This is discussed briefly in my comments on Simon Magus in chapter 8.

At this time, Greek, Roman, and Jew were united under one government and law. Roman law had developed from being very much a Roman entity to a system that was a rough average of the customs of its diverse peoples. The Romans placed great importance on law and the nations under their control were taught to respect and obey her laws. This was done through its strict and ruthless application. This had a leveling effect on the nations and helped civilize the empire. It has been said that "the universal law of Rome helped to prepare the way for the universal law of the Gospel"[5]

The Romans had been barbarian conquerors, destroying more advanced civilizations that stood in their way such as Carthage. When Rome vanquished the East, it did not destroy Greece but respected its civilization. The Greek language had become widespread through the endeavors and commercial success of the Greek republics in Sicily and Southern Italy. Following Alexander's conquest, Greek would be widely spoken throughout the Middle East and even as far as northern India and Egypt and around the Black Sea. About this time, a form of popular Greek developed called *koine* in which our New Testament would be written. When Rome took over the East it was too well entrenched to be replaced with the official language, Latin. The Greek language was also respected by the Romans, which was fortunate as it provided a better medium for expressing theological thought than Latin and so was the favored language of the Roman church for two hundred years.

The empire itself was becoming very cosmopolitan. Its legions were made of men from different nations rubbing shoulders, and traders from all nations mingled freely. With this came a readiness to at least try, if not accept, the ideas of other nations. Rome did not erase the gods of the nations but was tolerant even to the point of incorporating them into their pantheon. Judaism likewise was also similarly tolerated and declared a legal religion. Synagogues were found throughout the empire and would be the starting place for reaching the gentile world. The Jews themselves had been spread through the empire and all the large cities had a significant Jewish population. This interaction between Jew and gentile outside of Judea, at least, would have an important effect on the readiness of the world for the gospel. These Jews would start to shed much of their exclusiveness, a realization that they could be in the world without being part of it.

5. Renwick, *Roman Empire*, 4:212.

Many gentiles had been taught since the third century BC by the Stoic philosophers of a civic and moral brotherhood, where "all men were regarded as equal before the One; only virtue and vice were the differentiating factors."[6] Despite being a slave, a man could be free because his mind was free. Many accepted this philosophy but were repelled by the bankruptcy of paganism that it was clothed in and would be attracted to the ethical monotheism of Judaism. Many became proselytes or full Jews; others did not take the full step of circumcision and baptism and were known as *God fearers*. They were helped by the translation of the Hebrew Old Testament into Greek, (known as the Septuagint or LXX),[7] which was widely distributed throughout the empire. Others would abandon all religion and accept Epicureanism with its message of annihilation and its motto *carpe diem* (seize the day). Others sought comfort in magic, astrology, and the mystery religions. Few hoped for eternity. One writer said that "the human mind was declared vacant, and Christianity was at hand as the best claimant."[8]

THE GREEK PREPARATION

Alexander's conquest of the East in 334–327 BC was the turning point for the history of the ancient world, uniting East and West, i.e., the Greek world and the old Oriental civilization. This unity would last a thousand years till the conquest of Islam. This unity stretched from Egypt to the borders of India through Turkey to Greece. This process of union continued over the centuries and is called *Hellenism*, and through this, the ancient kingdoms became so united culturally that Rome could eventually dissolve the political entities and transform them into provinces of the empire.

With the coming of the Roman empire, a shift developed so that the eastern half of the empire was Greek and the western half Latin. In time the empire and the church would divide down these two groupings.

6. Renwick, *Roman Empire*, 4:210.

7. Sometimes referred to as the "Greek Old Testament," and its name is derived from the Greek for "seventy" as there were allegedly seventy-two translators. The sermons would most likely have been delivered in Aramaic with the quotations adjusted for a Greek-speaking audience.

8. Renwick, *Roman Empire*, 4:212.

The Contribution of the West

Such a union could not have been envisaged one hundred years before Alexander, with cultural thinking linked to the Greek polis (city-state) on one hand and the oriental class system on the other. Thinkers such as Socrates and Plato had developed the idea of abstract principles that applied to all mankind. The invention of the *logos*, the abstract concept, was one of the greatest discoveries of the human mind. Rational thought brought with it a universalism that could be learned and supported by logical argument. This thinking weakened patriotism and prejudice. By Alexander's time, even barbarians could say that they were Hellene, not by their birth but their education. A man came to see himself as a citizen, not of his *polis* but of the *cosmos*.

With the conquests, the native population could have equal rights with the Greeks through cultural and linguistic assimilation. The new cities were no longer sovereign states, but part of a centrally administered kingdom and the residents saw themselves as private people, something unheard of. Previously, men saw themselves and their responsibilities as citizens of a city. Hellenism didn't just happen, there was a deliberate merging of the cultures, typified by Alexander marrying ten thousand of his Macedonian officers to Persian wives in Suza. The books of 1 and 2 Maccabees record the attempted, forced Hellenization of the Jews.

The assimilating power of the Hellenic culture was enormous. The Greek language became a universal language, and, as cities like Antioch and Alexandria grew rapidly, largely from the influx of native residents, they still continued to retain their Greek identity. The center of Greek culture moved from Greece itself to the new cities of the East. People became converted to Hellenism as one would be converted to a different religion, and with the adoption of Greek names it became impossible to tell national identity. With the coming of the church, Hellenism changed from being a cultural and political identity to a pagan religious culture based around different interpretations of Plato's teachings. It would incorporate later heresies such as Mithraism as part of the tradition to be defended.

There were four phases of Greek culture:

1. Classical, which existed as a national culture;
2. Hellenism as a cosmopolitan social culture from 300 BC to the first century, a period represented by the great schools of philosophy;

3. Hellenism as a pagan religious culture (first century to the second century); and
4. Hellenism as a Christian culture, ending in the East with the rise of Islam.

The Roman Empire, with its rule of law and military power, adopted the Greek language and way of thought. The Roman poet Horace could say, "Captive Greece captured, in turn, her uncivilized conquerors."[9] That language has been described as "perhaps the world's most powerful and exact linguistic medium [for] the expression of abstract thought."[10]

The Contribution of the East

Military and political subjugation cannot explain what caused such universal acceptance of Greek culture. Often the victor succumbs culturally to the vanquished. Though the East was vanquished militarily by the Persians, they didn't bring cultural unity. One of the factors affecting this acceptance was that, apart from the Jews, there was a literary sterility with few books known from this period. This meant that if the East wanted to express itself it had to use the Greek language and forms. Also, a series of despotic rulers had broken the political spine of the local residents who would meekly accept each new ruler in succession. Only two cities, in fact, commercial rivals to the Greeks—Tyre and Sidon—gave Alexander serious opposition. At this time the empires were old and were bogged down in the inertia of tradition.

The Assyrian and Babylonian practice of transporting subjugated nations to a different land destroyed cultural growth and national identities, and so the vanquishers surrounded themselves with a cultural desert. All this led to a religious syncretism that would be a characteristic of Hellenism (see 2 Kgs 17:24–41). The removal of people from the cultic centers and the political function associated with them led to the development of abstract religious thought. Traditional religions became religious systems competing with other systems for the hearts and minds of men. Three major influences would emerge: Jewish monotheism, Babylonian astrology, and Iranian dualism.

9. Horace, *Ep.* 2.1.156.

10. Blaiklock, *Acts*, 134.

The East did not submerge totally under the flood of Greek culture. What could not be assimilated simply went underground. Dualism developed in which Eastern thought was expressed in Western garb, and this would impact back on pure Hellenic thought. The potency of this form and their grasping of the *logos* had a liberating effect on the East. Hitherto it had to express itself in images and symbols, presenting their religious beliefs in myths and rituals rather than in a logical manner. The strength of restated Eastern thought increased as it gained ascendancy over the West, a period covered by the Gospels and Acts. This was particularly evident in religious matters that became more and more tied up with cultural matters. At this time the Eastern religions gained prestige in the West as it presented old ideas in new clothing. These religions would challenge Christianity head-on at the close of the first century, and the greatest danger was that it would syncretize with them, as was tried with Gnosticism, and lose its identity.

THE JEWISH PREPARATION

From the time Israel left Egypt, it had a continuing battle with idolatry. The Northern Kingdom fell to the Assyrians in 722 BC, and the dispersion of the Jews started when they were deported from their land. Judah itself fell to the Babylonians in 586 BC, and the educated of the land were deported to Babylonia. This deportation had a dramatic effect on the Jews and the later establishment of the church. In Babylonia, away from their land and their temple in ruins, they found that their religion was greater than both and the synagogue emerged from their troubles. This institute would spread throughout the ancient world and was the starting point for preaching the gospel. Its form of service became the pattern of the church.

When a number of the decedents of the exiles returned from Babylon in 538 BC, we find the nation changed and it never again had the same attraction to idolatry. When the Seleucid king Antiochus tried to enforce Hellenism upon the Jews, some complied, but the nation rebelled and under the Maccabees threw out the Syrians after a protracted war between 168 and 142 BC. This success would ingrain a fierce pride in their own identity culturally and religiously. Rather than disobey the Law, a system of rules and regulations arose to interpret the laws and keep the obedient Jew from sinning. Many saw righteousness as an outworking of

God's obligation to man from his meticulous obedience to the law. The Pharisees came to prominence during this period. The nation stood out as uncompromising with either Greece or Rome in the syncretism that had overtaken the world, offering a clear alternative to the disillusioned. Many Jews themselves became very evangelistic.

The people were changing. When Antiochus desecrated the temple, the people rose in a united revolt. When Rome desecrated the temple and built a pagan temple on the site, there was no such uprising throughout the empire and those remaining in Judea. Increasingly they had come to see that good deeds were as valuable as sacrifices and that the temple was not essential to their faith. We do not hear them say, "How can we sing the song's of the Lord in a foreign land?" (Ps 137:4).

Jews are thought to have numbered about five million at the time, with half of these living in Judea. They made up roughly 10 percent of the Roman Empire.[11] Surprisingly, the Romans looked favorably upon the Jews, and they were exempted from military service and payment of pagan temple taxes. While there was often local opposition to the diaspora the official view from Rome was supportive. Under these circumstances, Judaism spread through the empire. Christianity was first seen as a sect of Judaism and as such enjoyed the freedom the latter was shown by Rome.

There had developed among the Jews a belief in the coming of three great men: the prophet like Moses, the servant of Isaiah, and the Messiah. All three would be rolled into one in Christ. At the time of Christ, the Jewish world was looking for the *eschaton*. This, they believed, would be the climactic end to this age with all its pain, suffering, injustice, and humility. It was a time when God would step into the course of history, roll it up like a worn carpet, and renew his creation. They believed they were living on the very brink of history. The Jewish eschatological hope is illustrated below.

The Eschaton

This age	The age to come
Sin	Righteousness
Sickness	Health
Demon possession	Health
Evil men triumph	Spirit triumphs

Table 1. The Jewish eschatological hope[12]

11. Bock, *Acts*, 43.

12. Fee, *Corinthians*, 84.

Coincidence or providence? The study of the timing of the entry of Christianity can only leave us amazed at how an apparently chaotic world would be running to time and plan. Evil men, rather than thwarting his purposes, were unwittingly doing his bidding.

2

The Church Is Born (Acts 1:1—2:47)

PREFACE (1:1–5)

While we may be full of praise for Luke's Gospel and his history of the early church, the fact remains that both books are intended for one man—Theophilus—and without him they might have gone no further.[1] When Luke first wrote to Theophilus, he addressed him as "most excellent Theophilus" (Luke 1:3), which suggests he was someone from the higher levels of society and so most likely to be a gentile.[2] It is not the way you would normally write to a Christian brother. We don't know who Theophilus was, though some have made the unlikely suggestion that it is just a general term for a believing reader as the name means "lover of God." More likely Luke was using him as a sponsor to publish his book.

Luke's Gospel is described as "all that Jesus began to do and to teach" (Acts 1:1), so Acts may then be described as what Jesus (through the Spirit) continued to do and teach. His Gospel appears to have had the desired result of giving Theophilus certainty of the things he had been taught (Luke 1:4) as he is now called "Theophilus" only. His second work would have nurtured that confidence, not by urging him to a more ethical life, but by recording sermons that focus on calling unbelievers to faith.[3] "*The whole Christian understanding of reality and ethics flows from the message of Christ's death and resurrection*,"[4] not ethics.

1. Lenski, *Acts*, 14.

2. This speaks against the misconception that early Christianity was exclusively a lower-class movement. The literary style of the book "suggests it is written for an educated part of society." Mitchell, *Fresh Look*, 37.

3. Johnson, *Message of Acts*, 142.

4. Johnson, *Message of Acts*, 142 (emphasis original).

The humanity of Christ's resurrection body is stressed with the words "appeared," "spoke," and "ate," which would counter the later heresies of Montanism[5] and Gnosticism where Christ only appeared to have a human body. Instead, the resurrection only revealed what Jesus always was,[6] and he provided abundant proof so there would be no doubt among his disciples who were described as "witnesses" (1:8). This was a multifaceted role. They bore testimony to the travesty of justice in Jesus' brutal and shameful death and God's vindication of him as being the judge of the living and the dead (10:41–42). Thy bore witness also to his miraculous signs and the harmonious testimony of scripture in foretelling these events.[7] For the Jews who were guilty of the murder of Jesus, they will be accusing witnesses in a law case. Yet to the repentant, the apostles will be as a herald of grace. Peter and John will also be witnesses to the Jerusalem church of the Spirit being given to the Samaritans and the gentiles.

With the expression, "taken up," Luke drew on language from the Old Testament and the Apocrypha, when God took the righteous directly to heaven.[8] In the place of Jesus, the Father will give the Spirit who is the promise of a new age (Luke 3:1–17), yet this is rooted in long-standing promises, and in Peter's first sermon he will quote the prophet Joel as evidence. He was already present as Jesus had been teaching the apostles through the Holy Spirit. His coming is so different it is described as a "baptism," with the association of cleansing (Ezek 36:25), but it is more than cleansing; it brought empowerment for mission.[9]

Luke further linked his two books by making an early reference to John the Baptist. In Luke's account of John's preaching, the baptism of the Spirit is coupled with "fire." To the Jewish mind, this would bring to memory the burning lamp from the covenant with Abraham (Gen

5. Named after its founder Montanus, it was known as the "New Prophesy" movement. Montanism differed from all the great second-century heresies as it began as a movement of religious fervor. The doctrine of the Paraclete and the second coming were everyday topics in the church so that to relate the prophetic word to the future in an extreme way was a short step. Montanus moved in this environment when he put his views forward. Things went from a more moderate position to the extreme position, where little credence was given to the written word and disproportionate attention given to the spoken word.

6. Bock, *Acts*, 36.

7. Johnson, *Message of Acts*, 145.

8. LXX of 2 Kgs 2:9–11; 1 Macc 2:58; Sir 48:9 (Elijah); 49:14 (Enoch).

9. Bock, *Acts*, 57.

15:17); the burning bush of Moses that did not consume but made holy (Exod 3:1–6); the shekinah that delivered (Exod 14:19–20), led (Exod 13:21–22), and sat on the tabernacle (Exod 40:34–38); the burning coal that touched the lips of Isaiah (Isa 6:7); and Isaiah's vision where the flame would dwell on every residence of Mount Zion (Isa 4:2–6). "In the promise of a baptism of fire they would at once recognize the approach of new manifestations of the *power and presence of God*."[10]

Jesus spoke of the "promise of the Father," which would include the passage from Joel that Peter would quote on the day of Pentecost. However, it is from passages they had heard Jesus speak about. The apostles use of Scripture in Acts was informed by Jesus' own explanation, such as on the night before Calvary in John's Gospel (John 15:26; 16:7–8, 13). Similarly, the necessity of the Christ to suffer as preached by Peter was "opened up" to the disciples on the road to Emmaus (Luke 24:13–35) and through the appearances Luke records over forty days.

THE ASCENSION (1:6–11)

In Luke's Gospel, the ascension is told in the personal terms of Jesus with his friends, recording his gestures and blessings. There is nothing of this in Acts. Here we see them, not so much as friends but as representatives of the church. As "apostles," they were to act as such with the full authority of the one who sent them.[11] The mention of the Spirit's coming would have raised Jewish hopes about the reversal of Israel's fortune, leading them to think in terms of the *eschaton*, where Jesus would be an earthly ruler.[12] They are warned sternly against trying to probe into the secret counsel of God. His reply points the apostles instead to the providence of God where this world in its chaos and injustice is still firmly under his governance. Their concern must be a person and his command, not a timetable. Neither his departure in a cloud reflecting the glory of God in the exodus (Ex 13:21–22), nor the coming of the Spirit meant the completion of the kingdom. It was more like the nobleman in the parable going to a distant country.[13] Though the day is coming when "not just an

10. Arthur, *Tongue of Fire*, 12; emphasis original.

11. Rengstorf, "ἀπόστελλω," 1:421.

12. Longenecker, "Acts," 9:256.

13. Gooding, *True to the Faith*, 41.

odd Pharaoh here or a proud Belshazzar there would be destroyed. All evil would be put down."[14]

The disciples were told to remain in Jerusalem until they were endowed with power, yet the Gospels attest these men already had experienced miracle-working power. Some equate this power with boldness and joy while imagining the apostles still "hiding with the doors locked in fear of the Jews" in the upper room as on the day of Christ's resurrection (John 20:19). But Luke assures us this is not the case as "they returned to Jerusalem full of joy; and they were constantly in the temple courts, blessing God" (Luke 24:52–53). This would have required great courage, yet what is the courage of an insignificant number compared with the millions in the Roman Empire and such an encompassing commission? The Spirit's coming gave power to live God-honoring lives (Rom 1:16–7), but in Acts the ten usages of *power* refer to miracles or their effects. However, this power should be understood as power to save through being witnesses as the three-and-a-half-year ministry of Christ left only a few hundred disciples, yet the church's first sermon would add three thousand (2:41).

The call to be witnesses would prove to be not just the role of the apostles. The origins of the spread of Christianity to the ends of the earth was not done by the apostles only but by ordinary though often persecuted believers. All who obey the call to repentance and faith in Jesus are God's servants and his witnesses. Obviously "sightless eyewitnesses are useless and only the Servant gives sight."[15]

Given that the Great Commission was the last words given by Jesus to the church, its importance cannot be overstated. Luke weaves his book around the progress of the Gospel to the ends of the earth. Jesus used a composite of words and ideas from Isaiah concerning the ministry of the Servant of the Lord (Isa 42–53; 61). The promise was that he would "heal the blind eyes and deaf ears of his servant people, so they could be his witnesses among the nations."[16] Specifically,

- The Spirit of God is poured out on his people (Isa 32:15)
- His people are witnesses to the saving acts of the only God (Isa 43:10, 12; 44:8)

14. Gooding, *True to the Faith*, 29.
15. Johnson, *Message of Acts*, 45.
16. Johnson, *Message of Acts*, 49.

- To the ends of the earth, pagans will abandon their idols and turn to God (Isa 49:6; 45:22)

The references from Isaiah are listed in appendix 1. The thirty-nine references to being witnesses in various forms means that everything in Acts "should probably be seen as subsumed under it."[17] The context of the Isaiah references is of the Lord's power (Isa 41:1–4) and the absolute powerlessness of the idols (Isa 41:21–23). In the case of the *Lord versus the idols*, both sides are called to be witnesses. (Isa 43:9–12; 45:20–22), but here only the Lord's servants are witnesses. He has led them from darkness to light and healed their blindness so they can testify against the empty gods and the blindness of those who follow them.[18] Being this witness, along with the command to preach, are actions in which the new church had no way of influencing its outcome other than through the gift of power.

Despite what Jesus meant by his commission to go to the ends of the earth and the way Acts documents the gospel's inclusion of the gentiles, this is not how the apostles first understood the commission. "When Jesus spoke of the 'Kingdom of God', they heard the 'Kingdom of Israel.'"[19] Yet the very command to evangelize Samaria where very few Jews lived pointed to the commission being inclusive of all people, not just the Jews of the diaspora. The Samaritans at least understood their Messiah was the "Savior of the world" (John 4:42). Such an unlikely message was given to the most unlikely messengers. Twice their nationality as Galileans, who were considered second-class Jews, is contrasted with their international ministry, (1:8–11; 2:9–11). Yet, unlikely as it seemed, the command is rooted in Isaiah where the Jews were to be a "light to the Gentiles" so that God's salvation might reach the ends of the earth (Isa 49:6; see also 48:20). The central focus of Acts would not be to Israel as "the message will go to all and is for all because Jesus is Lord of all (10:36)."[20]Acts will end with the gospel reaching Rome and all roads leading from there to the extremity of the empire.

The angel's message about Jesus' return was given on the Mount of Olives (1:12), the very spot Zechariah said the Messiah would come (Zech 14:4). The certainty of Christ's return in a similar manner to his

17. Longenecker, "Acts," 9:256.

18. Johnson, *Message of Acts*, 36–40.

19. Johnson, *Message of Acts*, 47.

20. Bock, *Acts*, 62.

departure is affirmed by two heavenly witnesses (Deut 19:15). The return will be as physical as the departure. However, Acts was written when the expectation of Jesus returning in the lifetime of the apostles, if such a belief ever existed, is being replaced with planning for the church being here for the long haul (e.g., 1 Tim 3:1–12). Paul did not believe that the conditions for Christ's return had been fulfilled (Rom 11). For Luke, it is of no concern for believers when the end will come; their concern is mission. He has a simple view: his return will happen but will not be as the meek Lamb of God but as the just judge of this world (Zech. 14:4–12; Acts 1:9–11; 3:18–22; 10:38–42; 17:30–31).[21] A believer simply must be ready. This has been described as "inaugural eschatology" with the fight of the early church resting on a person—Christ and his work—not a program or a date.[22] In the meanwhile, a Christian must live in the tension of a world that is passing away (2 Cor 4:16–8) and the "inexhaustible creative energy of God."[23]

The Messiah and the Mount of Olives

Jesus' departure from the Mount of Olives acted out Ezekiel's prophesy of how the glory of God would depart from the temple by way of the Mount of Olives, which was east of Jerusalem (Ezek 10:3–4, 18–19; 11:22–23). Haggai had spoken disparagingly of the second temple (Hagg 2:3) as it lacked the glory of Solomon's. There was no ark of the covenant nor any visible manifestation of God's presence (2 Chr 7:1–3). Yet Ezekiel also saw that God's glory would return by way of the East and enter via the east gate (Ezek 43:1–4), and Haggai promised that the glory would be greater than the first (Hagg 2:6–9). Five hundred years later, the triumphal entry of Jesus, with its strong messianic symbolism (Zech 9:9; 14:4), started at the Mount of Olives and would have followed this route. God himself had returned to the temple and he himself cleansed it. Matthew reports that the blind and lame came to him in the now-cleansed temple to be healed (Matt 21:12–15). As they were allowed in the court of the women, this is presumably the inner court, the temple proper.[24] Their healing in

21. Bock, *Acts*, 41–2.

22. Longenecker, "Acts," 9:215.

23. Johnson, *Message of Acts*, 56.

24. Razafiarivony, "Exclusion of the Blind," 109.

the temple that made "them fit for worship and appearance before God"[25] was a powerful sign that God's kingdom was at hand.

The Jews rejected Jesus, and on leaving the temple that day he returned to the Mount of Olives. Whereas he had previously described the temple as "my house" (Isa 56:7; Matt 21:13), it has become "your house" (Matt 23:38), which will be left desolate. God's glory had again departed by the east gate. On his way back to the Mount of Olives Jesus prophesied the destruction of the temple, and on his arrival there expanded on it (Matt 24).

The Impact of the Miraculous in Acts

When faced with the miracles of Jesus, his enemies did not deny them but ascribed their origin to Satan (Matt 22:24). The Pharisees and Sadducees had mocked Jesus by demanding that he prove that he was the Messiah by coming down from the cross, and, in his resurrection, God granted a miracle far greater than they had asked as proof. Though we associate the post-resurrection experiences of Christ with the church, we must recall that the enemies of Christ were the first witnesses of his resurrection (Matt 28:4). His resurrection, the greatest miracle of the church, left even the witnesses unmoved in their unbelief. The priests bribed the soldiers to say that the disciples stole the body as they slept. We will see in Acts that, contrary to some Christian teachers, miracles generally do not convert, rather lay open the heart of man, exposing corruption or the love of truth. The ascension, like all the miracles of Acts that follow, must not be seen as an action that gives proof but as an event that must be viewed and accepted with faith and discernment. Christianity will not allow itself to be proved.

MATTHIAS CHOSEN TO REPLACE JUDAS (1:12–26)

The room where they gathered would have been large as it could hold 120 people, and this suggests a wealthy supporter. It may have been where the Passover was held. Prayer is a key in carrying out the church's mission. It is mentioned thirty-one times and is only omitted in eight chapters. With the church's vivid awareness of Jesus' presence, prayer would not have been a duty or an obligation. Rather it was joyful and

25. Razafiarivony, "Exclusion of the Blind," 114.

confident and can also be for us when we really comprehend that "the one who is Lord and Christ is among us to discuss our needs."[26] Mixed into this praying, unified band were women. Their inclusion was a sign of the new order as they were excluded from full participation in Judaism.[27] Peter's address to "Brothers" (1:16) can be translated with the inclusive "Brothers and Sisters," suggesting all their involvement in the choice of Judas's replacement.

By referring to prophecy in Psalms (Pss 69:25; 109:8), Peter reminds the group that Jesus had not made a mistake when he personally chose Judas among the twelve apostles[28] through the leading of the Holy Spirit. They understood that what could be applied to the Servant of the Lord and the righteous sufferer in Psalms could be applied to Jesus. His zeal for God's house (Ps 69:9) caused him to cleanse the temple, yet Jesus did not cleanse the apostles, and Judas would be far worse than the priests.[29] He above all men was false. Still, the gospel had not been stopped through his treachery. As the community prepared itself through prayer for the coming of the Spirit, it is led to find his replacement.

Jesus had the opportunity over the forty days since the resurrection to appoint a replacement but left this task to the church as their first act in their exploration of the Holy Spirit. The traitor's work could not be redistributed among the eleven as Jesus had promised there will be twelve thrones (Matt 19:28; Luke 22:28–30). Memory of this may well have prompted Peter's call.[30] At Pentecost the twelve will be complete and represent the leaders of a fresh institution founded in continuation of God's promises.[31] The death of James (12:1–2) did not lead to a replacement apostle and a continuing apostolic succession. Yet a new community did not cancel out promises to Israel (Rom 9—11) who would still be involved in God's redemptive plan (Rom 11:15–6) and will be saved (Rom 11:25–9). We will not see in Acts a calling to abandon Judaism but more how Law-sensitive Jews and gentiles could coexist.

26. Johnson, *Message of Acts*, 28.

27. This is explored in my book *Women in Ministry: Paul's Advice to Timothy in Its Historical Setting*.

28. Only in Luke's Gospel are the Twelve called "apostles" (Luke 6:13).

29. To this day, Christianity has been plagued by appalling financial corruption, which will continue when there is a flawed relationship between the world and God.

30. Bock, *Acts*, 82.

31. Bock, *Acts*, 74.

Later in the New Testament, "apostle" would be used in a more general sense for one who is sent out. Here, the office is defined as "someone chosen by the Lord to be an authorized eyewitness of His ministry from his baptism to ascension."[32] The casting of lots was common in the Old Testament, with God having been asked to override the decision, e.g., "The lot is cast into the lap, but the decision is wholly from the Lord" (Prov 16:33). While casting lots was culturally acceptable at that time, the church would later look at personal qualifications, prayer, and some other way that Christ's appointment was clear to those seeking guidance.[33] Some feel that the church acted in haste to replace Judas, saying Paul was obviously the person God had raised up to replace Judas and that Matthias is never heard of again. But in 6:2 he is listed as one of the Twelve and most of the apostles are not heard of again. Paul does not meet the requirements of being a witness to Christ's ministry; his apostleship is something distinct.

Paul and Stephen are called witnesses to the risen Christ (7:56; 22:15; 20), and proclaiming Jesus was not limited to those specially selected people. However, Luke saw the role of the Twelve as different to those who followed them simply through their divine choice.[34]

Judas's death by suicide in Matt 27:5 would not have held the moral outrage for gentiles that it did for Jews.[35] Luke stresses the awful nature of his death, making clear it was God's judgment, and he will be the first of a number to be judged in Acts. The shocking nature of his death left the disciples perplexed about God's plan in including him in the Twelve, but a plan there was.[36] Concerning the profits Judas made from his betrayal of Christ, Alfred Edersheim noted,

> But from henceforth the old name of "Potters Field" became popularly changed into that of "Field of Blood" (Haqal Dema) and yet it was the act of Israel through its leaders: "They took the 30 pieces of silver—the price of him that was valued, whom they of the children of Israel did value and gave them for the potter's field!" It was all theirs although they would fain made it all Judas': the valuing, the selling and the purchasing. And

32. Wood, *Acts*, 28.

33. Longenecker, "Acts," 9:266.

34. Marshall, *Fresh Look*, 66.

35. Longenecker, "Acts," 9:264.

36. In Matt 27:5–6, the chief priests purchased the field and Judas hanged himself. A situation where both accounts can be reconciled is feasible.

> the potter's field—the very spot on which Jeremiah had been Divinely directed to prophecy against Jerusalem and against Israel: how was it now all fulfilled in the light of the completed sin and apostasy of the people as described by Zechariah![37]

The significance of Jesus being called "Lord" is explored in my comments on chapter 2, verses 25–33 but note here that the man Jesus "reads all hearts" (1:24), which is the prerogative of God. This includes the secrets of their hearts as with Judas.

THE GIFT OF THE HOLY SPIRIT (2:1–13)

2:1–4. Luke set the scene for the Messiah pouring out the Spirit in his Gospel (Luke 3:15–17; 24:47–49). The Jews knew the Spirit was with them (John 14:17), and some he even filled. John the Baptist was filled with the Spirit from birth (Luke 1:15), and his parents, Elizabeth and Zechariah, also experienced a filling (Luke 1:41, 67). But Jesus promised that after his ascension the Spirit would live in the believer (John 14:17). The Spirit was not just given to the church corporately as an instrument of service; it was also given individually[38] and to all who were present, making the relationship more intimate and personal. John the Baptist spoke of a time when God would baptize with the Holy Spirit and fire (Luke 3:16), and Jesus spoke of the events of Pentecost as the fulfillment of John's prophecy (1:5), but not just John's promise. This is not just another day of Pentecost but a day of "fulfilment," a term with a biblical ring.[39]

The day derives its name from the Greek word for "fifty" and refers to the number of days from the offering of the barley sheaf at the beginning of the Passover. On the fiftieth day was the Feast of Pentecost. Since the time elapsed was seven weeks, it was also called the Feast of Weeks (Exod 23:15–17; 34:22; Deut 16:10). The feast was proclaimed a "Holy Convocation" and no menial work was to be done. It was also one of the three pilgrimage feasts at which every male Israelite was required

37. Edersheim, *Life and Times*, 2:576. The margin references are Matt 27:7; Jer 19.

38. Longenecker, "Acts," 9:271.

39. Haenchen, *Acts*, 167. The word is used in the LXX and designates the prophesied climax of a period of time. Johnson, *Message of Acts*, 57.

to appear at the sanctuary. (Lev 23:21).[40] This explains why there were people from so many nations.

Pentecost was originally a harvest festival marking the wheat harvest. Two loaves from the recently harvested grain were offered as firstfruits to God (Lev 23:15–17), and similarly the day of Pentecost represents the firstfruits of a greater inheritance—a foretaste and guarantee of creation's final restoration.[41] Also, it had come to be remembered more for the giving of the Law at Mt. Sinai.[42] This was the time when the nation of Israel was converted and "all Jewish people became proselytes."[43] Luke's double reference to "sound" (2:2, 6) may be another allusion to the giving of the Law. Certain Jews believed that God caused a sound to come from Sinai, which changed to a fire that was then understood as a language.[44]

Despite the obvious Sinai connection between the new and the old covenant, neither Luke nor Peter makes this connection in the sermon that follows. Both the wind and the fire symbolize that God was powerfully present. In both Greek and Hebrew, "wind" and "spirit" are the same word, so the imagery of the rushing wind is giving clear evidence of the Spirit's presence. Wind was associated with God's appearance (2 Sam 22:16; 1 Kgs 19:11–12; Job 37:10; Ezek 13:13) and also with life (Gen 2:7) Their miniature pillar of fire, brought an association of theophany and glory, just as the burning bush (Exod 3:2) and the pillar of fire (Exod 13:21) were also a symbol of God's presence and glory, marking each recipient out as a temple where God's Spirit now lived.[45] The new creation of Pentecost fulfils Ezekiel's prophecy of the valley of dry bones where they are given life by God's breath. Following the murder of Jesus, the surprise is that the "tongues of fire" did not "consume the very stones of Jerusalem and all it contained."[46]

40. Freeman, "Pentecost," 964.

41. Gooding, *True to the Faith*, 33.

42. Deduced from the timing in Exod 19:1 and was the time of the annual renewal (Jub 6:17).

43. Eskenazi and Frymer-Kensky, *Ruth*, xxvi.

44. Philo, *Decalogue*, 45–47. Philo saw God's provision of food in the wilderness as the reason why his laws were known to be his pronouncements. This chapter will similarly end with the provision of food.

45. Johnson, *Message of Acts*, 59.

46. Gooding, *True to the Faith*, 52.

It is possible that the "house" where this occurred was the temple itself not the upper room.[47] The word Luke uses is frequently found in the LXX for the temple itself, which also had thirty halls that were described similarly. It was at the hour of prayer on a feast day, and it was their custom to be at the temple (Luke 24:53). However Luke uses a different word for temple. If not, they at least moved to the temple soon after, possibly a fulfilment of Ezekiel's prophecy of the river flowing from the temple (Ezek 47:1–12).

2:5–13. Pentecost can be seen as a partial reversal of Babel, where men built a monument to their pride. Now the people are gathered, and the language barrier is broken down and God's salvation is glorified. Speaking in known tongues, the first miracle of the church points to the paradox of miracles. It was only the devout men who wondered what this meant (2:12), and unlearned Galileans were the last people you would expect this from. Still, some obstinately refuse to see what God was doing. Instead of asking what it meant they said, "These men are drunk with partially fermented wine." Their very answer condemned them as that was not available till August, two months away.[48] The list mentions ancient kingdoms and modern entities. However, one group is singled out as being pilgrims, the visitors from Rome. This is where the story is headed, and these visitors may well have been the nucleus of the church there. Figure 2 shows the locations of the nations mentioned.

47. E.g., Bruce, *Acts*, 1954, 56.

48. Bock, *Acts*, 105.

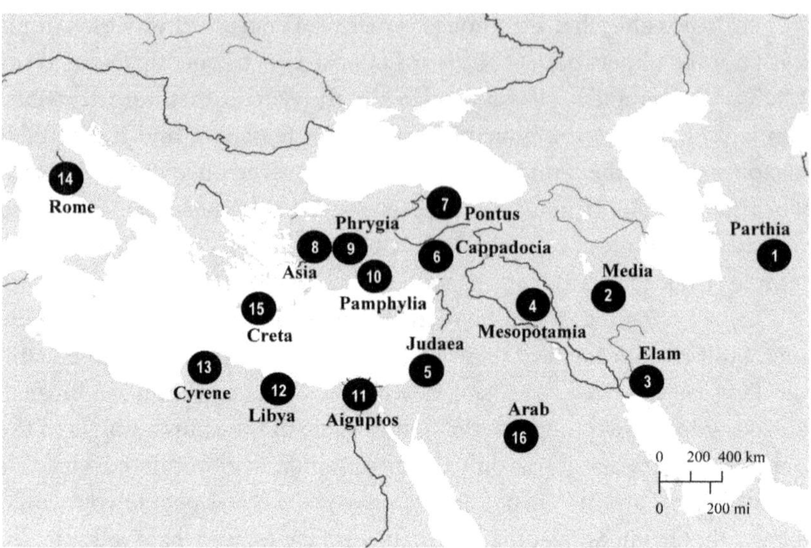

Figure 1. The people gathered on the day of Pentecost

The message was heard by pious men. John the Baptist introduced the idea that the Spirit's coming is associated with the ethical preparation of the people (Luke 3:7–17; Acts 10:2). However, their piety will neither excuse them from the corporate guilt of the death of their Messiah, nor the need to repent. Many of these men would be pilgrims visiting for the feast. God has taken the initiative in spreading the gospel as not only did the church gain three thousand members, it gained three thousand missionaries on its first day. Yet it is not till chapter 8 that the ethnic barrier will be crossed; even so, such a list of peoples and lands does point to a universal gospel. The LXX used "mighty deeds" to describe what happened in the past during the lead up to the exodus and in the wilderness, but here the apostles spoke of the mighty deeds of Jesus in the immediate past.[49]

Many of the older commentators saw the gift of tongues as a necessary tool for world evangelism.[50] This view also appeared when speaking in tongues reappeared in Scotland in 1828 and was also commonly held even with early Pentecostal churches. However, speaking in known languages does not occur again in Acts, nor is there any reason in Acts to see it as a continuing gift. Indeed, there was little need for it in the major

49. Bock, *Acts*, 104.

50. E.g., Dick, *Lectures*, 21.

centers. One commentator wisely points out, "I Corinthians is there to tell us that the ecstatic experience of the Spirit, to which modern presentations give so great a role in psychological reconstructions of Pentecost, does not impel people to preach in the streets but rather makes them cling together in a narrow circle; it was the 'Hellenists' . . . who first broke out from this reserve of the Jewish sect that believed in Jesus."[51] We will see it is radical theology, not ecstatic experiences, that will turn the world upside down. The theological term for speaking in unknown tongues is *glossolalia*.

PETER'S PENTECOST SERMON (2:14–39)

Luke and Acts have a first sermon near the beginning. We will see throughout Acts the theme of "as the master, so the servant," and in this vein Peter's sermon has parallels to the first sermon of Jesus at the synagogue at Nazareth (Luke 4:16–8). This includes

- the Lord's servant receiving the Spirit (Luke 3:22; Acts 2:1–4);
- a sermon explaining why the Spirit came (Luke 4:17–21; Acts 2:14–39); and
- a subsequent healing ministry with opposition (Luke 4:31–44; 5:12–26; Acts 3–4).

The Spirit's coming brought zeal, unflinching commitment to the risen Jesus, and the ability to preach with power, but it did not bring a clear understanding of the mission of the church. Thirty-odd years after Pentecost, both Luke and Theophilus knew the gospel was universal, however, Acts' unfolding account will show how slow the apostles were to comprehend this. Yet, the universality of the good news will be implicit in this first Christian message. Jesus had promised that the Spirit will guide into all truth (John 16:13), not grant everything immediately. Every Christian should have humility about his knowledge of God and his will. As the Puritans of old said, "There is yet more light and truth to break forth from His word."[52]

51. Haenchen, *Acts*, 189.

52. Taken from John Robinson's farewell sermon in 1620 to the Pilgrims leaving for New England.

The Apostolic Kerygma

Once the resurrection occurred, theological reflection of the life, death, and resurrection of Jesus started. In Peter's sermon, we have the undeveloped theology of the early church.[53] The Greek word *kerygma*, meaning "to proclaim like a herald," is the origin of the term given for this early preaching of the church. The "apostolic kerygma" regularly falls into four parts,[54] which are summarized as follows:

1. the announcement that the age of fulfillment has arrived;
2. a rehearsal of the ministry, death, and triumph of Jesus;
3. quoting of Old Testament Scriptures whose fulfillment in these events proved Jesus to be the Messiah; and
4. a call to repentance.[55]

These four elements are all present in Peter's sermon, but it is not the complete message, and Luke does not update the first messages to fit in with the later, developed understanding of the gospel. The ultimate subjugation of evil is not explored, as in 1 Cor 15:20–28, and we will also see in Paul's preaching the message of repentance from sin and faith towards God. What does not (and must not) change is that "Christian preaching begins with the name of Jesus"[56] and reaches its goal in him.[57] Peter's sermon typifies this.

The sermons in Acts are not self-help messages based on the latest popular thought but are "truth-centered, revelation-centered, God-centered and Christ-centered."[58] Their whole aim is to tell the truth derived from God's self-revelation and let that fall where it may. For some, the response was deep grief (2:37), for others it was furious anger (7:54),

53. The reliability of Luke's account is strengthened by the way he retained the less developed theology of the early church.

54. Others such as C. H. Dodd see a more complex pattern. He suggests: 1) the age of fulfilment has dawned; 2) this has taken place through the ministry, death, and resurrection of Jesus; 3) by virtue of the resurrection, Jesus has been exalted at the right hand of God as Messianic head of the new Israel; 4) the Holy Spirit in the church is the sign of Christ's present power and glory. 5) the messianic age will shortly reach its consummation in the return of Christ; and 6) the kerygma always closes with an appeal for repentance. Dodd, *Apostolic Preaching*, 21–23.

55. Bruce, *Acts*, 1954, 69.

56. Barrett, *Acts*, 140.

57. Bock, *Acts*, 119.

58. Johnson, *Message of Acts*, 159.

and yet for others it would bring incredible joy (8:39). It focuses on what God has done to get ones relationship right. This is only possible through Jesus, and so central was it that Paul would say, "For I resolved to know nothing while I was with you except Jesus Christ and him crucified" (1 Cor 2:2). Until a person is right with God, his relationship with others cannot experience a deep healing. Dennis Johnson, when commenting on the pressure modern preachers are under to broaden their repertoire, said,

> The preaching that builds people towards spiritual maturity does not take them beyond Christ. Rather it takes them more deeply into Christ so that their thoughts, attitudes, values, desires, reactions, words, and behavior are transformed by their death with Christ to sin and the resurrection with Christ to life and righteousness. . . . There is more than enough to keep the preacher occupied on a lifelong quest of new discovery and more than enough to address the needs of the human heart and human society.[59]

Word	First use	Second use
Pour out	17	33
Lord	21	36
Saved	21	40
Flesh	26	31
Abandon	27	31
Hades	27	31
Corruption	27	31
Sitting	30	34
Right hand	33	34

Table 2. Peter's use of rabbinic exegetical practice *gezera shawa* in his sermon[60]

Despite being seen as uneducated Galileans, Peter's extempore sermon is structured and sophisticated with reasoned argument, which shows the enabling of the Spirit of prophecy. The fisherman uses an exegetical device of the trained Jewish rabbis called *gezera shawa*, or "equal category" ( ). By this is meant an obscure passage can be illuminated by reference to another containing the same key word or term. Throughout

59. Johnson, *Message of Acts*, 161.

60. Modified from Bock, *Acts*, 134

Acts, "the dominating elements in the Spirit's witness would always be the spoken word,"[61] and while rhetorical practices will change over time and in different societies, the spoken word remains the Spirit's dominant witness.

2:14–24. Peter had captured the attention of his audience. He could easily dismiss any suggestion that they were drunk, as the Spirit was given at the time of prayer and before the first meal of the day. People don't get drunk first thing in the morning, especially on an important feast day.[62] He reminded them of the promise of the outpouring of the Spirit, longed for by Moses (Num 11:29) and explicit in Joel 2:29. There already was precedent for female prophets with Sarah,[63] Miriam (Exod 15:20), Deborah (Judg 4:4), Hannah (1 Sam 2:1–10), Abigail (1 Sam 25:23–35), Huldah (2 Kgs 22:14; 2 Chr 34:22), and Esther[64] being considered as prophetesses. Luke also called Anna a prophetess (Luke 2:36). There was no precedent, however, for what followed regarding slaves. The LXX, which Peter uses, is a deliberate mistranslation of the original Hebrew. It should read, "Even upon the menservants [slaves] and maidservants [slaves] in those days I will pour out My Spirit" (RSV). The old German commentators Keil and Delitzsch noted that the "Jewish expositors could not reconcile themselves to this announcement. The LXX by rendering [my servants] have put the servants of God in place of the slaves of men: and the Pharisees refused to the [slaves] even a knowledge of the Law (John 7:49). The Gospel has therefore broken the fetters of slavery."[65] Most of the slaves of the Jews were gentiles and for these to receive the Spirit implied that the gentiles would be blessed."[66] The universality of the gospel, which crossed every racial, gender, and social division, was not fully appreciated by the apostles until the specific call to minister to the gentiles (10:34). God will be directly accessible to all his people, including the most overlooked groups. He had not ignored even the slaves.

Some would see this as the fulfilment of those words of Joel. Peter instead saw the coming of the Spirit as the start of a decisive time of

61. Gooding, *True to the Faith*, 56.

62. Polhill, *Acts*, 108. The customary hour of prayer is the third hour, i.e., 9 a.m., and eating would occur at the fourth. The main celebrations on a feast day would be in the evening. Polhill, *Acts*, 108.

63. B. *Megillah* 14a.

64. B. *Megillah* 14b.

65. Keil and Delitzsch, "Joel," 6:212.

66. Lenski, *Acts*, 76.

fulfilment and judgment, blessing and trauma, when all will give an account. The clock is ticking towards a time of "blood and fire and billows of smoke [when] the sun will be turned to darkness and the moon to blood" (Joel 2:30–31). A time when creation is in upheaval and judgment. In his Gospel, Luke recorded the sun going dark (23:45) just seven weeks previous, adding an apocalyptic and eschatological element to the cross, making it a type of the day of the Lord. Peter later expands on this comprehensive judgment in 2 Pet 3. How imminent Peter thought the last day was on the day of Pentecost is uncertain. It would appear that the very early church initially expected it during the lifetime of the apostles.

The mighty works (2:19) where God gives evidence to the messianic end times combine salvation as well as judgment. The fierceness of the day of the Lord with its fire of judgment is contrasted with the "pouring out" of the Spirit, a term reflecting a torrential downpour on a parched land.[67] A key part of the sermon is placing Jesus alongside Yahweh. Whereas Joel urged his hearers to call on the LORD for salvation (2:21), Peter says to call on Jesus (2:38; 4:10–2) The fact that Jesus was from Nazareth was controversial, but that all pales into insignificance compared to the events that have just occurred.

Those who realized the seriousness of the actions of ungodly men are urged to repent as they are equally guilty. In a Western setting, Peter's hearers would defend their innocence, so the Jewish understanding of the corporate nature of sin must be appreciated (cf. 2:23 and 2:36 and verse 40; cf. Dan 9:5–8; Ezek 14:14; Isa 6:5–9). "Lawless men" would normally mean the gentiles without the guidance of Moses's Law, and the Romans did execute Jesus, but Israel through its lawless leaders and the mob were the driving force. This makes the whole nation guilty, and he accuses his hearers directly: "You, by the hands of lawless men, nailed him to a cross." The Jew was even worse than the gentile as Pilate tried hard to free Jesus. Yet "delivered over" is singular and suggests being handed over to God's plan. It is crucial to understand the death of Christ, not as the success of man or Satan but due to "the determinate counsel and foreknowledge of God." We are confronted with the mystery of God's predetermined plan and the responsibility of acting through the exercise of freewill.[68] As one commentator said, "It is a paradox without a ready solution. To deny it, however, is to go counter to the plain teaching of scripture."[69] By

67. Larkin, *Acts*, 53–54.

68. Gooding, *True to the Faith*, 46.

69. Longenecker, "Acts," 9:279.

attempting to overthrow God's rule through an act that brought their rebellion to a climax, the conspirators accomplished it instead.[70]

The injustice of Jesus' death was taken up by "the Supreme and Final Court of Appeal,"[71] and the resurrection is a reversal by the Father of man's judgment of his Son. (The divinity of Christ and his identification with Yahweh is stressed in verses thirty-four to thirty-six.) They had killed the author of life who was, in a wonderful mixed metaphor, loosed from the pangs of death. There was a new birth of the Messiah through the resurrection as "under severe labor pains the womb of the underworld must release the Redeemer."[72] This affirms the moral character of God who is just, loyal, and true. While the resurrection of Jesus was a singular event, Peter affirms the doctrine of the resurrection, without specifically saying so. It was a belief that some Jews (John 11:2–25), notably the Pharisees, held.[73] But the idea of an immediate resurrection was unknown.

The Messiah inaugurated his kingdom through his suffering. The preaching in Acts stresses the resurrection, an act where the verdict of unjust human judges is reversed by God. Through it, Jesus takes the role of "Christ, Lord, the giver of repentance, forgiveness, the Spirit, peace, and cosmic restoration."[74] Paul's focus on the cross is the atoning sacrifice that reconciles the sinner with God. The two are not contradictory despite the emphasis in the Acts' sermons being to the righteous servant who suffers for others (the cross is a tree of cursing [5:30; 10:39]).[75]

While Jesus had done mighty works, as would be expected by the promised prophet like Moses (Deut 18:15–22), Luke does not explore the Sinai themes, though there is a mention in chapter 3. Instead, the theme through the two psalms that Peter uses is Davidic and messianic. It it is hard to imagine, however, that the hearers would not have been making the associations with signs and wonders to evoke Sinai, especially at a time of pilgrimage. Jesus explained to the disciples on the road to Emmaus from the Law and prophets[76] how the Messiah must suffer

70. Johnson, *Message of Acts*, 146.

71. Gooding, *True to the Faith*, 50.

72. Bertram, "ὠδίν," 9:673.

73. The strength of the belief in the resurrection can be seen in 2 Macc 7, where the cruel martyrdom of seven brothers at the hands of Antiochus IV is recorded.

74. Johnson, *Message of Acts*, 146.

75. Johnson, *Message of Acts*, 147.

76. In the Hebrew Old Testament, the prophetic books included Joshua, Judges, 1 and 2 Samuel, and 1 and 2 Kings.

before being glorified (Luke 24:25–6). It is also hard to imagine how the many similarities with David, who was also betrayed by those he trusted, were not explained as they would have led Peter to his understanding of Pss 69 and 109.[77] Indeed, Jesus had quoted verse four which mentions being hated without cause and that psalm refers to vinegar and gall (Ps 69:21), which was pitilessly literal at the cross.

2:25–33. Peter's second proof text is Ps 16:8–11, where the vindication given to David is seen as a type or prophecy of the vindication of Jesus. Peter argues that the psalm ultimately is not about David. "Not seeing corruption" (Ps 16:10) is central as Peter repeats it in verse thirty-one where he is explaining the psalm and again in 13:35. It is not fully understood what is meant by Hades, the Greek equivalent of Gehenna or Sheol, but it was the place where the dead were gathered for judgment and contrasts being in God's presence. David spoke in the psalm as if his body would not decay but clearly that wasn't the case as his hearers knew where his undisturbed tomb was. His psalm referred to a specific person, the Holy One, someone who must be raised, not just some vague notion of the protection of David's dynasty which was promised to continue forever (2 Sam 7:12–13; Ps 132:11). Jesus was confident that his death will take him that very day to paradise, not Hades (Luke 23:43).

While it is important for the hearers to understand that Jesus is alive, it was also important to know where Jesus is now—at God's right hand (2:25), the place of favor (I Kgs 2:19; 1 Chr 6:39; Luke 22:69). God does not have a fixed locality so this introduces a very high understanding of Jesus who is capable of sitting everywhere and must mean a very close connection between the Father and Jesus. Sharing his glory points to Jesus' unique divine position. He works as the "middleman" in the giving and distribution of the Spirit, with the initiative coming from the Father. The whole of Acts shows that despite "sitting," Jesus is very active in the affairs of the new church, far beyond just giving the Spirit.

In the resurrection, Jesus did not become someone different, i.e., become "Lord"; rather he was shown to be "Lord" (see Rom 1:3–4; Luke 1:35) like a "public announcement."[78] Now, the Lord that is to be called upon is Jesus Christ and in his name they will be baptized. "Lord" was used by Palestinian Jews as a title for Yahweh,[79] and Jesus often appears as Lord in Acts, showing his lordship over salvation and distributing its

77. Gooding, *True to the Faith*, 46.

78. Mitchell, *Fresh Look*, 61.

79. Bock, *Acts*, 136.

benefits (4:33; 8:16; 11:17, 20; 15:11, 26; 16:31; 19:5, 13, 17; 20:21, 24, 35; 21:13; 28:31). His resurrection showed to the apostles that his authority is equal with the Father and could be used to refer to Jesus as Lord where the reference was to Yahweh (Ps 110:1, Joel 2:32; cf. Isa 45:23; Phil 2:10). They have crucified the one who shares the throne with God, and no greater sin against God was possible. Their act of baptism, not just words, showed they had "renounced their former position and attitudes."[80]

The sermon "highlights that it was God who acted through Jesus, God pours out the Spirit (2:17), worked miracles through Jesus, (2:22), then raised and exalted him (2:24, 32–3) thereby showing Jesus to be Lord and Christ."[81] Peter's use of Ps 16 looks back at the angel Gabriel's promise to Mary that Jesus would be given the throne of David and reign eternally (Luke 1:32–3). Jesus' kingship is not like David's who was anointed long before he was a king. While Jesus may not have sat on an earthly throne, his messianic power is on display now as it is he who gives the Spirit. He does this from being directly in the Father's presence. This was not just a claim to a fulfilled prophecy; they were witnesses to this unique person and event and it was what they were called to preach. It was so transformational that they cannot be silent (Luke 24:48; Acts 1:8).

2:34–36. For Peter's third proof, Ps 110:1, he took the lead from Jesus who used it to question whose son the messiah is (Luke 20:42–43). Psalm 110 was not clearly understood to be a messianic psalm at that time. It is linked to the fourth passage from Ps 16, a recognized messianic psalm, by the words "at my right hand."[82] Again, Peter argues that the passage cannot refer to David, instead it is about Jesus who is both Lord and Messiah. The titles of Lord and Christ, which Jesus was reluctant to use during his life, can now be used freely because of his resurrection as only then had he done the work of the Messiah.[83] Only then had he accomplished his mission of suffering and vindication and being exulted to the right hand of God.[84] It is this exultation God calls all to acknowledge,

80. Gooding, *True to the Faith*, 68.

81. Bock, *Acts*, 137.

82. Peter is using a talmudic hermeneutics rule called *gezerah shavah* (verbal analogy): "Where the same words appear in two passages, the same considerations apply." Longenecker, "Acts," 9:279.

83. Jesus was "accredited" by God as Messiah (2:22). This is a semi-technical term for office holders, both as someone either appointed or designated. The latter appears to fit better here. Polhill, *Acts*, 111.

84. Longenecker, "Acts," 9:280.

and for the Jews specifically, it involves the acknowledgment of Jesus as Messiah and the fulfillment of all Israel's hopes.

2:37–39. The crowds had been cut to the heart by John the Baptist and asked what they needed to do (Luke 3:10, 12, 14), and now this deep and sincere response is repeated by some. John had urged repentance in a Jewish framework, but Peter now urges them to respond to Jesus through repentance and baptism. Jesus could personally give forgiveness, and it was a promise now that had no racial boundaries. The only distinction now is between those who have been delivered from judgment and those of a crooked generation. Jesus is the one that distributes God's gifts of forgiveness and the Spirit. Repentance, a key term in Acts (2:38; 3:19; 8:22; 17:30; 26:20), means to make a deliberate turn towards God and his actions through Jesus, and Luke understands it as the response to the offer of forgiveness (2:38; 3:19; 5:31; 8:22; 26:18. 20; Luke 3:3. 24:47).[85] Repentance and faith are closely linked like two sides of the one coin.[86] One commentator described it this way: "Repentance stresses the starting point of the need for forgiveness whereas faith is the resulting trust and understanding that this forgiveness comes from God, the one turned to for the gift."[87] They are both blessings to be enjoyed immediately in this life.

But also, baptism, faith, forgiveness, and the baptism with the Holy Spirit are closely linked, and the nature of this linking has led to vastly different theologies, some of which stress the absolute necessity of baptism for Christian salvation. Others would say it has a saving power without the faith of the person being baptized.[88] What should be "the best of good news and should be read as the proclamation of that news [can be turned into] a set of theological problems."[89] A male proselyte entered into Judaism through circumcision and baptism, and when John preached a baptism of repentance the religious leaders reviled him, believing that

85. Bock, *Acts*, 141. The Greek meaning of *metanoēsate* is to change one's mind, but the Hebrew understanding is to turn, which is the understanding here. BAGD, "Μετανοέω," 516.

86. Marshall, *Acts*, 81.

87. Bock, *Acts*, 142.

88. The Roman Catholic view is that baptism works *ex opere operato*, which means "by virtue of the action," the sacraments are said to "cause that grace in the soul of man." Kennedy, "Sacraments," par. 13. As well, they have the power to sanctify. Buckley, *Council of Trent*, sess. 13.3. It is said not to be dependent on the faith of the recipient, provided they do not put obstacles in the way.

89. Longenecker, "Acts," 9:283.

their Jewish birth was sufficient. Jesus also baptized and preached the need for repentance. While Peter's baptism is still an individual response to the call for repentance, and the expected response, it is enriched as it is now done "in the name of Jesus Christ."

Baptism signifies that repentance has produced a cleansing that allows a person to be indwelled by the Spirit. Peter later explains that it is not the act that produces this cleansing but the response of a clear conscience to the resurrected Christ (1 Pet 3:21). In the Great Commission (Matt 28:16–20), Jesus had commanded his disciples to baptize in the name of the Father, Son and the Holy Spirit, but here they are to be baptized in the name of Jesus Christ (also 10:48; 19:5). This mirrors the earlier assurance that those who call on the name of the Lord will be saved (2:21). The word used for forgiveness is not the normal New Testament word but is common for Luke. It is a commercial term for cancelling debt.[90] Repentance, not baptism blots out sin, which is followed by the gift of the Spirit (also 10:43; 13:38–39). The seriousness of their sin had cut them to the heart, but God's response was gracious beyond comprehension.

The promise of the gift of the Spirit is to "all who are far off." We can't be certain how Peter understood this. As Peter was slow to understand the call to the gentiles, he may have meant future Jewish generations, or the diaspora. Whatever Peter understood, Luke at least saw the apostle saying more than he knew. Peter told his crowd to respond to his good news in various ways. The gospel is to be received, believed, they must call upon the name of the Lord, and also repent, but it is fundamentally the one thing, to "embrace God's grace through Jesus and the Spirit."[91] Salvation means that there is no judgment. Calling on the name of the crucified Jesus for forgiveness shows the authority Jesus has at the Father's side.

The Baptismal Formula

Peter's command to be baptized in the name of Jesus Christ has led to considerable debate over the years about the valid formula. Roman Catholics maintain only trinitarian baptisms are valid and saving,[92] but Protestants generally hold both wordings to be correct as the apostles

90. M. M. "Ἄφεσις," 96.

91. Bock, *Acts*, 147.

92. Miralles, "New Response," par. 3–4, 9.

obviously baptized in the name of Jesus Christ. It is possible that an even closer association with Jesus is intended as Peter may have been saying "baptized into the name." "Into the name" is a commercial term for the transfer of property. Thus, baptism into the name could be a public testimony that the baptized has become the property of Jesus. However, it is difficult to be dogmatic that this is the intention, though it certainly should be the outcome.

When Was the Spirit Given?

Theologians have debated since the earliest time an apparent contradiction between John's account of the giving of the Spirit at Easter and that of Luke at Pentecost. John said,

> Again Jesus said, "Peace be with you! As the Father has sent me, I am sending you." And with that he breathed on them and said, "Receive the Holy Spirit. If you forgive anyone's sins, their sins are forgiven; if you do not forgive them, they are not forgiven." (John 20:21–23)

So, "John tells us of one gift and Luke of another."[93] An attempt to harmonize these accounts was to reduce John's account to a purely figurative action, preparing the believers for Pentecost.[94] Another was to see them as different in their function, the first related to the forgiveness of sins and the second to the working of miracles. As John Chrysostom wrote, "One will not be wrong in asserting that they then also received some spiritual power and grace; not so as to raise the dead, or to work miracles, but so as to remit sins. For the gifts of the Spirit are of different kinds; wherefore He added, Whosesoever sins ye remit, they are remitted unto them, showing what kind of power Jesus was giving. But in the other case, after forty days, they received the power of working miracles."[95] Yet, another approach was to see this as the two writers describing essentially the same thing but reflecting the theological distinctions of the two writers with Luke being more authentic.[96]

93. Murray, *John*, 847.

94. An early proponent was Theodore of Mopsuestia (350–428) but condemned by the Second Council of Constantinople in 553. Brown, *John*, 2:1038.

95. Chrysostom, *Gospel of St. John* 86 (*NPNF*[1] 14:325).

96. Brown, *John*, 2:1039.

Ultimately, the relation between the two is obscure.[97] However, the very core of the Christian life is the Spirit's empowerment to live the life of Jesus. John's Gospel begins with an echo of creation, and, when Jesus breathed on his disciples, it ends with another (Gen 2:7). His words also echo the command at the valley of dry bones where the "son of man" was commanded to say, "I will cause breath (spirit) to enter you, and you shall live" (Ezek 37:5). Just as the Father was in the Son in his mission, so the Spirit's presence means that Jesus is in the disciples as they continue that mission.[98] The Spirit in the believers means, "The disciples must show forth the presence of Jesus so that whoever sees the disciples is seeing Jesus who sent them."[99]

The Baptism with the Holy Spirit

John had promised that Jesus would bring a baptism, not of water but with the Spirit and with fire. Before his ascension, Jesus referred to the day of Pentecost as a fulfilment of John's prophecy (1:5). This "baptism with the Spirit" is also called being "filled with the Spirit" (2:4) and these "metaphors (immersion in, drinking to the full of the Spirit) . . . imply a much greater experimental and visibly manifest reception of the Spirit than [experienced] in subsequent church history."[100] This could also refer to a more general term as when Peter received the Spirit's help when he spoke to the Sanhedrin (4:8, also 9:17; 13:9) and similarly of others (6:3, 5;11:24). But it could also be something that does not fit in preconceived theological frameworks as when Peter went to the centurion Cornelius and witnessed to Christ. There the Spirit came on all who were hearing the message, and they spoke in tongues but apparently not the known tongues of Pentecost. The depth of response among the gathered hearers (family, staff, and friends) would have been different, and they had not been baptized in water.

The Jews accompanying Peter were astounded that God would give the Spirit to gentiles, yet despite the differences in their experience, Peter equated it with their own (10:44–47). Though the word "baptism" is not used there, he does use it when recounting the events to the Jerusalem

97. Murray, *John*, 847.

98. Brown, *John*, 2:1036.

99. Brown, *John*, 2:1036.

100. Fee, *God's Empowering Presence*, 181.

church (11:15–17). The Ephesian believers who only knew John's baptism were re-baptized by Paul then the Spirit came upon them, and they spoke in tongues (19:1–7), so, while the term is not used it is clearly the same experience. This all led one Pentecostal writer to say, "Three times the story has been told, should the paradigm effect of these accounts lead us to expect the same things in our own experience of the Spirit?"[101] The more so as the promise of the baptism with the Spirit is given at the beginning of Jesus' ministry in the four Gospels and at the end of his earthly ministry (Matt 3;11; Mark 1:8; Luke 3:16; John 1:26; Acts 1:5).

Despite "baptism with the Spirit" being a perfectly biblical term, the mere mention of this term can bring contention and judgment (both ways) within all factions of Christianity. Some traditionalists have accused the "tongue talkers" of having a demon while some of those who do talk in tongues have accused the non-talkers of not being "saved!" The Acts record shows clearly that the Spirit was given prior to, at, or even after baptism (2:38; 10:44–47; 11:15–16; 15:8; 19:1–7). This was something far more than mere words as when the sorcerer Simon saw that the Spirit was given by the laying on of hands, he was prepared to offer Peter money to be able to do it also (8:14–17). It is very reasonable to understand that "there were definite observable signs of receiving of the Spirit"[102] and that it could be after the initial faith. But it could equally be argued that Cornelius, the twelve at Ephesus, and the Samaritans were unusual conversions while Acts 2:38 with repentance and baptism leading to forgiveness and the gift of the Spirit being normal. That does not take away from the giving of the Spirit in Acts being something recognizable and giving assurance to new believers as a sign of a new age.[103] Indeed it was something that could be experienced more than once to strengthen faith or renew the joy of it (4:31; 13:52).

The church in Acts shows the Spirit is constantly active, filling, guiding, giving powerful words of witness, and doing mighty deeds. For all that, Luke's teaching on the Holy Spirit has been described as having "loose ends and is 'untidy.'" That may be "inherent in the nature of the topic: the Spirit's working is not something that can be neatly categorized in a rational way but remains an element of the mysterious."[104] But what should the experience of the Spirit for a modern-day believer be? The

101. Lee, *Baptism in the Spirit*, 20.

102. Marshall, *Fresh Look*, 67.

103. Marshall, *Fresh Look*, 68.

104. Marshall, *Fresh Look*, 69.

Spirit enabling Christian living, which is an emphasis of Paul's Epistles, is an entirely different thing to the spiritual power needed to see the miraculous. Robert Anderson, in his *Silence of God*, describes the powerless situation of most western churches" when he said,

> The mystery remains that God who at sundry times and in diverse manners spake in time past unto the Fathers never speaks to his people now! The divine history of the favoured race for thousands of years teems with miracles by which God gave proof of his power with men, and yet we are confronted with the astonishing fact that from the days of the Apostles to the present hour the history of Christendom will be searched in vain for the record of a single public event to compel belief that there is a God at all.[105]

But that pessimism need not be the full story. The account of Andrew Murray's life includes the account of the start of the revival in Worcester in South Africa in 1860, which would see fifty men volunteer for ministry:

> On a certain Sunday evening there were gathered in a little hall some sixty young people. I was leader of the meeting, which commenced with a hymn and a lesson from God's Word, after which I engaged in a prayer. After three or four others had (as was customary) given out a verse of a hymn and offered prayer, a colored girl of about fifteen years of age, in service with a farmer from Hex River, rose at the back of the hall, and asked if she too might propose a hymn. At first I hesitated not knowing what the meeting would think, but better thoughts prevailed and I replied, Yes. She gave out her hymn-verse and prayed in moving tones. While she was praying we heard as it were a sound in the distance, which came nearer and nearer, until the hall seemed to be shaken, and with one or two exceptions, the whole meeting began to pray, the majority in audible voice, but some in whispers. Nevertheless, the noise made by the concourse was deafening.[106]

May my readers be blessed to know the Easter and Pentecost experience of the Spirit, who is continually manifesting himself in new ways. Yet one thing has not changed, the ministry of the church, like the

105. Anderson, *Silence*, 18. I would not go quite as far as Anderson but accept the general principal.

106. Du Plessis, *Andrew Murray*, 195–96,

ministry of Jesus, is dependent on the coming of the Holy Spirit. Further, it must be Christ-centered, and Spirit-directed.

The "Success" of the Church and the "Failure" of Christ

It is only fitting that Christ's ministry should reflect that of the Old Testament prophets (Matt 23:37; Luke 13:33–34) who preached a message of repentance to a people who would not listen. There is a further parallel between the death of Jesus and the nation of Israel. His death could be likened to the captivity in Babylon and his resurrection to the return from exile that would see the nation of Israel never again slip into the gross idolatry and immorality it had been guilty of before 586 BC with the fall of Jerusalem. Jesus stated his failure was due, not to his message but to his hearers, "even ungodly Tyre and Sidon would have repented" (Matt 11:20–24).

But the message is different. The Jews of Jerusalem did not respond to the message that we know of repentance from dead works and faith towards God. Through Peter's preaching they are convinced of their guilt in killing the author of life (3:15)—their Lord and Christ. This greater effectiveness, reconciling men to God, is evidence of the greater works promised to the church. Before the crucifixion, nothing could shake them from their system of righteousness by the deeds of the Law. But now some realized they were worse than the gentiles, at least Pilate found Jesus innocent and wanted to let him go. Whereas nearly all had abandoned Jesus, the later stability of his followers during persecution is largely because they realized how much they had been forgiven. "Having asked, one can trust God to provide it. After all, it is a promise that God gave much to fulfil."[107] "Christianity is optimistic about grace but pessimistic about human nature."[108]

THE FIRST CHRISTIANS (2:40–47)

In a city swollen for feast time,[109] three thousand believed Peter's pleadings, of which we only have a small portion, and were added to the new

107. Bock, *Acts*, 148.

108. Fernando, *Acts*, 117.

109. Estimated numbers vary dramatically and range from fifty-five thousand to two hundred thousand.

community. (Luke gives the count on a number of occasions—2:47; 4:4; 5:14; 6:1, 7; 9:42; 11:24; 13:43; 14:1; 17:10–12; 21:20.) The granting of the Law by God at Sinai was also commemorated at Pentecost, yet that was a day that saw the death of three thousand people (Ex 32:28). Showing the difference between life in the Spirit and justification by works (Gal 3:1–3), three thousand found eternal life when the Spirit was given. By mentioning signs and wonders, Luke links the apostles to the prophecy of Joel and the ministry of Jesus. God was supporting his new church. This caused the outside community to take careful and respectful notice of the believers. As a consequence, their numbers grew further.

Baptizing was not enough; Jesus had said it must be accompanied by instruction (Matt 28:19–20). What he did not speak about was the deep connection and joy that would come through the Spirit and the common experience of forgiveness that came at such great cost. The community was bonding together through being persistent in the four pillars of community life, apostolic teaching, fellowship, breaking of bread, and prayer. "Breaking of bread" may refer to having communion during a normal meal or just sharing meals. As it is sandwiched between teaching and fellowship on one side and prayer on the other, it is reasonable to see this as an agape feast. This is a communal meal "that emphasized the joy of communion with the risen Lord and of fellowship with one another, which Paul later quite 'legitimately' saw to have paschal import in line with the intention of Jesus."[110] Their fellowship was deep, a partnership drawn from what they shared in common[111] and all was made possible by the grace of God (4:33).

The first church demonstrated God's care by showing that they also cared. The extent of sharing of belongings could have been prompted by an expectation of Christ's early return, but Luke only gives the social reason behind the compassion. Luke emphasizes what the Spirit's activity does for the community rather than what he does for the believer.[112] A common theme of Acts is the community joined in prayer (1:24; 6:6; 8:15; 9:11, 40; 10:9, 30; 11:5; 12:12; 13:3; 14:23) The authenticity of the of the bond was shown through the community's compassion by voluntarily providing for the needs of their poor. It was not something forced on

110. Longenecker, "Acts," 9:288.

111. The word for "fellowship" in verse 42, *koinōnia*, and "sharing in common," *koina* in verse 44, have the same root, pointing us to an understanding of what Christian fellowship means.

112. Bock, *Acts*, 37.

them (5:4). This compassion was not restricted to Jerusalem but would prove to be community wide (2 Cor 8–9).

The importance of the radical change the Spirit worked in the early Christians in their relationship to their money must not be underestimated as many lived lives that were "economically marginal"[113] with very little to spare. Some Jews said that there was clear evidence for the validity of the Law given at Sinai in the way it was backed up by God's otherwise impossible provision of food.[114] Here it is happening again through the miracle of a believer's changed relationship to money. The model was not sustainable, however, and we know of two separate offerings for the Jerusalem church. The ideal community did not last as soon there would be division caused by favoritism in the giving of charity and deceit among the donors.

At this time, the church did not have a separate identity as Christianity and the temple are closely linked. This connection would only finally be broken in AD 70 with the destruction of the temple as part of the foretold judgment on Jerusalem (Luke 11:49–51; 13:34–5). So central is it that Luke began his first work in the heart of the temple with the promise of the coming gospel, reframes Jesus' final Jerusalem visit to appear that he never leaves the temple, and ends in the temple (Luke 24:53).[115] Despite this, its role in Luke–Acts is paradoxical as sometimes the temple is a place of peace and at other times a place of conflict.[116] Romans highly valued *pietas*, which included devotion to ancient temples, respect for ancestors, and preserving their customs.[117] Luke presents the life of Jesus in a way that it agrees with the Roman understanding of *pietas*, something continued with the apostles and Paul. Christianity was not a novel *religio illicita* (illicit religion), "but one firmly rooted in one of the ancient religions that existed and was accepted by the Roman Empire."[118] The emphasis Luke gives to meeting in the temple and the favor they were initially given leads to the conclusion that the believers saw themselves

113. Oakes, *Reading Romans*, 116.

114. Philo, *Decalogue*, 1.16.

115. Conzelmann, *Theology of Luke*, 75.

116. Monier, "Reading Luke," 115.

117. Augustus, *RG*. 24, 34.

118. Monier, "Reading Luke," 116.

"as representing all that is truly Jewish."[119] The temple would become the victim of its occupiers who were sacrilegious murderers.[120]

Tithing and Guaranteed Prosperity

Some modern preachers, using Mal 3:10, make a connection between prosperity and tithing. The Jerusalem church was the only part of the new community that can be expected to be diligent about tithing. It did not result in universal prosperity.

119. Longenecker, "Acts," 9:291.

120. Monier, "Reading Luke," 119–20.

3

The Church Advances (Acts 3:1—4:37)

THE HEALING OF THE LAME MAN (3:1–10)

Jesus used his own authority to bring times of refreshing and forgiveness. For three years the regular order of nature was suspended time after time. This was not done as a simple display of power but of the sovereign God offering a salvation beyond mere human powers. This "saving" is continued in his name[1] by Peter[2] and also by Paul at Lystra where similar terms are used of the healing of the lame man there. The healing of the crippled beggar is told not because it was the first or most notable miracle (sixteen more follow),[3] but because of the results that followed. The interest created through this undeniable healing saw another two thousand men added to the church. The beggar's prominent position sitting by the main temple's gate meant he was too well known for his changed circumstances not to have "awakened faith and to create controversy."[4] The new community was still reaching out to its Jewish neighbors from whom they were to experience their first opposition.

Jesus' compassion for and healing the lame is prominent in his ministry (Matt 11:5, 15:30–31, 21:14; Luke 7:22, 14:13, 21; John 5:3–9), but

1. The importance of the "name of Jesus" is discussed in my comments on chapter 4.

2. While Peter is the spokesman and overshadows John in this account, Luke's account, wherever possible, uses at least two witnesses.

3. Apart from general references to miracles, there are five healings (3:1–10; 9:10–19, 9:32–35; 14:8–11; 28:7–8), two raisings from the dead (9:36–42; 20:7–12), three accounts of persons being freed (5:17–26; 12:1–19 16:20–34), two exorcisms (16:16–19; 19:11–17), three judgments (5:1–11; 12:20–23; 13:4–12), one of transportation (8:39), and one preservation (28:3–6).

4. Bock, *Acts*, 164.

one of Luke's accounts (Luke 5:17–26) linked it to the authority to forgive sins, not just to release from suffering. As the beggar had been lame from birth, it raises the same question from John 9 about who sinned—this man or his parents that he was born lame (John 9:2). While the question may have been settled for Peter and John, it certainly was not for those attending the temple. The Pharisees at least would have considered him "steeped in sin" (John 9:34). Begging was not meant to occur under the Mosaic Law and there was not even a word for it.[5] It was the curse of the children of the ungodly (Ps 37:25).

The Law only forbade deformed priests from ministering in the temple (Lev 21:16–23) as they would have polluted it. However, David forbade the blind and lame from entering "the house," but was not specific about this was the palace or the temple (2 Sam 5:8). David's greatest son outraged the priests when he healed the lame and blind in what had to be the court of the men (Matt 21:14–5). He was in effect saying that the temple was an all-inclusive place where, "in the messianic age, the blind and the lame would be recipients of God's favor"[6] (Jer 31:8). As one commentator said,

> As Jesus heals the blind and the lame, he shows his authority to create purity in all those desiring to worship God, demonstrating that as the One who is greater than the temple (Matt 12:6) he fulfills the Old Testament prescriptions for cleansing that the temple practices required to come into the presence of God.[7]

This message of cleansing through Christ's forgiveness will be preached by Peter.

The gate of the temple[8] Peter and John used, called here the *Beautiful Gate*, was most likely the inner gate known as the *Nicanor* or *Corinthian Gate*, which separated the court of the women from the court of the men. Josephus describes how the nine gates to the temple, along with the jambs and lintels were covered all round with gold and silver but then describes one special gate:

> But there was one gate that was without the [inward court of the] holy house, which was of Corinthian brass, and greatly

5. Jastrow and Malter, *Begging*, 2:639.

6. Razafiarivony, "Exclusion of the Blind," 112.

7. Wilkins, *Matthew*, 692.

8. Luke is inconsistent with his use of the term "temple." We can't know if he is referring to the whole temple complex or one of the inner courts.

> excelled those that were only covered over with silver and gold. . . . Now the magnitudes of the other gates were equal one to another; but that over the Corinthian gate, which opened on the east over against the gate of the holy house itself, was much larger; for its height was fifty cubits; and its doors were forty cubits; and it was adorned after a most costly manner, as having much richer and thicker plates of silver and gold upon them than the other. These nine gates had that silver and gold poured upon them by Alexander, the father of Tiberius.[9]

The opulence of this gate is in sharp contrast to the poverty of the beggar sitting by it and the intent of the Law. It also stands in stark contrast to a community that shared their goods and where its leaders lived modestly.

The groans and cries of the deformed outside the temple of the creator of the universe begs the question of whether the creator does hear their cries. It should be remembered that, as he was outside the gate every day, Jesus would have passed by this man on a number of occasions, showing that healing is a sovereign act of God to be withheld or granted at his discretion (Exod 4:11). The beggar was condemned to sit outside the inner court, away from the associated presence of God only by men making the requirements of God more severe than they needed to be. His healing implies more than just the rectification of a physical problem. Peter takes the initiative, and the beggar is healed through faith in Jesus (3:16). Isaiah had promised the lame would leap like a deer (Isa 35:5–6), so the witnesses would have been asking if the messianic age had begun. No, it was a down payment on the healing that the Messiah's coming will bring, just as the judgment of Ananias and Sapphira will foreshadow the accompanying judgment. While this age may be passing away, in the messianic age, the restoration of all things is yet to come (3:18–21). The door is still open for repentance (3:26).

There is no indication there was any faith in the beggar. However, his subsequent actions show a perfect faith response through his praise of God. The modern Western church should ponder the words of Thomas Aquinas[10] when he called on Pope Innocent II when he was counting a large amount of money: "'You see Thomas, the church can no longer say silver and gold have I none.' 'True Holy Father, but neither can she

9. Josephus, *J. W.* 5.5.3.

10. Thomas (1225–1274) was a Dominican friar and priest and a leading philosopher and theologian. His work *Summa Theologica* is still very influential in the Roman Catholic Church.

say rise up and walk.' The moral of this story can be pondered by any Christian communion that enjoys a fair degree of temporal prosperity."[11] Fortunately, the most impoverished church can still say to anyone who is trusting Jesus that their sins are forgiven.

PETER'S SERMON IN THE TEMPLE AREA (3:11–26)

The sermon of Peter reported here also follows the pattern of the apostolic kerygma:

1. The age of fulfillment has arrived (3:21).
2. There is a rehearsal of the life, death, and resurrection of Jesus (3:13–15).
3. There is quoting of Old Testament passages proving Jesus to be Christ (3:18, 22–25).
4. There is a call to repentance (3:19–20).

3:11–16. As with Peter's first sermon, it is not personal sin that is denounced but their involvement in Christ's death. Who the alive and still-working Jesus is and what he does are inseparable. Instead, as with the sermon in Acts 2, Peter must start by correcting a misunderstanding. It is not their doing so: Peter directs the credit to God. The Father is again presented as reversing the verdict of sinful men (3:15). Those that realize their guilt are called to line up behind the Father and agree with him, otherwise they risk failing to heed the prophet like Moses (2:22–23

Peter linked God's fresh work firmly into the promises to the patriarchs and associates himself (our fathers, not your fathers) with the unbelieving members of the nation (3:13). Peter alludes to Jesus as the servant (Isa 52:13; see also Acts 3:26; 4:27, 30) and it was likely that the Son of Man saw his suffering through the lens of Isaiah's servant.[12] The Gospels clearly portray him as the suffering servant, but only Luke uses that term for him. In his Gospel it is through reference to the Servant Songs, and here the paradox of Jesus as Lord and servant is preached openly. It is men who should glorify God, so when God glorified Jesus, the order is reversed. This acceptance after suffering follows the pattern

11. Bruce, *Acts*, 1954, 84.

12. Bruce, *Acts*, 1990, 139–40.

of the suffering servant who was given over (3:13) in Isa 52:13—53:12. The inferences to Jesus as the servant are listed in Table 2.

Passage	Luke	Isaiah
Shine on those living in darkness and in the shadow of death	1:79	42:7
Your salvation, which you have prepared in the sight of all nations	2:31	52:10
A light for revelation to the gentiles and the glory of your people Israel	2:31	49:6
Numbered with the transgressors	22:13 also 3:3 by inference	53:12
The Spirit of the Lord is upon me	4:18–19	61:1–2
You are my Son, whom I love; with you I am well pleased	3:22	42:1 with Ps 2:7
[His life] which is poured out for you	22:20	53:12

Table 3.Luke's inferences to Jesus as the servant[13]

It had become recognized that for all the priest's actions to maintain the purity of the temple, it was the priests themselves who were defiling it, not the lame and blind.[14] The worshipers, however, went to the temple that morning, presumably content in their righteousness, only to be confronted with their wickedness, not their leader's (3:26). Peter only mentions the leader's guilt in passing (3:17) and lays the guilt firmly at the worshiper's feet. The leaders may have prompted the death of Jesus, but they were willing participants. Their sinfulness exceeded that of the gentile ruler Pilate who wanted to free Jesus (3:13); instead they chose "a murderer over one who reflects holiness and righteousness."[15] They rejected and then killed the author (or prince)[16] of life (3:15). By rejecting the holy and righteous one (3:14), they exposed their own blindness. They disowned him and killed him (3:13–17). However, the motif of substitution of the "righteous one," a term used to describe the Messiah (Isa 32:1. 53:11; Zech 9:9), for the wicked (3:14) should not be minimized. They were, after all, murderers themselves. Even his Roman executioner

13. Johnson, *Message of Acts*, 41–43.

14. CD V.6, 7; 1 QS V.19, 20.

15. Bock, *Acts*, 170.

16. Both are possible. As "Author" he creates the new life as he did with the cripple, as "Prince" he leads many to life. Given the healing and the reference to the life taker they preferred, "Author" is more likely. Bock, *Acts*, 171.

declared Jesus righteous (Luke 23:47). The apostles are witnesses, not just of the resurrection but also against them in the highest court.

> Peter now returns to his original contrast: the clash between the deed of the Jews and the act of God. They killed the Author of Life "whom God raised up from the dead" and this divine act is more than a contrast to the deeds of the Jews; at one stroke God nullified all that the Jews had done. He contradicted and condemned all that they had done; he approved and sealed his great Servant as being in fact the Author of Life, the Destroyer of Death. God accepted all of Christ's work and sacrifice as being full, complete, sufficient and crowned Jesus with infinite glory.[17]

Verse 16 has three references to Jesus' name and twice mentions faith and these are the source of blessing. "Faith" is a word frequently used in Acts and has a broad meaning. It can be an initial faith or the characteristic of a life, e.g., 6:5–7; 11:23–24, or the new movement itself. Here it is, the apostle's faith, and their faith in the name of Jesus healed the beggar bringing times of refreshing to a person whose situation was helpless. His response of exuberant praise has been the starting point for Peter's sermon to a group who are being made aware of their own wickedness, and likewise offered "times of refreshing" (3:19) if they will repent. Their response will play a part in ushering in the great events of the end time when the messiah returns.[18]

3:17–21. In verse seventeen Peter talks about their ignorance in crucifying Christ making his message more generous towards Israel than on the day of Pentecost. This does not in any way mitigate their sins. Ignorance "refers to the Old Testament distinction between sins for which sacrifices can be made (Num 15:27–29) and sins for which the sinner's soul is cut off (Num 15:30–31)."[19] This is not the ignorance of the gentiles who have not had opportunity to hear (17:30). A clear witness has been heard, and their ignorance will not be overlooked. Yet they were not past redemption (4:1–12) if they respond. However, Peter's message was not just a promise of judgment to those who were in danger of rejecting Jesus and his warnings a further time.

17. Lenski, *Acts*, 136.

18. Longenecker, "Acts," 9:297. The passage demands the assumed word "again" or "future."

19. Lenski, *Acts*, 139.

Just as the lame man had no reason to expect mercy that day, the offer of times of refreshing (3:20) and blessing (3:26) through turning to God and repentance (3:19) was extended to the wicked. Refreshing and blessing are built on the blotting out of their sins. The expression is a metaphor derived from the practice of washing or wiping off the ink on papyrus.[20] Ancient ink had no acid in it so did not soak into the paper.[21] It is an obliteration that leaves no trace. Surprisingly, Luke says very little about the significance of Christ's death and there is no mention in the Acts sermons of Jesus dying "for us" or "for our sins," though this is clearly part of Paul's theology. The only mention is in Acts 20:28 when Paul addresses the elders of the Ephesian church.

The repentance that Peter is urging on his hearers has no bearing on the timing of the messiah's return. This is not based on repentance but on specific timing established by God. Their repentance only allowed them to participate in the blessings. These are actively poured out by him now despite being in heaven and in the future on his return.

3:22–26. Peter lined up Jesus with Israel's great leaders, Abraham, Moses, and David. He further reminded his hearers that a suffering messiah was not something new, going beyond Isaiah's suffering servant to all the prophets (3:18), just as Jesus had expounded on them on the road to Emmaus (Luke 24:13–35). As to the future, it was also revealed by the prophets. The prophet like Moses that they were to heed was "raised up" (3:22), which could easily allude to the resurrection as Peter used this word in verse 15 and 26. Luke alluded to this Moses-like figure in his Gospel (Luke 9:35, cf., Deut 18:19) and further in Acts 7:22, 25, 30–39. However, the promised blessing from embracing the atonement of Jesus was not guaranteed to all Israel. There are severe consequences for rejection—"being completely cut off[22] (3:23)—which were also laid out by Moses. Notably, the passage referred to by Luke is about not keeping the Day of Atonement (Lev 23:29).

It is difficult to see a clear messianic prophecy from Samuel (3:24), so Peter's mention is more likely through Jesus' association with David. Samuel anointed David and prophesied the establishment of his kingdom (1 Sam 16:13; 28:17). But God's promises of blessing through his covenant with Israel go back to Abraham (Gen 12:1–3). As Acts unfolds the readers will become aware of the significance of that blessing as it

20. Stott, *Message of Acts*, 93.

21. Barclay, *Acts*, 35.

22. The word used by Luke describes utter destruction. BDAG, "ἐξολοθρεύω," 276.

was always God's plan to bless the gentiles (2:25; 11:15–18). The second time God gave Abraham the blessing is in the context of a father sacrificing his son.[23] Paul will stress the importance of the word "seed" being singular (Gal 3:8–29) and so referring to Jesus, the ultimate fulfilment of the promise. The goal was always to bless but it does require that his hearers turn.[24]

PETER AND JOHN ARRESTED (4:1–22)

4:1–4. In chapter 4 we will see the strategy of Satan starting to emerge as he attacks the church on three fronts. The council will use the not very subtle means of physical violence and even death. However, he will attack on two more fronts: in chapter 5 it will be by moral corruption with the account of Ananias and Sapphira and in chapter 6 by distracting the apostles from their key responsibility by occupying them with good works and administration.[25] We are confronted with the irrational and hardhearted response, first by the Sadducees and then the assembled council, to a miracle so astonishing that even they cannot deny it. Instead of rejoicing like the other witnesses, Peter's sermon in the temple is interrupted by the very high-level arrest of him, John, and the beggar (interruptions are a regular feature of Luke's recording of speeches—7:54; 10:44; 17:32; 22:22; 26:24). The Pharisees, who had the support of the people and were diametrically opposed to the Sadducees, were not present.

The arrest and subsequent interrogation are hardly surprising as the message of Jesus, resurrected and forgiving, would have been seen as inflammatory by many Jews.[26] The protagonists were the chief priest and the officer in charge of the temple police (number one and two[27] in the temple and drawn from the ruling families) accompanied by other Sadducees. The arrest was presumably in the evening, so they were put in

23. Luke's reference here more closely resembles the time it was given on Mt. Moriah. Bock, *Acts*, 180.

24. It is uncertain whether it is the audience who turns or the servant turns them.

25. Stott, *Message of Acts*, 105.

26. Witherington, *Acts*, 188.

27. Most likely the *sagan ha-kohanim* who had oversight over all the priests as well as the activities at the temple. Witherington, *Acts*, 189; Josephus, *Ant.* 20.6.2.

prison overnight, but this was not before five thousand more men[28] are added to the church.

Who Were the Sadducees?

The Sadducees, and the officials mentioned who would at the very least be closely aligned with them, traced their heritage back to Zadok, the high priest to David and Solomon. They claimed to represent the "views and practices of the Law and the interests of Temple and priesthood"[29] but had become thoroughly Hellenized. As a movement, they were "degenerated worldly-minded Epicureans."[30] Josephus said that the Sadducees only had the rich on their side,[31] and after describing the Pharisees, speaks of them this way:

> But the Sadducees are those that compose the second order, and take away fate entirely, and suppose that God is not concerned in our doing or not doing what is evil; and they say, that to act what is good, or what is evil, is at men's own choice, and that the one or the other belongs so to everyone, that they may act as they please. They also take away the belief of the immortal duration of the soul, and the punishments and rewards in Hades. Moreover, the Pharisees are friendly to one another, and are for the exercise of concord, and regard for the public; but the behavior of the Sadducees one towards another is in some degree wild, and their conversation with those that are of their own party is as barbarous as if they were strangers to them.[32]

Living a life without thought of God's judgment ensured that they acted in ways that promoted their own material comfort and protected their political power. They believed the Maccabean heroes had already ushered in the messianic age that was continuing under their supervision. The messiah was an ideal, not a person, and "the messianic age was a process, not a cataclysmic or even datable event."[33] The destruction of

28. Or possibly a total of 5,000 since Pentecost, up from 120.

29. Kaufmann, *Sadducees*, 630.

30. Kaufmann, *Sadducees*, 630. An Epicurean is devoted to the pursuit of sensual pleasure, good food, and comfort,

31. Josephus, *Ant.* 18.1.4.

32. Josephus, *J. W.* 2.8.14. The term may be derived from the Hebrew word for "righteous" but that is not universally accepted. Kaufmann, *Sadducees*, 630.

33. Longenecker, "Acts," 9:301.

the temple saw the end of the Sadducees. Paradoxically, the leader of these men, who loved the world so much, claimed to be the sole mediator between the people and God. If Peter could convince the people that they were in fact murderers, their authority would have been greatly diminished, if not destroyed. As Acts progresses, we will see that this elite did not speak for all priests.

4:5–7. After spending a night in prison, the apostles appeared before the council.[34] The singular resurrection of Jesus, something new in Judaism, cut across the authority of the Sadducees, particularly with the numbers responding to the new movement's message. They objected to the preaching of the resurrection and to any preaching that in any way related to Jesus as the Messiah. While the apostles did no more than make "an appeal and leav[e] the decision and consequences to individual response,"[35] the council believed they had the power and authority to compel compliance. The apostles' message was likely to "be politically, socially, and religiously destabilizing to their relatively good relations with Rome."[36] The ritual of the temple they presided over contrasted with the intimacy of the home-based ministry of the Way.[37]

The three men appeared before the "leaders," the very ones responsible for crucifying Jesus (Luke 14:1; 23:13, 35) the "elders" who were senior civic leaders, and the "scribes" (mainly Pharisees) who studied and interpreted the Law. In delivering a verdict, "it would be on behalf of the nation and influence the nation's perception of Jesus."[38] Only here do we have a high-priestly genealogy and appearing before them fulfills the prediction of Jesus that the apostles will bear witness to his name before rulers (Luke 21:12), starting in Jerusalem (Luke 24:47).[39] In verse six, Annas is called the high priest though he only held this position from AD 6–14. His son, Eleazer, followed him. Caiaphas, his son-in-law, was high priest at the time, serving from AD 18 to 36. Four of his other sons followed him as high priest. Annas is to be seen as having the power, if not

34. Possibly the Sanhedrin, a council of seventy elders plus the high priest who presided over all religious and many secular matters. It is called this in verse 15 though its existence at that time may only have been as an advisory role to the rulers. Witherington, *Acts*, 191.

35. Bock, *Acts*, 200.

36. Bock, *Acts*, 186.

37. Christianity is called "the Way" six times in Acts, where it is used in an absolute sense. It may refer back to Jesus' claim to be the way to the Father (John 14:6).

38. Bock, *Acts*, 191.

39. Edwards, "Parallels and Patterns," 488.

the position. John is possibly Jonathan, the son who followed Caiaphas in AD 36. The Aaronide priesthood and its rightful authority had ceased during the reign of Antiochus when it was purchased by Jason, the brother of the rightful high priest. Thereafter it had been dispensed at the will of Judah's political masters.

While others were present, the power lay with the Sadducees (5:17), all of them enemies of the resurrection and of any preaching about Jesus having risen from the dead. The two former fishermen from Galilee now had to face these powerful judges, whose verdict was absolutely made up in advance. Jesus had warned his disciples that they would face rejection and be hauled before judges just as it occurred to God's perfect servant, and they were prepared to be poured out like him. Yet, while Jesus had foretold that his followers would face prison, he also promised them that they would be given wisdom (Luke 21:12–15). Though the situation was hard, God empowered his servants by filling them with the Holy Spirit (4:8). This "filling" needs to be understood as separate from the filling of the Spirit at conversion and the "baptism in the Spirit" but an empowerment for a special task as the need arose. They were able to sustain a theological debate with the supreme religious court of the land.

The same adversaries had demanded of Jesus, "Tell us by what authority you are doing these things" (Luke 20:2), and Luke echoes these words in verse 7: "Who gave you this authority?" This is the first of a number of scenes throughout Acts that fulfil the words of Jesus, "The student is not above the teacher, but everyone who is fully trained will be like their teacher" (Luke 6:40). The Apostles quickly moved from the physical miracle to its spiritual significance. Jesus is responsible through them invoking the authority in his name. The name of Jesus is now powerful just as the name of the Father is powerful. There may also be, at least in the apostles' minds, a reference to the pious Jewish practice of using "the Name" as a substitute for God's name with its associated power and presence.[40]

Using Jesus' name expresses his very nature as God. God had promised that "wherever I cause my name to be honored, I will come to you and bless you" (Ex 20:24) and the psalmists spoke of it as a protective force (Pss 20:1; 54:1; 118:10–12, 26). However, unlike the views of some of the early church fathers, the expression "no other name" is not some almost magical saying that Christians use that can guarantee the

40. Longenecker, "Acts," 9:296.

efficacy of prayers.[41] The council of murderers considered that they had the authority to determine who could use this name.

4:8–12. By calling the council to account, the apostles were speaking with an authority above that which the religious leaders could ever possess. Peter's address is like that in chapter 3: "God has exalted Jesus, but you killed him" and "God declares the message, but you rejected it." Psalm 118 is one of the most commonly quoted passages in the New Testament (Matt 21:42; Mark 12:10; Luke 20:17; 1 Pet 2:4, 7), and here Peter gave a summary rather than a direct quote. He adds that the rejection was by "all of you" so making the rulers responsible for Jesus' death. What was scorned by them, God honored by making Jesus the first oversized "stone" in a new movement that will act as the reference for the entire structure. In the context of the psalm the cornerstone is of the gate through which the righteous may enter (118:20).[42] There are many references to the stone imagery in the Old Testament. The vision of Daniel of the stone not cut out by human hands (Dan 2:34–35) and his vision of the Son of Man (Dan 7:13–14) coupled with the similarity in Hebrew between "stone" and "son" led to the messianic association.[43] Jesus had earlier used Peter's quotation from Ps 118 in the parable of the vineyard and the rejected son (Mark 12:1–12).

By the name of Jesus, the lame man was "saved"[44] from his condition. The physical deliverance "symbolizes the fact that Jesus saves"[45] and is the setting for the double use of "saved" in verse 12. It was not new to call someone a "savior" and the Greeks had already applied this term to military leaders, the gods, philosophers, statesmen, and in emperor worship.[46] Jesus as "savior" is unique as he was not a conqueror, but a servant who offered forgiveness. The exclusive role of the risen Jesus does not allow any possibility of pluralism that was common in the Greco-Roman

41. The "name of Jesus" has power only when it is used with faith. The Jewish exorcists in Ephesus were trying to use it as a power-word to overcome the demonic by manipulating Paul's God. Likely other divine names were used as well. They were put to shame.

42. An alternative meaning could be to the capstone placed on the highest position of the temple to complete the structure. The psalms reference is used in this context in the *Testament of Solomon* (122–123). That work dates to c. 200 AD, however, both applications are perfectly acceptable as that is what happened.

43. Longenecker, "Acts," 9:304.

44. *Sesōtai* in verse 9 with *sōtēria* and *sōthēnai* in verse 12.

45. Bock, *Acts*, 192.

46. Stubbersfield, *Ephesus*, 18–19, 44, 51, 54, 73.

world[47] as it is now. It is also possible that "salvation" was used as a messianic title, which would strengthen Peter's claims for Jesus.[48]

People are normally rewarded for good works (4:9) but instead the apostles found themselves on trial. The miracle could not be denied as it was well known that the man was a cripple from birth (4:14). Yet they were unable and unwilling to draw the proper conclusion. The right conclusion would have been that the council should have been the ones on trial. As one commentator says, "If Jesus is healing, then he is alive, vindicated by God, and they are culpable for his death."[49] Instead, they kept silent. Not one voice is raised on behalf of truth, exposing their hardheartedness. Still, the apostles would not stir up the people against the council and even made excuses for their crucifixion of Jesus (3:17).

4:13–21. The ability of the Spirit to give courage to men who were previously fearful and to speak with an ability beyond any formal training they may have had (Luke 21:15) left the council astounded. In verse 13 they call the apostles ignorant men, which means they have not been through rabbinical schools, not that they could not read or write. However, they were not untrained, as they had been with Jesus. For all this, the charges made against Stephen, likely a Jew from outside Judea, when he was brought before the council will be very different to those brought against the apostles (see Table 4 and Table 6).

> While Paul would urge the believers to be subject to the governing authorities (Rom 13:1–7) the Apostles' response to the Council's threats shows there are limits to this obedience. The Jewish leaders no longer represented God's will.[50]

Their hard hearts in the face of the obvious miracle prevented the people from finding and acknowledging their Messiah. For their part, while rejecting the path of religious anarchy, the apostles refused emphatically to be silent. Yet even the hard hearts of the councilors had limits. The healed man was an obvious act of God approved by the worshipers so the council knew they could not safely punish the apostles. They would have been happy with the Christian service of the apostles without its message of sin and repentance. Little has changed. Christian

47. Stubbersfield, *Ephesus*, 105.

48 Longenecker, "Acts," 9:305.

49. Bock, *Acts*, 192.

50. Bock, *Acts*, 199.

good works must never be separated from the gospel. If they are only good works, they are not Christian works.

The apostles' growing power and influence are taken into account (4:16–17) as the council realizes it is involved in a "power struggle for the hearts of the Jewish people."[51] They threatened the two apostles commanding them not to speak or teach in Jesus' name again, a charge contrary to all reason and nature.[52] Jesus had said little when he stood where the apostles defended themselves eloquently and with authority.

It had been maintained among the critics that the appearance before the Sanhedrin in chapter 5 was a different account of the same story. It is now understood that these two events complement each other by accurately displaying Jewish jurisprudence. When ordinary people without theological training came before them in non-capital cases, they were to be given a warning before witnesses. They could only be punished if they committed the same act after being admonished. Luke clearly knew the precise details of Jewish legal practice.[53]

THE REPORT TO THE BELIEVERS (4:23–31)

On returning to their friends, they again all go to united corporate prayer, conscious of their dependence on God. They could have prayed for judgment on the council or to avoid persecution, but instead they asked that they would have strength to be about their mission and preach the message boldly.[54] The Way is thinking theologically about the opposition and set a model for us.[55] They address God in words drawn from Hezekiah's prayer after Sennacherib ridiculed God (Isa 37:16–20). There is a return to the doctrine of providence, God is in control despite the appearance that the counsel and raging of wicked men has prevailed. Rather, they are puppets in his hands. It is, after all, his creation.

The threats of the council were real but instead of being silent they encouraged themselves in the Scripture, quoting Ps 2, a Messianic psalm of the servant David. The psalm described the messiah's opponents well:

51. Witherington, *Acts*, 189.

52. Note the similarity to Socrates who declared before his judges that he would not stop teaching philosophy even to protect his own life. He replied, "Men of Athens, I respect and love you, but I shall obey the god rather than you." Plato, *Apol.* 29d.

53. Longenecker, "Acts," 9:300.

54. Bock, *Acts*, 202–3.

55. Bock, *Acts*, 205.

the "king" was Herod, the "ruler" was Pilate, the "gentiles" were the Romans, and the "people" were his own who should have received him. We can understand Herod and Pontius Pilate seeking to protect their power, but this unholy conspiracy involved, not just the Jewish leaders but the ordinary people of Jerusalem. Rather than God's intentions having gone horribly wrong, the players were all no more than pawns in a course of events predestined by the Father. As such, the "community leaves to God the moral judgment of the opponents and their actions."[56]

One commentator said of Ps 2 that the "two names of the Messiah which were current in the time of Christ—the name of Messiah itself, the Anointed, and the name, Son of God, owed their origin to this Psalm in its Messianic origin."[57] But more than just names, the community understood from this psalm that their relation to God was such that the rulers and their nations were nothing.[58] Now they understood that by identifying the messiah's enemies they could know God's enemies, which sadly now includes their own nation.

Referring to the "man" (2:22), Jesus being anointed as the Messiah (4:27) can lead to an understanding that Jesus was "adopted"[59] but this would be misleading. Luke's account of the infant Jesus shows he had the status of Messiah from before his birth. Elizabeth calls the unborn Jesus her "Lord" (Luke 1:43), the shepherds went to the newborn baby who was "Christ the Lord" (2;11) and Simeon calls the days old baby the "Lord's Messiah" (2:25–35)

They see themselves as God's bond servants, but in their culture slaves did not have authority to speak freely. For followers of the Way, submitting to the will of God is balanced by the right to speak freely and make requests.[60] They know from experience how God can act and are asking no more than the church might be enabled to act in ways that match his abilities.

As evidence that their prayer was heard, the house was shaken, and they were filled with the Holy Spirit. The filling of the Holy Spirit should

56. Bock, *Acts*, 209.

57. Plumber, *Psalms*, 38.

58. Bock, *Acts*, 202.

59. Adoptionism was an early Christian heresy popular from the first to third centuries that is anti-trinitarian. This belief saw Jesus, a righteous man, being adopted at either his baptism, resurrection, or ascension. This belief is still around in various forms today but was denounced by the Council of Nicaea in 325. The Council gave us the Nicene Creed.

60. Williams, *Acts*, 89.

not be considered as a once-only experience. Unlike salvation it can be repeated time after time. "Whitefield tells us in his journals that whenever he had a special visitation of the Spirit, he had come to feel that it was almost the harbinger of some unusual trial or difficulty, some terrible persecution or some such cause of distress. This has often happened, and not only to individuals but to communities. . . . God, as it were, then rewards His people for having gone through the trial in such an excellent manner."[61]

The request for boldness in the proclamation was heard and also the request that God's compassion would continue to be displayed (4:29–30). The salvation of God would be proclaimed in both words and his sovereign actions. Chapter 4 will conclude with the church itself taking the initiative showing compassion. The early Jerusalem church was not backwards in asking great things of their Lord with a matched expectation that he would hear. The church today can be guilty of asking small things because they expect little. Augustine clearly saw that the absence of present-day miracles will leave the church open to disbelief in the greatest miracle.[62]

Christian witness took place in a very hostile environment. The encounter with the Jewish authorities will be the first of about twenty encounters with them, state authorities, or mobs. The pattern of non-retaliation and prayer remains a pattern to be followed.[63]

THE PRACTICAL COMPASSION OF THE EARLY CHURCH (ACTS 4:32–37)

In chapter 3 we saw a beggar sitting at the luxurious gate to the temple. That situation flew in the face of Israel being a place where there were not to be any poor (Deut 15:4). Luke's words deliberately mirror the promise for faithfulness. The new community was committed to each other through "risky liberality"[64] and was living out the intention of being a people without abject poverty. All held their property loosely (4:32),

61. Lloyd-Jones, *Romans*, 335.

62. Augustine, *Civ.* 1033. Following Augustine's practice of recording the miracles that occurred in his diocese (seventy alone in two years in just one locality), I have made a practice of recording testimonies from my own church. These are found in my book *So Much Blood: And Other Stories from the Potato Field.*

63. Marshall, *Fresh Look*, 80.

64. Johnson, *Message of Acts*, 79.

but some went further by selling excess property (4:34). Unlike those who joined the Qumran community,[65] Christians were not required to dispose of all their property. This was a more difficult choice as responsibility rested with the believer, not another. It meant that they lived lives in the community where their actions were on display daily, and they were responsible for their motives, which needed to be constantly probed.[66] The sale of land was not forced on anyone, and Ananias and Sapphira in chapter 5 were reminded that their property was theirs to sell and use as they saw fit (5:4). This sharing was spontaneous and came from seeing "each other as family and friends worthy of compassionate care."[67] Jesus had said that men would know the disciples by their love for one another (John 13:35). Such was the power of the new life created through forgiveness and the indwelling of the Spirit. The call of God is to heal and to have compassion and beyond the account of Acts the church would understand that as extending to all of God's creation.

It is not possible on a sustained basis to sell your asset base as eventually the resources within the church would be eroded to a situation where they were worse than before. Yet we "have no liberty to dismiss it as a rash and foolish mistake."[68] The poverty of the Jerusalem church must have been crippling and made worse when persecution of the believers began. We read on two further occasions in Acts that outside funds had to be injected, and then it was by the gentiles. How widespread this communism of goods was practiced in the Jerusalem church is uncertain; it was not a "New Testament pattern" followed by the gentile churches or even all the Jerusalem believers. More likely we are talking about landlords selling excess property. Mary, the mother of John Mark, retained her own home (12:12). The idyllic Christian community as illustrated by 2:44–46 and 4:32–37 was not to last long as shown by Ananias and Sapphira (chapter 5) and the dispute over the distribution to the widows (chapter 6).

The administration of the church was relatively simple, and everything is revolving around the apostles. Their message was centered around the resurrection of Jesus, which showed God's vindication of him. But there was something going on among ordinary believers. The

65. Likely Essenes, a Jewish ascetic sect who lived in the Judean desert and were responsible for the Dead Sea Scrolls.

66. Johnson, *Message of Acts*, 78.

67. Bock, *Acts*, 215.

68. Stott, *Message of Acts*, 107.

commission of Jesus to the church was to evangelize to the ends of the earth, but nothing was said about the social ministry of believers. But Jesus had spoken in his very first sermon that the coming of the gospel would be good news for the poor (Luke 4:18) It is fair to ask if it was indeed good news "unless it offered them justice as well as salvation, the abolition of poverty as well as the remission of their sins."[69] The coming of the Spirit was transforming the community. The needs of the poor did not just arrive after Christ's ascension, rather their Spirit-led response to it changed.

Community life is meant to be both mission and community care.[70] In the midst of an explosion of spiritual power Luke could place a very strong "emphasis on food and money on buying and selling on houses, fields, estates and possessions."[71] As an example of a balanced Christian life we are introduced to Paul (9:26–27) and Barnabas, a Levite[72] from Cyprus, a Jew of the dispersion. He is shown as a big-hearted man, not only generous but responsible for the acceptance of the first gentile church by Jerusalem (11:22). Barnabas is called "the son *paraklēseōs*" which can be translated as advocate, consolation, or encouragement. The similarity to the name given in John's Gospel (14:16) to the promised Holy Spirit, *Paráklētos*, should be noted. While we often hear of calls to be like Jesus, his life shows what it is like to be like the Holy Spirit.

Against this balance of Barnabas, Luke chose to include three instances of appalling behavior by certain members of the early church: Judas, Ananias and Sapphira, and favoritism in the giving of charity. All this was behavior that was immediately repudiated,[73] which suggests, as one commentator noted, that "in the eyes of the early Christians a proper realignment of one's attitude to material possessions was a necessary result of true faith in Jesus"[74]

69. Stott, *Message of Acts*, 108.

70. Bock, *Acts*, 218.

71. Gooding, *True to the Faith*, 21.

72. Only the Levite clan headed up by Aaron and his sons were chosen to be priests (Exod 28); the other family clans were first assigned the menial service of the tabernacle (Num 1:47–53). At the temple they continued service such as policing the area but also took on a spiritual role through copying the Law and instructing in it. Eusebius said that he was one of the seventy called by Jesus. Eusebius, *Hist. eccl.* 1.1.4 (*NPNF*[2] 1:81).

73. Gooding, *True to the Faith*, 22.

74. Gooding, *True to the Faith*, 23.

4

The Church Experiences Setbacks (Acts 5:1–6:7)

ANANIAS AND SAPPHIRA PUNISHED (5:1–11)

The account of Ananias's and Sapphira's failure shows the honesty of Luke and the wisdom of God when writing this history.[1] There is no place in a balanced understanding of the church for an empty triumphalism, rather it must be able to come to terms with its humanity and at times a very sordid past. Just as the lame man's leaping foreshadows the full healing that will occur when the Messiah returns, the judgment of Ananias and Sapphira "was a sign foreshadowing the full and final judgment of deceivers at the Messiah's coming."[2]

The failure of these two was the second way the evil one had found to harm the ministry of the church but Peter is shown to be prophet-like in that he can read minds.[3] The passage also seems to show the Peter of old who wanted to call fire down on the Samaritans (Luke 9:54). While he is accused of acting "without the compassion or restraint of his Lord Jesus,"[4] it is God, not Peter, that judges and acts. We are not told why the burial was so quick, nor why Sapphira was not told; the account is simply too brief.[5] The swift judgment of the two, told without pity and

1. Contrast this to the official history of the Assembly of God (AoG) in Queensland, which deliberately leaves out the problem areas: "The problem areas are best left out." (Hunt, *Queensland Conference*, 31).

2. Johnson, *Message of Acts*, 81.

3. Bock, *Acts*, 221.

4. Longenecker, "Acts," 9:314.

5. Longenecker, "Acts," 9:315.

apparently without the opportunity for Ananias to repent, is in sharp contrast to the directions given in Matt 18:15–7. Nor does it match with the advice given in 1 Cor 5 with a man who is to be delivered to Satan and that his spirit may be saved. Yet, puzzlingly, 1 Cor 11:30 talks about people having died through taking communion inappropriately and we might view that as a "lesser" sin. The quick, harsh judgment "challenges any soft understanding of God which divests him of a judgmental role."[6] Their judgment prevents us from turning down the impact for us of other passages of Scripture. Church discipline is necessary, but it tends to swing from being too severe to being too lax.[7]

At the destruction of Jericho (Josh 7), Achan coveted what belonged to God and pilfered some of the things dedicated to the Lord. He was stoned and burned for this. By saying to the Holy Spirit (5:9) that the full amount was the Lord's but holding a portion back, their action was similar and both interrupted the progress of the people of God.[8] The Spirit has come to make Christ's church a community of integrity as well as love, yet we may ponder why those whose sins were far greater, such as the high priest and Herod, were not judged so quickly. Also, later horrendous sin in the church did not meet with similar divine retribution but only the patience of God. The opportunity for repentance was seldomly grasped. The pair's filling by Satan (5:3) was in contrast to the community having been filled with the Spirit (2:4). Satan may have prompted the pair, but responsibility lay with them as it did with Judas who also was likewise filled (Luke 22:2–3). Money was involved in both cases.

However, the issue was not that they did not make a big enough sacrifice by withholding money as Ananias and Sapphira were under no compulsion by the apostles or God to give all, or perhaps even any of the money to the church. The church was so completely intertwined with the vitality of the Spirit that deceiving the former was to attempt to deceive the latter and ultimately God himself[9] who searches the heart and requires integrity. Jesus was creating a holy community where people parted with their money to help the needy and where the example of Barnabas and others set an example and expectancy for the pair to emulate. The couple

6. Mitchell, *Fresh Look*, 104.

7. This is an incredibly difficult subject. John Stott gives a "good general rule that secret sins should be dealt with secretly, private sins privately, and only public sins publicly." Stott, *Message of Acts*, 112.

8. Bruce, *Acts*, 1954, 110.

9. Bruce, *Acts*, 1990, 61.

were performing an act of charity for human eyes and this counterfeit compassion showed paradise was not yet achieved.[10] A concern about their reputation required the sale of the land but their greed considered it too high a price to pay for this fame. "Between the two passions, the dexterity of hypocrisy suggested a compromise."[11]

Ananias and Sapphira were treated by God as an unclean presence in his church.[12] It is often discussed whether Ananias and Sapphira were saved. On one hand, Luke had said, "All the believers were one in heart and mind. No one claimed that any of their possessions was their own, but they shared everything they had" (4:32). This leads to the conclusion that "if that is what true believers were and did, Ananias and Sapphira were not two of them."[13] On the other, one preacher, after looking at the way the Lord dealt with David's sin with Bathsheba and murdering Uriah (2 Sam 11:1–15), said,

> Had God [held his peace] concerning David it might have resulted in David "getting away with it." If so, would David have been better off? No, neither would the name of God. (2 Sam 12:4). This seems to be why God visited Ananias and Sapphira with sudden death. (5:1–11.) I am fully aware that some do not believe Ananias and Sapphira were ever fully converted. There is not a single passage in Acts that leads us to believe Ananias and Sapphira were not genuine believers. What is equally true of Simon Peter before them, that they were saved but gave into the flesh.[14]

Anyone who has encountered hypocrisy in the church would dearly love to know the answer to this difficult question. It cannot be resolved here.

Luke sums up the whole life of faith and piety in the phrase the "fear of the Lord" (9:21; Luke 1:50), which is rooted in the assurance of God's holiness, constancy, and justice. "Fear is the appropriate response when God's presence and power are revealed in the midst of frail human beings."[15] The result of the judgment caused people to believe that God was at work in their midst and to treat the church respectfully, leading

10. Johnson, *Message of Acts*, 88.
11. Dick, *Lectures*, 77.
12. Bock, *Acts*, 225.
13. Gooding, *True to the Faith*, 97.
14. Kendall, *Once Saved*, 117.
15. Johnson, *Message of Acts*, 82.

to a willingness for many to seek the apostles for the miracles that follow (5:12–6). The first reference to the "church," or *ecclesia*, in Acts is found in verse 11. What was emerging would be a "collection of distinct local communities distributed worldwide" (20:28).[16] At this stage, however, the Jewish Old Testament community and the New Testament church are not two separate groups but the one congregation of the Lord to which the doors had now been thrown open, the *scandalon* over which many Jews would stumble.

CONVERTS MULTIPLIED (5:12–16)

The bridging paragraph to the second encounter with the Sanhedrin contains the third summary of the state of the church. Like the ones before, it focuses on signs and ministry (2:42–47; 4:32–35), but this time it looks at its relationship with outsiders.[17] The ministry of the church is shown as barely extending past the walls of Jerusalem due to its strong connection to the Temple. Solomon's porch was a public area on the east of the temple,[18] and likely where Jesus taught (John 10:23). By teaching there the message was able to go out to men and women without discrimination. The combination of both men and women can be seen in judgment with Ananias and Sapphira (5:1), but also positively in belief (17:12, 34), baptism (8:12), and persecution (8:3; 22:4).

The apostles' boldness along with healing miracles are answers to the prayers after first appearing before the hostile council (4:24–31). The public held the church in high regard as the powerful miracles of healing showed that God was at work in and through them. (Luke does not confuse sickness with being oppressed by evil spirits.) Jesus had promised greater works than he had done (John 14:12), and Luke uses language that reflects Moses in the Old Testament (Deut 34:10–12) for this powerful healing and deliverance ministry. While healing is often associated with laying on of hands, the reference here is singular and likely refers to their labor in ministry. If the authority given to the apostles' words through the healing of one lame man made the temple authorities angry, these multiple healings must have made them furious beyond measure at their continued teaching. Like master, like servant, Luke will reveal that

16. Bock, *Acts*, 227.

17. Bock, *Acts*, 229.

18. Josephus, *J. W.* 5.5.1.

the Council were happy to have a pretext to kill them (5:33) just as they were with Jesus.

Who are "the rest" who would not join (associate with) the apostles in the temple? Is it the rest of the Jews or the rest of the believers? And were they afraid because of the judgment on Ananias and Sapphira or fear of being arrested by the high priest? No doubt many unbelievers had an "awestruck reserve,"[19] but many are believing, so that would seem to rule out the non-believers. While the swift judgment likely had an impact, it should not have affected the honest. One commentator assesses this in a way that is pertinent to modern missions: "Perhaps the view is, why should we place ourselves in unnecessary risk? It is one thing to be an object of persecution and be prepared for it. It is another for a group knowingly to seek it when this is not necessary, as others are successfully performing the ministry of healing."[20]

Many critics believe the reference to Peter's shadow is mere superstition on the part of the sick, however like Jesus (Luke 7:1–10) and Paul (19;12), healing can be done at a distance. The virtue is not in the shadow but in recognizing and approving Peter as an approved messenger of God. Seeking healing through close association with him was no different from the woman seeking healing by touching the hem of Jesus' garment (Luke 8:43–48). Even if their ideas were tainted with superstition, that did not stop God from being gracious.

THE APOSTLES IMPRISONED (5:17–26)

The Sanhedrin was largely responsible for keeping peace in the temple area and was delegated affairs that Rome did not wish to deal with, such as religious matters.[21] It had tolerated the blatant disobedience of its strict orders not to teach in Jesus' name, but, "finally, without an especial cause or occasion, the cord snapped."[22] Only Peter and John incurred the wrath of the Sanhedrin in chapter 3, but the scope of the persecution was expanded as the twelve apostles are publicly arrested, so as to make a strong public point. With a later arrest said to be peaceful (5:26) and given the guards' reputation for violence, this was likely a very

19. Haenchen, *Acts*, 113.
20. Bock, *Acts*, 231.
21. Bock, *Acts*, 245.
22. Lenski, *Acts*, 212.

unpleasant experience.[23] They had after all been warned and now, under Jewish jurisprudence, the Sanhedrin could take full action (see comments on 4:13–21). The whole movement is threatened with extinction by the removal of all its leaders. Though the Sadducees are the strong dominating influence with more to lose, the Pharisees are also present (5:34) and apparently in agreement. Whereas jealousy is the motive for the Sadducees, misguided zeal is more likely for the Pharisees. However, in verses 27–40 we will also see their moderating influence.

The public arrest and miraculous release are told with "maximum brevity." Like the resurrected master, like servant, they had escaped a sealed and guarded prison,[24] the leadership's worst fear. God was making a much stronger public statement about the importance of the message of the unique life provided in Jesus. It is far more important than obeying corrupt leadership. The angel (not the angel of the Lord which is used of God himself in the Hebrew Scriptures) then instructed them to return to the temple to "tell the people all about this new life"[25] (5:20). This is the first of three prison releases (Peter in 12:5–11; Paul and Silas in 16:25–26), showing the leadership powerless before God when he chooses to act. The martyrdom of Stephen and James and Paul's long imprisonment means they are not totally powerless though. Whatever the outcome, Luke revealed that God is still present, so encouraging the believers to remain strong in their faith in Jesus.

The message of new life raised such concern that the apostles were to answer, not just to the religious leaders but to "every available leader at every level."[26] Unaware that they have been released, the high priest summoned the apostles from the prison only to find it secure and well-guarded but minus the occupants. For the Sadducees that would not conceive of any divine action, this would have been extremely perplexing (5:24) though less so for the Pharisees. The leaders who should be leading Israel into truth had gathered instead to pass judgment on the apostles and their message. God had already passed judgment on unbelief in the church and was publicly passing judgment on the leader's unbelief.

23. B. *Pesachim* 57a.

24. Gooding, *True to the Faith*, 100.

25. Life and salvation are synonymous in the New Testament. Both are used to translate the Hebrew word for "to live." Longenecker, "Acts," 9:319.

26. Bock, *Acts*, 240. The terms are the *synedrion* and the *gerousian*, sometimes translated as the "senate."

The worshipers did not see the apostles as religious criminals and had a much better understanding of who Jesus was and the situation regarding their release. This had all been too public to sweep under the carpet and the guards sensed their own danger if they used violence to rearrest them. Given the mood of the crowd on seeing the blasphemy against God's messages, the apostles could have escaped had they wished, but like Jesus, they did not use violence. The apostles' preaching, attested by signs, brought respect but not always faith. This will quickly change in chapters 6 and 7, as some will gladly stone the church, or at least one part of it.

THE APOSTLES BEFORE THE SANHEDRIN (5:27–42)

5:27–33. The miraculous release from prison with a direct command from the angel to continue to preach the message openly in the temple completely put to rest any question about whether to obey the rulers over God. It was impossible for murderers and those with the message of "this life" to live in harmony. The council showed their hypocrisy in verse 28, where they are indignant at any suggestion that they are guilty of the death of Jesus.[27] The leaders had conveniently forgotten that they had urged the crowd to call down the blood of Jesus upon themselves and their children (Matt 27:25).[28] Perhaps they really did believe they were innocent, considering Jesus had brought it all on his own head by claiming to be equal with God (John 5:18). Their hatred of Jesus was so strong that they could not bring themselves to repeat his name (5:28). Without hesitation, Peter accepts the charge and repeats his previous claim that God reversed of their ungodly killing of Jesus by raising him (2:24, 32; 3:15; 4:10; 10:40; 22:14). The apostles' prayer for boldness (4:29) after their first encounter with the leaders had been answered.

Peter and the apostles again declared to them that God exalted Jesus to his right hand as supreme leader (5:31), with shared responsibility with him.[29] As Savior he can give repentance to Israel (5:31). The hand of God in the Old Testament is a symbol for his powerful intervention, but from the context of Acts 11:21 the hand that is equipping the evangelist

27. Christianity has a shameful record of anti-Semitism that has been justified by quoting this and similar verses. Peter's response was valid, but it was done as a loyal member of Israel. Gooding, *True to the Faith*, 98.

28. Stott, *Message of Acts*, 116.

29. BADG, "Ἀρχηγός," 112.1.

is Jesus himself. For the Sanhedrin, the death of Jesus on the cross was proof of his blasphemy whereas the apostles had argued that Jesus was unjustly accused and did not deserve the shame brought upon him. Standing before the council the apostles did not talk of "crucifixion" but hanging on a "tree" and so drew attention to the circumstances of his death and the associated curse. The comments of G. B. Caird on this need to be taken to heart:

> Surely no Christian preacher would have chosen to describe the death of Jesus in terms which drew attention to the curse of God resting upon the executed criminal, unless he had first faced the scandal of the cross and had come to believe that Jesus had borne the curse on behalf of others.[30]

Luke has previously emphasized God's sovereign purposes in the life, death, and resurrection of Jesus. Here, with a trinitarian response, he stresses those same purposes in the way that salvation is received through Jesus. God was not seeking revenge nor justice but the leader's repentance for murdering Jesus and repentance also through acknowledging the need for salvation.[31] Through giving repentance to Israel, "The exalted Jesus celebrates his enthronement by bestowing on enemies the change of heart that leads to forgiveness."[32] Repentance is a gift given by Jesus now that he is exalted (5:31; cf., 11:18), in the same way it will be God's choice that the gentiles believe after hearing the word through Peter. Jesus is also the Savior because of the gift of the Holy Spirit. Acts emphasizes that God's decision is not only behind the mode of salvation but "people's reception of its benefits."[33] That is not a defense of a simple impersonal determinism. The planned power and mercy of God draws people to faith in Jesus and the announcement of what God has done must motivate people to repent.[34]

In response to the gracious offer of the Holy Spirit through repentance, the Sadducees are "cut to the heart" (5:33) (as used of the hearers on the day of Pentecost [2:37]) but in anger through unbelief. The council wanted to kill the apostles (5:33), and though they didn't strictly have that power, that was only a technicality as their actions with Jesus

30. Caird, *Apostolic Age*, 40.
31. Gooding, *True to the Faith*, 99.
32. Johnson, *Message of Acts*, 25.
33. Johnson, *Message of Acts*, 151.
34. Johnson, *Message of Acts*, 151–2.

showed. (5:31). The apostles' escape from prison should have served as a "warning not to add an atrocious crime to an already grievous guilt,"[35] let alone attempting to stop the spread of the message of life.

Who Were the Pharisees?

In Luke's Gospel the Pharisees are the main opponents of Jesus, meaning we can easily see them simply as vile hypocrites,[36] but Acts is much more favorably disposed towards this group as were the people. Their name is derived from the Hebrew *Pərūšīm*, the separated ones, and though not very numerous, (Josephus indicated about six thousand at the destruction of the temple),[37] they were as respected as the Sadducees were reviled, and everything they said about the king or high priest was believed.[38] The Pharisees, with their simple living and strict observance of the Law,[39] were seen as religious patriots and spiritual leaders.[40] Unlike the Sadducees, they believed that the spirit lived beyond death and that it was judged, and unlike them, they believed that God sometimes acted in human life. While the Sadducees only accepted the Law, the Pharisees also accepted the Prophets and the Writings as we do but added the oral law. They looked forward to the messianic age.

Pharisees democratized Judaism by teaching from the Law that the whole people of Israel had a priestly sanctity and claimed for their own meals the same holiness as those of the priests in the temple. This explains their emphasis on ritual purity in the Gospels. This democratic view of their faith was also behind the establishment of the synagogues and instruction of sons in the Torah.[41] They were also less rigid in the way justice was administered.[42] Pharisees also held women in higher regard, freeing them from many of the burdens of ritual purity and protected them with the introduction of the marriage document.[43]

35. Gooding, *True to the Faith*, 100.

36. Even in Judaism, the presence of hypocrisy was acknowledges as seven types of Pharisees were recognized and only two of them were good. B. *Sota* 22b.

37. Josephus, *Ant.* 17.2.4.

38. Josephus, *Ant.* 13.10.5.

39. Josephus, *J. W.* 18.1.3.

40. Josephus, *Ant.* 13.293.

41. Kohler, "Pharisees," 9:661.

42. Josephus, *Ant.* 13.10.6.

43. Kohler, "Pharisees," 9:663.

The prestige of the Pharisees gave them a stronger voice on the Sanhedrin than their numbers suggested. Not only did the teaching of Jesus have similarities to this group—Paul still called them "brothers" after many years of Christian ministry—the commentator Ernst Haenchen points out,

> It is not Judaism and Christianity which confront each other as enemies, but only Sadducees and Christians. For Pharisee and Christian are at one where belief in the resurrection, the nucleus of Christianity is concerned (even if the Pharisees failed to draw the necessary conclusions in respect of Jesus' resurrection). Christianity is not a falling away from Judaism; on the contrary, its doctrine of resurrection is the basic teaching of Israel, which only the [Sadducee] disputes.[44]

5:34–39. The Sadducees had "risen up" in jealousy (5:17), but in verse 34 the voice of moderation, the Pharisees represented by Gamaliel, "rises up" when he addressed the Jewish leaders in private. Paul would boast of being taught by him and with good reason. He was one of the six great teachers given the title *Raban* ("our teacher"). His prestige was such that it was said, "When Rabban Gamliel the Elder died, the honor of the Torah ceased, and purity and asceticism died."[45] Subsequent events were to show Paul to be out of step with his teacher, at least on this day. (The Babylonian Talmud speaks of "that pupil" that Rabbi Gamaliel had among his disciples who gave him much trouble, manifesting "imprudence in matters of learning."[46] The quotation is believed to refer to Paul.) Though not a believer, Gamaliel did show mature wisdom in his opposition. His is the first speech of a non-Christian in Acts and the second adversary within Luke–Acts who, when taking a close look at the new movement, does not make a decisive judgment. Pilate had judged Jesus as innocent of any crime deserving death (Luke 23:1–25).

Based on his understanding of the hand of God in the history of Israel, Gamaliel counselled the members to do nothing but to wait and see, as he expects the movement to simply die out like earlier uprisings (5:35–8). His warning that they might be fighting against God may have been prompted by the apostles' inexplicable release from prison and their boldness. Luke's point is that Christianity is not like the popular but

44. Haenchen, *Acts*, 223.

45. M. *Soṭah* 9:15.

46. B. *Shabbat* 30b.

short-lived revolts and that the leadership is in danger because of their unbelief and fighting with God (5:39).[47] Gamaliel's advice was followed, likely driven as much by the potential for disrupting the public peace and the brutal Roman crackdown that would follow the theological argument.[48] The history of redemption was a favorite theme of the Jews. Seeing God's hand in their history was so vital in their understanding of the nature of God that the historical books Joshua, Judges, Samuel, and Kings were classed as prophecy. Stephen teaching on the nature of God and the church would be based on the actions of God in history.

Gamaliel's viewpoint that if Christianity is not of God it will come to nothing is generally a sound deduction but is not always correct as can be seen in many heresies and religions. Christianity itself has also collapsed in places in the face of strong opposition. The one example Gamaliel quoted—Judas—was the founder of the zealots who were still active. This was typical Pharisaic teaching: "God is over all, and needs no help from man for the fulfillment of his purposes; all men have to do is obey and leave the issue to him."[49] While the words of Gamaliel do amount to "fence sitting," in the face of all such entrenched unbelief there was probably nothing more that could be said and it did save the apostle's lives.[50]

5:40–42. Gamaliel's advice is taken and the Twelve are beaten. The Law allowed for forty strokes to be delivered but the practice was to deliver only thirty-nine, lest they miscount and be guilty themselves. Such is the blasphemous treatment of the messengers of the one who fulfills the Law. While not the same as the Roman scourging of Jesus, this was still horrific and could leave people close to death.[51] The church and the temple are inseparable at this stage and Christianity could be taken as a branch of Judaism. His advice would have been different if the apostles were answering the same charges levelled against Stephen in chapters 6 and 7. He had reached radical "conclusions that related to the primacy of Jesus' messiahship and lordship and the secondary nature of Jewish views about the land, the Law, and the temple."[52] This was heresy

47. Bock, *Acts*, 251.

48. Bock, *Acts*, 252.

49. Bruce, *Acts*, 1954, 146.

50. Gooding, *True to the Faith*, 101.

51. Detailed instructions on how the whip is to be made and applied is found in M. *Makkot* 3.10–14.

52. Longenecker, "Acts," 9:324.

to them, and, far from being a moderating voice, we see one of their own emerging as the main protagonist.

Rather than grumble, the apostles take honor in what others would consider a disgrace. This introduces us to the concept of *kingdom pain*, as opposed to *human pain*.[53] Despite the beating and the leaders command to stop, they obey the angel and continue the daily journey to the temple to teach. However, the unwilling separation of Christianity from Judaism was being forced upon it from outside. In verse 42 we are first introduced to that word at the foundation of Christian ministry: *evangelizeō*, "to preach the good news."

An Apparent Historical Error

Luke apparently reports Gamaliel disagreeing with Josephus by reversing his chronology of the revolts. Josephus gives the revolt of Judas of Galilee the founder of the Zealots, which arose because of the census of Quirinius, at about AD 6. This agrees with Gamaliel,[54] but Theudas's uprising occurred roughly ten years after Gamaliel spoke, not before.[55] However, Josephus wrote of the time after Herod the Great's death, saying, "There were ten thousand other disorders in Judea, which were like tumults, because a great number put themselves into a warlike posture."[56]

The only similarity between Luke and Josephus is the names, yet liberal scholars have used this apparent discrepancy to claim Acts was historically unreliable. By contrast, the archaeologist and former skeptic, William Ramsay, argued, "A writer who proves to be exact and correct in one point will show the same qualities in other matters. No writer is correct by mere chance or accurate sporadically."[57] It is best to leave this matter to our general ignorance of this period and the actors, especially as Theudas was a common name.[58]

53. This is expanded in my book *Pain and a Powerful God*.
54. Josephus, *Ant.* 18.1.1.
55. Josephus, *Ant.* 20.5.1.
56. Josephus, *Ant.* 17.10.4.
57. Ramsay, *Trustworthiness*, 80.
58. Bock, *Acts*, 250.

THE APPOINTMENT OF THE SEVEN (6:1–7)

Division was arising in the church. The devil's schemes against the church first involved threats, then moral corruption from within, and in chapter six, distracting the Apostles from their core work with necessary and even spiritual Christian ministry by attending to the problem themselves. The sharing of property that should have shown Christian unity threatened to disrupt it with "a crack that could have become a chasm."[59] The churches had brought with them into Christianity the prejudice between the Hebrews and the Hellenists who were likely meeting in separate home churches due to the language issues. The result was that the widows of the Hellenists did not receive a fair distribution of the daily food distribution. It may well be that the problem occurred, not out of malice but simply that the organizational structure of the church did not keep up with its fast growth.[60] The matter had to be set straight immediately before it grew and was largely resolved when both parties take responsibility to solve it.

Jews of the dispersion, also known as the Hellenists, were Greek-speaking. On returning to Jerusalem, their language was a barrier to the Hebrew or Aramaic-speaking Jews. However, the division was more complicated than just language. Paul, a Jew from Tarsus, was a Greek speaker yet classed himself as a Hebrew (Acts 22:3; 2 Cor 11:22). Dispersion Jews had to practice their faith far from the temple and were forced to answer the question of how much pagan culture could be accommodated while still being faithful to the Lord. Among this group there were widely different views. Some would strictly maintain their difference from the pagans and others would try to build bridges even to the extent that Judaism was forced into existing pagan philosophical frameworks.[61] As Acts progresses, the corresponding question comes to the fore: How much must a formerly pagan gentile change to be in service to God? Stephen's opponents in chapter 6 were returned Jews from the diaspora and likely included Hellenists. Their violent opposition shows that they were not a homogeneous group.

The Spirit had been leading the church to a new understanding of its relation to material things. Peter and John would remind Paul

59. Johnson, *Message of Acts*, 23.

60. Bock, *Acts*, 258.

61. E.g., Philo of Alexandria (20 BC–AD 50) interpreted Judaism in a Neoplatonic framework.

to remember the poor (Gal 2:10) and James said that pure and faultless religion was not just keeping oneself morally spotless; it had to go hand in hand with looking "after orphans and widows in their distress" (Jas 1:27). Their care by God was an Old Testament promise but it took compassionate people to actually do it. The church was learning that its compassion can be measured against the way it cares for the widows and homeless, and even for those outside its own community (3:1–6). Instead, the unity of 2:46 had been replaced with murmurings. The same word for murmuring is used in the LXX of the murmuring of the Israelites against Moses (Ex 16:7; Num 14:27; 1 Cor 10:10), suggesting that the complaints were really against the apostles.[62]

This was not the last ethnically diverse church that became difficult to manage.[63] Too frequently, believers have embraced the cross that removes the alienation between man and God but are repulsed by the notion that the same gospel should remove the barriers between different kinds of people. In God's wisdom, this racial division would prove the catalyst that led to the spread of the gospel outside of Jerusalem. The Spirit was poured out on Hebrew and the Hellenistic Jews alike; however, cultural tensions were arising even before the church started on the task entrusted to them of being a community open to all.

The seven men were not chosen by casting lots or divine vision or by appointment by the apostles but by the whole church, yet there is confidence that this, too, was God's will. Church elections should not mean that God has abdicated his throne and replaced that with the will of the people. Rather, those casting votes were to represent Spirit-baptized people who can discern the Lord's will and appoint leaders who are full of the Spirit.[64] The task also required the divine wisdom of Jesus to bring justice to the poor (Isa 11:2, 4).[65] That suitably equipped men were available meant that the problem was foreseen by God and there was already an answer in their midst. The words Luke used in the apostle's direction to choose seven[66] men reflect the command of Moses when appointing Joshua and the other servants (Num 27:16).

62. Stott, *Message of Acts*, 120.

63. Bock, *Acts*, 255.

64. Johnson, *Message of Acts*, 88.

65. Johnson, *Message of Acts*, 102.

66. There is likely to be a Jewish significance in the number seven but it is not explicitly stated.

Use of "choose"	Acts 6:3	Num 27:16 (LXX)
Must have the Spirit	Acts 6:3	Num 27:18
Leadership followed after laying on of hands	Acts 6:6	Num 27:23
Take the lead in carrying God's dominion into spiritually polluted gentile territory	Acts 8:4–8, 26–40,	Gen 15:16; Lev 18:27–8

Table 4. Similarity of Joshua to the seven[67]

The seven may have all been Hellenists as suggested by their Greek names, meaning that the division must not have been too deep, but that is speculation as some Jews had Greek names at that time.[68] It is more likely that a mixture of both groups were appointed.[69] Stephen is introduced as a man full of faith, and the Spirit is preparing us for his martyrdom. Nicholas[70] is a convert to Judaism from Antioch heralding the start of world evangelism from that city. Philip will become an evangelist in Samaria. The ministry of Steven and Philip is likely to be representative of the other five. With the introduction of Stephen and Philip, Luke is preparing his readers for a missional church but not before the scattering of the Hellenist Jews, the ministry in Samaria, the conversion of the Ethiopian and Cornelius, and above all, Saul of Tarsus.

With the appointment of the seven, a second group of leaders is introduced working alongside the apostles. The two aspects of the church's ministry—preaching God's salvation and relieving human suffering—cannot be separated, but they had to be distinguished from each other.[71] In these two ministries we can miss that the apostles put prayer alongside preaching as indispensable to the spiritual health of the church.[72] However, there was not a clear-cut distinction into "spiritual" with the apostles and "secular" with the deacons. The seven are frequently

67. Johnson, *Message of Acts*, 92.

68. The apostles Andrew and Philip had Greek names.

69. Lenski, *Acts*, 246.

70. There is strong evidence from the early church fathers that the Nicolaitans of Revelation claimed their authority from the deacon Nicholas. See, e.g., Irenaeus, *Haer.* 1.26.3 (*ANF* 1:352). There is also little difficulty in assuming that they unjustly claimed this relationship. Harnack, *Sect of the Nicolaitans*, 421.

71. Johnson, *Message of Acts*, 90.

72. A prayerless church should take to heart my notes about James the brother of Jesus when discussing 15:13.

called "deacons," and though the word is not specifically used of them, as servants of the church to the poor this is what they were.[73] As the church grew the role would evolve. If a New Testament pattern can be established, it is that administrative structures must evolve to meet needs.

The role of "deacon" required the seven to be "full of faith" and the Holy Spirit (6:5, 8–15), indicating that their ministry was not just distributing food but involved preaching. Indeed, their effectiveness in preaching was one indication that they were full of the Spirit. By the time Paul wrote the Pastoral Epistles, the definition of what constituted "full of the Holy Spirit" had become muddied as seen in the extremes in Corinth. Paul would advise selection of church officers only after an examination of their character and a period of probation. While the seven were all men, the role in 1 Timothy and Titus is expanded to include women.[74] The task is also likely to be much broader as well.

When the Apostles said that it would not be right to leave off the preaching of the gospel to distribute charity to the poor, this was not a moral choice about what was right and wrong but about priorities.[75] The ministry to the poor was important, too important to be trusted to just anyone, but the Apostles were called to preach and pray. The seven were appointed to their role with prayer and the laying on of hands. This is largely symbolic as the community has already recognized that they are full of the Spirit and equipped for the task. However, it is unlikely to be totally symbolic with an acknowledgment of a shared responsibility and likely imparting some extra gifting.

Paul, in his practice, did not fully agree with Peter that it was not right to leave off preaching to "serve on tables" as he did this on at least two occasions. He left his teaching ministry in Antioch to bring an offering to Jerusalem, and, later in his life, he was to postpone his preaching trip to Rome for the same reason. James stressed how the care of orphans and widows is just as much of a life that is acceptable to God as is living a separated life (Jas 1:27). However, to accommodate a world that is ready

73. The distribution in verse 1 and the apostles' ministry in verse 4 is *diakonia*, while the distribution in verse 2 is *diakonein*. It seems of little significance that the seven are not actually called *diakonos* or, in English, "deacon."

74. For an in-depth discussion, refer to my book *Women in Ministry: Paul's Advice to Timothy in Its Historical Setting*.

75. Bock, *Acts*, 259. There is a warning in this story about the danger of pastors being robbed of ministry time by what can be a very heavy burden of administration. Stott considers it essential to have an administrator, which frees the pastor from unnecessary administration. Stott, *Message of Acts*, 123.

to accept the compassion of the Holy Spirit delivered through his messengers, yet have no tolerance for the evangelistic message of how to get right with God, is a "criminal dereliction of duty to both God and man."[76]

In verse 7 we are told that "the word of God spread," much like a seed, almost directing its own growth to a time of harvest. As part of this growth, many priests joined the church. There were so many priests[77] that they only served for two weeks per year and then returned to their normal living. A large proportion of a significant number represented significant numerical growth in the church,[78] which, in turn, would have tied the church even more strongly to the temple. This would have further alarmed the Jewish leaders. Stephen's sermon would show that the temple was now obsolete, and, on the dispersal of the Greek-speaking Jews, God's presence would be scattered wherever they travelled.

The positive response of many priests will be followed by the stubborn unbelief of the members of the Synagogue of the Freedmen. Most priests would have lacked the social standing of the high priestly families but are more likely to be more pious and therefore more receptive to the gospel.[79] The commentator Darryl Bock, reminds us that when "measuring successful end results [we] may need to take into account both those who enter the church and those who react against it as was the case in Jerusalem."[80]

76. Gooding, *True to the Faith*, 104.

77. Josephus said there were at least twenty thousand priests. Josephus, *Ag. Ap.* 2.8. Others put it at less but still at a very large number.

78. Bock, *Acts*, 265.

79. Longenecker, "Acts," 9:333.

80. Bock, *Acts*, 265.

5

The Church's First Martyr (Acts 6:8—7:60)

THE ARREST OF STEPHEN (6:8–15)

Stephen, already described as "full of the Spirit and wisdom" (6:3) as well as being "full of faith and the Holy Spirit" (6:5), is now said to be "full of grace" as was Jesus (Luke 4:22) and the early church (4:33). That grace enabled him to have a ministry that is portrayed as no less than the apostles despite "serving on tables." The members of the Synagogue of the Freedmen were made up of Cyrenians and Alexandrians,[1] as well as those from Cilicia[2] and Asia, and this represents opposition from a vast geographical region. The situation is starting to change for the church, which has, up to this point, had the approval of the general public. These men were unsuccessful when they debated with Stephen as Jesus had promised (Luke 12:11–12, 21:12–5). So they bought him before the Sanhedrin on false charges of blasphemy against Moses and against God. Moses is put first, showing the importance placed on the Law, the foundation of the nation's worship. The later Mishnah stated that a person was only liable to that charge if they mentioned God's name and cursed it,[3] though Num 15:30 gave a much broader definition: "But anyone who sins defiantly, whether native-born or foreigner, blasphemes the Lord and must be cut off from the people of Israel." The agitated group was not likely to be debating different definitions. They were so agitated that, to make their case before the Sanhedrin about defending the Law of

1. Cyrenians came from Northern Africa, and Alexandria is in Egypt.

2. Cilicia is in the Northeastern Mediterranean.

3. M. *Sanh.* 7.5.

Moses, the Synagogue of the Freedman had to bring false witnesses, the very thing forbidden by the Law in its fundamental covenant, the Ten Commandments. Some things to note:

1. The scene has switched from temple to synagogue.
2. This is likely to have been Paul's synagogue; Tarsus is in Cilicia, i.e., Paul could not refute Stephen's arguments.
3. Stephen's preaching was more radical than the apostles': "The issue of Jesus is before the Sanhedrin for the fourth time . . . only Jesus and Stephen were accused by the Sanhedrin of predicting the destruction of the temple. However, Stephen alone was charged by this body with speaking against Moses or the Law."[4]

The charges laid at the various trials are tabled below and illustrate graphically that Stephen was "in tune" with Jesus. Similar claims will be leveled at Paul (21:28, 24:6), which he will deny (25:78).

Jesus	The Apostles	Stephen
Mark 14:58, destroy this temple	1. Acts 4:2, proclaiming Jesus and the resurrection from the dead 2. Acts 5:28, continued teaching and bringing Jesus' blood on them	Acts 6:13 1. Speaking against the temple 2. Destroy this place 3. Change our customs

Table 5.Charges when bought before the Sanhedrin

As an observant Jew, Stephen was likely to have experienced forgiveness in the once-a-year ritual when the high priest entered the holy of holies with the blood of the animal sacrificed for the nation. Complete forgiveness now came along with the gift of the Holy Spirit for those who, through repentance, put their trust in the crucified, risen, and glorified Jesus.[5] Not only was forgiveness being dispensed through the authority of Jesus, the Son of Man, the reality of it was also being reinforced possibly almost daily (2:42) in the Lord's Supper where the blood of the new covenant is poured out for the forgiveness of sins (Matt 26:26–8). God had promised through Jeremiah that there would be a new covenant, that it would not be like the old (Jer 31:32), and that "the people of God

4. Wood, *Acts*, 110.

5. Gooding, *True to the Faith*, 119.

[could not] be related to God under the terms of two different covenants simultaneously."[6]

Jesus had foretold the destruction of the temple in Luke 21:5–36, not that he would do it personally—that would be done by outsiders due to Israel's sin. This was saying no more than what Jeremiah prophesied and had already happened under Nebuchadnezzar. To speak about the destruction of the temple this way was in effect to say the leadership was corrupt and an insult to them. The Qumran community were also saying in no uncertain terms that the temple was polluted and its priests were so wicked that people could not worship in such a place.[7] Unlike Stephen, they were hoping for a day when it would be purged and they could return, but even without the destruction or purging of the temple, Jesus had said to the Samaritan woman, and Stephen had understood that "a time is coming and has now come when the true worshipers will worship the Father in the Spirit and in truth" (John 4:23). Simply, Stephen had grasped that the temple had become obsolete. The Law was not scorned, but it was fulfilled.

While God had chosen for his presence to dwell for centuries in the most holy place the veil that forbade access was torn by God on the day Jesus was crucified. He had spoken of a new temple which was his body, destroyed and rebuilt after three days. The Apostles only understood this after his resurrection (John 2:22). Instead of being excluded, this was the temple where people could go directly to the Father through the living Christ by the Spirit. There were now no divisions where only priests or high priests could go, there was no court of the women and of the men.

These views are most clearly expressed in the book of Hebrews, which speaks of a better covenant founded on better promises (Heb 7:22; 8:6). That writer also understood that the physical temple had "served Israel well as a God given 'parable,'"[8] but the invitation was now to enter boldly into the most holy place (Heb 10:19–22) in the heavenly temple. Christians did not understand this all at once and God did not rush the understanding of the difference between the two covenants. How clear Stephen was in his understanding of the radical nature of the new covenant and access to the heavenly temple found in Hebrews and in Paul's writings (Eph 2:18) we cannot know. What Stephen did understand could not be compromised and was worth dying for.

6. Gooding, *True to the Faith*, 120.

7. Vermes, "Dead Sea Scrolls," S:215.

8. Gooding, *True to the Faith*, 123.

Steven had calmness in the face of his accuser's rage, but it went further. With the face of an angel, he was touched by God's glory[9] as was Moses when he returned with the Law (Exod 34:29). This was God's vindication of Stephen's interpretation of the Law.[10] At the conclusion of my comments on chapter 7, I will draw parallels between Jesus and Stephen and show that an authentic imitation of Christ was not just the prerogative of the apostles.

THE OBEDIENCE OF ABRAHAM (7:1–8)

The most striking feature of Stephen's defense is its inability to create strong emotions across the whole spectrum of commentators. The liberal scholar Martin Dibelius said of its apparent lackluster content, "The major part of the speech (7:2–34) shows no purpose whatsoever" and of its "compressed reproduction of the story of the Patriarchs and Moses," "the most striking feature of this speech is [its] irrelevance."[11] The atheist George Bernard Shaw described Stephen as a "quite intolerable young speaker," and by stoning him to death "it was a severe way of suppressing a tactless and conceited bore."[12] Even when I first studied Acts, my conservative tutor G. O. Wood echoed my own understanding at the time: "It seemed no more than a long historical review . . . and I found it more interesting to skip from 7:1 to 7:51. The sermon simply appeared to review so tediously things I already knew."[13] Yet Stephen's profound reinterpretation of four epochs of Israel's history, which his accusers had reveled in, made them white with rage. For Luke to have contributed so much space to this event when others are told briefly must mean we are dealing with something profound, even if we did not immediately perceive it.

The consequences of his defense became the turning point of the church, as seen from what follows and the amount of space given to it compared to those of Peter and Paul. Yet, in this masterful testimony to Christ, Stephen only mentioned Jesus once (6:52), and neither does he explicitly mention the Old Testaments references to him. This may

9. Bock, *Acts*, 275.

10. Stott, *Message of Acts*, 129.

11. Dibelius, *Studies in Acts*, 168–69.

12. Shaw, *Preface to Androcles.*

13. Wood, *Acts*, 111.

be more because his address was cut short rather than by design. Still, his defense "laid the theological foundation for the dispersion of the believers, the scattering of the New Israel."[14] His message challenges the permanence of the temple, and rabbinic Judaism would be forced to continue without the temple in less than forty years. He went further by demonstrating that only those who followed Jesus were listening to Moses.

Stephen's address showed that possibly the most spiritually aware person in the church was not in charge. It appears that the apostles were accommodating the Way into traditional Jewish life as they had not yet seen the full significance of Christ's work as it applied to the Law and the temple. A further sign of Stephen's greatness was that he did not seek a higher position. Now facing the Sanhedrin, he shows an utter lack of concern for his own safety. Stephen did not attempt to clarify what he had said or explain any misconceptions. The main thrust of his defense was to show through the Scriptures themselves that what at least some of those who followed Jesus were saying was not blasphemous, irrespective of what the popular view was at the time. He considered these changes to the way believer's worship, which were so important that he would not back down from them and rather die.[15]

Genesis describes how mankind's original knowledge of God descends into almost universal polytheism, idolatry, and immorality. By revealing himself to Abraham, the witness to the world for the only God would begin through this man's descendants. This revelation was gradual over different times using different people, and Stephen focuses on four of these periods: 1) Abraham in Haran and Canaan; 2) the Patriarchs in Canaan and Egypt; 3) Moses in Egypt and Midian, again in Egypt, and later Sinai; and 4) finally in the promised land through the kings David and Solomon and later through the prophets. Each stage initiated new movement and "a more extensive experience in God's provision for their redemption."[16] Also, each new stage of revelation required Israel to begin acting in a different way.

When the high priest, likely Caiaphas,[17] asked Stephen if the charges were true, except at the end he respectfully addressed his accusers as "brothers and fathers." In 7:2 he further adds, "Our father Abraham,"

14. Johnson, *Message of Acts*, 92.

15. Gooding, *True to the Faith*, 118.

16. Gooding, *True to the Faith*, 124–5.

17. Caiaphas was high priest till 36 or 37 AD.

so linking Christianity to God's revelation to the patriarch. His defense begins to lay a foundation through showing that Abraham believed and worshiped God before the Law and the temple. He will point out the unbelief of Israel, which is in sharp contrast to the belief of Abraham (7:51–3). In fact, the Law and temple did nothing to check Israel's habitual tendency of unbelief.

Abraham was the son of idol worshipers (Josh 24:2), but it was not a series of prohibitions and commands that drove Abraham out from the pagan gentiles. Rather, "It was the revelation to him of the superlative glory of the living God, and the vision of the eternal city God promised him."[18] Not only was this the start of his journey of faith, but it also became the foundational spiritual experience behind the birth of Israel. God's glory,[19] revealed far from the temple, drew him on a path of pilgrimage where he would stand conspicuously apart from the nations. Abraham was set apart so that all the polytheistic and idolatrous nations can be blessed.[20] Chapter 7 will also end with the glory of God (7:55–56). Paul, a Hebrew of the Hebrews, will likewise be blinded by God's glory and be sent back into the nations as a missionary. The commentator David Gooding made the searching observation, "How can we witness effectively to our modern pagan idolatrous world unless a similar sight of the glory of God has first broken within us that 'love of the world' which 'is not of the Father'?"[21]

Though living in the land promised to him, all Abraham would own was a cave in which to bury his wife, yet he was unwavering in his trust in the repeated covenant promise that his numerous descendants would be a nation with a land of their own (Gen 12:7; 13:15; 15:2, 18; 17:8; 24:7, 48:4). In effect, Stephen is saying that the very fact that they are now living in that land despite being enslaved in Egypt (and carried off to Babylon [7:43]), shows God is faithful to his promises. Also, by implication, according to his covenant promises, wherever Abraham and his descendants were, there God's presence was also, going with them to a polytheistic land. For someone living the pilgrim lifestyle, holy ground was wherever God meets his people. Worshiping at "this place" (7:7) could refer to either Canaan or the temple itself, but the point of

18. Gooding, *True to the Faith*, 112.

19. Though the Genesis account does not talk about a revelation of God's glory, it is assumed.

20. Gooding, *True to the Faith*, 110–11.

21. Gooding, *True to the Faith*, 112–13.

the passage is that it was the land that was the promise, not the temple. Circumcision as a sign of the promise that was made without obligations on Abraham's behalf was given before the Law.

The Death of Abraham's Father

Stephen spoke of God's call coming to Abraham in Ur in Mesopotamia moving from the place of his call to Haran with his family including his father. Only after his father died (7:4) did God send Abraham on a life of promise. Genesis 11:27–32 tells the account of Terah, Abraham's father, leaving Ur for Haran with his family, but later in 15:7 God speaks of leading Abraham from Ur. For brevity, Stephen may be simply telescoping the events.[22] Abraham may have been unaware of the significance of the move from Ur under God's leading with the specific call coming in Haran. The timing of Terah's death is the problem as the Hebrew text places his death at sixty years after the departure.[23] There is no easy solution, though it has been suggested that the seventy years of Gen 11:26 may be referring to the birth of Abraham's oldest brother.

THE AGE OF THE PATRIARCHS (7:9–17)

Stephen's defense moved on from Abraham to the patriarchs, and his interpretation of Israel's history focuses on the activity of God saving a stubborn people. Driven by jealousy, and far from the faith of Abraham, Joseph, one of Jacobs sons, is betrayed by his brothers and sold into slavery in Egypt. Yet, despite such an evil act, this betrayed brother is the source of salvation to the betrayers. Luke draws a parallel between Stephen and Joseph as both had the favor of God (6:8; 7:10), and both were betrayed by their own.[24] The brothers in their betrayal and failure to recognize their "savior" set the pattern for the unbelief of the nation, matched only by "God and his goal of saving his stubborn people."[25] Stephen does not draw the obvious parallel to Jesus though the inference

22. Bock, *Acts*, 282.

23. Terah was 70 years old when Abraham was born (Gen 11:26), Abraham was 75 years old when he left Haran (Gen 12:4), and Terah died at age 205 in Haran (Gen 11:32).

24. Bock, *Acts*, 286.

25. Bock, *Acts*, 287.

may not have been lost on his hearers. As with Jacob and Moses, so there are two visits from Jesus.[26]

Stephen compressed the burial accounts. Jacob was buried at Machpelah near Hebron in the cave Abraham had purchased (49:29–32; 50:13), but Joseph was buried in Shechem (Josh 24:32) in Samaria, though still in the promised land. The command by Joseph for reburial in the promised land (Gen 50:24–26) was an act of faith that God would keep his word, and this was before seeing little progress on another key promise fulfilled. From one son of promise, Isaac, the family had increased to seventy-five by the time it entered Egypt and greatly increased in number there.

This continuing revelation was not erratic, and the centuries in Egypt away from the promised land was not an abandonment of the plan but a stepping stone. Abraham had been told that the time in Egypt would happen. And when Jacob was told to go to Egypt (Gen 46:2–4), he was only doing what God told Abraham would happen.

MOSES IN EGYPT AND SINAI (7:18–36)

Stephen's account of Moses is longer than the others because he has been accused of speaking against him. There is no agreement on how the chronology of the Old Testament intertwines with that of Egypt, so it is impossible to speak with any certainty as to who the pharaoh was that did not remember Joseph. His plan to diminish Abraham's descendants failed in part because of what happened to Moses, a beautiful child "before God" (7:20). Stephen introduces extrabiblical information about Moses (7:22), describing how he was "well equipped and trained as a leader"[27] during the first forty-year block of his life, and this equipping was by God's enemies. When equipped, God gave Moses the thought[28] to visit his brothers (7:23), but he saw injustice and confronted it. The first day he found one being attacked by an Egyptian. In the process of saving the man, Moses killed the oppressor and then buried him to hide the deed. The following day he found two Hebrew men fighting and questioned them. Stephen's point was that Jews should be reconciled to

26. Johnson, *Message of Acts*, 118.

27. Bock, *Acts*, 291.

28. The expression used by Luke is used in the LXX to describe God putting a thought into someone's heart (2 Kgs 12:5 [English 12:4]; Isa 65:16; Jer 3:16).

each other, which is the same reason he was preaching Jesus to them. The oppressor pushed aside a "prince" of Egypt, demanding to know, "Who made you ruler and judge over us?" (7:27). "Ruler" and "judge" were exactly the roles Jesus, God's deliverer and the prophet like Moses (3:22), was to take, though this is not explicitly stated till speaking about the burning bush (7:37). Stephen concentrated on the hostility among the Hebrews.

Similarly with Jesus, God's deliverer Moses was originally rejected (7:25–27), and his Law was also rejected (7:40–43). Yet God promised to raise up a prophet like Moses (7:37), and Jesus, like Moses, was rejected. "The repeated rejection of Moses had a contemporary analogy for Stephen in the Sanhedrin's repeated refusal of Christ. The second refusal of Moses was in the character of religious apostasy 7:39–41."[29] Some themes are found that show Moses as an implied type of the promised prophet:

1. The rejected person becomes the leader.
2. He is a deliverer through signs and wonders.
3. He is a prophet and forerunner of the one to come.
4. He receives and gives words of life.

Had Steven finished his speech it is likely you'd have drawn the further parallel of Moses and Jesus giving revelation on how Israel should live.[30]

Like Abraham, Moses lived as a sojourner for a time, finding a home and a family in gentile territory in Sinai. At the end of the second forty-year period, Moses, approved by God yet the rejected deliverer, encountered the Lord in the burning bush. For all the talk of an angel (7:30), it was the Lord's voice. His meeting with God at the burning bush was far greater than what was encountered at the most holy place in the temple as God was never said to have appeared there. Moses was told to remove his sandals because he stood on holy ground (7:30–33), yet there appeared to be no restrictions against worshipers wearing sandals in the temple. This shows that *no* place possesses an innate sanctity of its own, not even the temple. The council would not accept the premise that anywhere God is becomes holy. A theme of Stephen's speech is that God is faithful in sending leaders to his people and they constantly reject them.

29. Wood, *Acts*, 113.

30. Bock, *Acts*, 298.

Stephen emphasizes God's choice of Moses by using the expression "this one" five times between verses 35 to 38 and preparing the way for Jesus, the one like him.[31] The rejection of Jesus is of a different order because the salvation he delivers is different as he delivers to eternal salvation. There is no one to follow on from Jesus as he did with Moses, only those who act on his behalf.[32] Moses was appointed to his role by angels (7:30, 35, 53),[33] but God himself sent Jesus. The deliverance from Egypt is told briefly.

After a slow start, Stephen built the tension, especially with the double emphasis "this is that" when referring to Moses in verses 35 and 36, the one he is accused of speaking against.

REJECTION OF MOSES AND THE LAW (7:37–43)

Moving to the third forty-year period of the life of Moses, and like the two before, God continued to be with him. It is not until the wilderness that is there any mention of sacrifices and offerings. Stephen reminded his accusers that Moses promised that God would raise up a man like him that they were to listen to (Acts 7:37; Deut 18:15).[34] Without belittling Moses, he saw that "Israel cannot limit divine revelation and redemption to the confines of the Mosaic law."[35] Rather than looking towards this man with his angelic revelation, they look back with longing to Egypt (7:39). When Peter referred to the new Moses, he addressed his audience as sons of the prophets who should hear Jesus, but for Steven, his hearers are those who rejected Moses and killed the prophets (7:51–53). They rejoiced at the golden calf made with their own hands (7:41). Steven is preparing for his comments about the temple made without hands (7:48), which is Jesus.

Very quickly they rejected the identity that God had for Israel as the unique people, embraced polytheism (7:40), and celebrated in a blatant violation of the first commandment (7:39–41). To reinforce

31. Bock, *Acts*, 296.

32. Witherington, *Acts*, 270.

33. It was a common belief in Judaism that the Law was given through angels. Jub 2:1; Josephus, *Ant.* 15.5.3.

34. Later rabbinic sources would link this person to Old Testament characters such as Samuel or Jeremiah, possibly as a reaction to Christian usage. There was at the time a firm belief in a messiah who would be like Moses. Peter made reference to this person also (3:22–26), expecting his hearers acceptance. Longenecker, "Acts," 9:343.

35. Longenecker, "Acts," 9:343.

the detestable conduct of their forefathers, Stephen quoted Amos 5:26 with the expression from the LXX of "giving over," which Paul repeats in Romans regarding God's judgment of the world (Rom 1:24, 26, 28). In their case, God gave them over to the worship of the heavenly bodies (7:42).

Steven was far from being critical of the Law and Moses, but he goes on the attack and reminds his accusers that their own Scriptures condemn them. C. K. Barrett put it very clearly: "Never had a people been so privileged or so completely negated their vocation."[36] Despite receiving the living words (7:38) from Moses through angels, the offerings made by their forefathers in the wilderness were not brought with a pure heart. It was still the case in Amos's day and was very evident to Stephen at his time and will continue till the day of the Lord (Amos 5:18). The gods that are referred to by Amos are open to discussion as it is not clear how the Hebrew should be read,[37] though it is of little concern as the "gods" change with different generations. Stephen mentioned the tent of Molek as an introduction to the tent of God, which is spoken of reverently (7:44–6). The apostasy in the wilderness brought judgment, and Stephen was implying similar unbelief, which may allude to judgment of his generation.[38] Peter also alluded to this judgment in his sermon on the day of Pentecost (2:16–36). Amos mentioned "beyond Damascus" (Amos 5:27), but Stephen updated it to Babylon (7:43), the judgment that saw the exile and destruction of the first temple.

God had promised there would be a new and better covenant but not like the old (Jer 31:32), it would be founded on better promises (Heb 7:22; 8:6). There is no point having a new covenant if the old was satisfactory; through the Lord's Supper Jesus was constantly reminding Stephen that it was his blood sacrifice that ratified the forgiveness and acceptance of the new covenant. Clearly "the people of God [could not] be related to him under the terms of two different covenants simultaneously."[39]

36. Barrett, *Acts*, 367.

37. E.g., the Hebrew can be read "Sikkuth your king" and the LXX, which Stephen follows, has "the shrine of Moloch" and "Kiyyûn" for "Rephan."

38. Bock, *Acts*, 300.

39. Gooding, *True to the Faith*, 120.

A PLACE TO WORSHIP GOD (7:44–50)

Joshua, whose name is the Hebrew equivalent of Jesus, brought the tent into Canaan, and God did a powerful work of deliverance in the conquest (7:45). The tabernacle was constructed carefully following a pattern handed down by God to Moses (7:44), and he was content to localize his presence there in the wilderness and, after the conquest, in Canaan (7:45; 1 Chr 17:4–6). Abraham had seen the glory of God, but the revelation to Moses in Sinai was much deeper as the Lord was beginning to teach his people what it was to have him dwelling among them and for them to dwell with him.[40] Without being derogatory to either, Stephen appears to view the Tabernacle, not the temple, as the epitome of Jewish worship. The mobility of a tent contrasted the fixed stone structure, which "was a restraint on the status quo mentality that had grown up around the temple."[41] James, the brother of Jesus, would look to the tabernacle of David as being the ideal; there worshipers could come before the ark of the covenant (15:16).

When Stephen spoke of David finding favor with God (7:46), he was referring to the especially close relationship God had with him (1 Sam 16:13; 18:12, 14). David wanted to replace the tabernacle with a grand and permanent place of worship that would "solidify the relationship between God, land, and dynasty."[42] In response to David's desire to build a permanent temple, God sent Nathan with a promise that his own house (or lineage) would be established forever (2 Sam. 7:16; 1 Chr 17:4–14). The actual construction of his magnificent temple was left to his successor (1 Kgs 8:27), yet Stephen calls what Solomon has built, not a "temple" with its association of holiness but simply a "house" (7:47). By doing so he does not give the present building undue importance.

Even Solomon admitted that God could not be confined to a locality, saying in 1 Kgs 8:27, "The heavens, even the highest heaven, cannot contain you. How much less this temple I have built!" However, Stephen quoted Isaiah 66:1–2a, but the remainder of verse 2 is implied to his hearers: "These are the ones I look on with favor: those who are humble and contrite in spirit, and who tremble at my word."

40. Gooding, *True to the Faith*, 126.

41. Longenecker, "Acts," 9:346.

42. Bock, *Acts*, 301.

The temple built by Solomon and "made with hands"[43] (7:48) stands in contrast to the temple of Christ's body made without hands (Mark 14:58). It was never part of Jewish teaching that God actually lived in the temple but spoke of his Name and presence being there. In practice this was often denied.[44] They simply should not have regarded it in any literal sense as God's home.[45] They should neither have so identified the Lord with the temple as to see it's continued existence as guaranteeing them protection, nor it's destruction as a sign of abandonment. How could a building constructed on earth contain the one who created the universe? If God could not be contained to a location, the implication may be that he cannot be confined to a specific people.[46]

The criticism of an unduly exulted value placed on temple worship is less an attack on Judaism as a whole "than on a religious cult that allowed no room for God to work in a new way."[47] It was not wrong to have built the temple as it served Israel well as a God-given parable, a copy of the things in heaven and as a place to put his Name and meet his people. The old temple never gave people freedom to enter into the most holy place, yet once a year one man was allowed to come into the presence of God on earth. On Christ's death the veil of the temple was torn, allowing people unimpeded access to the Father (Eph 2:18).[48] If the Son of Man, the ideal male, could enter God's presence in heaven so could his followers. This did not repudiate the idea behind the high priest's yearly visit, rather it fulfilled it.[49] Likewise, the coming of the messiah was no surprise as Moses and the prophets had announced it; David had foretold a new priesthood after the order of Melchizedek.

The tent in the wilderness with its God-given plans, furniture, and ceremonies was expanded upon in Solomon's temple, but even this was not God's final word as it could not be an adequate fulfillment of Nathan's prophecy. The temple his accusers so prized would be gone by AD 70, leaving Israel without a place to offer sacrifices for sin and forcing

43. This was a common expression used to denigrate something (Lev 25:1; Isa 2:8; 46:6. Acts 19:25; Eph 2:1)

44. Longenecker, "Acts," 9:346.

45. Stott, *Message of Acts*, 138–39.

46. Bock, *Acts*, 304.

47. Marshall, *Fresh Look*, 69.

48. Some see it as a sign that God's presence had departed from the most holy place. Very likely we are meant to see both possibilities at once.

49. Gooding, *True to the Faith*, 128.

them to substitute prayer. Everything Stephen said had "already [been] promised, warned about, or declared."[50] The body of Jesus was not just a temple when he was on earth; it would be raised from the dead and rebuilt as God's temple. The eternal kingship was established in Christ, and the "house" is the Redeemer of God's elect along with his elect (Eph 2:19–22; John 2:20).

AN UNBELIEVING GENERATION (7:51–53)

Stephen's argument that Jews had failed to keep the Law could imply that Christian Jews were not opposed to keeping it.[51] His opponents didn't just not keep the Law; they also rejected it. As with Joseph and Moses and with the prophets to whom they paid great tribute (Matt. 23:30), Jesus assured them that they were true sons of their fathers, as also did Stephen (7:51–52). Throughout Israel's history they persecuted the prophets, but Jesus had told his generation that they would be liable for their blood (Luke 11:50–51). The wickedness exceeded that of their predecessors as they had not killed a prophet but the author of life. Moses and the prophets had accused the nation of being "stiff necked." Now Stephen lays the same charge against his accusers. For all their trust in the physical act of circumcision, the leaders were accused of behaving like the heathen and being unfaithful to the covenant through being "uncircumcised in their heart and ears" (7:51). This was an implied call for them to repent.[52]

There is a shift from "our fathers," which Stephen has used consistently up to this point to "your fathers" (7:51). His address had concentrated on how the nation resisted the covenant-keeping God but Stephen changes that to resisting the Holy Spirit. He was saying there is a division in Israel between those who obey and those who resist the Holy Spirit. Stephen has already been described as a man full of the Spirit and whoever responds to his message responded to the Spirit. Their fathers had persecuted and killed the prophets with the message of the coming righteous one and finally exceeded their wickedness by doing the same to the author of life. They are still resisting the leaders God had chosen. Nothing has changed.

50. Bock, *Acts*, 303.

51. Marshall, *Fresh Look*, 69.

52. Bock, *Acts*, 304.

Instead of Stephen, it is the accusers that have broken the Law given to them by angels (7:53); their behavior is what is bringing about the separation of the two communities. But it was not sought by the followers of the Way. Those following the new faith were truer to the promise and the Law.

Stephen's address is summarized in Table 5 below:

Where God blessed		Who the Jews Resisted	
Person blessed	Where	Who	By Whom
7:2 Abraham	Mesopotamia	7:9 Joseph	Patriarchs
7:4 Abraham	Haran	7:27, 39 Moses	Israel
7:10 Joseph	Egypt	7:52 Prophets	Their fathers
7:11,15 His brothers	Canaan	And now they resist Jesus	
7:17, 38 Israel	Egypt, Sinai		

Table 6. Stephen's sermon summarized

7:54–60 THE STONING AND DEATH OF STEPHEN

Stephen's argument is too much for his accusers, but he looked into heaven and saw the glory of God, ending this story as it began with God's glory being revealed to Abraham. He saw Jesus, as the Son of Man[53] (7:56), exulted as Peter preached in chapters 2 and 3 and standing beside God. For his hearers, this is a blasphemous act that attacked God's uniqueness.[54] Those who had been accused of having uncircumcised ears (7:51) covered them to not hear the truth. Whereas every other New Testament reference to Jesus is to his being seated with the Father, here he is seen as momentarily rising to greet his first martyr. Jesus also stands as a witness before God to his witness on earth. The words Stephen uses were those on which Jesus was found guilty of blasphemy (Luke 22:69). The brutal execution is described very peacefully: "He fell asleep" (7:60).

The Mishnah describes a death by stoning:

> Four cubits from the stoning place the criminal is stripped . . . the drop from the stoning place was twice the height of a man.

53. This was Jesus' favorite description of himself and refers to the everlasting ruler of Dan 7:13.

54. Bock, *Acts*, 309.

> One of the witnesses pushes the criminal from behind so that he falls face downwards. He is then turned over on his back. If he dies from the fall that is sufficient, if not the second witness takes the stone and drops it on his heart. If this causes death, that is sufficient. If not, he is stoned by the whole congregation.[55]

Unfortunately, it is an idealized reconstruction of a later period. The Sanhedrin could not condemn a man to death without Roman approval. This was an illegal execution, yet by having the witnesses stone Stephen they tried to give it legitimacy (7:58). A verdict had not even been pronounced.

The attitude of Stephen is exactly the opposite of the high priest Zechariah, who cried, "May the Lord see this and call you to account" (2 Chr 24:22). Instead, Stephen's words echo Jesus' crucifixion where he cried out and gave up his spirit (Luke 23:46) but not before asking God to forgive, not his own sins but those of his accusers (Luke 23:34).[56] God is doing a new thing with his people as even then Stephen was caring for his murderers. It was easier for his accusers to kill Stephen than to admit he was right about them and the Law. Fearful of the spread of Stephen's views, the Sanhedrin persecuted the whole church, though we will see that this largely fell upon the Hellenists. Peter had preached that Jesus was the only means of salvation for the whole earth (4:12) but had not taken this to its logical conclusion. From "Stephen's perspective that the gospel be divorced from Jewish cultic practices [it] opened the way for carrying the gospel across the borders of language, race, culture, religion, and sex."[57]

Stephen's exposure of Israel's stubbornness had prepared the reader for Saul's entrance, a young man guarding the clothes of murderers from local thieves (7:48). The two communities could not be compared more starkly. Saul may well have been one of the accusers as he was from Cilicia (6:9). When Paul could not resist Stephen's arguments, he was forced to realize that there was a different way to read the Scriptures than how he was taught by Gamaliel. "The implications for the Gentile nations are

55. M. *Sanh.* 7:3.

56. There are many similarities to the account of the death of James, the brother of Jesus, and Stephen, including the prayer for forgiveness. Eusebius, *Hist. eccl.* 2.23 (*NPNF*^{2} 1:125–28).

57. Wood, *Acts*, 124.

that God can speak to them also."[58] He also saw that there was a different way to act.

Michael Griffith noted that "the New Testament writers seem to go out of their way to demonstrate how the followers of Jesus reflected on His life, imitated it and in some degree repeated it."[59] Stephen's ministry clearly shows this imitation of Christ and his role as a second Christ. Luke wants us to see that the authentic imitation of Christ was not just the prerogative of the apostles but was demonstrated also by the new believers.

The Lord Jesus	Stephen
"in the power of the Spirit" (Luke 4:14) "full of grace and truth" (John 1:14)	"full of God's grace and power" (6:8)
"by miracles, wonders and signs" (2:22)	"great wonders and miraculous signs" (6:8)
"no-one dared to ask him any more questions" (Luke 20:40)	"could not stand up against his wisdom or the Spirit" (6:10)
"many false witnesses" (Matt. 26:60)	"they produced false witnesses" (6:13)
"I am able to destroy the temple" (26:61)	"Jesus . . . will destroy this place" (6:14)
"eyes of everyone . . . fastened on him" (Luke 4:20)	"all . . . looked intently at Stephen" (6:15)
"the Son of Man will be seated at the right hand of the mighty God" (22:69)	"I see . . . the Son standing at the right hand of God" (7:56)
"Father, into your hands I commit my spirit" (23:46)	"Lord Jesus, receive my spirit" (7:59)
"Father, forgive them" (23:34)	"Lord, do not hold this sin against them" (7:60)
"Joseph . . . a good and upright man" (23:50)	"Godly men buried Stephen" (8:2)
"a large number . . . mourned and wailed" (23:27)	"and mourned deeply for him" (8:2)[60]

Table 7. Comparison of Stephen to Jesus

58. Griffith, *Example of Jesus*, 62.

59. Griffith, *Example of Jesus*, 59.

60. Table taken from Griffith, *Example of Jesus*, 60.

6

The Scattered Church Includes the Outcasts (Acts 8:1–40)

THE CHURCH IS SCATTERED (8:1–4)

Saul, later Paul, is introduced and is contrasted to the devout men who buried Stephen (8:2). The way they are described suggests they were not Christians, much like the way Jesus was not buried by his own. The Mishnah stated that it was only permissible to grieve silently but not lament the executed,[1] so their loud lamentation was a defiance of the Sanhedrin and a declaration of Stephen's righteousness.[2] While it is possible that Saul was a member of the Sanhedrin (26:10), it is not certain. There has been a rapid transformation in Saul as he goes from guarding cloths to actively, violently,[3] and systematically seeking out Christians. Likely, he understood the significance of what was said more than others, possibly even the apostles themselves. We will come to know Paul as the apostle or ambassador of Christ, but the wisdom of God is staggering when we consider that this man was first "the apostle of the Law" (8:3; 9:1–2). Inadvertently, Saul in his great rage would start the spread of the gospel among the gentiles. The word *evangelizeō*, from which get "evangelize," has only been used once before (5:42) but is found five times in this chapter,[4] so popularizing the word.

1. M. *Sanh.* 6.5–6.

2. Bock, *Acts*, 319.

3. The word in the LXX in Ps 79:14 (English 80:13) is used to describe a boar ripping up a vineyard. See BADG, "λυμαίνω," 604. It is especially used of "the ravaging a body by a wild beast." Bruce, *Acts*, 1954, 175n8.

4. Twice it is the object of the verb, and three times it is the object of the news itself.

In the Old Testament, a scattering would have been seen as God judging a rebellious people by excluding them from the temple.[5] If anything, this one was a judgment on Jerusalem as the testimony about Jesus had diminished. But the temple was now obsolete, as Jesus was the new temple. The "tongues of fire, miniature glory clouds, resting on each disciple of Jesus at Pentecost, sealed the presence of the Spirit of glory and of God wherever believers might be scattered (see 1 Peter 4:14)."[6] It should be a very natural thing for wandering Christians to spread the gospel as "nameless amateur missionaries,"[7] but Saul did not know that yet.

The church, conservatively estimated at this stage at twenty-five thousand[8] in Jerusalem and surrounds, is to undergo its first major persecution, yet not the whole church. The Hebrew Christians don't seem to be as affected by the persecution, as the apostles remained in Jerusalem apparently in relative safety and a church also remained. Why the apostles were able to stay in Jerusalem we are not told; perhaps they were too well known and regarded or they took the risk.[9] Philip (8:5–8) was one of the original deacons and most likely a Hellenist; the founders of Antioch were also Hellenists (men of Cyprus and Cyrene). These men would take the gospel beyond Jerusalem.

As the Jewish nation had been dispersed through the nations, so now the new Israel is dispersed (8:4). The Spirit had been poured out on Hebrew and Hellenistic Jews alike, making them equally equipped in taking the good news to the ends of the earth.

PHILIP IN SAMARIA (8:5–13)

Despite Jesus clearly telling the church to preach the gospel to the Samaritans (1:8), it took persecution for it to happen. However, the cultural and religious leap when Philip, one of the seven, preached to the Samaritans in an unspecified city must not be underestimated. Luke has prepared us to look favorably on the Samaritans with the parable of the good Samaritan and the thankful leper (Luke 10:29–37, 17:18). However, they were hated by the Jews (John 4:9). Eating with them would bring

5. Johnson, *Message of Acts*, 95.
6. Johnson, *Message of Acts*, 95.
7. Stott, *Message of Acts*, 146.
8. Lenski, *Acts*, 311.
9. Bock, *Acts*, 318.

ritual impurity, which is why the Samaritan woman was surprised that Jesus would share a vessel with her (John 4:9). They have been described as occupying "a sort of covenantal 'no man's land'—not belonging to Israel, but not quite pagan Gentiles either."[10] They were not racially pure but "polluted" by immigrants brought into Samaria by the Assyrians after the destruction of the Northern Kingdom in 722 BC.[11] Neither were they religiously pure as they mixed the worship of God with their own gods. They had their own temple[12] (John 4:20) on Mount Gerizim, in conjunction with their half yearly bread religion. As they accepted the Books of Moses,[13] they did have a belief in a coming messiah (John 4:25), and Philip would build on this. In many ways they did not differ fundamentally from Jewish beliefs and could be even more diligent in the observance of the Law.[14]

Being mistreated by the religious officials in Jerusalem over their attitudes to the temple may have helped Philip build a sense of kinship with the Samaritans.[15] Even so, to acknowledge that the messiah would not be a Samaritan and that salvation is from the Jews was a very big admission given their history.[16] Like Stephen, Philip's preaching was accompanied by powerful miracles despite not being an apostle. He also had a strong deliverance ministry, something not mentioned in relation to the Jewish church. It is possible that this strong demonic influence was directly due to the sorcerer Simon (see commentary in the section titled Simon Magus). We will be introduced to Elymas, another sorcerer, in chapter 13. In a time where life for many could be crushing and oppressive, the promise that magic offered was very tempting. It promised control over fate and the power to gain control over the unseen and uncontrollable forces that people believed were at play. Simon's power was so impressive that when they said of him "This man is rightly called the Great

10. Johnson, *Message of Acts*, 97.

11. It could be said that the hostility goes back a thousand years to the dividing of the kingdom after Solomon's death.

12. The temple was destroyed in 128 BC by John Hyrcanus, but the site was still used for that purpose.

13. There were a number of changes, such as supporting Mt. Gerizim over Jerusalem.

14. Cowley and Huxley, *Samaritans*, 10:674.

15. Longenecker, "Acts," 9:355. He suggests that had the first ministry among the Samaritans been by the apostles they likely would have been rebuffed as in Luke 9:51–56. Longenecker, "Acts," 9:359.

16. Gooding, *True to the Faith*, 142.

Power of God" (8:10), they were attributing some divine power to him.[17] Many had followed Simon when speaking of himself and his abilities, but Phillip spoke only of "the good news of the kingdom of God and the name of Jesus Christ" (8:12). We have a parallel to the magicians in Egypt that could not match the signs of Moses. However, it was the message of God's rule that caused the Samaritans to come to faith, not the powerful miracles and deliverances that only bore witness to the message.[18]

Where previously the Samaritans had been amazed by Simon and his signs, he in turn is further amazed by the powerful ministry of the apostles, especially their ability to give the gift of the Holy Spirit (8:13, 18–9). Simon had been unable to deliver the Samaritans from their afflictions because, presumably, they lacked the funds to engage his services, but ultimately, he lacked the power. Simon himself believed and was baptized (8:13). It is possible that he thought that if he followed the stream, he would retain his adherents.[19] Views vary considerably among the commentators about whether, in the midst of a genuine work of the Spirit, Simon's faith is superficial, but it is not presented that way. As in other cases in Acts, baptism is immediate, but here there is a separation between baptism and the receipt of the Spirit; this is so abnormal that Luke draws attention to it (8:16).

The Magic of Simon

When we think of "magicians" our first thought is of skilled illusionists, but we are introduced to something much darker and beyond the experience of most of my readers and myself. However, when I was a much younger man, our family was very good friends with a former district commissioner from Tanganyika. He administered an area that was remote and backward at the time. Only after he had been in that area for about twelve years did he become aware of a very dark form of witchcraft that was hidden and not spoken about. His investigations led to about a dozen people being hung for murder of different close family members. His account of those times defies belief; however, I was able

17. It is known that in the fourth century the term "Great Power" was used by the gnostics as a divine title. Johnson suggests that Simon was claiming to be the incarnation of a deity. Johnson, *Message of Acts*, 170. The Samaritan religion would have prevented them from saying he was divine.

18. Johnson, *Message of Acts*, 171.

19. Bruce, *Acts*, 1954, 179.

to meet other former colonial service officials that were involved and verified his account. While this is not the place to expand upon these matters, what I am trying to say is we need to keep an open mind about what is being said here and to heed Luke's warning that there are spiritual forces and spiritual experiences that are beyond our comprehension, and they are not all good.

THE HOLY SPIRIT IS GIVEN TO THE SAMARITANS (8:14–25)

Philip had acted on his own initiative, so when the church in Jerusalem heard that the Samaritans had believed, they sent Peter and John to confirm the validity of the reception of the gospel across the first major religious barrier. We are not told how they knew the Spirit had not been given. Apart from Simon, there is no hint that the Samaritans' faith response was inadequate, nor that Philip's message was defective. The apostles approved and built on Philip's ministry by praying for the Samaritans to receive the Holy Spirit. When the Spirit later fell on Cornelius and his family, it was spontaneous and confounded many as they could not believe that God would give his Spirit to uncircumcised gentiles (11:1–3). In Samaria, the apostles laid hands upon the believers, "indicat[ing] fellowship and identification" prior to the Spirit falling. This was obviously a supernatural manifestation, likely with tongues.[20]

John Stott considers verse 16 as the most extraordinary statement in Acts.[21] The Samaritans were "only" baptized, suggesting that water baptism and receiving the Spirit were expected to occur together. The break between baptism and receipt of the Spirit goes against Peter's promise in his Pentecost sermon (2:38), and implications are drawn from it in Catholic and Pentecostal practice. It is used to justify the Catholic practice of a separation between baptism and confirmation with apostolic hands and can be used as a defense of Pentecostal practice of laying on hands to receive the baptism in the Holy Spirit.[22] However, it could also signify no more than an apostolic witness was needed for such a groundbreaking change, as it would be with Cornelius. It could equally

20. Bruce, *Acts*, 1990, 222.

21. Stott, *Message of Acts*, 150.

22. Most mainline Pentecostal groups would say that someone cannot be converted and not have received the Spirit. They would understand the baptism in the Spirit as something generally subsequent to salvation, not necessary for it.

be argued that chapter 2, with conversion, baptism and receiving the Holy Spirit occurring at the one time, is the normal practice.

It was not the sole right of the apostles to give the Spirit, making it something a mere evangelist could not do. Ananias will do this in chapter 9. The giving of the Spirit was not controlled by the apostles,[23] and there is no set pattern in Acts. The Samaritans were used to being hated by the Jews and were given special evidence to show that they had been fully incorporated in the faith. This delay could well have avoided a "Samaritan curtain," where the two parties found Christ without finding each other.[24] Only a few years previous, John, along with James, had wanted to be like Elijah and call down fire from heaven to consume the unbelieving Samaritans (Luke 9:54). Now Peter and John will acknowledge them as brothers and sisters and call down holy fire upon them. The time had come for the fulfilment of Jesus' promise to the Samaritan woman at the well, that the time was coming when people would not have their worship centered on a physical location but worship in Spirit and truth (John 4:21–4).

In Acts, the gospel workers never receive payment, but Simon thought that "God's grace [was] a business commodity,"[25] so he asked to buy this power.[26] Integrity is an issue as with Ananias and Sapphira and the charity to the widows. Simon's offer showed him to be an enemy of God and that his heart was not straight before God (8:21) despite having believed and being baptized. Peter's strong denunciation used words similar to those of the psalmists, who described the Israelite generation that died in the wilderness as not having a straight heart (Ps 78:37), and of Moses, who warned against those who turned from the Lord having a root of bitterness (Deut 29:18). "Simon, the spokesman for ancient magic, confessed the superiority of the word of Jesus after his attempts to enfold its power into his own syncretistic system were rebuffed."[27] The magician appears to repent but his failure to pray for himself hints of him being unregenerate (8:24), and Peter says as much: "You have no part or share

23. Bock, *Acts*, 330.

24. Stott, *Message of Acts*, 158.

25. Johnson, *Message of Acts*, 171.

26. The practice of purchasing ecclesiastical office is called "simony." From the earliest days, there were teachers who regarded Christianity as a source of profit, and even Paul found it necessary to warn against it (1 Tim 6:5).

27. Johnson, *Message of Acts*, 172.

in this ministry" (8:21).[28] Luke deliberately left this section open-ended, perhaps leaving it to the reader to make his/her own conclusion. Later church history speaks loudly against the sincerity of any deep repentance (refer to section titled Simon Magus).

After expanding on the preaching of Phillip, the apostles return to Jerusalem by way of many Samaritan villages where, following Jesus' example (Luke 9:51–56), they also preached. In Jerusalem they are not subject to the questioning that will follow Peter's preaching to and eating with the gentile Cornelius.

Simon Magus

What we hear of Simon in 8:24 and 8:13 when he repented of his sin contrasts with what the church has to say of him. He is portrayed as a well-known opponent of the early Christians and the arch heretic. Luke may have included this material to explain Simon's tenuous relationship with the Christian community and to indicate to his readers that Simon did not have a divine or apostolic approval. While Simon's final words seem ambiguous, the whole of Luke's narrative in fact has a negative attitude towards Simon. Peter's speech seems to reflect Luke's own judgment on Simon's Christianity: it was false.

While Christianity and Gnosticism emerged on the scene at about the same time, they are distinct religions though some argue the latter is derived from the former.[29] The church fathers unanimously claimed Simon Magus was from Gitta, a pagan area of Samaria, and was the arch-Gnostic, though Luke only refers to him as a magician (8:9–24). He went to Rome under Claudius, accompanied by a prostitute from Tyre called Helen who he called his *Ennonia* ("First Thought"). He considered himself to be a god and that this "Thought" leaped forth from him in the beginning and generated the angels who made the world. Helen was then seized by the angels and held captive in various bodies down the ages (Helen of Troy and the "lost sheep" of the Gospels) until appearing as a common prostitute. Simon came in the form of a man to save her and to offer salvation through his knowledge. He would appear to the Jews as

28. The validity of Simon's conversion and repentance is debated among the commentators with wide varieties or opinion.

29. Yamauchi, *Pre-Christian Gnosticism*, 21.

Son, to the Samarians as Father, and to the nations as Holy Spirit.[30] Two things separated Simon from later Gnosticism, though: Simon claimed to be divine and salvation came from recognizing him, not through any self-knowledge.[31] He later founded the cult of the Simonians, which lasted till the third century.

CONVERSION OF THE ETHIOPIAN (8:26–40)

After three accounts of mass conversions, Luke then tells three stories of the salvation of individuals. We may find it surprising that God asked Philip to leave a successful work in Samaria to go on a long journey to save just one person.[32] But this one person would herald the international expansion of the kingdom across every conceivable barrier. It was also a down payment on the promise of the inclusion of the Ethiopians and eunuchs (Ps 68:31; 87:3–4; Isa 11:10–11; 56:3–7). However, the apostles were also slow to realize that they had a mission to the gentiles as well, and they also had to be directed to go to them by angelic mediation (see chapter 10 with Cornelius and Peter). It is not surprising then that this account has a number of similarities to Jesus opening the Scriptures to his disciples on the road to Emmaus.[33] "The house of prayer for all nations was . . . located (among other places) at a wadi beside a wilderness road in old Philistine territory, where a castrated Ethiopian was cleansed for priestly service through faith in the Lamb of God who 'was led like a sheep to the slaughter' (8:32 quoting Isa 53:7)."[34]

While an angel said go to Jerusalem to the Gaza Road, it is still the Spirit's leading[35] for Philip to approach the Ethiopian in the old Philistine stronghold. The location itself signaled that those who were formerly outcasts were to be included. The first gentile, who was not a

30. Irenaeus, *Haer.* 1.23.1–5 (*ANF* 1:347–48); Justin Martyr, *1 Apol.* 1.26 (*ANF* 1:171–72). Justin was from Samaria and died in AD 165 and was very aware of Simon's continuing legacy, which strongly suggests the validity of the connection with Simon Magus and the founder of the Simonians.

31. Yamauchi, *Pre-Christian Gnosticism*, 62.

32. The details of the events from the election of the deacons, the martyrdom of Stephen, the Samaritan ministry, and the Ethiopian eunuch could have been learned when Luke stayed with Paul in Philip's home for several days (21:8–10),

33. Edwards, "Parallels and Patterns," 489–90.

34. Johnson, *Message of Acts*, 100–101.

35. For similar angel/Spirit leading in Luke, see Luke 1:26–35 and Acts 10.

full proselyte, was about to be added to the church and so set an example to the young church to the extent of the barriers that were to be broken down by the gospel. His salvation would be considered impossible on the following grounds:

1. He was not a Jew but an Ethiopian.
2. He was black and descended from Ham, (Ham's progeny is cursed Gen 9:25).
3. He could only be a "proselyte of the gate" since he was barred from entering the inner temple courts because of his castration (Deut 23:1).

These second-class proselytes were bound only to the Noachian commandments in Gen 9:4–6 and its seven commandments against idolatry, blasphemy, disobedience to magistrates, murder, fornication, robbery, and eating of blood. This class of proselyte was extremely common at that time, and it was from that group that the church was to grow in other nations.

"Ethiopian" is a misleading term. The word used is for Sudan, which is confirmed by the official title Candace for the queen (probably the queen mother). As a high official he would have been expected to worship the state deities, including Apedemak, the lion god, Amun from Egypt, along with a host of lesser deities from Egypt and Sudan. Among this gross heathenism and demonic forces, he had heard of Yahweh, God of the Jews, an example of his sovereign call. Refusing to enter that life and being barred from full entry to Judaism with its temple free of images, God graciously opened a new door for him.

As with Peter and his three-fold vision, Philip's understanding of what God wanted only unfolded as he obeyed the Spirit's command. His intentions were made clear when Philip heard[36] the Ethiopian reading about the unjust death of the Lord's servant that Isaiah told with irony and his request for a guide. The question of who Isaiah was writing about, though clear to us, would not have been clear to the Ethiopian. While Jesus identified with Isaiah's servant (Mark 10:45; 14:24; Luke 22:37), there is no evidence in early Jewish writings connecting the servant with the messiah.[37] The Samaritans were presented as unstable and credulous, but this high public servant is shown "as a thoughtful seeker after the

36. Reading was generally done aloud at that time.

37. Longenecker, "Acts," 9:365.

truth"[38] who readily admits his ignorance. Starting with this passage (note God's providence), Philip proclaimed Jesus to him.

> The Spirit has to expressly tell Philip to join with the Ethiopian who he finds is reading the Septuagint of Isaiah 53:7–8 where Isaiah is depicting the great servant of God in his suffering and his death. He cannot understand. The prophet says, "His generation who considered?" and then states why the question is asked "because taken away from the earth was his life." Taken from the earth how could he have a generation? Yet behold what a vast generation is his. All these believers in all ages. The Septuagint is correct who shall declare, recount, set in detail his generation.[39]

Without a heavenly vision like Paul and Cornelius, and only the reading and explanation of the Scriptures, the Ethiopian believed. His connection to the Jewish faith would have made baptism a natural next step and, at his request, is baptized. Immersion is suggested. Verse 37 is not in the best manuscripts, but something like this needed to have happened. It could have been part of an early baptism liturgy.[40] The rhetorical question by the Ethiopian about whether there was anything to prevent him from being baptized (8:36) is repeated with Cornelius (10:47). Nothing is said of the Spirit coming upon the eunuch but there was a Spirit encounter that left him rejoicing. No questions were raised at this point about fellowship between Jews and gentiles, and the question of circumcision did not arise with the Samaritans as they were already circumcised.

In one instant Philip was walking alongside the eunuch, in the next, by the Spirit of the Lord, he was found in Azotus (Ashdod) amid the land of the "uncircumcised Philistines." The issue of gentile ministry will not be raised explicitly until Cornelius. This instantaneous removal validated the ministry to the eunuch and among the gentiles in the region from Azotus to Caesarea, the Roman capital of Judea and possibly the fifth largest city in the empire.[41] Nothing is said of Philip's attitude to faith and circumcision among his converts, which would have been an issue for the Jerusalem church. When Paul visited Caesarea on his last journey

38. Stott, *Message of Acts*, 163.

39. Lenski, *Acts*, 334. It is hard to imagine Philip didn't point him to the whole of chapter 53.

40. Stott, *Message of Acts*, 161.

41. Bock, *Acts*, 370.

to Jerusalem along with Luke, Phillip was still living there along with his four prophetess daughters (21:8–9).

7

The Church's Persecutor Is Converted, People Healed (Acts 9:1–43)

SAUL'S CONVERSION (9:1–9)

To drive home the importance of Paul's dramatic conversion to the infant church, Luke told it three times. Rather than containing contradictions, they complement each other. Here, the story is recounted by Luke, then told in Paul's own words to the angry mob in the temple precincts (22:1–21), and again to king Agrippa (26:12–20). Before the mob, he emphasizes his heritage, and before Agrippa he emphasizes the promises made through the prophets whom the king believes. All three record his call to the gentiles. There can seem to be a disconnect between the Paul of Luke's Acts and the Paul of his Epistles. When Paul spoke in his Letters of his own religious experiences he was reserved (2 Cor 12:1–4), which was a reaction to the exaggerated claims of the false apostles who stressed signs and wonders rather than personal witness.[1] However, Luke is concerned with the apostle's ministry in the larger concerns of the church, not "local church politics or issues."[2]

There are two themes at play in the story of Paul's conversion. The first is of God's just judgment on Saul while the second is of being rescued from that judgment and being called by name twice[3] through grace to be to the Lord's messenger. By using multiple inferences, (see Table

1. Marshall, *Fresh Look*, 92. Refer to my comments on Acts 9:23–25.

2. Bock, *Acts*, 350.

3. A sign of intense emotion. Bock, *Acts*, 357. For a double calling of the name, see also Abraham (Gen 22:11), Jacob (Gen 46:2), Moses (Exod 3:4), Samuel (1 Sam 3:4, 6), Absolom (2 Sam 19:4), Martha (Luke 10:41).

7 below), Luke wanted his readers to see Saul's conversion in the same vein as that of Moses who spoke directly to God and Samuel, the founder of the subsequent prophetic tradition, along with Daniel, Ezekiel, and Jeremiah.[4]

Moses (Exod 3:4) and Samuel are called by name twice (1 Sam 3:10).	Saul is called twice (Acts 9:4).
Moses' call came while watching the sight of the burning bush (Exod 3:3).	Paul's call is associated first through a vision given to Ananias (Acts 9:10) and then to Paul (Acts 9:12).
Moses and Samuel reply, "Here I am" (literally, "Behold I [am here]") (Exod 3:4; 1 Sam 3:4).	Ananias replies, "Yes Lord" (literally, "Behold I [am here]") (Acts 9:10).
On asking, the Lord reveals to Moses that his name is "I am" (Exod 3:4).	On asking, Paul is told, "I am Jesus" (Acts 9:5).
Moses is told to say, "The God of your fathers . . . has sent me" (Exod 3:13).	Ananias tells Paul that "the God of our fathers" has commissioned him (Acts 22:14–15).
Moses pleads, "I ask Lord, choose[5] another person" (Exod 4:13 LXX).	Ananias says to Paul, "The God of our fathers has chosen you" (Acts 22:14).
Daniel was the only one who saw the vision of the messenger of God. His companions fled and hid (Dan 10:7).	Saul's companions only experienced a frightening and powerful phenomenon (Acts 9:7).
Ezekiel fell to the ground when he saw God's glory, was commanded to stand, and was then commissioned to proclaim God's word (Ezek 2:1–3).	Saul fell to his feet and was commanded to stand (Acts 9:4–6).
The Lord promised to rescue Jeremiah in his ministry of building up and tearing down (Jer 1:8–10).	The Lord promised to rescue Paul from his own people and the gentiles (Acts 26:17).

Table 8. Similarities of Paul's call to that of Moses, Samuel, Daniel, Ezekiel and Jeremiah[6]

Saul did not decide for God, rather God decided for him and was the driver of Paul's complete transformation from beginning to end. Going to arrest Christians, Christ took hold of him (Phil 3:12), suggesting that he was the one arrested.[7] For a Jew with such impeccable

4. Johnson, *Message of Acts*, 114.

5. The word for "choose" used by Moses and Ananias is rare in biblical Greek. Johnson, *Message of Acts*, 114.

6. Johnson, *Message of Acts*, 113–14.

7. Stott, *Message of Acts*, 170.

credentials as Saul to be called to take the gospel to the gentiles was so radical that God's initiative and the genuineness of the vision, like the twofold revelation to Cornelius and Peter, was needed to be confirmed through a second revelation to Ananias.

For a strict and zealous Pharisee, the Messiah proclaimed by Stephen who had foretold the destruction of the temple was anathema. Further, Jesus had been condemned by the Jewish leaders and was executed in disgrace.[8] God's disapproval of Jesus was obvious to all as the Law had warned that anyone who hung on a tree was cursed (Gal 3:13). As a Christian, Paul would come to embrace the stumbling block of the curse of the cross (1 Cor 1:23; Gal 5;11), understanding that Christ, the sinless one, became a curse on behalf of others. Jesus who knew no sin became sin for us (2 Cor 5:21). Through his faultless observance of the Law, Paul had sought to acquit himself but came to an understanding put so eloquently by Luther:

> Thou, Lord Jesus, art my righteousness, but I am thy sin. Thou hast taken upon thyself what is mine and hast given to me what is thine. Thou has taken upon thyself what thou wast not and hast given to me what I was not.[9]

Saul saw himself "obligated to heed the command, 'you must purge the evil from among you' (Deut 17:7)."[10] An "evil" was spreading among women as well as men, so he threw himself with doubled effort into the persecution of the church. He "laid waste" the church (8:3), a word used to describe the damage done to a vineyard by a wild boar or a wild animal ravaging a body, a trail of utter destruction. The allusion is continued with him being described as "breathing out murderous threats" (9:1), recalling the snorting of a wild beast.[11] He did all this being fully aware of the earnestness and stamina of his opponents and the suffering it would cause.[12] He could justify his actions by the following:

- The biblical example of cleansing sin such as at Baal-Peor (Num 25:1–5, see also 25:6–15)

8. Johnson, *Message of Acts*, 109.
9. Luther, *Instructions to the Perplexed*, 110.
10. Johnson, *Message of Acts*, 109.
11. Stott, *Message of Acts*, 169.
12. Longenecker, "Acts," 9:368.

- The historical example of Mattathias and the Hasidim removing apostasy (1 Macc 2:23–28, 42–48)
- The belief at that time that keeping the Law was necessary for the Messiah to come[13]

With such precedents, Paul would be expecting God's commendation[14] for his systematic door-to-door searches. On hearing that there was a group of Christians in Damascus, a significant and prosperous city 250 kilometers north, he was empowered by the high priest and the Sanhedrin (22:5) to carry them back to Jerusalem. Though Damascus was in a foreign nation, the Romans had permitted the power of the Sanhedrin to spread over all Jews in all nations. Damascus[15] had a large Nabatean Arab population, but the Jewish population was also high, as in AD 66 between ten and eighteen thousand Jews were recorded as being killed there by the Romans.[16]

Despite the apparent resolve of the "apostle of the Law," Paul was a man under conviction. Here, and when retelling the story before Agrippa, Jesus used a well-known expression of the day for a man at war with his god:[17] "It is hard for you to kick against the goads" (26:14). A goad is a pointed stick that was used to control animals. This figurative term would have given his Greek-oriented audience a better understanding of Jesus' literal question, "Why are you persecuting me?"[18] This learned man was likened to a dumb ox who had been fighting the forces around him that were directing him towards his call.

This image suggests that Paul had a half-conscious conviction that Christianity was true.[19] Saul had been cut to the heart (7:54) by Stephen's defense and had seen his face shine like that of an angel. How could he not have been moved by Stephen's death and prayer? But also, "From within him, it was his own spiritual experience of the Law"[20] (see Rom 7 where Paul describes the roll of the Law). William Barclay describes

13. E.g., M. *Sanh.* 97b–98a.

14. Longenecker, "Acts," 9:369.

15. Damascus became part of the Roman empire in 64 BC and was one of the ten cities of the Decapolis (Mark 5:20; 7:31).

16. Josephus, *J. W.* 2.20.2; 7.8.7.

17. E.g., Euripides, *Bacch.* 794–95; Aeschylus, *Ag.* 1624.

18. Longenecker, "Acts," 9:552–53.

19. Bruce, *Acts*, 1954, 491.

20. Barclay, *Ambassador for Christ*, 47.

this: "Paul found himself in the position of knowing what he ought to do and wanting to do it and yet being unable to do it. He found himself knowing what he should not do and not wanting to do it yet not being able to stop himself. Here was an agonizing situation which could drive a man mad. The better the man was the more agonizing the situation was, Comparison of Stephen to Jesus."[21] He discovered if he tried to rule his life by the Law and nothing else, that in a completely paradoxical way it was actually the cause of sin (Rom 7:7–25). As for Paul's conversion,

> It is often said that Paul was converted on the road to Damascus. Strictly speaking this is not the fact. His conversion began in the encounter with the Law, but it was not accomplished until the Gospel entered his heart by faith and that did not occur on the road but in Damascus.[22]

After a lonely week (a Pharisee would not associate with the police), he neared Damascus. Traveling was normally done in the cool of the morning, the cool of the late afternoon, or early evening. But during the burning heat of noon the caravan rested. The fact that Paul was pressing on at midday (26:13) showed that "he was driving himself and his companions to the limit of human endurance, so that he could get away from these thoughts of his and find solace in violent action."[23]

While Damascus was the first city outside of Israel said to have had Christians, it cannot be the only one as Saul's journey to Damascus was not his first attempt at persecuting the church in foreign countries. Luke describes this as "on one of these journeys" (26:12). His reputation for merciless persecution went ahead of him (9:13–14). While not murdering anyone personally (9:1), with Stephen's death he had shown that he would accept the outcome of the Sanhedrin's mock trials. The suddenness and power of the light sent Saul and all his companions (26:14) to the ground cringing in terror but the ability to understand the words spoken were for Saul's ears only.[24] Salvation appears to be found only by one of the group, and that the least worthy. The others could only report that something very significant had occurred. The account has a similarity to the time when God spoke directly to Jesus about glorifying Jesus, but the

21. Barclay, *Ambassador for Christ*, 48.

22. Lenski, *Acts*, 355.

23. Barclay, *Ambassador for Christ*, 54.

24. The second retelling says that his companions did not hear the voice (22:9) but likely refers to understanding the voice.

crowd heard it indistinctly and said that either an angel spoke to him or it thundered (John 12:29).

Saul was told a little about his call to the gentiles, though we do not learn about this till he retells it before Agrippa (26:16–18). To this point, Saul would have been willing to accept gentiles if they had forsaken idolatry for trust in the God of the Jews, been circumcised, and obeyed the Law like a Pharisee, but he otherwise would have shunned them contemptuously. Yet, as David Gooding expressed, "Despite his strenuous zeal, Saul the persecutor was the climax of Israel's rebellion against the Lord."[25] Paul's vision revealed him to be "an enemy, persecutor and blasphemer against God. Who shall say that his blasphemy was less serious than that of Gentile polytheism?"[26] He had been rejecting God all along (Luke 10:16), and the knowledge of this likely cured him of any feeling of superiority towards formerly polytheistic believers.[27] What happened to Paul was not just a slight adjustment of his spiritual compass but a total realignment of all that he believed God was and expected.

Stephen had testified that Abraham had seen the glory of God, now Paul also, though not as a friend but as an enemy under condemnation. Saul called the unknown heavenly visitor "Lord," showing high respect without necessarily calling him divine, yet surely with the beginnings of the theological overtones it would have in his Letters.[28] Jesus, who revealed himself to Paul in his glory, not the resurrection body of chapter 1, still connected to his humanity by calling himself "Jesus the Nazorean" (22:8), and identified himself with his servant's suffering (9:4). This very close identification, forcefully impressed upon Paul, was expanded later in life as he explained our union with Christ and of the church as the body of Christ. This association is a two-way relationship, as the suffering and death of Jesus belong to his people.[29]

On the road, Paul sees and speaks to the Lord who commissions him as the apostle to the gentiles. In his Letters, he understands his vision as comparable to that of the twelve (1 Cor 9:1). Paul would later write about Jesus as a cosmic spiritual figure to whom we can be united, but for "Luke, Jesus is a living being who can speak directly to people (9:4) and

25. Johnson, *Message of Acts*, 112.

26. Gooding, *True to the Faith*, 154.

27. Gooding, *True to the Faith*, 154.

28. Stott, *Message of Acts*, 173.

29. Johnson, *Message of Acts*, 117.

appear to them in visions (18:9; 23:11: cf. 27:23–24)."[30] The bright light did not blind Paul's companions, but he had seen the Shekhinah; blind, he needed to be led by hand to the house of Judas in Damascus. Paul was blind for three days, during which time he prayed and fasted, a sign of his repentance from his great sin in persecuting the church. Paul's blindness was full of symbolism, tracing back to the covenant curses. Moses had warned that for their disobedience, "The Lord will afflict you with madness, blindness and confusion of mind. At midday you will grope about like a blind person in the dark" (Deut 28:28–9). Similar thoughts are found in Isaiah where, because of their sin, Israel would grope at midday "like those having no eyes" (Isa 59:10). In the same vein is the physical blinding of Zedekiah, the last king of Judah, and the blinding of the Jewish false prophet on Cyprus (13:6–12).[31]

Until he saw himself as a person desperately in need of rescue from the consequences of his own sins, Saul was a blind man who needed a guide. He was in the process of becoming a guide to lead the blind but that could only happen when he recognized the depth of his sin and called on the name he had been trying to eradicate. Like Isaiah, he could not speak God's message until a "burning coal from the altar of God touched his lips to purify them and remove his guilt."[32] Saul's conversion gives insight into how God deals with his enemies and how we should also.

ANANIAS RESTORES PAUL'S SIGHT (9:10–19A)

As Ananias had only heard secondhand about Saul (9:13), he is unlikely to be an escaping Hellenist and, apart from being a particularly godly man, he does not appear to be anybody special in the church, just "a certain disciple." Before the Jerusalem mob Paul would stress Ananias's impeccable Jewish pedigree, he was highly respected because of his devout practice of the Law (22:12). We don't hear of him again. However, his reply, "Here I am Lord," mirrors the obedient servants of the past (e.g., Abraham, 22:1–2, 11–12). His natural reluctance to commit what would otherwise be suicide by calling on Paul in Straight Street[33] is

30. Marshall, *Fresh Look*, 61.

31. Johnson, *Message of Acts*, 110.

32. Johnson, *Message of Acts*, 115.

33. Straight Street, where Paul was staying, still exists in Damascus as its main east-west road. At the time, there were major halls with colonnades on both sides and two great city gates at each end. Haenchen, *Acts*, 323. It was a very fashionable address.

overcome by the Lord in the vision when he assured Ananias that the feared persecutor was having a similar vision. Second visions signify that the matter was firmly determined by God, as with Pharaoh (Gen 41:32) and Cornelius. Jesus had spoken to Saul on the road about his commission to be a witness to what he had seen (26:16–8), but Ananias added that he was to be God's "chosen instrument" to take the gospel to Jew and gentile alike, even before their rulers (9:15). But it would also be a life of suffering where the persecutor becomes the persecuted (9:16).

Annanias, who Luke calls a "disciple," refers to the believers in Damascus as "those who call upon your name" (9:14) and, for the first time in Acts, "saints" (9:13). Christians are described in many ways in Acts—saints, followers of the Way, brothers, witnesses—each looking to a different aspect of what it meant to follow Jesus. But "those who call on the name of the Lord" highlights the difference between Judaism and Christianity. These words are a standard Old Testament description of praying to God (Gen 4:26), so to call on the name of Jesus as Lord would have previously been as blasphemous to Saul as "to call on the name of Baal" (1 Kgs 18:16–46) and worthy of similar punishment.[34]

Paul had handled many Christians before but very roughly. The first Christian to handle Paul is completely the opposite in word and deed, which must have had a profound effect upon a blind man. On the road, the persecutor had called the heavenly vision "Lord," but Ananias knew exactly who that was; he had been sent by the Lord, by Jesus, to perform the miracles of restoring sight and filling with the Holy Spirit (9:17). Saul's sight was miraculously restored by Ananias, who told Saul to be baptized and wash away his sins (22:16, 2:38) while calling on "his name,"[35] i.e., the righteous one, Jesus (22:14). This is the first time the Spirit is recorded as being received outside of Israel. The limitations of verse 9 are immediately reversed: Saul can see, he eats food, and he drinks. Saul's blindness was typical of his nation's blindness, but now,

> Saul was appointed as the Lord's servant and witness, restored to sight so that he might "open eyes that are blind" and "release from the dungeon those that sit in darkness" (Isa 42:7 NIV). He had seen the righteous servant in his glory (Isa 52:13; 53:11), and that sight had brought to light hidden blindness—and

34. Gooding, *True to the Faith*, 154.

35. Calling on a name is an expression pointing to salvation (Rom 10:12–3; 1 Cor 1:2).

> cured it. . . . Apart from the Spirit, zeal for God is blind, the blind zeal blunders its way contrary to God's purposes.[36]

We live each day as it comes, not knowing what lies ahead: good or ill. We read part of what Paul suffered in 2 Cor 11:23–33. For most men, the knowledge that this was ahead would be too much to bear. For Paul, in receiving as good as he gave, it would be a sign of God's favor and an earnest of his reward. Never again would he persecute, nor would he raise his hand against those who persecuted him.

PAUL PREACHES IN DAMASCUS (9:19B–22)

After regaining his bearings among those whom he had come to persecute, Paul made no hesitation in preaching the Way. So complete was his turnaround that the Jews were not only "amazed," but they were also "confounded" as Paul himself had been in the Synagogue of the Freedmen. His message was Jesus, the Son of God, the only place in Acts where he is called this (9:20). He is now preaching as an eyewitness of the glorified Jesus. The more Saul preached Christ the more powerful he became, likely because of his growth in the understanding of his commitment to Jesus as Messiah.[37]

PAUL ESCAPES TO JERUSALEM (9:23–31)

Likely, the Jews had persuaded the governor of the city under King Aretas to arrest Paul whose preaching has what will prove to be the usual results: the Jews plotting to kill him. The time span of "many days" is probably three years following Paul's time in Arabia[38] (Gal 1:18). He escaped by being lowered over the wall in a basket. Paul will have to continually defend his apostleship (e.g., 2 Cor. 11:16–12:13), and it is not surprising. Compare him to the "real apostles": under persecution, they don't run but remain (8:1), and when they get into trouble the "real" apostles are delivered miraculously. Instead of being like the soldier who was highly honored for being the first to scale the wall in battle, Paul had to escape down the wall in a basket in the middle of the night (2 Cor 11:30–33).

36. Johnson, *Message of Acts*, 46–47.

37. Longenecker, "Acts," 9:276.

38. It has been speculated that the three years in Arabia is when Jesus revealed the gospel to Paul (Eph 3:3; Rom 16:25; Gal 1:11–12).

Instead of being able to give the content of great visions and revelations, he must speak about physical weaknesses (2 Cor 12:1–10)! Remember also that the "true" apostles could not leave off preaching to serve on tables, and what does the "fool" boast in? Weaknesses! Paul is indeed what his opponents claim; even more so! He has been in more weaknesses than even they know about (2 Cor. 11:21–29).

Paul fled to Jerusalem, possibly staying with his sister (22:16). The three-year disappearance could have made the Jerusalem church more suspicious of Paul.[39] However, he was introduced to the apostles through the intermediary action of Barnabas who worked to maintain the unity of the church. In Galatians, Paul is fiercely independent of the Jerusalem church so their recognition of him in 9:27 does not mean subjection to them.[40] Paul in Gal 1 shows his authority was from God. It was not until after fourteen years (Gal 2:1) that he conferred with the apostles about the content of his preaching. In Jerusalem, Paul took up outreach to the Hellenistic Jews (9:29), but they were no longer disputing with Stephen but a superbly educated Pharisee.[41] It is possible that with the death of Stephen and the expulsion of the Hellenistic Christians that this had been neglected.[42]

His preaching got him into trouble again, and, in a rerun of Damascus, the Hellenistic Jews planned to kill him. On learning of this, the apostles (Peter and James) arranged for him to escape, but Paul may not have initially been in agreement. Paul later told how, in the temple, he went into a trance and the Lord told him to flee.[43] He went to Caesarea, the principal Herodian port, and from there to what appears to be relative safety in his home city of Tarsus (see Gal 1:18–24).[44] His warm reception in Caesarea on his third missionary journey suggests an earlier association with the believers there.

Nothing is said directly about Saul's time in Tarsus, a city in Cilicia, but from Galatians there is an indication that he preached in both Syria and Cilicia (Gal 1:21–24). This may also be the time he was lashed five

39. Bock, *Acts*, 363.

40. Mitchell, *Fresh Look*, 93.

41. Blaiklock, *Acts*, 92.

42. Longenecker, "Acts," 9:278–8.

43. Longenecker, "Acts," 9:379.

44. As Tarsus was on the boundary of the land of Japheth, there is a possibility that, in terms of Jewish salvation history, Paul is doing the opposite of Jonah who was fleeing to avoid preaching to the gentiles. Bock, *Acts*, 370.

times by the synagogue leaders (2 Cor 11:24), and the hardships he experienced (2 Cor 11:23–7) possibly from being disinherited by his family (Phil 3:8). None of this is mentioned in Acts. If so, such a strong response may be attributed to Saul already working effectively with gentiles.

Despite the possibility of persecution breaking out again, the believers were at peace and were strengthened. Even in the presence of persecution the church has grown numerically (nothing has been said about the start of the Galilean church), and its commitment to the Lord has been encouraged and/or comforted[45] by the Spirit. Usually the term "church" refers to a community of believers in one location but here the three communities—Judea, Galilee, and Samaria—are referred to as one church (so also 20:28).

To this point there has been nothing to date the events of the church, but it is believed that Paul's ministry started about AD 33. The 2 Corinthians account of Paul's escape (11:32–33) from Damascus after having spent time in Arabia (Gal 1:17–18) occurred because the ethnarch, under the authority of Aretas, king of the Nabataeans, guarded the city. Aretas reigned from 9 BC to AD 40. The date was now likely to be AD 37–39.

A Seeming Error in the Timeline

Paul said that after his conversion he did not consult anybody but went to Arabia for three years and does not mention a prior ministry in Damascus (Gal 1:13–20). Luke's account has Paul going from Damascus to Jerusalem after avoiding an assassination plot by escaping in a basket through the city wall. In Acts, the plot was at the instigation of the Jews, and in 2 Cor 11:32–33 it is the secular governor. Paul's preaching was causing a disturbance, and he could easily have been denounced to the governor. The Romans cracked down heavily on unruly behavior, so he would have similar interest in seeing Paul removed from the scene. Some see this as a conflict that is impossible to reconcile.[46] The issue disappears if we acknowledge that Paul was only retelling the main points in such a way as to establish the genuineness of Saul's conversion.[47] This would

45. The word used has a wide range of meanings and is the same term that is used of Barnabas. His ministry typifies the work of the Spirit.

46. E.g., Barrett, *Acts*, 460–62, 466.

47. Longenecker, "Acts," 9:377.

allow for a brief ministry starting in Damascus prior to travelling to Arabia and then returning there after a three-year hiatus, i.e., what the Galatians version says (Gal 1:17). The northwest tip of Arabia reached almost to Damascus, so Paul may not have travelled far from the city,[48] making a return a logical move. The period in Arabia has no bearing on Luke's purpose.

Paul bows out of the story until 11:25, and the narrative is given over to the ministry of apostles and unknown Hellenists.

PETER HEALS AENEAS (9:32–35)

With Paul safely away in Tarsus, the story returns to Peter with the healing of a man in Lydda who had been paralyzed for eight years. From the next few chapters, we see the general work that the twelve apostles would have likely been doing. The infant church lacked the organization that we now know, and these visits by the apostles would have been very important for church stability. There was no New Testament, doctrines, creeds, etc., yet calling the believers "saints" is unusual for Luke but they are referred to this way three times in chapter nine (9:13, Ananias of the saints in Jerusalem; 9:32 of Aeneas; and 9:41 of Tabitha) and not again till 26:10. This may be intentional as chapter 10 has a long story about what constitutes holiness in the new order.[49]

Luke is building up to the account of the conversion of the first full gentile with accounts of Jesus working miracles through Peter in areas with a significant gentile population, Joppa especially, yet with no loss of power. It is reasonable to assume that Peter was ministering to Jews who were generally less stringent in obeying the Law. This was done without making the jump to minister to gentiles with the subsequent gift of the Spirit. That will have to wait for Cornelius.

Lydda was a large village[50] about forty kilometers northwest of Jerusalem on a main trade crossroads[51] and was in the area that Philip had evangelized. With both Aeneas and Tabitha, Peter will use the command *anastēthi* or "get up" (9:34, 40); the verb *anistēmi* is the same

48. Stott, *Message of Acts*, 176.

49. Gooding, *True to the Faith*, 169.

50. Josephus, *Ant.* 20.6.2.

51. Lydda was on the intersection of the main highway from Egypt to Syria and from Jerusalem to Jaffa. It is the location of the legend of St. George slaying the dragon in 303 AD.

word used of raising Jesus. This is hardly an accident.[52] Both miracles will be reflections of the work of Jesus. Peter did not pray for a healing but declared it to Aeneas as he did with the beggar at the temple gate (3:1–10). As Jesus told the paralytic at Capernaum—"Take your mat and go home"—Peter similarly told Aeneas to take up his mat. (Paul will also mirror Peter by healing a lame man [14:8–12], refer to in Table 16).

We have seen how the gift of the Spirit brought changes in the believer's attitude to money and how good works were the evidence of a changed heart. The theme of good works is continued with Tabitha and her gifts to the poor widows and Cornelius whose gifts to the poor were acceptable to God (10:4). Aeneas, through no fault of his own, could not boast of any actions "deserving" God's mercy but is still a "saint." The healing ministry of the church was primarily driven by compassion by returning people to health and usefulness. But their broader effect was to cause people to turn to the Lord (9:35), as in the healing of Aeneas at Lydda. The Bible uses "all" rather loosely and here refers to a number of people.

TABITHA RAISED FROM THE DEAD (9:36–43)

Joppa had been the main port for Jerusalem as it had the only natural harbor on the Mediterranean between Egypt and Ptolemais (modern Acre). Because the Jews there hated Herod, he built the artificial harbor of Caesarea about 45 kilometers north. While Peter was in Lydda, a saintly woman from the nearby city of Joppa died. At the urging of the saints from Joppa, Peter went to the city (a five-to-six-hour journey) and Tabitha was restored to life. Tabitha is from the Aramaic for a "gazelle doe" and Dorcas, the other name used of her, is the Greek equivalent. She was obviously a woman full of faith but is remembered because of her "practical holiness" in works directed towards destitute widows. "Good works grow from faith and are but the very Word of God in its deed and fulfillment which has been implanted in us by faith."[53]

In Jesus' miracles he was using the template of Elijah with the widow of Zarephath (1 Kgs 17:23) and Elisha with the Shunamite widow's son (2 Kgs 4:35). Peter, the servant who is not above his master, mirrors his miracles. As with the centurion's servant, both parties,

52. Stott, *Message of Acts*, 183.

53. Lenski, *Acts*, 384, quoting H. Mueller (source not given).

who were renowned for their good works, sent messengers with urgent requests (Luke 7:2–10). The raising of Jairus' daughter is also mirrored through emptying the room and especially with the words "Tabitha arise"[54] (Mark 5:35–43; Luke 8:41–56). Placing the body in an upper room seems strange, possibly in the hope that something was to happen. Placing bodies in upper rooms has been associated with restoration of life accounts (1 Kgs 17:19, 2 Kgs 4:10, 21). After Aeneas was healed after being paralyzed for eight years, they may have thought it was only a slight extension of divine power to raise the dead.[55]

Peter stayed on at the home of Simon the Tanner. Despite the usefulness of their products, many commentators say that tanning was an unclean profession. This would mean that Simon was as unfit for table fellowship as Cornelius, meaning that Peter was already ignoring Jewish purity laws. However, there is disagreement as to whether being a tanner made someone unclean. Rather, it appears there was a strong disdain for tanners because of their stench and perceived lack of morals and poverty rather than an issue of purity.[56] Living with Simon would not have been pleasant and would have involved Peter disregarding these Jewish scruples. He had already been with John and Philip in Samaria, so the old Jewish legalism is dropping away. The next chapter will show a decisive and complete break.[57] At the very least, Peter was already halfway to accepting what the Spirit would reveal.

54. If Peter was speaking Aramaic, there would have been only one letter different between the words of Jesus in Mark 5:41 and those of Acts 9:40.

55. Longenecker, "Acts," 9:382.

56. Oliver, "Simon the Tanner," 55–56, 58. As the Ethiopian eunuch was excluded from the temple, so were tanners because of their offensive smell. B. *Chagigah* 7b. A tanner's wife could demand a divorce if she could no longer endure the conditions. M. *Ketub.* 7.10.

57. Lenski, *Acts*, 392.

8

Peter Ministers to Gentiles and the Fallout (Acts 10:1—11:30)

CORNELIUS'S VISION (10:1–8)

The scene has moved to Caesarea, a modern, major, artificial port city[1] with a heavy Roman presence as it was the provincial capital where the Roman prefect lived. Most residents were gentiles. The amount of space given to the story of Cornelius reflects how momentous the actions of chapter 10 were. The Jews perceived the borders of God's kingdom to be the borders of Israel, and his family was restricted to Jacob's family. The wall dividing Jew and gentile, which prevented gentiles from joining the church, was about to open wide.

Like the calling of Paul, there were two complimentary and very clear visions (10:3, 11). In the visions of chapter 9 and 10, the most unlikely people are sent a messenger of deliverance. The Ethiopian eunuch who was baptized perhaps years earlier was a modest preliminary, and Cornelius would be the preliminary to Antioch. Despite Paul being called as the apostle to the gentiles, it would be Peter who would be the first to preach the gospel to them. The keys to the kingdom had been given to Peter (Matt 16:9). With them he had opened the kingdom to the Jews at Pentecost, to the Samaritans, and in this chapter, to the gentiles.

The early Jerusalem church resisted the evangelism of gentiles without them becoming full Jews first, which involved circumcision for the men. In Acts, the gentiles are described in seven ways, which point to their need for salvation: They are:

1. The construction of Caesarea is recounted by Josephus. Josephus, *Ant.* 15.9.6.

- ignorant with an arrogance that leads to idolatry (17:22–31);
- rejecting Gods purpose and revelation in history, especially in their hostility to God's people the Jews and in Pilate's rejection (7:18–20; 4:25–28);
- idolators (most evident in Ephesus in Acts 19:23–41);
- materialistic (16:16–19; 19:24–27);
- engaged in unethical behavior (20:17–35);
- under Satan's power (16:18); and
- subject to judgment (10:38–42).[2]

Yet, as unlikely as it seemed, there was no mistake in opening the gospel to the gentiles as it was all directed by God. Standing outside this were men like Cornelius, "God-fearers" or a "proselytes of the gate" who were semi-converts. They were gentiles who had forsaken idols, rejected polygamy, and adopted monotheism, following the basics of Jewish morality.[3] Jewish attitudes to them varied dramatically as the men had not been circumcised. Still, his faith had a big impact on those around him (10:4) and was pleasing to God.

A centurion, the commander of one hundred men[4] and roughly equivalent to our captain, would have risen through the ranks by his ability, and those encountered in the Gospels and Acts are all recorded favorably. We may be less kindly disposed to an army officer, known for very strict discipline and whose daily task could include the supervision of a crucifixion with absolute barbarity (Matt 8:5–9) or a flogging (22:25). As an experienced soldier, Cornelius is likely to have looked an enemy in the eyes and killed him with his sword. Combining that with being (most likely) a Roman citizen[5] and part of an occupying army, Cornelius would seem an unlikely person to receive grace. And yet, he has true spirituality, access to, and approval by God, but, apart from God's revelation, Peter could never have viewed him that way.

2. Bock, *Acts*, 35.

3. Jacobs and Hirsch, "Proselyte," 10:221.

4. There were typically six units of one hundred men in a cohort and ten cohorts to a legion.

5. As part of the Italian cohort, it is most likely that he was a Roman citizen. A cohort by that name is known to be in Syria a little later, but that does not preclude a second cohort of the same name or that Cornelius was doing duties at headquarters. Speidel, "Roman Armies," 233–38.

A striking feature of the account of Cornelius is the repetitions. Peter's three visions are mentioned twice (10:16; 11:10) and the centurion's four times. Of these four times, once is by Luke (10:3–7), then by Cornelius servants (10:22), followed by Cornelius himself (10:30–2), and eventually Peter (11:13–14). The emphasis changes in their retelling. The angel's words—"Your prayers and gifts to the poor have come up as a memorial offering before God" (10:5)—emphasize the centurion's piety in words that reflect the Old Testament. His prayers and the generosity of his almsgiving were like the cries of the Hebrew slaves that went up to God (Exod 2:23) and the grain offering that was a memorial and a pleasing aroma to the Lord (Lev 2:2).[6] Notably, a sacrifice honored by God was made, not in the Jerusalem temple[7] but in the home of an uncircumcised gentile in a pagan city.[8]

The Jews only called a full proselyte a *ger ha-ẓedeḳ*, or a *ger ha-berit* (a sincere or a righteous proselyte),[9] yet God, in effect, is calling uncircumcised Cornelius just this. And not just him, but Luke casts the whole family as devout and God fearing (10:2). Like the centurion in Luke's Gospel (Luke 7:5), he is commended for his generosity to God's people, particularly the poor, a sign of a faith that is pleasing to God. He was like Jesus in this sense as he also "went around doing good" (10:38). Cornelius's prayer time was attuned to that of the Jerusalem temple. Yet, the Jewish concerns about holiness acted as a barrier to taking the gospel to such a person.[10] Despite having God's approval, which is of more value than Peter's, he still lacked, but what did he lack?

The retelling of the angel's message moves towards the need to hear Peter's message (10:22), which will be further explained as the message of salvation (11:13). But does a man whose good deeds and prayers are a sweet fragrance to the judge of all men's hearts need to be "saved" when just welcoming a righteous person as a righteous person is sufficient to receive a righteous person's reward (Matt 10:41)? Still, like the pious Jews at Pentecost, he and his household must be "saved" (2:21). The fullness of his relationship with God will come through faith in one he has only

6. Johnson, *Message of Acts*, 127.

7. Bock, *Acts*, 387.

8. The city contained a temple in honor of Rome and Augustus. This was forbidden in Israel, but Caesarea was technically in Phoenicia, and Herod claimed he was forced to build it by the Romans.

9. Jacobs and Hirsch, "Proselyte," 10:221.

10. Gooding, *True to the Faith*, 172.

heard of (10:36) and yet will shower him with forgiveness and the gift of the Holy Spirit. The message is to be proclaimed to Jew and gentile, pious and irreligious alike.

The angel, described as a man in shining clothes (10;30), gave clear instructions on how to find Peter, and he dispatched two of his staff and a soldier that Luke records as pious (10:8). With a God-fearing family (10:2), we can assume that the two staff were also, or they would not have been trusted with this important spiritual task.

PETER'S VISION (10:9–16)

The next chapter will show that the thorny issue with Cornelius was not preaching to a gentile but eating with one. Israel's distinctive diet, given by God, signified its holiness and separation as a people of God by protecting from the pollution of the gentile nations (Lev 20:25–6). They were important because when they were ignored Israel "generally became as corrupt as the other nations."[11] The separation led to an unwarranted sense of superiority to the gentiles, combined with a confusion of moral and ceremonial holiness. To complicate matters, devout Jews believed that simply eating with other Jews who were lax about kosher laws would bring defilement, as ceremonial defilement could come by touch.[12] The intractable problem of separation needed direct action by God. This new path that upends the dietary laws was hinted at by Jesus with his own, much-criticized action of eating with sinners and tax collectors. He had said,

> "Are you so dull?" he asked. "Don't you see that nothing that enters a person from the outside can defile them? For it doesn't go into their heart but into their stomach, and then out of the body." (In saying this, Jesus declared all foods clean.) He went on: "What comes out of a person is what defiles them. For it is from within, out of a person's heart, that evil thoughts come—sexual immorality, theft, murder, adultery, greed, malice, deceit, lewdness, envy, slander, arrogance and folly. All these evils come from inside and defile a person." (Mark 7:18–23)

There was not a big jump from this to not call anything unclean that God had cleansed. The passage from Mark's Gospel is followed by Jesus

11. Gooding, *True to the Faith*, 176.

12. Johnson, *Message of Acts*, 129.

healing the daughter of a Syrophoenician woman. Peter will be directed to go to Phoenicia.

At midday, as the three men from Cornelius drew near, Peter went to the roof of Simon's house to pray undisturbed. The normal prayer times were 9 a.m. and 3 p.m. to coincide with the temple sacrifices, yet some pious Jews also prayed at midday using the example of Daniel (Dan 6:10) and the psalmist (Ps 55:17). Peter went into a trance, receiving the first of three visions where he saw heaven open and what looked like a large sail filled with animals and a voice that he identified as the Lord's telling him to sacrifice and eat. The very fact that he is told to "sacrifice" pointed to this being a religious act.[13] The sheet contained the same three categories as Noah's ark: four-footed animals, reptiles, and birds (Gen 6:20), but a distinction was made between clean and unclean (Gen 7:2). Peter's vision did not make that distinction.

Luke records Peter's refusal in similar words to those of Ezekiel when the Lord commanded him to eat food prepared in an unclean way:

> Then I said, "Not so, Sovereign Lord! I have never defiled myself. From my youth until now I have never eaten anything found dead or torn by wild animals. No impure meat has ever entered my mouth." (Ezek 4:14)

Ezekiel's prophetic act was foretelling a situation where the wall of Jerusalem that kept out the pagan gentiles was to fall but not before the inhabitants were defiled and Israel rejected. Peter's equally shocking vision "announced the cleansing and reception of the Gentiles."[14] There were no clean and unclean people as such. Matters such as contact with death and disease or matters of diet were only superficial. Defilement lay at the very core of the human heart and for Jew and gentile alike; any "cleansing must permeate it deeply."[15] Peter was scandalized by "an almost inscrutable riddle,"[16] yet these visions were given by the Lord. As with Philip and the Ethiopian (8:29), the meaning became clear when he obeyed what the Spirit said and traveled to Caesarea.

The visions of both Cornelius and Peter did not come as vague apparitions or shadows or dreams but with the full force that the breach of the wall was God's work. It is therefore fitting that there is a shift of

13. Barrett, *Acts*, 507.

14. Johnson, *Message of Acts*, 129.

15. Johnson, *Message of Acts*, 131.

16. Longenecker, "Acts," 9:387.

terminology from "holy one," "Messiah," and "servant" in chapters 2 and 3 to "Lord" here (10:14). He has the authority to declare the unclean, clean. There was a belief that, as all animals were permitted to Noah and therefore clean (Gen 9:3), when the messiah came the unclean animals will be made clean.[17] Peter's vision was not just an allegory about the Lord cleansing the gentiles. Jewish food laws were at the heart of the separation between Jew and gentile and the cleansing of the food. The removal of the dietary laws made it possible for the two to have table fellowship. He will find, however, that the vision had less to do with food, but everything to do with "unclean" people (10:34–6).

Food and eating with gentiles will be spoken about in chapter 15 at the Council of Jerusalem, but there it is in the context of what is wise to do when they are trying to reach Jews for the faith (11:5–21). Paul will speak about it in the context of conscience, not the Law (1 Cor 10:25, 27).[18]

CORNELIUS SENDS FOR PETER (10:17–23A)

Peter was perplexed about the vision, and the Lord intervened again to tell him to go with Cornelius's servants who arrive at just the right time. In verses 22–23, we see the first repetition of the events that characterize this portion. Luke was stressing the divine direction opening the doors to the gentiles—the story has had an angel of God (10:3), a voice from heaven (10:13–5), and finally the Spirit directs Peter (10:19). Peter has been portrayed as a faithful Jew in his strict observance of the food laws, but his attitudes were already changing as he invited the three men into Simon's home as his guests. Fellowship is implied, especially with a pious soldier.

The choice of the first gentile was not apparently random like the pagans on Paul's missionary journeys since Cornelius is said to be well known among the Jews for his piety. This did not lessen the shock of what was to happen, and many of the Jews will criticize Peter for his actions (11:1–3). The answer that they accepted was, "'Who was I to think that I could stand in God's way?' When they heard this, they had no further objections and praised God" (11:17–18).

17. *Midrash Tehillim*, 146.

18. Bock, *Acts*, 390.

PETER'S VISIT TO CORNELIUS (10:23B–33)

Jonah had fled from Joppa to avoid preaching to the gentiles, angry with the knowledge that God would be merciful to them (Jonah 4:1–3), but now Peter willingly goes. He set out early with six Christian men (11:12) who will be witnesses to the momentous events that were to follow. These six would have had to overcome the same issues as Peter but without the benefit of a vision. They arrived at Cornelius's home to find many of the centurion's friends and family waiting to see and hear Peter. Faith was already evident on both sides of the Jew–gentile divide.

Peter's actions in entering the home of a gentile were unbecoming and against their Law (10:28). Cornelius's actions were also unbecoming as he appeared to "worship" Peter, and there was a Greek belief in divine men. It is more likely that "Cornelius was not paying divine honor to Peter but was going beyond the limit that a minister of God or angel can accept."[19] His bowing to Peter reflects the promise of Isa 45:14—"They will bow down before you and plead with you, saying, 'Surely God is with you, and there is no other; there is no other god.'" Peter assured him that he was no different to him, just a man (10:26).

PETER'S SERMON TO CORNELIUS (10:34–44)

The apostle starts with an admission that he had been wrong in making a distinction between people based on race. Peter had been proclaiming to the Jews that Jesus is "Lord," but now that the time has come for God to extend his kingdom over the gentiles, he is "Lord of all" (10:36). If he is Lord of all, the gospel can go to all.[20] Until now, when Peter had spoken about repentance, he has been talking to the Jews of Jerusalem about the sin of crucifying their Messiah. There, the repentance is agreeing with God. Because Cornelius was a God fearer the Old Testament prophecies would have been meaningful, so he started with the good news of peace (10:36). The call to believe implies repentance for personal sin as there has been a reference to John the Baptist (10:37) and of judgment by Jesus of all men (10:42), but this is alongside the offer of forgiveness (10:43). Note that the apostolic kerygma is still present:

1. time of fulfillment has arrived (10:36–37);

19. Lenski, *Acts*, 412.
20. Bock, *Acts*, 397.

2. rehearsal of the life of Jesus (10:38–40);
3. Old Testament quotations (10:43; remember this is a summary of the sermon); and
4. call to repentance, or at least a prelude to it (10:43).

Before a gentile, Peter confesses what the Jewish nation did to Jesus. The "saints," the people with their religion revealed by God and a zeal for righteousness and all their privileges, "killed the supreme doer of good."[21] The Jewish method of execution was stoning, but the religious leaders were adamant that Jesus was to be crucified, which is referred to as "hanging him on a tree" (10:39). This is not being poetic, but refers to Deut 21:23: "Anyone who is hung on a pole is under God's curse." In this way the temple authorities "proved" that Jesus did not have God's favor, whereas the priests did. They condemned the "fairest life that ever lived as though it were the foulest."[22] A crucified Messiah was and still is a stumbling block to the Jews. Jesus bore, not simply the punishment for our sin but rather the guilt of our sin. As John Stott said,

> The life, death and resurrection of Jesus were more than significant events; they also constituted the gospel, which *he commanded us* (the apostles again) *to preach*, in the first instance *to the people, that is*, the Jews. But the scope of the gospel was universal.[23]

As Peter travelled to Caesarea, he had come to a deeper understanding of the vision and comprehended the Old Testament message. God is not one who plays favorites and "deals impartially especially in his love for the alien, the Gentile dwelling in the midst of Israel"[24] (Deut 10:14–18). Israel was never to forget that they were once aliens and found protection among gentiles (Deut 10:19). The only division was between those who fear the Lord and those who don't, and the centurion's actions showed that he and his family did fear God, which was the beginning of wisdom (Prov 1:7) and led to actions that demonstrated their piety.

Peter reminded Cornelius that he knew the account of Jesus. The apostle would later say to Agrippa that the good works and miraculous ministry of Jesus (and the church also) was not done in a corner, and

21. Gooding, *True to the Faith*, 182.
22. Gooding, *True to the Faith*, 182.
23. Stott, *Message of Acts*, 191; emphasis original.
24. Johnson, *Message of Acts*, 132.

some knowledge about Jesus and his work would have been known to all. He could refer to John the Baptist who served as a bridge between the two ages without any explanation. How much Cornelius knew is a matter of conjecture, however he was able to know very intimately the details of his crucifixion. It is hard to imagine the account of the centurion at the crucifixion was not spoken of among soldiers of equal rank. The resurrection is spoken of as a fact. Jesus, not an apparition or angel, ate and drank with his followers (10:41), and now his followers are eating and drinking with gentiles.

The blessings of the age to come are given to people who believe in Jesus; to Cornelius and his friends it is the forgiveness of sins (10:43) and this is without circumcision and the observance of the Law. Peter's message of Jesus as judge of the living and the dead (10:42) and the need for belief in him would be expected to lead into the call for repentance, but the Spirit fell before Peter could finish or the group respond. Salvation was granted outside of the "required" response.

GENTILES RECEIVE THE HOLY SPIRIT (10:45–48)

Luke draws attention to the fact that the witnesses are all circumcised (10:45) and emphasized the fact that Cornelius and his group were not. Yet, with this multitude of witnesses and the independent visions, it excluded the possibility that expansion of the gospel to the gentiles was simply Peter's idea but firmly rooted instead in the will of God. Despite being in the midst of a strongly Spirit-led event, everyone was astonished when the Holy Spirit fell spontaneously upon the gentiles without repentance and baptism. The giving of the Spirit, without apostolic prayer or laying on of hands, was something visible and indisputable, accompanied by speaking in tongues (10:46). As the audience was united with one language, it is likely to be ecstatic utterances rather than the known language at Pentecost. Peter saw what happened as identical to what happened on the day of Pentecost (11:15–7). Peter's question—"Can anyone forbid water?" (10:47)—implies that had the Spirit not fallen there would have been many that would have said, "Yes." Peter went further by staying a few days with Cornelius, presumably discipling the group. This required table fellowship.

The word "prevent" is reminiscent of the Ethiopian's request about what is stopping him from being baptized (8:36). Peter takes this word up again when reporting to Jerusalem that not to have done so would have been to try and "prevent" God's will (11:17). God himself welcomed the gentiles and set his seal of approval on their faith without being circumcised. And this was on "all who heard" in a household (11:14) very likely to have slaves. God had made his will clear at Caesarea. The gentiles were to be seen as "clean" as he had forever brought down the dividing wall between Jew and gentile. Surface matters such as circumcision and dietary rules had their place up to the coming of the Messiah but only the forgiveness that he offered with the gift of the Spirit could provide the deep cleansing and separation from pollution that must occur. Instead of external laws, the Spirit was given to believers who will lead them into right living and demonstrate his presence through the evidence in righteous living (Gal 5:22–3).

The relationship of the church to the gentiles as to whether it was "either lawful or obligatory to evangelize them" has not been settled. What had happened was an exceptional divine intervention and Peter was forced to preach to Cornelius and his associates.[25] The issue will arise again at the Council of Jerusalem where Peter declared that requiring circumcision after baptism would make somebody guilty of wanting to test God (15:7–11). Many in the early church had trouble keeping up with what God was doing and wanted the cultural and religious differences in the Torah to remain. Judgmental attitudes about peripheral matters can be very strong still in today's church, forgetting that God has accepted the one who has seen the horror of his sin and receiving his forgiving grace.[26] The Trinity has been active in all this. God initiated it, Christ was preached as the center of the plan of redemption, and the Spirit confirmed all of this by falling at his discretion.[27] The church had only been following God's lead.

THE RESPONSE BY THE CHURCH (11:1–18)

Luke uses similar wording of the reports reaching Jerusalem about the preaching of Philip to the Samaritans and for the conversion of Cornelius (8:14; 11:1). The Samaritans' conversion foreshadowed the inclusion of the gentiles. It was not Cornelius that was the problem but what he

25. Longenecker, "Acts," 9:384.

26. Johnson, *Message of Acts*, 136.

27. Bock, *Acts*, 401.

represented—gentiles—and even almost certainly slaves being brought into one church with faithful Jews while bypassing what had been revealed to Moses. The Jewish church, which held with obeying fully the Laws of Moses, was very upset, yet Peter would have been no different if he had not had his vision.[28] They had good reason to be concerned. The Jews in Jerusalem had turned on the Hellenists with their more liberal views, and now Peter had gone beyond anything they had done through eating with gentiles. The commentator Richard Longenecker sums up the situation: "What goodwill still remained towards believers in Jerusalem would be quickly dissipated."[29]

Peter retold the story ensuring the Jewish believers had an accurate account on which to base their judgment.[30] What they heard was very likely to have been distorted. When Peter's version, corroborated by the six witnesses (11:12), is heard, they were willing to put aside their prejudices and their concerns, acknowledge that this was the Lord's doing, and praise him (11:18) at least for a time. To do otherwise would have been to have been to stand in God's way (11:17), and they, like Peter, must accept what God had done without hesitation (11:12). However, this prejudice will resurface later in Antioch (Gal 2:11–4). Their attitude initially was that you must be a Jew before you can become a Christian (salvation by works). This was to change to gentiles could become Christians, but they had to become Jews as well (faith plus works; 15:1–3). This is not resolved till chapter 15 where it was determined that gentiles did not have to become Jews, nor, what they likely feared, did Jews have to become like gentiles. Outside of matters touching the core of the faith, the church did not have to be uniform.[31]

Peter avoided telling the critics about how he hosted gentiles overnight, nor did he tell how God had already approved Cornelius's faith prior to Peter's visit but introduces a part of the angel's message that Peter will bring a message of salvation (11:14). Perhaps this was a tactful way of bypassing prejudices. The gift of the Spirit was evidence that gentiles had been "granted repentance that leads to life" (11:18). God had worked alone by preparing their hearts without any involvement of Peter.[32] Peter remembered after the Spirit fell that John had a baptism of repentance,

28. Bock, *Acts*, 406.

29. Longenecker, "Acts," 9:369.

30. Bock, *Acts*, 407.

31. Bock, *Acts*, 410.

32. Stott, *Message of Acts*, 194–96.

and repentance is a necessary part of the gospel, but Jesus had promised to baptize with the Spirit, the power for living a new life. John had told the religious leaders not to glory in their descent from Abraham as God could raise up children of Abraham out of the stones (Matt 3:9), and he was basically doing just that with the inclusion of the gentiles.

THE GENTILE CHURCH AT ANTIOCH (11:19–21)

The story returns to the Hellenist Jews who were fleeing from the persecution following Stephen's death. The aim of the persecution had backfired, with the church instead expanding through those who were oppressed. Unnamed Christians, though possibly including Simon Niger and Lucius of Cyrene (13:1), took the gospel to Phoenicia and Cyprus (the home of Barnabas) and even to Antioch, but there the message somehow crossed over to the Greeks or Hellenists[33] "also." These Greeks very likely had some connection with the synagogues, initially at least.[34] There had been no input from Jerusalem, nor was that church recorded as being connected with deliberately initiating any mission. What was such a drama for Peter that it required three visions and has taken from 10:1—11:18 (that it was acceptable for Peter to preach the gospel to the gentiles without going through Judaism), the Hellenist Jews did on their own authority. Such a momentous event where Jewish and uncircumcised gentile believers come together as equals in a church, not a Christian Jewish synagogue, is told with great brevity.

The evangelization of the gentiles by these unnamed Hellenists doesn't appear to have been intentional. They had success because "the Lord's hand was with them" (11:21). This is almost word for word what Luke wrote about John the Baptist (Luke 1:66). The expression "appears some 200 times in the OT in one form or another [and is] a metaphor for divine sovereignty."[35] Only Luke uses this expression, but here and in his Gospel it is the Lord working "with" rather than "coming upon." These Jews, with their vision broadened through living in the gentile world, were more radical in their theology and realized that their faith did not require circumcision, the Law, or temple. They understood that the

33. "Hellenists" here is focusing on a group within the gentiles and using the term in its original meaning.

34. Longenecker, "Acts," 9:400.

35. Edwards, "Parallels and Patterns," 491.

division was no longer between Jew and gentile but "between Christian Jew and Gentile on the one hand and non-Christian Jew and Gentile on the other."[36]

Luke has been telling the account of the conversion of very unlikely individuals but here switches to the most unlikely location. Antioch was founded roughly three hundred years prior by Seleucus I Nicator, one of Alexander's generals, and became the capital of the Seleucid Empire. A descendent, Antiochus IV Epiphanes (215–164 BC), persecuted the Jews and sacrificed pigs on the altar of the Jerusalem temple, the abomination of desolation of Daniel. The Lord's new temple would be set up in his capital two hundred years later.[37] According to Josephus, Antioch, a cosmopolitan city full of gods and situated on the Orontes River in what is now southeastern Turkey, was the third largest city of the Roman world[38] after Rome and Alexandria, with a population of perhaps a half million. One in seven may have been Jewish[39] and had the rights to follow their own laws.[40]

The city, which had become the capital of the Roman province of Syria (also known as Antioch by Daphne to distinguish it from fifteen other Antiochs), was sophisticated and cultured but also renowned for its lax morals. The "morals of Daphne" was "a phrase which was proverbial in the ancient world for loose and immoral living."[41] The region's corrupting influence led Juvenal[42] to call the Tiber the "sewer of the Orontes."[43] Sufficiently close to the city to be described as a suburb was a large center and a place of pilgrimage, the grove of Apollo, which was a beautiful pleasure park with associated temple prostitution and "the scene of an almost perpetual festival of vice."[44] It was so corrupting that a later general forbade Roman legionnaires to go there.[45] The gentiles and Jews that turned and believed (11:21) would have found their new faith

36. Gooding, *True to the Faith*, 189.

37. Johnson, *Message of Acts*, 95.

38. Josephus, *J. W.* 3.2.4. Other estimates put the population much lower.

39. Longenecker, "Acts," 9:399.

40. Josephus, *Ant.* 12.3.1.

41. Barclay, *Ambassador for Christ*, 58.

42. Juvenal was a Roman poet active in the late first and early second century.

43. Juvenal, *Sat.* 3.60–65.

44. Latham, *Daphne*, 731. For a description of Daphne and what went on there, see Gibbon, *Decline and Fall*, 2.23.

45. Capitolinus, "Avidius Cassius," 6.

extremely countercultural and needed the power of the Spirit to live a holy life in that environment. The teaching of Barnabas and Paul would have been critical (11:26).

The Ongoing Importance of Antioch

"The church at Antioch from the outset had an ethos quite different from that of the Jerusalem church."[46] After the destruction of Jerusalem in AD 70, Antioch was to become the most important home of Christianity in the early church. Its legacy to today's church is in the missionary vision and its hermeneutical school.

> It has been said that the first Protestant school of hermeneutics flourished in the city of Antioch of Syria, and had it not been crushed by the hand of orthodoxy for its supposed heretical connections with the Nestorians [who emphasized the real manhood of Christ], the entire course of church history might have been quite different. The Christian community was influenced by the Jewish community and the result was a hermeneutical theory which avoided the *letterism* of the Jews and the *allegorism* of the Alexandrians.[47]

Moreover, "This school had a remarkable influence in the Middle Ages and became the pillar of the Reformation, and finally became the 'principal exegetical method of the Christian Church.'"[48]

THE RESPONSE OF THE CHURCH (11:22–26)

The church in Jerusalem heard of what had happened in Antioch and sent, not Apostles but Barnabas, a trusted emissary, to investigate. Given what was happening in Samaria and Caesarea, it was likely that many thought things were moving too fast and were out of control. The inclusion of gentiles into the church is not resolved until chapter 15. Barnabas is described as being "full of the Spirit and faith" (11:24), which marks him out as a second Stephen and views the ministry in Antioch as an extension of his life.[49] Their choice of envoy was the best possible; he is

46. Bruce, *Acts*, 1954, 241.
47. Ramm, *Protestant Biblical Interpretation*, 48; emphasis original.
48. Ramm, *Protestant Biblical Interpretation*, 50.
49. Johnson, *Message of Acts*, 95–96.

the only one called "good" in Acts. William Barclay described him as "the man with the biggest heart in the church."[50] When the "son of encouragement" saw the grace of God at work (11:23), he lived up to his nickname by "encouraging" the believers. Imagine, at this crisis point, how long the gentiles would have been barred from the church had Jerusalem sent a narrow, legalistic Jew like those who visited later. Yet the separation between Jew and gentile was so strong that it later became a short-lived but serious matter of contention between the two teachers (Gal 2:13).

Many turned to the "Lord," but it is uncertain whether this means the Father or Jesus, but more likely Jesus as he is the one they need to be faithful to (11:23). So many followed Jesus that Barnabas needed help, and perhaps knowing of Paul's call to the gentiles, maybe even working with them already, he travelled to Tarsus to bring him back to share in the ministry of teaching (11:26) and encouraging (11:23). It was especially important given the moral setting of Antioch. This continued for a year.

The believers had got the attention of Antioch's unbelieving citizens who saw them as a separate group. The name "Christian"[51] is not from the church itself (who called themselves the disciples, believers, the church, brethren, saints, and the Way), nor is it Jewish (they called the church the Nazarenes). Antioch had a gift for sarcastic speech and fixing nicknames to people. They were lighthearted and respected no one. The name was given in contemptuous jest. The church was not too proud as not to bear any stigma. Those outside saw what the church would only perceive later, that "Christianity was no mere variant of Judaism."[52] This ran the danger of Christians losing their protection as a *religio licita*, which it did soon after the ending of Luke's account.

FIRST MISSIONARY OFFERING (11:27–30)

A prophet, Agabus, from Jerusalem told the Antioch church of an impending famine, and in response they sent an offering to Jerusalem with Paul and Barnabas. (See 2 Cor 8–9 for the second offering.) The Jews believed that the spirit of prophecy ended with the last of the written

50. Barclay, *Acts*, 90.

51. The word mixes the Greek form of the Hebrew word for "messiah," i.e., "Christ" with the Latin ending for a group.

52. Longenecker, "Acts," 9:402.

prophets, but with the coming of the Messiah it would flourish again.[53] Christians not only proclaimed that Jesus was the prophet like Moses (3:22; 7:37), but they also saw prophecy as a living manifestation of God's Spirit among them. It is ranked next to being an apostle (1 Cor 12:28; Eph 4:11). The reasoning behind the offerings is described in 2 Cor 9:10–15; it would tend to knit together the hearts of the Jews and the gentiles as well as providing material support. The exchange of gifts continues the two ministries of word and table established in Jerusalem.

This support was not just "feel-good" tokenism but was the difference between life and death. Famine at that time did not necessarily mean that no food was available but that it was priced out of the reach of the poor.[54] Claudius reigned from AD 41 to 54, and while no empire-wide famine was reported, localized famines were a major problem for him.[55] Josephus recorded a famine in Judea (see Josephus's account below), but this is after the death of Herod in AD 44, which is the subject of the next chapter. While later than the predicted famine, it gives a good indication of what happened. The prediction of Agabus must have been somewhere between AD 39 and 42. The gift is sent to the elders in Jerusalem, the first mention of the group. They appear to be functioning alongside the apostles and likely took care of the day-to-day matters of the church.[56]

Had the extreme generosity of the early days left the church very vulnerable? The communal ownership of property that occurred in Jerusalem did not happen in Antioch, but individuals set aside as each one was able (11:29), as with the second offering (2 Cor 9:7). The decision to make an offering was made apparently on their own initiative and went against all the old prejudices that had divided Jew and gentile. Still, a changed heart made the impossible possible, and it was sent with Barnabas and Saul to Jerusalem. Barnabas and Paul arrive in Jerusalem in time for a renewed persecution of the church and Peter's escape from prison.

The Council of Jerusalem in chapter 15 will formally discuss the freedom of the gentiles from circumcision and make a ruling. The account of Gal 2 of when Paul came to Jerusalem as the result of a revelation fits better at this point. This would mean that "there were two meetings to discuss the same basic issue, the place of the Gentiles in the church, one of a more informal and private nature . . . and the other of a more formal

53. Longenecker, "Acts," 9:403.

54. Gapp, "Universal Famine," 263.

55. Suetonius, *Twelve Caesars*, 172; Cassius Dio, *Hist. rom.* 7.60.11.

56. Bock, *Acts*, 418.

character at the time of Paul's visit to Jerusalem in Acts 15."[57] However, there is considerable debate about this and far from universal agreement.

Josephus's Account of a Jerusalem Famine

Queen Helena of Adiabene (an ancient kingdom in norther Mesopotamia) was a devout convert to Judaism and went to live and worship in Jerusalem. Her son, King Izates, sent her with a very large sum of money. Josephus records her actions in AD 46 or 47 during what is unlikely to be the same famine:[58]

> Now her coming was of very great advantage to the people of Jerusalem; for whereas a famine did oppress them at that time, and many people died for want of what was necessary to procure food withal, queen Helena sent some of her servants to Alexandria with money to buy a great quantity of corn, and others of them to Cyprus, to bring a cargo of dried figs. And as soon as they were come back, and had brought those provisions, which was done very quickly, she distributed food to those that were in want of it. . . . And when her son Izates was informed of this famine, he sent great sums of money to the principal men in Jerusalem.[59]

57. Mitchell, *Fresh Look*, 95.

58. Gapp, "Universal Famine," 260–61.

59. Josephus, *Ant.* 20.2.5.

9

The Church Loses a Leader and Its Consequence (Acts 12:1–24)

JAMES KILLED; PETER ARRESTED (12:1–5)

The Antioch offering was needed sooner than expected when the church again underwent political persecution, which cloaked itself as defending the faith against heresy. It would have looked as if irremediable damage was to be done to the fledgling church, yet the Spirit would soon lead the Antioch church to make a great leap forward in the progress of the gospel. The good favor that the church first knew is now gone (12:3), likely compounded by ministry to the gentiles.[1] And some of the leaders were put into prison including James, the brother of John, who was put to death by Herod Antipas. Herod was a very popular leader; Josephus describes him as the complete opposite to Herod the Great in many ways, who worked hard to maintain his subject's approval, and was very devout when in Jerusalem.[2] He was close to the Pharisees[3] and had to keep on good relations with the Sadducees. To the shame of the church, Herod's practice later became "widespread throughout Christendom, indeed almost universal."[4]

The relations between the Jews and Christians were such a low state that they were pleased by the murder of a leader of the group denounced by the religious leaders (12:3). Herod likely murdered James

1. Bruce, *Acts*, 1990, 280.

2. Josephus, *Ant.* 18.5.3; 19.6.1; 19.7.1. He was not very pious when in Rome.

3. The Babylonian Talmud records a king that is guided by the queen and that queen was guided by Gamaliel. B. *Pesah.* 88b. The timing makes the king Agrippa I.

4. Gooding, *True to the Faith*, 190.

to demonstrate his faithfulness to Moses and so increase his popularity. James, the second reported martyr, was one of the three who was privy to much more than the other disciples, e.g., the transfiguration. We may think it strange that someone who could have been of much value to the church was taken so early as it is now only AD 42 or 43.[5] However, Jesus had hinted at it (Mark 10:38). Peter died c. AD 68 and John c. 90. Why should one of the special apostles live and another die? The answer can only be seen in God's sovereignty. While the complement of twelve is restored after Judas' death, there is no replacement for James.

Peter, who may have been out of town during the imprisonment of James, is himself arrested. And the timing, at Passover, a feast celebrating religious freedom,[6] mirrors the imprisonment of Jesus. Also, just as the resurrection of Jesus was a reversal of the ruling of the Sanhedrin and the government, so Peter's release "nullified Herod Agrippa's political discrimination and religious persecution."[7] He was guarded with four squads of four soldiers (12:4), two of which were shackled to him (12:6). A single shackle was normal,[8] so this was extremely high security, and, further, at night the soldiers normally served three hours at a time so there would be no chance of them falling asleep.[9] Peter's fate was sealed. However, the church was praying earnestly (12:5); as undoubtedly they did for James; while unanswered for James, it is seen as the catalyst for Peter's deliverance. Prayer is "the only power which the powerless possess."[10]

There are several Herods mentioned in the Gospels and Acts. The following simplified family tree will help distinguish one from the other.

5. Herod was in Rome in AD 41 and died before Passover in 44.

6. Gooding, *True to the Faith*, 193.

7. Gooding, *True to the Faith*, 195.

8. Josephus, *Ant.* 18.6.7; Seneca, *Ep.* 5.7.

9. Vegetius, *Epitome*, 3.8.

10. Stott, *Message of Acts*, 209.

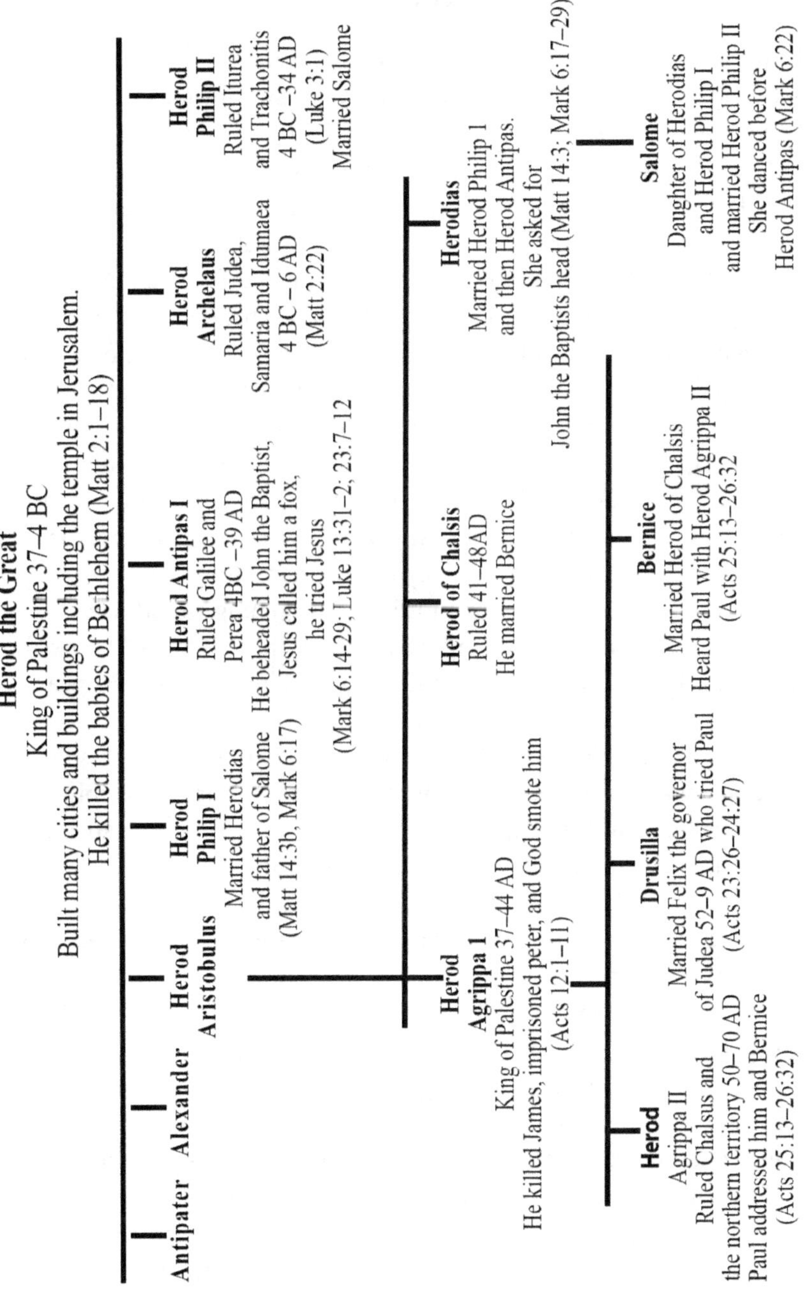

Figure 2. The lineage of Herod the Great

12:6–19 PETER DELIVERED FROM PRISON

Unlike the persecution of Stephen's time, the apostles are the main targets, and it coincided with the expansion of their ministry to the gentiles. The security was stringent; no one would have forgotten the events of Acts 5:25 where the twelve apostles were arrested but "escaped" and were later found preaching in the temple. How embarrassing. This was not going to happen again, and Herod had proved it with James. Yet, the night before Peter is to go to trial, he was released from jail by an angel who appeared in his glory. Luke is certain that this deliverance was not through human intervention. There would have been no doubt as to the verdict and sentence Peter was facing, yet his inner peace allowed him to sleep deeply (12:7). The angel of the Lord "struck" Peter to wake him (12:7), a play on words of the Lord striking Herod for his blasphemy (12:23). The shackles fell from his wrists, the angel told him to dress, and led him out of the prison past guards and through securely locked doors, which opened automatically before them until they were on the street. The noise, especially of an iron door opening would have woken a guard even if he was sleeping deeply, something done at the peril of their life. The angel then went with Peter for a block before disappearing. Understandably he thought this was all a vision.

We are introduced to John Mark (12:12), whose mother's substantial home was one of the centers of the Jerusalem church. Possibly much of the material in his gospel was learned directly from the apostles at this house. Not all of the believers sold their possessions. Church prayer meetings have changed little; no longer is the building shaken, nor, it seems, is there an expectation that the prayers will be answered. When Rhoda answered the door to find Peter outside, she ran to tell the gathered saints (in her excitement leaving Peter standing in the cold street). Rhoda was likely a slave,[11] yet she is remembered with a name and participates in the joy of the moment, pointing to the promise that maidservants will share in the outpouring of the Spirit. Their reply was "You are out of your mind" (12:15), and continued praying for Peter's release no doubt. Luke had a sense of humor. A further parallel to Jesus is the response to Rhoda's news and the announcement of the resurrection (Luke 24:10–11); once again a woman's testimony is rejected. They reluctantly concede she may have seen his angel (Matt 18:10).

11. Bock, *Acts*, 428.

Peter continued to knock until the gate was opened, and presumably after already rousing half the street (yet another deliverance?), Peter silenced the group. He explained that the Lord had delivered him, even if he had used an angel. After recovering from their astonishment that God had answered their prayers, arrangements were made for Peter to travel to a safer place. The instructions to tell James show the Lord's brother had reached a leadership position by AD 42 or 43, one he maintained until he was murdered in c. AD 62.

The soldiers who guarded the prison are carefully examined, likely under torture, and, as Herod believed they must have been complicit in the escape, were put to death. The soldier's fate was normal for letting a prisoner escape, which makes a mockery of the Sanhedrin's orders to the soldiers who guarded Christ's tomb to say that the disciples stole his body while they slept! So severe could be the consequences for letting a prisoner go that a guard might kill his prisoner to avoid it (27:42) or kill himself should it happen (16:27). Herod's action in killing the four soldiers was an exercise in saving face. He had the record of the twelve escaping (5:19–24), the extra high security, and the steel door. He must have known a higher hand was behind all of this, yet while the record of persecution ceases, it is likely it did not, though Peter did return after Herod's death. Herod's rebellion against God will have a dreadful end.

The account of Peter being delivered from his chains should have caused Herod to have taken note of an incident in his own life. He was placed in chains when in Rome for an intemperate remark about Tiberius. When Caligula followed in AD 37, he was freed and the new emperor presented him with a gold chain of equal weight to the iron ones he wore.[12] These were deposited in the temple treasury as a testimony of "how great soever they are, may fall; and that those that fall may gain their former illustrious dignity again."[13] The next passage will see God's judgment on him.

THE DEATH OF HEROD (12:20–24)

For all the mercy shown by God to Peter it will be balanced by judgment upon the arrogant persecutor of the church. Herod Agrippa had gone from Roman chains to controlling all the areas ruled by Herod the Great.

12. Josephus, *Ant.* 18.6.10.

13. Josephus, *Ant.* 19.7.1.

At the midpoint of Luke's Gospel is the glorification of Jesus and halfway through his Acts we have the false glorification of Herod. Is this intentional? For some unknown reason, Herod had cut off the food supply to Tyre and Sidon in Phoenicia. This was a serious matter needing to be put right any way the Phoenicians could, whether by bribes, which may well be how Blastus the chamberlain was "persuaded," or with flattery, which they were going to use with Herod. At a speech in Caesarea at a festival in honor of Caesar,[14] his speech was continually interrupted by cries of "voice of a god, not of a man" (12:22).

Josephus tells us that the flattery was in response to the dazzling sunlight being reflected from the clothes made of pure silver, giving the impression of "glory."[15] Luke refers to this as "royal apparel" (12:21). (Josephus's version allows us to contrast this with the true glory of the angel in the prison cell [12:7]). Herod was too good a "Jew" to believe it, but he said nothing against the ignorant idolatry of the Phoenicians. There are times when it is equally as wrong to say nothing as to partake. The sin can even be greater if there is more enlightenment. Josephus agrees with Luke that his death was God's judgment, but Luke's version sees this as a part of God's activity on behalf of the church in Jerusalem. While the focus will move to the empire-wide gentile mission, God was not neglecting the Jewish believers.

The Mishnah records, "When Herod Agrippa was reading the law of the Kingdom, (Deut. 17:14–20) as a Jewish King must do in the Sabbatical year at the feast of Tabernacles he wept when he read 'Thou shalt not set a stranger over thee who is not thy brother'—but the people cried out repeatedly 'Be not dismayed, Thou art indeed our brother.'"[16] Despite the Jewish opinion of him as a godly man, his death, which involved being eaten by maggots while alive, was associated with particularly ungodly men (e.g., Antiochus III (a type of the antichrist) who sacrificed pigs in the temple). "And so the ungodly man's body swarmed with worms, and while he was still living in anguish and pain, his flesh rotted away, and because of his stench the whole army felt revulsion at his decay" (2 Macc 9:5–9 RSV). The same thing happened with Herod the Great.[17] However, for Herod Agrippa, he is punished by an angel, not directly by

14. Josephus, *Ant.* 19.8.2.

15. Josephus, *Ant.* 19.8.2.

16. M. *Soṭah.* 7:8.

17. Josephus, *Ant.* 17.6.4.

God (12:23). His death, likely in March AD 44,[18] is a key to dating events in Acts.

The death of Stephen is in striking contrast to that of Herod. Stephen, full of the Holy Ghost, saw God's glory and forgave his murderers, his face looking like an angel's. Herod was full of worms, and after allowing others to place God's glory on himself, died under God's judgment in great pain. The chapter started with Herod in triumph as James was killed and Peter soon to be killed. It ends with the freedom of Peter, the death of the persecutor, and the gospel flourishing. Human plans had been overthrown by God's. Yet, in God's sovereignty, Manaen, a foster brother of Herod, would become a leader in the Antioch church (13:1) and be instrumental in the gentile ministry.

18. This could be at the quinquennial games started by Herod the Great at the founding of Caesarea to honor Augustus, but it could also be to honor the birthday of his patron, Claudius, in August. Longenecker, "Acts," 9:413.

10

Paul's First Missionary Journey (Acts 12:25—14:28)

BARNABAS AND SAUL COMMISSIONED (12:25—13:3)

Barnabas and Saul returned from Jerusalem taking with them Barnabas's nephew John Mark, and, with that, the focus on and initiative for expansion is with Antioch. The ministry at the church in Antioch does not appear to be noted for its miraculous nature but for its teaching and its teachers. The Spirit had gifted its leaders without regard to ethnicity,[1] and the church worked smoothly without regard for those differences. Simeon may be the Simon of Cyrene who carried the cross of Jesus, and he, along with Lucius, may have been black.[2] Manaen, who had been bought up with Herod Antipas, displays the sovereign grace of God in calling one man and rejecting another. Whereas Herod had just been judged by God for, among other things, opposing the church, Manaen is now to be used by the Holy Spirit to make a gigantic leap in advancing the church. This parallels Moses and Pharaoh who grew up in the same household.

The release of Barnabas and Saul from pastoral duties by the church in Antioch and their commissioning to take the gospel "to the ends of the earth" (1:8) was the work of the Holy Spirit in response to prophets and teachers seeking God through worship and fasting (13:2). It was also likely in response to the whole church as they are mentioned in verse 1, and the pair reported to the church on their return (14:27). Prayer rather than sacrifice is a key ministry of believers/priests, and, as the church drew near to God, they also understood the need to reach

1. Bock, *Acts*, 438.

2. Cyrene is in modern-day Libya.

out to unbelievers. Yet the two knew of this commission well before the church, as Jesus had already called them to it. Barnabas had a similar call to Paul, but we are not told of it. However, God had given him a great heart full of compassion, and surely that is the most valid motivation for evangelism. They followed this with further prayer and fasting, so testing the vague call and interceding for the two they were sending out.[3] After commissioning them by laying on hands they set off. The Father, Son, and Spirit were at work in the one task, but the church was not passive. Stott sees the interaction of Spirit and church as a healthy balance to two dangers: individualism, as the apostles did not act on their own despite their calling, and institutionalism, where decision making is done without any reference to the Spirit.[4]

In line with Luke's selective account, which from this point focuses on Paul, we are not told about the expansion of the church to the east or south or of work done by other apostles and evangelists. Thomas, for example, is believed to have reached Kerala in southern India.

BARNABAS AND SAUL IN CYPRUS (13:4–13)

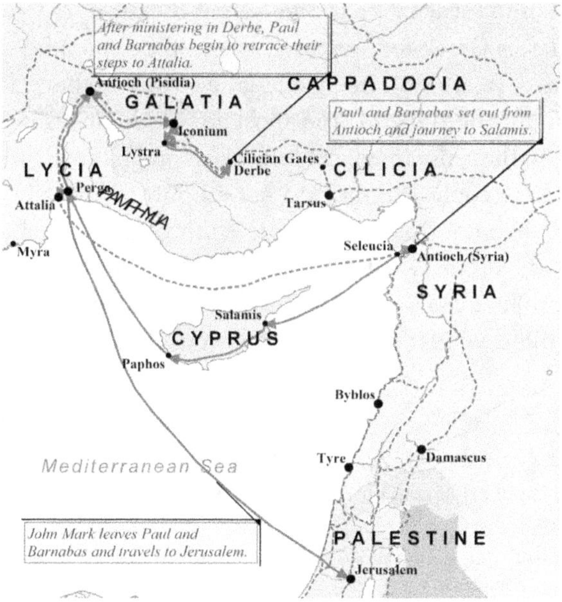

Figure 3. The first missionary journey

3. Stott, *Message of Acts*, 216,
4. Stott, *Message of Acts*, 218.

Barnabas and Saul, assisted by John Mark,[5] were sent on their mission by the Spirit who had commissioned them and the prayers of the Antioch church. They travelled first to Seleucia, the port of Antioch, and then to Salamis, the largest city in Cyprus. As Cyprus was the home of Barnabas, they started in familiar territory. There had already been some evangelism in Salamis as it would have been the Jewish center of the island (11:19). Their mission began in a synagogue in line with Paul's practice of only going to the Greeks after the gospel was rejected by the Jews (Rom 1:16). As Christ had already been preached in the synagogues some time before (11:19), it is surprising that they were still able to preach the gospel. They proceeded from Salamis to the other major city, Paphos, which was the administrative center and where the team ministered among gentiles.

The Jewish false prophet Bar-Jesus is introduced before the proconsul[6] Sergius Paulus and in more detail. Unlike Simon who claimed to be able to do great acts, Bar-Jesus had access to the proconsul through his claims to have divine knowledge through prophecy. Bar-Jesus may have been his name, but this was also a Semitic way of describing a person's character.[7] His name meant "son of Joshua" or "son of salvation," but Paul will call him for what he is: the "son of the devil" (13:10). His other name, Elymas, is Greek for "sorcerer,"[8] and, like Simon, he was a *magos*, meaning "wise" (8:9; 13:6). Being a Jew, he is likely to have done this as a so-called prophet of the Lord. The apostate world Bar-Jesus was working in was "real, in the sense that it actually exists and has real powers," which is what attracts people, but they do not ask if it is "morally and spiritually true."[9] When confronted with the truth of the gospel preached by Barnabas and Saul, now called "the faith," his reaction showed that he was a false prophet. He is called "an enemy of righteousness" (13:10) and was struck blind with the sign of the covenant curse (Deut 28:28–29),

5. His role is not explained, but it is quite possible that he was an eyewitness to the ministry of Jesus.

6. A proconsul was a Roman magistrate that governed a senatorial province, i.e., one that did not need an army.

7. Johnson, *Message of Acts*, 173.

8. Possibly a transliteration of an Arabic word meaning "to know" and equivalent to *magos*. Hunter, "Bar-Jesus," 1:431.

9. Gooding, *True to the Faith*, 209.

just as Paul had been.[10] Both needed to be led by the hand (9:8). In this power encounter, the gospel was greater than the occult.

The gentiles were described as a people lacking understanding (Rom 10:19, quoting Deut 32:21), but Sergius Paulus was an insightful man. He wanted to hear the word of God (13:7), as presumably reports of the disquiet that invariably follows would have reached him. When he "saw" God's judgment of blindness on Elymas, who had being making the straight ways of the Lord crooked (13:10), he believed and was amazed at the teaching of the Lord brought by the missionaries. There is no mention of the proconsul being baptized, but his belief cannot be taken to mean any less than in other cases where it is mentioned without baptism (14;1, 17:34, 19:18).[11] Sergius Paulus became the first gentile convert recorded that had no prior connection with Judaism through the synagogue.

Again, Luke points to the preached word being the primary means employed in the Lord's conquest of the nations. Elymas had used his spoken words to manipulate the forces surrounding Sergius Paulus, "but the words of God's messengers address the conscience of the hearers, bending their will to the lordship of Jesus."[12] As with Simon, the ending for Elymas is inconclusive, but as the blindness will only be for a time (13:11), the door was open to repentance. Contrasting the blindness of the false prophet was the message of the two missionaries who were called to be a light to the gentiles (13:47). From this point they were ministering among gentiles, but we have to wait till the evangelists reach Asia Minor to hear anything of the content of their messages. It was common for a Jew to have a Greek or Roman name as well and as Saul likely takes the lead in the mission, he becomes Paul and is never called by his Jewish name again.

PAUL'S SERMON IN PISIDIAN ANTIOCH (13:13–43)

After Leaving Paphos in Cyprus, Barnabas's native country, the three sailed about 180 kilometers to that of Paul's homeland, Asia Minor, and arrived in Perga in Pamphylia, a small and economically poor province on the Southeast coast of what is now Turkey. There, John Mark deserted

10. Johnson, *Message of Acts*, 174.

11. Longenecker, "Acts," 9:421.

12. Johnson, *Message of Acts*, 175.

the team and returned to Jerusalem. We are not told why but some possibilities include the following:

1. He was put out by his uncle being demoted.
2. He got cold feet when the dangers of preaching to a hostile audience, the risk of disease, or physical rigors came home to him.
3. He lacked conviction.
4. He disapproved of the ministry direct to gentiles.

Whatever the reason, Paul considered it desertion (15:38). When Barnabas wanted to include him in the second journey, it led to a "sharp disagreement" and a split between Paul and Barnabas. Barnabas took John Mark. God was not finished with this man despite his failure(s). The quitter is accredited by church tradition as founding the church at Alexandria. Later he would emerge as a fellow worker (Phlm 24), a profitable servant of Paul in Rome, a man most wanted at the end. Peter would describe him as "Mark my son" (1 Pet 5:13). Papias, an early church historian, said of the gospel he wrote, "Mark who was Peter's interpreter, wrote down accurately, though not in order all that he recollected of what Christ had said or done."[13] This man could have been easily lost to the church; we owe his "redemption" to Barnabas whose big heart was again to change the history of the church. Barnabas's greatness was possibly not in what he did for God, but what he made possible for others to do for Christ, including Paul, the Antioch church, and John Mark.

The two walked approximately 150 kilometers, from Perga over the Taurus mountains through robber-infected regions (2 Cor 11:26), to the cool of Pisidian Antioch in Phrygia Galatia,[14] a Roman colony and an administrative and military center. There was also a large Jewish population there.[15] Evangelism in Perga only occurred on the return visit (14:25). Pisidian Antioch, at its highest, was over twelve hundred meters above sea level, and it is often suggested that the pair had to travel to higher ground as Paul was ill and suffering from something that was debilitating

13. See Eusebius Church History 3.39.15 (*NPNF*[2] 1:172).

14. It was near the border of Pisidia, called that to distinguish it from a city of the same name in Galatia; Galatia is Greek for Gaul. It took this name after King Nicomedes in 278/277 invited a horde of Celts to Bithynia to serve as his mercenaries. They escaped his control.

15. Josephus, *Ant.*12.3.4. He records that two thousand Jewish families were brought into the region.

and appeared to disfigure him as well as affected his eyesight (Gal 4:12–15). He may have been suffering from malaria. Up to Paul's sermon at Pisidian Antioch (13:16–41), the couple had always been mentioned as Barnabas and Saul. For the remaining journey it is Paul and Barnabas. The content of that sermon was revolutionary and is what separates Saul the persecutor of the church from Paul the apostle to the gentiles. He is never called Saul again. His sermon has all the elements of the apostolic kerygma:

1. the age of fulfillment has come (13:23–25);
2. a rehearsal of the life of Jesus (13:27–31);
3. citation of Old Testament Scriptures (13:32–35; 40–41); and
4. a call to repentance (13:38–40).

But where it did differ is that justification by faith as we know it is first clearly proclaimed, as opposed to the works of the Law (13:38–39), and to Jew and gentile alike:

> In these two short verses [13:38–39] we have Romans and Galatians in a nutshell. Justification by faith alone—*Sola Fide*—is an endless inexhaustible theme. "The way to salvation, so slowly and with such difficulty prepared for us—slowly through the time of preparation in the old covenant—with difficulty through the bitter suffering and death of Jesus: and yet so short and so pleasant for us to travel—short, for all that we need is to embrace the cross of Christ by faith—pleasant, for here we find remission of sins, life, and salvation."[16]

Paul's first recorded sermon is preached before a mixed audience of Jews and God fearers in the synagogue in Pisidian Antioch. The policy of Paul and Barnabas in all the cities was to go to the synagogue first. There are two reasons for this. Firstly, the gospel was to go to the Jew before the gentiles (Rom 1:16; 2:9–10) as salvation was worked through the history of Israel. Paul only went to the gentiles after the Jews had rejected the gospel. Secondly, though Paul was the apostle of the gentiles, he probably had a greater burden for the Jews than any of the apostles (Rom 9–11). "I have great sorrow and unceasing anguish in my heart for I could wish that I were cursed and cut off from Christ for the sake of my brothers. Those of my own race, the people of Israel" (Rom 9:2).

16. Lenski, *Acts*, 544.

An offshoot of his ministry in the synagogues was his access to the God fearers, gentiles who had turned from the idolatry and immorality of pagan society to Judaism where they found an acceptable God, a divine revelation through the Scriptures, and an ethical morality. The God fearers, not being circumcised, were on the fringes of Judaism, but these men would become the core of many churches.

After the apostate Jew Bar-Jesus, we now see in the synagogue at Pisidian Antioch Judaism at its best—studying, preaching, and attracting gentiles.[17] It is possible Paul was dressed as a rabbi leading to the invitation to speak.[18] His hearers knew the Scriptures and had a reverential attitude towards them, which guided his content through the repeated appeal to the prophetic Scriptures (Ps 2; Isa 55; Ps 16). This changed as he moved into totally pagan areas where there were no synagogues. The sermon has similarities with the sermons that have preceded. As with the first sermon of Peter, he interpreted Ps 16 as being fulfilled by the resurrection of Jesus, not by David (13:35–7). He also reflected Peter's sermon in Solomon's Colonnade by attributing the death of Jesus to wickedness and ignorance on man's behalf and the purpose of God declared through the prophets (13:40–41). There is also a strong similarity to Stephen's sermon through the rehearsal of Israel's history (13:17–23). But there are noticeable differences. Paul told Israel's history in a way that emphasized, not its rebellion but God's faithfulness through the gracious election of Israel that he caused to prosper through his provision of leaders. The covenant relationship is acknowledged despite the gospel going to gentiles if the Jews rejected it.

13:16–22. Paul's sermon, like Stephen's defense, started with "the great confessional truths of Israel's faith,"[19] and by recounting their history of saviors, Paul led up to the greatest savior. He focused on God's saving action and only in verse 21 is he not the subject of the main cause in the history of Israel; where the people are mentioned, it is in the context of rebellion. He briefly mentioned the patriarchs, who were chosen without merit (13:17), the time in Egypt and the deliverance from slavery there (13:17), and then the wilderness wanderings (13:18) where again God's mercy saved them from extinction (Exod 32:10–14; 34:5–10). God was the deliverer who allowed one nation to defeat seven in Canaan (13:19). Following this was the time of the judges when their constant

17. Gooding, *True to the Faith*, 210.

18. Longenecker, "Acts," 9:423.

19. Longenecker, "Acts," 9:425.

Lawbreaking bought God's judgment, and they were mercifully provided with a savior (Judg 2:18). This is followed by Samuel (13:20). The people grew tired of the saviors God provided and demanded a king (1 Sam 12:8–12), but Saul, the people's idea of a savior, did not have the wisdom or power to deliver them and even rejected David, the God-given savior, and drove him from the land.[20] This history climaxes with David, who in due time returned and became king and did what was asked of him. This elevation to kingship is called being "raised up" (13:22; a word play on Jesus being raised up in 13:30, 37).

What Does the 450 Years Refer To?

Harmonizing the dates for the time in Egypt, the wilderness wanderings, conquest, and period of the judges is extraordinary difficult. The 450 years mentioned by Paul likely is meant to cover the period of the enslavement in Egypt, the forty-years, and the conquest.[21]

13:23–39. Paul then jumped a millennium to the promise of a "savior" to come from David's line (13:23) who he identifies as Jesus. "Savior," while not a common description of Jesus in Acts and the Gospels (Luke 2:11; John 4:42; Acts 5:31), focuses on his role as "deliverer."[22] The bridge between the promise to David of a descendent who will be a "son" to God (2 Sam 7:14) and its realization in Jesus was repentance preached by John the Baptist. Repentance is mentioned (13:24) and is implied in the promise of forgiveness of sins (13:38), but the message's emphasis is clearly on faith.[23] At the time of writing, the term "savior" was frequently given to prominent people and rulers, but this "savior" was so far above any earthly deliverer that even John was not worthy to remove his sandals (13:25). As Jewish slaves were allowed to keep their dignity by not being forced to untie the thongs of sandals, it was a very strong statement by John of his (and our) unworthiness before Jesus.[24]

Despite there being no charge to answer, Jesus was condemned to die on the "tree" (13:29). Paul does not avoid Deut 21:22–23 where anyone who is hung on a tree is under God's curse but stresses the injustice

20. Gooding, *True to the Faith*, 214.
21. Merril, "450 Years," 246.
22. BDAG, "Σωτήρια," 801.2.
23. Johnson, *Message of Acts*, 157.
24. Bock, *Acts*, 454.

thrust upon the innocent (11:28). Despite the Prophets being read every Sabbath they were not understood as Jesus was not recognized but was instead rejected by the nation (Isa 53) and condemned as was predicted (13:27). By using God's Law to attack the Messiah they showed that it could not "change the heart's basic hostility to God."[25] In their ignorance, they were carrying out all that was written about Jesus (13:29) yet the outcome of this tragedy is good news. Just as there was no ambiguity about the death of Jesus who was laid in a tomb (13:29), there was no question about how God vindicated Jesus by reversing that sentence (13:30). The first step in salvation was to save the Messiah himself from death.[26] This was not done in secret as Jesus was seen by many of his disciples (13:31), and at the core of the gospel would be his witnesses to the people.[27] This four-part confession is mirrored in 1 Cor 15:3–5, but his witnesses are now no longer just those Jesus appeared to after his resurrection as Paul used "we" to include his followers (13:31).

The confession of Israel and the church are linked as the witness of Jesus' disciples is supported by that of the Scriptures, and Paul quoted three of these. They contain the coming promise to their ancestors (Ps 2:7), the promise extending beyond David (Isa 55:3), and the predicted raising of Jesus (Ps 16:10 also in Acts 2:25–28).[28] Peter had already explained how Ps 16 could not be about David as his tomb was known. Psalm 2, a royal psalm and therefore ultimately about the Messiah, predicted the completion of God's redemption by the sonship of Jesus being made evident[29] and from where he is actively working. While the promise is now realized, the Isaiah quote shows the scope is far beyond David and extends to Jew and gentile (13:38) alike who hear and respond by believing (13:39) the preaching of forgiveness.

13:40–43. Likely sensing the mood of the congregation, Paul set before them two very stark alternatives. The first is the release from sin by seeking forgiveness. They can only do this if they have believed (13:39) in the salvation brought by "this man" (13:38) Jesus, who Paul called Savior (13:23), Son (13:33), and Holy One (13:35). The preaching of Jesus offered far more than the Law with its associated sacrifices could: total forgiveness or "justification." This way they would be made right or

25. Gooding, *True to the Faith*, 216–17.

26. Gooding, *True to the Faith*, 217.

27. Bock, *Acts*, 455.

28. Bock, *Acts*, 455.

29. Refer to my comments on Acts 1:1–5 and 4:27 for "adoptionism."

"justified" before God (13:39). Paul emphasizes this by the double use of "justified" in Acts 13:39. God's declaration of righteousness enabled the gift of the Spirit. Only here in Acts do we encounter the term "justify" (13:39), a term very important in Paul's Epistles. No longer are we dealing with sins of ignorance for which there was forgiveness under the law, but justification and forgiveness that the Law could not confer.[30] The second is judgment. Paul quoted a shortened version of the LXX version of Hab 1:5[31] to warn them that by rejecting the new work God was doing they would perish (13:40–41). The "work" is likely to mean God's working in Christ and the message about it.[32]

At the conclusion of the service and the Jews had left, the gentiles asked that they might hear more of the message on the following Sabbath (13:42). There were some, both Jews and gentiles, who believed and followed the two evangelists. While usually distinguished, they are now addressed as one group who must remain faithful in God's grace.

THE GOSPEL GOES TO THE GENTILES (13:44–52)

On the next sabbath a large crowd gathered to hear the gospel and not just God fearers but gentiles who would have been idolators. The Jews' response to seeing their synagogue treated like a "common theatre or town hall"[33] is called "jealousy." Their zeal for the covenant prevented them from seeing the ultimate promise of the Law and the breakthrough change that had occurred. Paul quoted the command for the servant to be a light to the gentiles and bring salvation to the ends of the earth (13:47 quoting Isa 49:6). Simeon had already called the baby Jesus this when he was purified in the temple (Luke 2:32). Now as "commissioned servants," they cast themselves as doing the work of the servant,[34] and before Agrippa Paul would testify to this being his calling (26:17–8). Just as Jesus was blasphemed against (Luke 22:65), so also the evangelists are hated (Luke 21:17) and their message blasphemed. Paul reminded the scoffers of his warning a week earlier, that in rejecting the message they bring themselves into judgment (13:41) and so do not consider

30. Johnson, *Message of Acts*, 155.

31. The Habakkuk text is in relation to God raising up Babylon to judge Israel's sin.

32. Bock, *Acts*, 461.

33. Longenecker, "Acts," 9:429.

34. Bock, *Acts*, 462–63; 404.

themselves worthy of eternal life (13:46). Only in this passage are salvation and eternal life equated (13:46, 48). The responsibility for their judgment is theirs, but those who responded with faith were "appointed for eternal life" (13:48). Human responsibility and a very strong statement of divine sovereignty and activity stand side by side in this passage. They were then free to take the gospel to the gentiles, which they did.

There appears to be a presumption that if the Jews reject the message it should go to others. The spontaneous reaction to the preaching of the good news at Pisidian Antioch (13:48) is a divine prompting and is a confirmation that the call to minister to the gentiles was legitimate (see also 14:27; 16:14).[35] The missionaries did not believe this to be an innovation on their part as it was justified by the commission given to the Jews to be a light to the gentiles (Acts 13:47; Isa 49:6). Paul would later teach in Romans that Jew and gentile stood equally in condemnation and access to God (Rom 2:1–3:31), which allowed ministry direct to gentiles.

Opposition came from the unbelieving Jews who used their influence with devout gentile women to stir up discord with the leaders who in turn expelled them from the region. Shaking the dust from their feet, an action that was instructed by Jesus (Matt 10:14; Mark 6:11; Luke 9:5; 10:10–11), symbolized that the responsibility for the rejection of salvation lay with the residents and that the evangelists removed the defilement of the city. They have not rejected the messengers but Jesus. However, before leaving the city for Iconium, the message had penetrated all levels of society with Jews, proselytes, God fearers, devout women of high standing, gentiles, and leading men mentioned.[36] Some responded with belief and were filled with joy and the Holy Spirit, and Paul would soon write to the Galatians reminding them that their joy is a fruit of the Spirit (Gal 5:22). Again, persecution only spreads the gospel.

MINISTRY IN ICONIUM (14:1–7)

Leaving Pisidian Antioch, the pair chose the southeastern route that would take them to three very different cities in Southern Galatia. The Romans subdivided Galatia into different regions and Isauria, Pisidia, Phrygia, and Lycaonia are known to us. The first city, Iconium (modern Konya), was a city on a high plateau at about 1,027 meters above sea

35. Marshall, *Fresh Look*, 70.

36. Bock, *Acts*, 451.

level in the steppes of Turkey and connected to Pisidian Antioch by a well-known Roman road called the Via Sebaste or Royal Road.[37] Strabo described Iconium as a small, well-built town but the area was cold and bare with little water.[38] The city remained largely Greek and resisted Roman influences by attempting to retain "the ethos of an old city state."[39] The pattern emerges whereby they preach, Jews and gentiles respond, but opposition causes them to flee. Sometimes it is dealt with briefly as in Iconium, and in other cities it has more detail. Nothing is known of the Jewish population, but there was a synagogue that the evangelists visited.

The Greeks here are most likely God fearers and the response of Jew and gentile is told in terms of "belief," (14:1) not repentance. The refusal to believe by the others is disobedience to God and consequently "poisoned" the gentiles against the new believers who are called "brothers" (14:2). Given their distrust of the gentiles and the way they kept separate, it is surprising that the Jews sought help from the gentiles along with the city leaders[40] (14:5) to resist the evangelists.[41] Despite the city splitting (14:4), they kept preaching in Iconium for a considerable period, preaching the message of God's grace, a wonderful description of the gospel, which was confirmed with signs and wonders (14:3). Paul lays stress upon his apostleship in his letters, but Luke reserves that term for the twelve; only in chapter 14 does he refer to Paul and Barnabas as "apostles" (4, 14).[42]

When writing Galatians, Paul appealed to these miracles as evidence that what he preached was approved by God (Gal 3:4–5). Yet, the miraculous element of their ministry did nothing to convince the unbelieving Jews who planned to stone the pair, so judging their message as blasphemy. The cooperation of the gentiles to bring about a lynching means that they also saw the gospel as seriously affecting the wellbeing of society (14:5). There is a fascinating account of the split in Iconium in the *Acts of Paul*, which includes a description of Paul: "A man of small stature, with a bald head and crooked legs, in a good state of body, with

37. Witherington, *Acts*, 418.

38. Strabo, *Geogr.* 12.6.1.

39. Longenecker, "Acts," 9:431.

40. As a Greek city, it would have been governed by an assembly of citizens. Longenecker, "Acts," 9:432.

41. Bock, *Acts*, 470.

42. The twelve were apostles of Christ; Paul and Barnabas were apostles of a church, sent out with a specific mission. Stott, *Message of Acts*, 229.

eyebrows meeting and the nose somewhat hooked, full of friendliness, for now he appeared like a man, and now he had the face of an angel."[43] It is tempting to think the account may have been built on some actual incident that was remembered.

On learning of this, they fled thirty-three kilometers south of Iconium to Lystra and Derbe (ninety-six kilometers southwest of Iconium and ninety-five kilometers southeast of Lystra) in the province of Lycaonia.[44] Persecution is again spreading the gospel, but the choice of these two towns is surprising. The area was rustic, and the people were generally poorly educated. The geographer Strabo describes them as militant and non-Roman in their lifestyle with little regard for civil law. The area was full of robbers, causing the Romans much trouble as many were protected by living in mountain caves.[45] Luke showed the universality of the gospel across different levels of civilization.[46] The archaeologist William Ramsay asked, "How did the cosmopolitan Paul drift like a piece of timber borne by the current into this quiet backwater?"[47] The pair may have fled across the border to this backwater for the safety of a different administration,[48] waiting for the inflamed situation to subside. However, as a result of their evangelizing in these small communities, Timothy from Lystra would be added to their group on the second journey (16:1), and Gius from Derbe would accompany him on the third (20:4).

MINISTRY IN LYSTRA (14:8–20)

Paul's ministry in Lystra and Derby is a dramatic change as they were ministering in cities where there was presumably no synagogue, and the inhabitants are virtually all gentile and pagan. Yet it is likely there were some Jews as Timothy's mother Eunice was a Jewess (2 Tim 1:5). Further, there was no knowledge of the Scriptures, so the gospel had to be presented in a manner that was sensitive to their background and limited

43. Wilson, "Acts of Paul," 1–25. The description is 3.3. It does not read like an idealization.

44. Ramsay has shown that only between AD 37 and 72 was Iconium on the Phrygian side of the regional border. Ramsay, *Trustworthiness*, 39–45.

45. Strabo, *Geogr.* 12.6.2–5.

46. Bock, *Acts*, 471.

47. Ramsay, *Cities of St. Paul*, 408.

48. Ramsay, *Trustworthiness*, 45. Ramsay also noted that for the pagans, it would not only be against the law but against the frontier-gods to pursue them.

understanding of God. This required tremendous flexibility in style and emphasis to find points of contact yet without sacrificing the core of the gospel.[49]

With no synagogue and the Greek practice of public oratory, especially with the philosophers, the missionaries[50] preached in the open in Lystra. Paul saw a man lame from birth that had sufficient faith to be healed (14:9). Luke stressed his condition three times, suggesting how dire it was. By using similar phrases, Luke linked Peter's healing of the lame man at the temple with Paul's in Lystra, so underscoring Luke's aim of showing Paul as equal to Peter but with different areas of ministry.

Lystra	Jerusalem
Lame from his mother's womb (14:8)	Lame from birth (3:2)
Fixed his gaze on him (14:9)	Peter looked straight at him (3:3)
Leaped up and was walking (14:10)	He jumped to his feet and began to walk (3:7)

Table 9. Similarities between the two accounts of healing a lame man

The idea of the gods healing was not foreign to the pagans,[51] but the residents of Lystra had a tradition that Zeus and Hermes once walked among them as strangers and performed miracles but brought severe judgment on those who were inhospitable.[52] When Paul, a stranger, raises the lame man, the residents thought history has repeated itself and wanted to avoid the severe retribution from the earlier visit. His stare and loud voice are further associated with the gods, which helped the pagans come to the wrong conclusion.[53] Barnabas was called Zeus, the chief Olympian god, suggesting he was the leader of the group, and Paul they called Hermes, the messenger of Zeus and his son (14:12). To the evangelists' horror, the priest of Zeus even tried to sacrifice bulls to them. For all their rustic nature, their enthusiasm and ability to see the

49. Stott, *Message of Acts*, 232.

50. Luke may have been attributing the address to both evangelists (14:14). They both shared in the preaching (14:1, 3, 7, 21, 27).

51. Asclepius was a god of healing and his rod with a snake entwined remains a symbol of medicine today. His sites contain tablets recording claims of miracles.

52 The account of Baucis's and Philemon's encounter with Jove and Hermes is found in Ovid, *Metamorphoses*, 8.920–1105.

53. Strelan, "Recognising the Gods," 488–97.

supernatural at work stands in sharp contrast to the cultured philosophers of Athens who want nothing to do with the supernatural.[54]

The missionaries were at the extremes of the Roman province of Galatia, and Greek was not the common language (14:11) so they did not fully appreciate what was happening. It was only with difficulty that they stopped the sacrifice. Whereas Herod accepted worship (12:20–23), the two vehemently rejected it in accordance with the first commandment (Exod 20:3). Nor would they use the incident as a stepping stone on which to build as they did have a message that God had come down from heaven and walked among men. They could easily have taken advantage of their gullibility for their own benefit. Barnabas and Paul were men of like passion to the Lystrians, but not totally as they were of like passions to their gods.[55] Their gods were not the creators and only ruled over certain areas. After a war among the gods, Zeus received heaven, Poseidon the sea, and Hades the underworld, the areas Paul mentioned as ruled by the living God (14:15).

In the first sermon to purely pagan gentiles and without having access to the Scriptures, the missionaries directed the residents of Lystra to the abundant evidence that God, through his providential supply of the good things necessary for life. He had shown himself as the creator of the heavens, the earth, the sea, and everything in them (14:15). This veiled reference to the Sabbath requirements in the Ten Commandments alone should be sufficient to turn a person from such "empty things" (14:15) to the only one worth worshiping. Paul will later explain in his Letters how they were without excuse (Rom 2:14–16; 1 Cor 1:20–1).

Pervading the whole of Acts is the call to the grace of repentance, which can only come through honestly facing the ugliness of sin. The Jews had brought their history of rebellion to a climax and needed to turn. Paul explained that the true God of the universe had no longer abandoned people to the foolishness of paganism. The gentiles outside of God's covenant must also "turn" from the empty worship of idols. This was what God called them to through Isaiah: "Turn to me and be saved all you ends of the earth" (Acts 14:15; Isa 45:22). This turning through repentance was a public sign of a transfer of allegiance to the one they opposed.[56] This was not a matter of a person being changed through simply

54. Bock, *Acts*, 476.

55. E.g., Zeus was extremely immoral and fathered many children through union with the gods and humans.

56. Johnson, *Message of Acts*, 152–53.

changing one philosophical system for another but a call to commitment to a living person built on the firm foundation of the resurrection.[57]

So quickly after people wanted to worship them, Jews from Antioch and Iconium turned the crowd, and they stoned Paul and dragged him out of the city thinking him dead (14:19; 2 Cor 11:25; Gal 6:17; 2 Tim 3:11). His recovery as the newly won disciples looked at his body appears miraculous (14:20). A man who says he is just like the Lystrians has healed a lame man and now, for all intents and purposes, has risen from the dead like the one he preached. Despite his preaching being cut short, it was effective. As mentioned, Timothy, Paul's beloved assistant, is from Lystra and possibly a convert at this time, and his mother and grandmother are commended for their faith (2 Tim 1:5). A close bond will develop between the two and he will later accompany Paul on his second and third journeys.

On the following day, the pair left for Derbe, which was about ninety-five kilometers southeast of Lystra and on the border of Galatia.[58] This would have been a hard walk for Paul following his almost fatal stoning. When Paul wrote Galatians some months later, he said, "From now on, let no one cause me trouble, for I bear on my body the marks of Jesus." These *stigmata* may have been the results of the stoning. His thorn in the flesh (2 Cor 12:7) may have been the ongoing effects of the persecutions he suffered.

THE RETURN TO ANTIOCH (14:21–28)

Making many converts in the small town of Derbe would have made a major impact on the community yet Luke does not record that the preaching met with any opposition. This must have been a welcome relief. On making the decision to return to the commissioning church, they did not take the shortest route, which is east through Tarsus, but made the courageous decision to retrace their steps through the cities they formerly had to flee. Luke does not inform us how the apostles gained access to the cities, but a change of magistrates is a possibility.[59] Their concern was not just to evangelize but to pastor the new churches as best they could, so in each city they strengthened and encouraged the believers to remain true

57. Johnson, *Message of Acts*, 154.

58. Strabo, *Geogr.* 12.6.3.

59. Ramsay, *St. Paul*, 120.

to the faith and warn them about trials to come. There can be a heavy price in receiving the free gift of forgiveness and peace with God.[60] In Romans, Paul writes of the troubles between the first and second coming as "birth pangs" (Rom 8:12–25). Christianity is now referred to as "the faith" (14:2) which points to "the dynamic that drives the community."[61] The "kingdom of God" (14:22) normally refers to his entire program but here is limited to the vindication after death. Their encouragement to remain steadfast in the faith contrasts the encouragement of the gentiles to do evil at Iconium (14:2).[62]

Paul and Barnabas appointed elders in every city,[63] and, as with their own commissioning, this was accompanied by prayer and fasting as they committed to the Lord those whom they (elders and church) trusted. This turned an administrative exercise into a spiritual one. Leaving there, they returned to Perga where they now evangelized. Illness may have prevented it on the first visit. From Perga they travelled to the port of Attalia[64] and from there back to Antioch. The work that the grace of God committed them to (13:1–2) had been completed (14:26). They did not report to the church what they had done but what God had done and how, despite their persecutions and hardship, it was God who opened the door of faith to the gentiles. In chapter 15, the church will have to determine if this faith is sufficient. The pair stay an indeterminate but long time in Antioch. Stott estimates that the first missionary trip took about two years.[65]

Churches, Not Missions

Stott points out something we could easily overlook: the evangelists left behind churches when they went home, not missions, which has been the practice of Western evangelism. These churches could be left to

60. Gooding, *True to the Faith*, 224.

61. Bock, *Acts*, 482.

62. Bock, *Acts*, 482.

63. Critics can see the appointment of elders as a something that only occurred after Paul and the church lost their Spirit led dynamic. See, e.g., Campenhausen, *Spiritual Authority*, 80. They point out that the term "elder" is only used by Paul in the Pastoral Epistles, which they hold to be forgeries. This view has no merit.

64. As with Antioch and its port Seleucia, Perga is situated some distance inland from its port, Attalia. This helped protect against pirates.

65. Stott, *Message of Acts*, 235.

the faithfulness of God (14:23b) and the Spirit living in the believers. However, they had an established doctrine called "the faith" (14:22b) to which believers had to remain true (14:22a), as well as a recognized and plural leadership appointed from their own midst (14:23a).

But it is not that simple. Paul was building on the ground already well prepared through Jewish mission and the core of members drawn from the God fearers who already "had a strong Old Testament background in doctrine and ethics."[66] A church could not be built and governed in a few months by a congregation that had all just come from paganism. He concludes, rightly so, that there is a place for both approaches, but the ideal situation is when foreign workers are guests, not leaders.[67]

66. Stott, *Message of Acts*, 238.

67. Stott, *Message of Acts*, 235–39.

11

The Church's First Council (Acts 15:1–35)

JUDAIZERS ATTACK THE CHURCH IN ANTIOCH(15:1–4)

Luke recorded that the Jerusalem believers praised God over the conversion of Cornelius (11:18), and there was subsequently a glowing assessment by their envoy Barnabas of the ministry in Antioch (11:23). However, the church was not a monolithic block. The audacious ministry of Paul and Barnabas turned the trickle of gentiles to the church into a torrent.[1] These new believers were coming into fellowship through baptism, not circumcision. Sometime after returning from their first missionary journey the Antioch church was visited by believing men from Jerusalem who taught that you must also be circumcised to be saved (15:1). For them to be taken so seriously, it is likely that they claimed to have the authority of the Jerusalem church behind them. In Galatians, Paul spoke of men sent from James (Gal 2:12), but it is not entirely certain that this was the same visit.[2]

Earlier the church was divided into Hellenistic and Hebrew Christians, and here there was an attempt to divide it into gentiles and Jews. By saying, in effect, that most of the church in Antioch weren't saved, the visitors were rejecting those who God had accepted. Faith in Jesus Christ was not enough, not even faith plus works motivated by faith but faith plus one requirement, circumcision, was essential. Even if it was only introduced as part of the covenant with Abraham (Gen 17:9–14),

1. Stott, *Message of Acts*, 240.
2. It is not said that they represented James's views. Refer to appendix 2.

and as a sign of belonging to God's people, the entire legal system of Moses would soon follow (15:5). These men reduced Christianity to no more than a reform movement within Judaism where Moses must complete what Jesus started.[3]

The Problem of Timing

The Galatian church experienced similar pressures to those found in Antioch. It is difficult to harmonize the Acts account of Paul's three visits to Jerusalem with the two visits recorded in Gal 2 and how that fits in with the Council of Jerusalem. Generally, Acts 9:26–30 is seen as matching the first visit. The issue is with the second and scholars deciding that either:

1. Acts 15 represents Gal 2:1–10;[4]
2. Acts 11:30 equates to Gal 2:1–10;[5]
3. the matter cannot be resolved;[6] or
4. the Council of Jerusalem is a fabrication.[7]

Rather than agreeing that Luke has written a fictional story, "because he knows that his readers will retain only what he puts before them in grand impressive animated scenes,"[8] it is important to attempt to harmonize Acts and Galatians. However, this debate will be of little interest to the "everyday Christian," so I have included it as appendix 2. Sufficient to say here is that I have concluded that Paul wrote Galatians to the churches mentioned in chapters 13 and 14 and before the Council of Jerusalem, i.e., option 2 above.

How serious this problem was can be seen from Gal 2:11–21 where Paul takes a strong stand on the lesser matter of table fellowship between Jew and gentile, rather than salvation. The scene is something like this (with reservation): Paul and Barnabas return to Antioch and sometime after that Peter arrived doing his apostolic rounds. James commissioned

3. Stott, *Message of Acts*, 241, 243.
4. Lightfoot, *Galatians*, 230–1.
5. Bruce, *Acts*, 1990, 330–31.
6. Johnson, *Acts*, 270.
7. Haenchen, *Acts*, 457–58.
8. Haenchen, *Acts*, 458.

some men to go to Antioch for some purpose or other, but while there they overstep their authority and reject table fellowship with gentiles; with that would be sharing the Lord's Supper. The church was sharply divided, causing Peter and, more surprisingly, Barnabas with his big heart to be intimidated for a time (Gal 2:13). At a later stage, more men from Jerusalem visit Antioch and go further, saying that salvation requires circumcision. There is a deep division of opinion that bewildered the church. The issue is too deep, and the implications were too far-reaching for the matter to be resolved in Antioch, so they sent a deputation to Jerusalem for a ruling (15:2). On their way to Jerusalem, they told the churches of Phoenicia and Samaria (15:4), both founded by Hellenists, what happened with the gentiles. Everyone outside of Judea rejoiced, showing it was only the small minority, the Pharisees (15:5), that insisted on circumcision.[9]

THE COUNCIL OF JERUSALEM (15:5–21)

15:5–6. The Council occurs roughly halfway through the book, which has been building up to the watershed decision that freed Christianity to go to all nations and "give the Jewish-Gentile church a self-conscious identity as a reconciled people of God."[10] Jerusalem will recede further into the background along with Peter while Paul will come to prominence. The situation came to a head when groups were acting as if gentiles could become part of God's people simply by accepting the Jewish Messiah. At issue was whether to consider the church as a completed Judaism with its circumcision and the Law, or see these as a national characteristic of Jews rather than a characteristic of the new people of God.[11] A very robust, if not violent debate was expected from the way that this chapter starts, but if so, it was not reported that way.[12] Everyone has a chance to plead their case and Luke briefly summarized what must have been a much longer discussion. Leadership of the church by Peter and the rest of the twelve has given way to leadership by James and the elders.

A minority who were also Pharisees demanded circumcision plus obedience to the laws of Moses, but Luke did not record their argument.

9. Haenchen, *Acts*, 458.
10. Stott, *Message of Acts*, 241.
11. Marshall, *Fresh Look*, 73.
12. Barrett, *Acts*, xxxvii.

Wasn't circumcision and the Law gifts from God to be valued and had not the prophets foretold that the nations would go to the house of the Lord in Jerusalem (Isa 2:2; 11:10; 25:8–9; Zech 8:23)? They had simply added belief in Jesus to their existing practices and went further than what was first demanded at Antioch as observance of the Law was added to circumcision (15:5). If the Council was to give way to this matter, they would also soon be demanding obedience to the traditions as well. Judaism had shown that when someone approaches God through works, rules get piled upon rules upon even more rules and so become a burden too great for even the Jews to carry (15:10). While the Law was holy, its demands could not be kept (Rom 7). Righteousness earned through obedience, or even grace plus merit earned through obedience, is diametrically opposed to the inward purity of the heart given through faith.

15:7–12. Without recourse to Scripture, Peter retold his missionary role in God's call of the gentiles and declared the universality of God's grace: "We believe that we will be saved through the grace of the Lord Jesus, just as they will" (15:11). This grace was unsought and undeserved and rested totally with God's initiative. Peter had forgotten this when he was at Antioch a short while before. Because the Spirit fell on Cornelius prior to baptism and circumcision, we could easily have thought that the matter of the unburdened inclusion of gentiles had been settled. Even then, the bone of contention in chapters 10 and 11 was not that Peter evangelized Cornelius but that he ate food with him that had not been prepared according to Jewish food laws.[13] As a result they would be ritually defiled. The recognized mechanism for fellowship was circumcision and observing the Law.

Peter issued a very strong warning to the opponents who thought that what God had done was not good enough[14] and wanted to add further regulations on people that God had already approved. Doing that would be to "test" God (15:10) or perhaps better understood as "trying God's patience," just as their forefathers "tested" God in the wilderness (Exod 17:2). God had taken the lead by showing through giving the Spirit that they had been completely accepted, their hearts cleansed and forgiven.[15] Circumcised Jews and uncircumcised gentiles are both equally saved by grace, so therefore, circumcision is ultimately nothing. Peter's gospel message of salvation by grace for Jew and gentile alike (15:11) echoes

13. Marshall, *Fresh Look*, 41, 71.

14. Gooding, *True to the Faith*, 231.

15. Bock, *Acts*, 500.

Paul's censure of him in Galatians when he withdrew from fellowship from the gentiles (Gal 2:16).[16] The heavy yoke of the Law that cannot be borne (15:10) should be contrasted with the easy yoke of Christ (Matt 11:28–30).

Peter spoke with such authority that the whole assembly fell silent and were ready for Barnabas and Paul to speak. The assembly listened in silence as they told how God has acted in a sovereign manner through them with signs and wonders with their ministry to the gentiles. This, along with the gift of the Spirit, proved God must have approved not only their preaching Jesus to the gentiles (15:12) but the gentiles themselves. However, nothing of their argument for acceptance of the gentiles on faith alone is recorded. Barnabas is mentioned before Paul, possibly because he was more highly respected in Jerusalem.[17] Their diminished role in the Council may simply reflect that they were seeking a churchwide solution so there would be other major actors.[18]

15:13–21. Yet, experience alone is insufficient to weigh the matter. James, the brother of Christ, took control of the meeting and put the experiences of Peter, Barnabas, and Paul to the touchstone of Scripture and found that prophetic Scripture and their experience agreed and brought the two together for a solution. He made no mention of Barnabas's and Paul's argument, possibly being tactful. They were, after all, gathered to pass judgment on the evangelists' work. He spoke of God taking a people for his Name from among the gentiles (15:14), which described their call in a similar way to the call of Israel (Deut 26:18–21; 32:8–9; Ps 135:12).[19] This, then, would preclude proselytizing the gentiles for Judaism but see this as a fresh work.[20] Critical to James's argument that this new way was an old promise is what he meant by "restoring again the Tabernacle of David" (Amos 9:11–12).[21]

There are two options for understanding this. One is that it refers to the restoration of David's royal house and dynasty destroyed by Nebuchadnezzar and that God's people will inherit what is left of Edom

16. Stott, *Message of Acts*, 245–46.

17. Longenecker, "Acts," 9:445.

18. Bock, *Acts*, 491.

19. Bock, *Acts*, 502.

20. Larkin, *Acts*, 224.

21. James cites the LXX of Amos 9:11–12, which differs substantially to the Masoretic Text (MT), though still appropriate. However, his reading matches a known variant.

who, along with other nations, will be called God's people.[22] A restored Israel, i.e., Jewish Christians, will inaugurate the gentile mission so "the rest of mankind may seek the Lord" (15:17). The other is to see this as the tent containing the ark of the covenant, which was pitched inside the walls of old Jerusalem on Mount Zion before the first temple was built (2 Sam 6:17).[23] It was in "opposition" to the tabernacle of Yahweh, which was at Hebron at that stage and was supposed to be the home of the ark. It appears David's tent had free access for all Jews (Ps 15:1). It is the house of the Lord in David's psalms and appears as a place of fellowship, joy, and praise (Ps 42:4). Sacrifice was not a major part of its function, as that remained with the tabernacle in Hebron (2 Sam 15:7–12). Compare this freedom with the temple later to be built on Mount Moriah. This was a picture of the limits of even the best of Judaism, where access was barred, to the freedom of access that was to apply to the church. This freedom of access predates the temple just as the covenant of Abraham predates the Mosaic covenant. Both seem very appropriate, but the Davidic line is the option usually favored.

15:19–21. The apostles, and also the elders, informed laymen, discussed the matter. They did not put it to a majority vote. "Mere numbers do not increase wisdom and Christian essentials are not decided by numbers and majority vote."[24] What would the answer have been if this matter came up just a few years previous when ministry to gentiles was not envisaged?

The principal issue of the necessity of circumcision was resolved when James made a "firm proposal"[25] that no barrier is to be placed in the way (over and above faith) (15:19), but a practical matter remained. While Jewish believers must accept gentile believers, many still obeyed the Law regarding food. This was not going to change overnight, and their consciences must be respected. Their way of life goes back to "the earliest time" (15:21), so some compromise and sensitivity was necessary for church unity. The reading of Moses every week could either be a call for sensitivity to those who read him or for where a gentile could go to understand the matter better.[26] To make fellowship between gentiles and

22. Fitzmyer, *Acts*, 553.

23. Lenski, *Acts*, 609–10.

24. Lenski, *Acts*, 596.

25. Stott, *Message of Acts*, 248.

26. Marshall, *Acts*, 254.

Jews possible, some simple matters were to be avoided. These matters were:

1. pollution from idols;
2. immorality;
3. meat from strangled animals; and
4. blood matters.

These restrictions, all of which are amplified in Lev 17–18, cover more than table fellowship. As well as having sensitivity to Jewish restrictions on blood, the restrictions may have been a call for faithfulness to the true God who requires moral worship.[27] The Jews had a sacred association of the life of an animal being in its blood (Lev 17:10–14). Often the animals could be strangled so not bled,[28] and sometimes the pagan temple was the abattoir so they could have been sacrificed to an idol. Possibly the sexual immorality especially envisaged was association with pagan rites including temple prostitution, a particular issue in Antioch. Importantly, no work of the Law was added as a requirement for salvation. What is not included are the positive duties such as loving God or abstention from the major moral concerns like murder and theft,[29] but these are likely so basic they were assumed everyone would comply.

James believed that the apostles and elders should write to the gentile church outlining their decision. It boiled down to simply asking, as a matter of love, that gentiles were not to flaunt their liberty.[30] It could be argued that the Council made a decision based on pragmatism rather than on principle. Luke does not clearly answer the question of, with Christ's coming, whether it brought a new people of God into existence into which both Jew and gentile enter by faith, or whether there was a continuing people into which the gentiles were added.[31] Still, it is easy to overlook that the decision of the Jerusalem church "was one of the boldest and most magnanimous in the annals of church history."[32] Every advance in the worldwide gentile ministry would bring further difficulties

27. Bock, *Acts*, 506.
28. Philo, *Spec. Laws*. 4.122–3.
29. Gooding, *True to the Faith*, 237.
30. Wood, *Acts*, 231.
31. Marshall, *Fresh Look*, 75.
32. Longenecker, "Acts," 9:450.

to the Jewish church in their own homeland,[33] the more so with the rise of zealotism over the next two decades leading to the destruction of Jerusalem. Still, even after the third missionary journey, the Jerusalem church is standing by its decision (21:25).

Paul was called to his gentile mission by God and the Council has legitimized his ministry through the decision. One matter that the Council did not address was how Jewish believers were to view keeping the Law. Paul shows two options, the first being scrupulous observance with a view to evangelizing the Jews or less scrupulous so they can evangelize the gentiles (1 Cor 9:19–22; Rom 14–15). This was to be done within the limits of what their conscience would allow and without forcing their decision on another.[34]

The Names of James, the Brother of Jesus

The names by which James was known should shame us. One was "Camel Knees." Eusebius records an early church historian, Hegesippus (c. AD 110–ca.180), who said James "was frequently found upon his knees begging forgiveness for the people, so that his knees became hard like those of a camel."[35] Eusebius also recorded Hegesippus saying, "Because of his exceeding great justice he was called the Just, and . . . 'Bulwark of the people.'"[36] He won many people to the Nazarene fellowship by his manner of life and earnest testimony to Jesus as the door of the sheepfold and the true way of life." No doubt the legalists thought they would have an ally in James. But they did not have the measure of the man.

THE COUNCIL'S LETTER (15:22–29)

The Council's decision repeats the expression "it seemed good" three times (15:22, 25, 28): good to the Apostles, elders the church, but also the Holy Spirit. The apostles and elders followed James's advice and chose two of the leading church members and prophets (15:32), Judas and Silas, and sent them back to Antioch to communicate the Council's decision. Nothing more is said of Judas, nicknamed Barsabas (Son of the Sabbath)

33. Longenecker, "Acts," 9:450.

34. Bock, *Acts*, 493.

35. Eusebius, *Hist. eccl.* 2.23.6 (*NPNF*[2] 1:125).

36. Eusebius, *Hist. eccl.* 2.23.7 (*NPNF*[2] 1:125).

beyond chapter 15, but Silas would accompany Paul on the second missionary journeys. He is usually considered the Silvanus of 2 Cor 1:19; I Thess 1:1; and 1 Pet 5:12. The letter is addressed to the churches in Antioch, Syria, and Cilicia and the context infers that Paul was involved in the establishment of them all though Luke did not record any ministry in Syria. The Jerusalem leaders accept that they sent the troublemakers that caused them so much distress (15:24), but that they had overstepped their remit. The original troublemakers are left in no doubt, they did not have the authority or support of the home church. Jerusalem also set in place the remedy and key to this was the vindication of Barnabas and Paul. They are called "beloved" (15:25), and their work for Jesus among the gentiles at peril to their lives (15:26) is acknowledged.

After the earlier stress, they did not wish to burden the gentiles beyond the very minimum needed so to not give offence to Jews and God.[37] It should be stressed that the conditions (abstaining from food sacrificed to idols, from meat with blood, and immorality) had nothing to do with salvation. They were carefully aimed at eliminating any hindrances to fellowship between an orthodox Jew and a gentile. Circumcision is the major sign of the Mosaic covenant, if what is listed here is a way of salvation. It would have included circumcision, not just minor portions of the ceremonial law. Christian freedom, it must be remembered, means that the Jewish Christians are free to eat kosher. With the ruling that the church did not have to be "monochromatic in its practice,"[38] the need to spread the contents of this letter would prompt the second missionary journey.

The Relation to the Council of Jerusalem to Galatians and 1 Corinthians

Galatians was written directly to counter the challenge of Judaizers who were influencing the churches in Galatia in the same way as the church in Antioch had been. So why didn't Paul quote from the Council's decision? The explanation in this commentary was that Galatians was written before the Council's decision. The Council's decision was c. AD 50 and 1 Corinthians was written c. AD 55 so the decision was still "fresh" but

37. Bock, *Acts*, 512.

38. Bock, *Acts*, 514.

whereas Paul will not permit sexual immorality (1 Cor 6:12–20), he will permit the eating of food sacrificed to idols (1 Cor 8:1–13; 10:22–33).

The prohibition of immorality was not for immorality's sake but in the context that some Christians were saying that their Christian freedom permitted them to attend the temple feasts (which could become orgies) (1 Cor 6:18–20; 10:14–22). They even boasted about their freedom and what it permitted (5:1–2). Paul is more concerned about the abuse of Christian freedom than upholding the Council's decision. They were in effect saying, "Look how far I can stretch my Christian freedom." Paul would reply that he is free to give up his freedom to advance the faith.

Possibly Paul did not consider the Council's decision as binding for all circumstances but an expedient for where the Hebrew Jews had not broken with tradition. Corinth was different (especially as in many cities the temples were the registered abattoirs) with its Hellenistic Jews who would realize that an idol is nothing (1 Cor 8:4) and that their food has nothing to do with our relation to God (1 Cor 8:8). Of course, they had to use discretion when eating with weaker brothers, e.g., someone straight out of idolatry who had some experience of the spiritual forces behind the idolatry.

After his hard stand for freedom in Galatians, why did Paul appear to compromise in Jerusalem and not quote it when it appeared appropriate (Rom 14; 1 Cor 8–10)? Ultimately, the answer cannot be known but some suggestions include the following:

1. Galatians was written before the Council (refer to appendix 2);
2. Paul did not fully agree with it but accepted it for the sake of unity;
3. he had no confidence that they, like any other community, would not change their mind;
4. the Judaizers were not interested in the Council's decision as they may not have accepted it;
5. the "superspirituals" in Corinth may not have accepted an "ecclesiastical statement";[39]
6. the church was already fully aware of the Council's decision; or
7. Paul was basing his argument on his own authority as it was a gift and calling direct from God (Gal 1:1, 1:11—2:21).

39. Longenecker, "Acts," 9:452.

THE RETURN TO ANTIOCH (15:30–35)

The two prophets encouraged, or perhaps better "comforted" the Antioch church after their distressing time of uncertainty, which caused them great joy (15:31). The envoys stayed for some time, encouraging and strengthening the church and then at least Judas returned to Jerusalem. Paul and Barnabas took up where they had left off, teaching the good news but it is not the same. The addition of many to the number of people teaching points to the empowering ministry of Judas and Silas (15:35). Also, with the position of the believing gentiles clarified, it may have given more confidence for others to join in teaching.

12

Paul's Second Missionary Journey (Acts 15:36—18:22)

PREPARING FOR THE SECOND MISSIONARY JOURNEY (15:36–41)

The first journey started through a revelation of the Spirit during a time of worshiping and fasting (13:1–3), but for the second his guidance is hidden. Paul's suggestion to Barnabas to go back and see how the believers in the newly evangelized areas were faring seems very like the decision of the Jerusalem church that "it seemed good" and driven by pastoral concern. Luke recorded that the Spirit's leading became obvious only after the decision was made to go (16:6–10; 18:9–10). Paul had a very fruitful partnership working alongside Barnabas for years, yet this did not stop them from having a strong disagreement. Barnabas considered reclaiming Mark for the ministry so important that Paul was the dispensable one. This restoration proved so complete that Peter would think of him as a "son" (1 Pet 5:13) and Mark would record what the apostle taught about Jesus.[1] He would be a fellow worker with Paul (Phlm 24) and one of the people most wanted with him at the end of his life because of his usefulness (2 Tim 4:11). Church tradition says Mark founded Christianity in Africa when he established the church in Alexandria and became its first bishop.[2] Coptic tradition has him being martyred there. Given the hard times of the second trip, perhaps both were right, but it was not handled well.

1. Eusebius, *Hist. eccl.* 2.15–16 (*NPNF*² 1:115–16).

2. Eusebius, *Hist. eccl.* 2.24.1 (*NPNF*² 1:128).

Paul mentions Barnabas in 1 Corinthians (9:5–6) and any resentment appears well healed. Tradition says that Barnabas was preaching the gospel in Salamis in Cyprus when local Jews and Jews from Syria who were frustrated with his success dragged him from the synagogue where he was debating, and, after torturing him, stoned him to death. Mark then buried him.[3]

PRELIMINARY TO PAUL AND SILAS WORKING IN EUROPE (16:1–10)

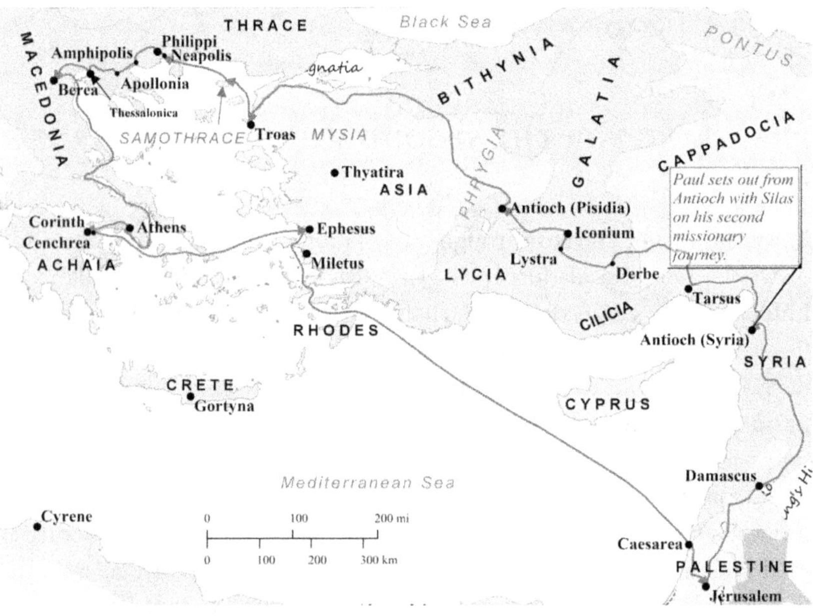

Figure 4. Paul's second missionary journey

As Luke proceeded to tell the story of the early church his content changes after the Council. Apart from the address to the philosophers in Athens there are no more summaries of Paul's sermons; there is little point. What does follow is how the Spirit led Paul and his companions, and at times how that same Spirit sought out individuals that would never be considered subjects of God's mercy. In this chapter the story turned to an emphasis on individuals and not cities or regions.

3. Fleetwood, *Life*, 600.

16:1–5. Paul and Silas started their journey walking westwards and first visited Derbe and Lystra and other towns in Southeast Galatia. Despite being left to their own devices for some time without an apostle or the New Testament to guide them, the churches appeared healthy and were even stronger by the time the pair left. The church has spread wider without Paul's help as ministry in the region is now "from town to town" (16:4). There they delivered the letter from the Council, which put an end to the question of the need for gentiles to be circumcised. While this is now a dead issue for modern Christians, Paul's fear of separate factions has become a tragic reality. While circumcision is no longer an issue, Stott suggests modern replacements for "the gospel of God's sufficient grace" can be philanthropy, religious observances, or experiences.[4]

However, in Lystra, Paul asked Timothy, the son of Eunice (2 Tim 1:5), a Jewess, and a Greek father (possibly dead),[5] to join them but not before circumcising him. Timothy was "spoken well of" by the Christians in Lystra and Iconium. This may well have been the time Timothy was commissioned and given gifts through prophecy and the laying of hands by the elders of the church (1 Tim 4:14). Paul was not being inconsistent regarding circumcision. Jewish descent through the mother is assumed here and this is a very long held belief, possibly from the early second century or earlier.[6] What is surprising is that someone who was taught the Scriptures from infancy (2 Tim 3:15) by his mother and grandmother, two very devout women, had not already been circumcised. The uncircumcised son of a Jewish woman would have been considered "an apostate Jew, a violator of the covenant,"[7] perhaps why he was also "known" among the Jews though not "spoken well of" as in the church (16:3). What was necessary for acceptance with God is not the same as what is acceptable to men,[8] so to prevent any distractions as Paul ministers to the Jews, he circumcised him. This was not a salvation issue but a matter of practicality and not giving offence to the Jews as they ministered (1 Cor 9:19–20; similarly 21:17–26 with Jewish purification

4. Stott, *Message of Acts*, 256.

5. Many commentators note that he "was" the son of a Greek. If so his lack of circumcision is more surprising.

6. Bock, *Acts*, 523.

7. Bock, *Acts*, 523. Descent in Greek culture was through the father,

8. Stott, *Message of Acts*, 254.

rites). One commentator noted, "Being a good Christian did not mean being a bad Jew."[9]

16:6–10. Phrygia and Galatia could refer to the ethnic groupings but if Luke meant the Roman divisions, it would mean their journey would have taken him back through Iconium and Antioch, which was the stated aim (15:36). They then proceeded to go northwest towards Mysia, the northern and western portion of the Roman province of Asia where the capital Ephesus is located. This great port was the gateway to Europe and Asia, but the Holy Spirit prevented them from preaching there. However, Paul would later spend over two years in the city (19:8–10). They then proposed to go north to Bithynia, but the "Spirit of Jesus" prevented them. This term is only found elsewhere in Phil 1:19. It is unlikely that a distinction is meant as the Spirit was the other counselor sent by Jesus. With the mention of God (16:10) there is a trinitarian reference in the guidance. We are not told the specifics of how they were prevented from preaching[10] where they had intended but it is distinguished from what followed: a vision (16:9). They then walked to the port of Troas on the northwestern tip of Asia Minor. By this stage they have travelled about 950 kilometers as the crow flies. The first "we" section starts in verse 10 so Luke must have joined en route or at Troas. For the pair to have found a believer mature enough to be of assistance in an area unevangelized by Paul speaks to the Spirit's work in spreading the gospel.

After uncharacteristically been stopped from preaching in Troas, Paul had a vision of a Macedonian man asking him to come over and help them, which he took as positive guidance after two doors had been firmly closed. Rather than acting rashly on one person's vision, the group discussed it and came to the conclusion that they were to go to Macedonia. Stott points out that "God's guidance is not negative only but positive . . . not circumstantial only, but also rational."[11] They travelled over the Aegean Sea on the first available ship. We are not told how much planning went into their journey, the Spirit's presence did not exempt them (or us) from this nor from courageous leadership. As has been observed, "It does demand that we not take *our* plans too seriously. . . . The presence of Jesus demands that we formulate and reformulate our fallible plans in order to keep in step with his invisible plan."[12]

9. Longenecker, "Acts," 9:455.

10. It was necessary to pass through Mysia to get to Troas.

11. Stott, *Message of Acts*, 261.

12. Johnson, *Message of Acts*, 27–28.

PAUL AND SILAS MEET LYDIA (16:11–16)

It appeared that Paul's plans would have taken him to Ephesus, possibly the fourth largest city in the empire, which would later prove to be a valuable hub for spreading the gospel through the Roman province of Asia. Instead, the Spirit had an appointment with a sole devout Jewess on the side of a river. As in all the "we" sections, Luke notes the ports used for departure and arrival of his sea voyages and the daily progress (20:6; 21:1–8; 27:2–44; 28:11–14). After all the changes to their plans, sailing with favorable winds may have encouraged the group that the Lord was with them and had a pressing agenda in Macedonia. They quickly made the 240-kilometer journey to Philippi via the island of Samothrace, then the next day to Neapolis (modern Kavalla), the port of Philippi. The return journey took five days (20:6). It is questionable whether Paul would have visited this area by choice, but the Spirit led him to establish a church that would be a source of joy and financial support in his later years when many had deserted him.

Philippi, was named after Philip II of Macedon, father of Alexander the Great. Macedonia had been a great power under Philip II and Alexander four centuries earlier but had been a Roman province following its conquest by the Romans in 168 BC. Macedonia was divided into four districts, and Philippi was one of the main cities of one of these. After the assassination of Julius Caesar, Mark Antony and Octavian (later to be known as Augustus) led an army from Rome to Philippi in 43 BC and there defeated the conspirators Brutus and Cassius. They committed suicide there. After the battle, the victorious soldiers were given fertile soil, the city was expanded[13] and became a Roman colony (16:12), which gave it the status of a Roman city. This was followed by further colonists after the battle of Actium in 31 BC when Octavius defeated Mark Anthony and Cleopatra. The residents would appear to be proud of its military connections as Paul used many allusions to the military in his Epistle to them. It is likely to have the feel of a small Rome[14] with a strong allegiance to it (16:21). It wasn't, however, the leading city; the capital was Thessalonica. It is suggested that Luke expressed pride in what may have been his home city.[15]

13. Strabo, *Geogr.* 7.41.

14. Bock, *Acts*, 533.

15. Stott, *Message of Acts*, 262.

The Jewish influence in Philippi was negligible. Even after spending some days in the city getting their bearings, they had to make an educated guess as to where the Jews met on the Sabbath, if indeed there was such a place.[16] This city was all but unreached by Judaism. Ten men were needed to form a synagogue, but we only read of some women meeting beside a river at a place of prayer.[17] The new work of the Spirit saw a church being started by a group of women, and Paul's dealing with them shows a greater openness than was normally allowed in Jewish life. Under Judaism, "No number of women could compensate for the absence of even one man necessary to complete the quorum of ten."[18] A Jewish male would thank God each morning that he has not been born a gentile, a slave, or a woman. The greatest barrier of all these was between Jew and gentile. This was not always a disparagement of these three groups as lesser persons but a recognition that they "were excluded from religious privileges only open to Jewish males."[19] These traditional barriers are crossed in Philippi as these three groups considered at arm's length from God are the subject of God's mercy.

Paul had already said that these distinctions should not exist in the church as they were all one in Christ (Gal 3:28). Among the women gathered there was Lydia,[20] a seller of purple cloth from Thyatira, a center for the purple dying trade in Roman Asia. She is likely a widow or unmarried, but her profession of dealing in extraordinarily expensive dye and cloth[21] assumes she was wealthy. She was also a "pious woman," which may describe a former polytheist who worshiped the God of Israel but did not follow the Law completely.[22] It is possibly the case here. On hearing Paul, the Lord initiated the response by opening her heart (16:14).

16. Lenski, *Acts*, 655.

17. The term is unusual for Luke as he normally uses "synagogue." While there may have been a building it is not certain. In the absence of a synagogue, Jews could meet in the open air by water. Philo. *Flaccus*, 14. The location by water would facilitate the ceremonial washings needed.

18. Bruce, *Acts*, 1954, 331.

19. Bruce, *Galatians*, 187.

20. Thyatira was in the ancient kingdom of Lydia, hence her name or possibly her trade name.

21. The edict of Diocletian in AD 301 set the maximum price of purple died wool at 50,000 denarii per three hundred grams; in silk 150,000 denarii; pure gold at 50,000 denarii, also for roughly three hundred grams. The highest paid artisan only earned 75 denarii per day. Frank, *Rome and Italy*, 328, 412.

22. BADG, "Σέβω," 746.2a.

She and her household were baptized, and her home became the center for evangelizing the city. Lydia was adamant that they must allow her to be associated with Paul and his companions. Again, with the jailer, Luke will use a gender pair as the main focus of salvation.

The mention of the baptism of the household brings many questions: Were there children? Were there servants that had not believed the message but were instructed to do so? We simply are not told.

PAUL AND THE DEMON-POSSESSED GIRL (16:16–21)

Luke had already recorded Simon Magus and Elymas who were making money from religion; here there is an enslaved fortune teller, while the Ephesian books of magic will follow. Unfortunately, Christianity also has not freed itself from this scandal. Like a syndicate owning a very valuable racehorse, this very valuable girl was owned by a syndicate. The slave girl and her owners offered demonic guidance at a high price, but they met with men led by the Spirit and who preached the gospel without charge. Another comparison was the role of business in the spread of Christianity. It is safe to assume[23] that Lydia as a seller of purple cloth also made "a great deal of money" (16:16) and was also pointing to Paul as telling the way to be saved, (16:17) something she had experienced. The two women were the opposite ends of the social and spiritual spectrum.

In the Lord's lawsuit against the idols in Isaiah, he declared that his ability to foretell the future proves his power to control the future (Isa 42:8–9; 46:9–10). The idols were powerless to do this even though there was no shortage of people who claimed to do this in their name. The Lord, for his part, not only rules the future but also overrides the predictions made on behalf of the idols (Isa 44:24–26). Moses had forbidden anyone from practicing divination, etc. from living in the land or for anyone to consult such a person (Deut 18:9–15). Yet into the foundation of the church in Philippi came the very confusing scene of a spirit-possessed, fortune-telling slave declaring loudly that the "most high God" was bringing salvation to Macedonia through his servants (16:17). "The way of salvation" was in danger of being confused in the public mind with spiritism, which may have presented it as "a way of salvation."[24] The terms

23. She had servants and a house large enough for at least four guests and the means to support them.

24. Gooding, *True to the Faith*, 14. Trebilco, "Paul and Silas," 64. "Salvation" in the Greco-Roman world could also be a very diminished concept to that of Christianity.

she used for God would also have very different meanings to a gentile in Philippi to that of a Jew. The term was also used of Zeus[25] but could mean a supreme god of your choice.[26]

The girl was controlled by "a python spirit" (16:16). This term is derived from the serpent oracle Python, which, according to Greek myths, the god Apollo slew to establish his famous oracle at Delphi southwest of Philippi in Achaia.[27] Just as Jesus had silenced the testimony of the demons who declared him to be the holy one of God (Matt 8:28; Mark 1:34; Luke 4:41), so Paul silenced the spirit in her by casting it out, though waiting for some days (16:18). Without any rituals or incantations, the spirit simply came out on the authority of Jesus Christ. "The servants of Jesus rejected convenient alliances with religious systems that are, at the heart, lies."[28] Paul's distress and days of hesitation may have been because the consequence of depriving the girl's owners of a lucrative income; the accusation and imprisonment was almost certain and could almost end the mission to Philippi.[29]

As the spirit "went out" (16:18) so also her owners hope for profit "went out" (16:19). As with Simon, their motive was "neither the quest for truth nor the pursuit for holiness."[30] The exorcism liberated the slave, but the wellbeing or dignity of the slave did not register with them. Twice, "profit" is mentioned (16:16, 19). Like the Ephesian silversmiths (19:24–28), the owners masked their greed by a call to civic duty with the addition here of Roman pride (16:21). (Timothy, a half gentile, and Luke, a gentile, are exempt, likely because anti-Semitism is also at play.) Her owners denounced Paul and Silas for "announcing" customs that were unlawful for Romans. Their slave had heralded the missionaries as "announcing" the message of salvation. Having made others pay for the knowledge she revealed, the owners demonstrated that they did not believe her.[31]

It is possible that her owners saw Paul's act as "magic," as something supernatural had happened in the name of Jesus and using magic to

25. Aeschylus, *Eum.* 28–29.

26. Trebilco, "Paul and Silas," 63–64.

27. Graves, *Greek Myths*, 60, 61, 79, 83–85. The priestesses were called "Pythia."

28. Johnson, *Message of Acts*, 177.

29. Trebilco, "Paul and Silas," 51–52, 60.

30. Johnson, *Message of Acts*, 177.

31. Johnson, *Message of Acts*, 178.

harm someone was forbidden by Roman law[32]. Her owners were able to provoke a mob drawing on the biases and fears of the citizens. They prayed on their Roman pride by highlighting the evangelists were Jews[33] and possibly implying that Christianity was an unsanctioned religion. Paul has been led to this point by very clear leading by the Spirit, and the ancients, knowing nothing of God's plans, were no different in seeking supernatural guidance for a very uncertain life. This was a superstitious age, and removing the ability of the local soothsayer to predict the future would have been very frightening. The residents must have put much of trust in her predictions as they made a lot of money from her (16:16). However, her owners only formally accused the pair of disturbing the peace and introducing an unsanctioned foreign cult to Roman citizens and by so doing brought their "crimes" into the jurisdiction of the magistrates. This was the first formal charges against the pair; however, the only violation of Roman law will be the imprisonment and beating of the missionaries.

Jesus had warned that an exorcism without the person getting their heart in order could mean the spirit might return along with seven others worse than itself (Matt 12:43–5). If the slave girl was only "delivered" and not incorporated into the church as a believer, she was not truly "delivered" in a Christian sense, so we should infer this had happened.[34]

PAUL AND SILAS IN PRISON (16:22–40)

In the first major legal trouble, Paul and Silas faced similar charges to their master: disturbing the peace (Luke 23:2, 5). Faced with a riot, the magistrates chose to simply flog the pair publicly without any hearing. The magistrates were answerable only to the emperor. This was likely to be done in the public square in front of their judgment seat or *bema*.[35] Their actions give an insight on how Roman justice was administered on a local level,[36] something Paul called "outrageous" (1 Thess 2:2; cf. 2 Cor

32. De Vos, "Finding a Charge," 57.

33. Claudius had expelled the Jews from Rome (18:2), which would not have gone unnoticed in this little Rome.

34. Stott, *Message of Acts*, 265.

35. Schneider, "ῥαβδίζω," 6.971.

36. Bock, *Acts*, 539. About five years later, Paul would write to the Corinthians, saying he had been beaten with rods three times (2 Cor 11:25). We do not know any details of the other two instances.

11:25). Roman citizens were not to be whipped,[37] yet the pair appear to say nothing about their Roman citizenship at this stage. The slave girl was released from obvious bondage to the powers of darkness, but the actions of the citizens of Philippi showed they also needed release from a "spiritual prison. God's next move in that direction was to get two of his servants into the physical goal at Philippi."[38] While the events may have caused some to question the Spirit's leading, the Lord had already shown Paul how much he must suffer for his name (9:16) but with also the promise of deliverance (26:17). They were brave men who accompanied Paul!

To make an example of the pair, after they were beaten the magistrates handed them over to the jailer for safekeeping, and he, in turn, exposed them to further indignity by placing them in an inner cell with their legs in stocks (16:24). As well as being tight, the holes could be aligned so they kept their legs spread in a painful position.[39] There is no mention of torture as such, but the jailer was likely to have at least supervised this on others, if he had not actually performed it himself. Jailers were often retired soldiers and not likely to be the milk of human kindness. At midnight the other prisoners were listening, not to the pair cursing men but praying and singing hymns. There was an earthquake, which opened all the doors and freed the chains from the wall. Earthquakes were a relatively common occurrence in the area, but ordinary earthquakes do not lose the fetters, open stocks and open doors without collapsing buildings in the process.

Not surprisingly, the earthquake woke the jailer who rushed to the prison, and, when he saw the doors were open, intended to kill himself and would have done so if Paul had not stopped him. Death was the likely consequence anyway for letting prisoners escape, but the jailer could at least avoid the extra unpleasantry that went with it (12:19; 27:42). While the ancient world's code of shame and honor was at play,[40] there was likely more. Hellenism considered earthquakes as a theophany,[41] which may

37. Cicero, *Orations*, Ver. 2.5.162. Cicero (106–43 BC) was a distinguished Roman lawyer and statesman. Caning and chaining of a Roman citizen was forbidden by at least three codes: those by Valerian (509 BC), Porcian (248 BC), and Julian (23 BC). There were heavy penalties for doing so. Conzelmann, *Acts*, 133.

38. Gooding, *True to the Faith*, 275.

39. Eusebius speaks of stretching the feet of the saints to the fifth hole in the stocks. Eusebius, *Hist. eccl.* 5.1.27 (*NPNF*[2] 1:214).

40. Bock, *Acts*, 540.

41. Ovid, *Met.* 9.782–3; 15; 15.669–78.

have caused him to think that they were angry because of the punishment of men who had greater spiritual power than the spirits that controlled the slave girl. He had to wonder who these prisoners were who could sing hymns in such a dark situation and apparently stop all the inmates escaping, but they had been listening to the hymns (16:25). Critics such as Haenchen dismiss this account: "The whole episode is such a nest of improbabilities that it must be struck out as unhistorical. Its absence does not produce any gap whatever."[42] Improbable, yes, except that it was a divine moment.

The jailer called for a light and, trembling with fear about who they had imprisoned, fell at the feet of Paul and Silas, asking how he could be saved (16:30). Likely he knew of the slave girl's testimony that they proclaimed the message of salvation from the charges brought against them that required his special care. The account of the trial is very abbreviated and presumably there was some knowledge of what they were preaching as this was part of the charge. The evangelists had already saved his life by staying, so he was asking if there is a way to "escape God's reaction to the injustice in which the jailer has played a role."[43] Only personally trusting the one they have been proclaiming can save him and his household (16:31). The promise that salvation could extend to the household was made before he met them and knew whether it comprised children or not (16:32) and before he had judged the response when he preached to the family (16:32). The involvement of the household is mentioned three times. Paul considered the proclamation of salvation in the Lord Jesus so important that he did it there at that jail even before his wounds were tended to (16:33) and before he ate. Showing his penitence, the jailer tended the wounds of Paul and Silas. As Chrysostom noted, he "washed them and was washed: those he washed from their stripes, himself was washed from his sins: he fed and was fed."[44]

Whereas Paul had told the jailer to "believe in the Lord Jesus" (16:31), the household "believed in God" (16:34) so Luke again links the two. As a result of their faith, the household was baptized, perhaps from the jail as well. As with Lydia's household, we do not know if this involved children. Only then did the jailer go into the house and prepare a meal for Paul and Silas, which would have been "unclean" by Jewish standards. We are left to ponder the impact on the prisoners and guards from witnessing

42. Haenchen, *Acts*, 501.

43. Bock, *Acts*, 541–2.

44. Chrysostom, *Acts of the Apostles* 36 (*NPNF*[1] 11:224).

the reconciliation the gospel had by immediately taking a fearful enemy, a man likely immune to the suffering of others, to joyfully meeting the needs of others with care and hospitality. To know God means to show the same care he would. There is no mention of receiving the Spirit, but it can be implied as there is great joy from one who was ready to commit suicide moments earlier, along with his household (16:34).

In the morning, the magistrates sent officers to the jail, possibly the men who beat the pair, with instructions that they were to be released, and the jailer told Paul and Silas they could leave and "go in peace" (16:36). The magistrates' bravado in severely beating the two changed to them sheepishly trying to get rid of them "quietly" (16:37). These were not ordinary men they had flogged without a trial, and it is hard to imagine that word of the events the night before had not reached them; it was their job to know. Perhaps also they may have started to hear rumors about their citizenship.[45] When given their freedom, Paul and Silas refused it and only then played their ace card: the magistrates have flogged Roman citizens without a trial!

Luke's account does not suggest that the evangelists could not get the attention of the magistrates over the roar of the crowd, so why would Paul and Silas chose not to mention their Roman citizenship? Perhaps they did not want to deny their Jewish culture and religious loyalties and/or avoid suffering for the cause of Christ.[46] To have pleaded Roman citizenship when the others could not "would be a violation of his oneness and solidarity with them."[47] To have called others to suffer when they could avoid it by pleading Roman citizenship would be hypocritical and left the church open to the charge it was only for Romans.[48] Paul later stood on his rights (and for the rights of any who are arbitrarily treated), not so much for his own sake but for the believers as it was important that their innocence and the injustice be recognized as publicly as their beating. Without clearing the faith under Roman law, the fledgling church could have also been subject to further arbitrary attacks.

45. The outrageous behavior of the magistrates would have been discussed at Lydia's home, and she would have had contact with them as their togas had a purple stripe. While in the realm of conjecture, she or others may have informed them of the real reason for the accusation against the pair.

46. Bock, *Acts*, 539. Paul is quick to appeal his citizenship when later faced with a scourging (22:25), which was murderous by comparison.

47. Bock, *Acts*, 539.

48. Witherington, *Acts*, 502.

The magistrates were alarmed to learn they had beaten Roman citizens. This could have cost them their lives! Roman citizenship was regarded as so sacred that Cicero, when accusing the Roman magistrate Verres, said, "It is a crime to bind a Roman citizen; to scourge him is a wickedness; to put him to death is almost parricide. What shall I say of crucifying him? So guilty an action cannot by any possibility be adequately expressed by any name bad enough for it."[49] Conversely, to claim Roman citizenship falsely was a capital offence,[50] but no one asked for evidence. Knowing of their greater power than the "python spirit" and hearing of extraordinary events of the night before may have been sufficient. No doubt the appeasement involved profuse apologies and likely strong words of advice from Paul regarding the treatment of the now-vindicated church. The Lord's guidance to Philippi was matched with his deliverance.

The magistrates asked the pair to leave the city, possibly to ensure peace and the evangelist's safety, but equally possible to stop the outrage against the magistrate from the Roman colonists.[51] They graciously agree but also because the work was established and they could minister elsewhere. The request is similar to the deliverance of the demoniac of Gerasene where the financial loss of the pigs led to the population asking Jesus to leave (Mark 5:1–20). But they did not leave before going to Lydia's home and encouraged the brothers and sisters. Luke remained as the "we" sections do not return till 20:6 at the conclusion of Paul's third missionary journey when he leaves Philippi. The amount of time Luke spent in Philippi and the detailed account of the time there suggest to many commentators that Luke was a resident of Philippi.[52] Perhaps also Luke, the beloved physician (Col 4:14), was a product of the school of medicine at Philippi that sent its doctors widely abroad.[53]

49. Cicero, *Ver.* 2.5.66.

50. Suetonius, *Twelve Caesars*, 176–77. Claudius beheaded those falsely claiming Roman citizenship.

51. Lenski, *Acts*, 689.

52. E.g., Longenecker, "Acts," 9:458.

53. Longenecker, "Acts," 9:460.

PAUL AND SILAS MINISTER IN THESSALONICA (17:1–9)

Paul and Silas, no doubt still sore from their beating, along with Timothy, walked fifty-three kilometers south-southwest along the Via Egnatia from Philippi to Amphipolis, formerly the capital of one of the four subdistricts of Macedonia, and then a further forty-three kilometers west-southwest to Apollonia, another district capital. Though these were major cities, they did not stop to evangelize but continued a further fifty-six kilometers to reach Thessalonica (modern Saloniki). Strabo described it as the "metropolis of Macedonia"[54] and, as such, had excellent sea and road connections for spreading the gospel. Macedonia was very loyal to Rome. It, like Crete, was a senatorial province, meaning it was governed by a proconsul as it did not need an army to maintain peace. Thessalonica was a free city with the right to govern on a Greek model.

Paul and Silas taught from the Scriptures in the synagogue over three Sabbaths[55] and were conscious of God giving them the strength to do so (1 Thess 2:2). They showed how the scriptures predicted that the messiah must suffer and die and then rise again and that this man was Jesus (17:3). There was no precedence for a resurrection before the *parousia*, which made the message difficult to receive and could only be believed when the Spirit opened a heart, as with Lydia. Paul evangelized without imposition or manipulation, rather presenting the gospel through "reasoning," "explaining," and "proving" (17:2–3), by which some were "persuaded" and "joined" (17:4). Consistently, while some of the Jews and God fearers believed the message (17:4), others became very hostile (17:5). Luke did not mention any miracles here or in Berea to further validate their teaching, but Paul implies it in his first Letter (1 Thess 1:5).

The major success is with the gentiles across the social strata (17:4)—women, some of high status, are again mentioned. Aristarchus and Secundus (20:4) were probably converted at that time. The unbelieving Jews were incensed and egaged some of the rabble from the marketplace to cause trouble. The Jews' reaction is described as "jealousy," or perhaps being "zealous," (17:5) and may mean that they were zealous for

54. Strabo, *Geogr.* 7.7.21.

55. The two Letters to the Thessalonians suggest a longer stay; three weeks is likely the period of Jewish ministry. The ministry in Thessalonica and Berea is told very briefly.

God's glory and the Law.[56] They went to the home of Jason, intending to drag out Paul and Silas to take them to what was likely to be a public assembly of citizens responsible for judicial matters. Possibly, they thought that locals would be more tolerant of their riot.[57] They only found Jason and had to make do with him and some other believers instead and took them to the magistrates[58] (17:6). Paul and Silas may have been hidden by the believers.

The Jews must have had some knowledge of the trouble that followed Paul and Silas and used this as the basis for charging them with causing a public disturbance, not just in their city but across the whole world (17:6), and, for good measure, the new believers were also harboring these people (17:7). The rabble final accused the evangelists of having a political manifesto with their teaching about the Messiah (17:7). Presumably, the Jews twisted Paul's teaching—about Jesus coming as God's Son (1 Thess 1:10; 4:15), his kingdom (1 Thess 2:12), and questioning the world's peace (1 Thess 5:3)—to make it political. They claimed Christianity was treasonous to the state, and for elements within Judaism it was political and there had already been insurrections.[59] For the Greeks also, the idea of a messiah would have involved kingship,[60] and Jesus was a king but not in any sense the Greeks understood. There was no attempt to overthrow Caesar.

Despite being alarmed (17:8), the magistrates did not bow to the mob[61] as happened in Phillipi but simply took a legal security from Jason who would be guaranteeing the evangelists do not break Roman law. As

56. Larkin, *Acts*, 246.

57. Larkin, *Acts*, 247.

58. As an indication of the reliability of Luke as a historian, he calls the magistrates *politarchs*, a word found in inscriptions in Macedonian cities but not found elsewhere in Greek literature. Bruce, *Acts*, 1954, 344.

59. The AD 40s had been a very turbulent time in Rome's dealing with the Jews. Claudius had to threaten the Jews in Alexandria who were "stirring up a universal plague throughout the world." Sherwin-White, *Roman Society*, 51. There was trouble in Palestine on the death of Herod Agrippa 1 and Claudius expelled the Jews from Rome at the instigation of "Christus." Suetonius, *Twelve Caesars*, 176–77.

60. Bock. *Acts*, 548. The Greek word for the "emperor" was *basileus* which is most likely the word used by Paul for Jesus as king. Bruce, *Acts*, 1954, 346.

61. Conzelmann found it strange that prominent women could not use their influence to stop the riot but that does not take into account the spontaneous nature of the riot. Conzelmann, *Acts*, 135, The influence of these women is more likely seen here as the judgment is sane. Bock *Acts* 552.

part of this deal, Paul is likely banished[62] before he answers that charge. Once Jason had posted the bond, Paul's hands were tied, at least during those magistrates' tenure.[63] When writing to the Thessalonians, he seems to indicate that he wanted to remain and then to return but was stopped by Satan (1 Thess 2:14–18). Luke's writings make clear what is meant by preaching Jesus as Messiah. Twice this charge is raised by the Jews (17:5–7; 18:12–13) and twice by gentiles (16:19–21; 19:24–27); twice it is partially believed (16:19–21; 19:24–27) and twice it is rejected (18:14–17; 19:35–40).[64] As one commentator noted, at this stage "the world's jury is still out on the new faith, but it is not the clear threat some make it out to be."[65]

There is consistency between Luke's account in Acts and Paul's first Letter to the Thessalonians. Paul spoke of how they came to the city after the outrageous treatment in Philippi (1 Thess 2:2) and how they received the message amid severe suffering (1 Thess 1:6; 2:14–15). Further, Paul acknowledged the hostility of the Jews and how they tried to stop the gentiles from hearing the message (17:16). Also, there is his time alone in Athens (1 Thess 3:1), and sending Timothy to them (1 Thess 3:2) fits well. The city remained faithful despite persecution, giving great joy to Paul.

PAUL AND SILAS MINISTER IN BEREA (17:10–14)

Paul and Silas only started their seventy-two-kilometer southwest walk to Berea (modern Veria) at night, suggesting there was an urgency. The mob may not have been happy with Jason only posting a bond. Timothy would later join them (17:14). The town was off the beaten track[66] but still had a sizeable population. It would be necessary to pass through the city to go to Athens, Paul's next stop, but it is not certain that it was planned. There must have been a significant Jewish population as there was a synagogue. Luke does not have a complete stereotype of the diaspora Jews[67] as these were described as "more noble" (17:11). Instead of

62. Bock. *Acts*, 553.

63. Bruce, *Acts*, 1954, 345.

64. Witherington, *Acts*, 502–3.

65. Bock. *Acts*, 549.

66. Cicero, *In Pis.* 36. The content of Cicero's mention of Berea is in relation to a conspirator in a murder plot against Nero escaping Thessalonica at night for Berea.

67. Witherington, *Acts*, 502.

hostility, they eagerly received the message and checked the Scriptures daily to see if what Paul was saying was true (17:11).

We are not told the subjects he spoke on, unlike in Thessalonica (17:3), but they must have had very similar content as Paul compares the Berean response to that in the city he fled. As a result, many believed including God fearing men and especially leading women who were also God fearers. One convert, Sopater, son of Pyrrhus, is with Paul on his next journey to Macedonia (20:4). The Jews in Thessalonica heard that Paul was preaching in Berea, so they came and stirred up a second crowd. The ruling in Thessalonica was from a different jurisdiction,[68] so there was no guessing how the magistrates would respond. The Berean believers probably recognized that no place in Macedonia was safe for Paul, so they escorted him to the coast (17:14). The route to Athens is normally by sea (313 kilometers south-southeast, 160 kilometers as the crow flies) as Mount Olympus blocked the way by land, making a very long journey but Luke does not say.[69]

PAUL PREACHES IN ATHENS (17:15–18)

Friends from Berea escorted Paul to Athens, likely to ensure his safety. Though Paul only spent a few weeks in Athens, the account is about the same length as that of Paul's time in Corinth where he spent a year and a half, showing Luke's selective use of his information. Though the government of the Mediterranean was Roman, the strongest cultural influence was Greek, especially with its language. Athens had an empire with colonies and settlements throughout the Mediterranean but, by the time of the New Testament, it was a relatively small and quiet city (perhaps between twenty and twenty-five thousand people). It was no longer a player on the world's political stage though still a center for culture and a university town.[70] Stott called it "the empire's intellectual metropolis,"[71] and it was a center for art, but this was focused on Greek idolatry. While Paul preached here and had some success, the New Testament does not

68. This is similar to when Paul and Barnabas fled from Iconium to Lystra and Derbe on the first journey.

69. Luke normally mentions the port, so its absence may mean that Paul took the land route to lose those following him. Based on varying readings of this verse, Bruce favors the land route. Bruce, *Acts*, 1954, 347.

70. Fant and Reddish, *Biblical Sites*, 14–15.

71. Stott, *Message of Acts*, 276.

portray Athens as a center for evangelism. The household of Stephanas in Corinth will be called the first converts in Achaia (1 Cor 16:15).

It appears that Paul had intended to wait for Silas and Timothy to join him before starting to evangelize (17:16), though, as normal, he did reason in the synagogue. Paul was well acquainted with paganism but what he saw in Athens was at a different level and deeply disturbed him so he could not remain silent. What the Athenians saw as their glory, Paul saw as their shame. This sets the scene for his argument against idols. When he reasoned in the agora to anyone who would listen, he could see the four-hundred-year-old Parthenon with its twelve-meter statue of Athena.[72] There were at least twelve temples to different gods, let alone statues and shrines to lesser ones.[73] Pliny reported there were as many as three thousand statues in Athens, many would have been to gods.[74] So pervasive was the polytheism that there was a proverb: "The gods walk abroad so commonly in our streets that it is easier to meet a god than a man."[75] It is not that Paul could not see the beauty, rather God-given ability to create that beauty was being used instead for idolatry.[76]

Athens was also the city of Socrates and Plato and the adopted home of Aristotle, Zeno,[77] and Epicurius. Luke confirms the stereotype of Athenians having itching ears wanting to hear the latest ideas (17:21). Thucydides wrote about them: "No men are better dupes, sooner deceived by novel notions, or slower to follow proved advice. You despise what is familiar, while you are worshipers of every new extravagance."[78] As Paul's prominence grew, the more important men and professional Stoic and Epicurean philosophers demanded to hear more about these new gods—"Jesus" and "Resurrection."

The curiosity of the philosophers was not the same thing as openness to the gospel, though as they had a long history of antagonism against foreign gods and killing their messengers[79] they used a very derogatory term of Paul which might be roughly translated "seed picker"

72. Her polished spear tip was said to be visible for over sixty kilometers. Blaiklock, *Acts*, 137.

73. These are described by Pausanias. See Pausanias, *Descr.* 1.17–29.

74. Pliny, *Nat.* 33:17.

75. Petronius, *Satyricon*, 17.

76. Stott, *Message of Acts*, 277–78.

77. Zeno of Citium (224–c. 262 BC) was the founder of Stoicism.

78. Thucydides, *History* 3.38.5.

79. Josephus, *Ag. Ap.* 2.38.

(17:18). It was a contemptuous term used to describe someone who picks up bits of information here and there and cobbles them together without understanding.[80] As mentioned, it appeared to them that Paul joined together a Jewish god "Jesus" along with a Greek goddess or idea known as "Resurrection"[81] (17:18). The concept was totally foreign to them as verse 32 will show. Pliny described it as a mad idea and that death was nature's supreme gift.[82] Luke portrays the Athenian intellectual arrogance against the reality that they lacked even the most basic understanding of the truth about God. Yet, despite the derogatory name they called Paul, did they recognize something different in him?

Who Were the Epicureans?

Epicureans, followers of the Athenian Epicurus (341–270 BC), believed the gods probably existed, but they were totally disinterested and removed from human affairs, which had only come into existence through random chance. As such, they would neither reward good or bad living, nor respond to any supplications. Reason was sufficient as "by which means Religion, brought down under our feet, is bruised in turn; and his victory sets us on a level with heaven."[83] They lived for pleasure, but this was generally not understood as a life of indulgence but a state of trouble-free tranquilly. The wise person sets out to live well and die well with no regard to the gods.[84] They were like the Sadducees in believing that there was no existence after death and therefore no judgment or justice. Death was neither a concern for those who are living, nor for those whose lives are ended.[85] They were critical of superstitious religion, but the sources show them inconsistently following the traditional religions.[86] It could later become a cover for self-indulgence and when combined with a withdrawal from public life was the antithesis of Roman virtue.[87]

80. BADG, "Σπερμολόγος," 762.
81. The term is feminine.
82. Pliny, *Nat.* 7.190.
83. Lucretius, *De rerum natura*, 1.62–79.
84. Diogenes Laertius, *Epimenides*, 10.126.
85. Diogenes Laertius, *Epimenides*, 10.125.
86. Jipp, "Paul's Areopagus Speech," 577–78.
87. DeLacy, "Cicero's Invective," 50–55.

Who Were the Stoics?

Stoicism was more followed than Epicureanism. Instead of rejecting the Greek gods, the Stoics reinterpreted them and their myths. They believed that a mind, which they called "Logos" or "Reason," permeated the whole universe. This Logos was seen as divine and could be personified as Zeus.[88] With this force permeating everything, i.e., they were pantheists, and their conviction that the gods love mankind and knew the future, there was a rational defense for magic and omens.[89] Also, because the Logos permeated everything, mankind had a spark of the divine within him leading their poets Chrysippus and Aratus of Soli to say, "We are his offspring."[90] Paul will use this in his address. This led to a belief in a *cosmopolis*, or world state where truly free souls had equal citizenship rights, so breaking down national and class distinctions.[91] A stoic would attempt to try and live in harmony with the Logos which would lead to "a contentment impervious to external events or fluctuating emotions."[92]

Death, the one act free of all discrimination, was inevitable, but the Stoic could refuse to fear it. The body had a soul that interacted with each other, but on death they separated.[93] Views differed about what happened after that, but there is no "indication that the survival of the soul after death had any direct benefit to the individual or that the Stoics used this as a motivator toward ethical or intellectual behavior. There is no heaven or hell in Stoicism; the time to live one's life and to perfect one's virtues is in the present."[94] Like the Epicureans, they also were inconsistent as they at least gave lip service to the pagan gods. Their commitment to "stern, unbending endurance" greatly attracted the Romans.[95]

As the commentator Longenecker noted, "Post-Christian paganism has been unable to come up with anything better"[96] than these two philosophies.

88. Cleanthes, "Fragment," 67–68.
89. Chrysippus, "Fragment 1169," 68–69.
90. Cleanthes, "Fragment," 67–68. Aratus of Soli, *Phaenomena* 5.
91. Bruce, *Acts*, 1954, 330.
92. Johnson, *Message of Acts*, 195.
93. Durand, *Stoicism*, 37.
94. Rubarth, *Stoic Philosophy*, 20.
95. Blaiklock, *Acts*, 139.
96. Longenecker, "Acts," 9:474.

PAUL BEFORE THE PHILOSOPHERS (17:19–34)

It is not certain whether Paul was arrested. It is possible as the word suggests that Paul was forced to attend the meeting of the Areopagus, which was a very powerful body. Against that, he was not held in custody after his defense. Very likely it was a hearing to understand Paul's message and determine if he would be given the freedom to continue teaching.[97] Luke is usually clear about any legal implications.[98] It is not surprising that the philosophers thought Paul was talking about foreign gods—since the conquest of the East and Egypt by Alexander, the Greeks were being exposed to many foreign gods that were new to them. What was a surprise was that Paul told the philosophers at the Areopagus that his "gods" were not foreign, as the Athenians already knew of and had unknowingly worshiped the God he was now preaching.

Speaking to them,[99] Paul quoted the poet philosopher Epimenides—"For in him we live and move and have our being"[100] (17:28)—and reminded them of the largely forgotten, unknown god. Who was the "unknown god"? Pausanias, a second century mythographer and travel-writer, wrote of altars to unknown gods (plural) in Greece,[101] but this altar is to an unknown god (singular). During the second year of the Peloponnesian War (430 BC) between Athens and Sparta, Athens appeared to be winning until a plague broke out. Its severity was such that no one had seen the like. The disease showed no regard to a person's piety towards the gods and their temples; where people from the countryside had fled, they become places of special misery. The plague is estimated to have killed somewhere between seventy-five and one hundred thousand people, or 25 percent of the then overcrowded population. The residents sacrificed to every god, but the plague did not abate. The constant funeral pyres caused the Trojans to withdraw and the Athenians' trust in their gods was shaken.[102] The Athenians sent to Crete for Epimenides, a

97. Longenecker, "Acts," 9:474.

98. Bock, *Acts*, 563.

99. This can refer to a physical location, a hill northwest of the Acropolis or the Athenian governing body.

100. From his poem "Cretica," which Paul also quotes in Titus 1:12. Rendal, "Cretians Always Liars."

101. Pausanias (c. AD 110–c. 180) was a traveler and geographer. Pausanias, *Descr.* 5.14.8. This reference is to Olympia.

102. Thucydides retells the plague in detail. Thucydides, *History* 2.49–54.

philosopher and poet, to advise how to cleanse the city and so placate the gods. Diogenes Laertius, writing in the third century AD recounts,

> He took sheep, some black and others white, and brought them to the Areopagus; and there he let them go whither they pleased, instructing those who followed them to mark the spot where each sheep lay down and offer a sacrifice to the local divinity. And thus, it is said, the plague was stayed. Hence even to this day altars may be found in different parts of Attica with no name inscribed upon them, which are memorials of this atonement.[103]

This unknown god had proven himself more powerful than all of the idols they had sacrificed to and had compassion on them when they were without hope, yet they did not seek to know him. By making the unknown God known, Paul was not declaring a new God to them. Now, to these philosophers, the truth was less important than intellectual novelty (17:21). Luke reverses the accusation and in effect calls them the "seed-pickers."

Before telling the philosophers about God being their judge, he had to explain what kind of God he was referring to.[104] In his address, Paul did not quote any Scripture, but he did quote this same Epimenides at the same spot the sheep were released. Yet in his reference to God giving mankind breath and life (17:25), his thoughts were firmly rooted in the Old Testament in Genesis where God was the creator and gave life and breath (Gen 2:7), but especially to a strongly monotheistic section of Isaiah where this is given to every generation (Isa 42:5).[105] From at least the fifth century BC the Athenians believed in what they called "Autochthony," where their common ancestors had sprung from the earth of Attica, that a people had always lived there, and that they had started the process of civilization earlier than the migrating people around them. This made them think they were better than others and even their lowest citizen was of nobler birth than a non-citizen regardless of wealth.[106] The idea of all men originating through Adam, though not specifically mentioned, cut across their uniqueness and superiority and put all men

103. Laertius, *Epimenides* 1.10.

104. Gooding, *True to the Faith*, 248.

105. The philosophers following Plato believed that God created the universe using an intermediary called the "demiurge." This was a major part of later Gnosticism.

106. Rosivarch, "Autochthony and the Athenians," 301–3. This belief in the equality and dignity of its citizens was at the core of the development of Athenian democracy.

on an equal standing. It also means that God is not a stranger in any part of his universe, and no part could claim him as their own property.[107]

He took ownership of the altar to an "unknown God" (17:23) to remind the intellectuals of Athens of their admitted ignorance (17:23, 30) and their foolishness in worshiping idols. As for the perceived cleverness of their philosophical constructions of God, it was no more than groping in the dark (17:27). Yet their poets were given sufficient light to realize this, had they followed their insights to their logical conclusion. If the offsprings of God have flesh and blood, how can an inanimate idol be a god (17:29)? They had realized that the qualities that they saw in humankind had to be found in the divine in at least equal quantities. The creation could reason, hear, and see, but had not made the connection that humankind is relational. Christianity was a superior "philosophy" to that of the "superstitious"[108] Athenians in that not only did it admit that the idols were nothing, but its followers are consistent as they refuse to honor them. Temples and cultic services were nothing. It had also followed the insights of the philosophers to their logical conclusion.

It is difficult to be certain what Paul meant by God marking "out their appointed times in history and the boundaries of their lands" (17:26). It could refer to the biblical periods allocated to the nations (Deut 32:8; Dan 8) but could also refer to the "philosophical rendering of 'the boundaries [of the season's geographical zones] for habitation'"[109] The "appointed seasons" may be no more than this as it was in Lystra (14:17) as "by whose sequence annual provision is made for supplying men with food."[110] Paul may have meant one thing, and the philosophers heard another. Either way, the point is that God is sovereign.[111]

Paul portrays them as humans seeking God in their own imperfect way, like a blind man groping in the hope of getting hold of God. Paul portrays the understanding of God's glory as attainable because he is close by as Epimenides said and his altar testified, yet creation does not reveal

107. Gooding, *True to the Faith*, 301–2.

108. An alternate rendering of "religious" in Acts 17:24. Paul was not giving them a compliment and compliments were forbidden when addressing the Areopagus as it was considered a trick attempted to sway their judgment. Lucian, *Anach.* 19.

109. Jipp, "Paul's Areopagus Speech," 582. E.g., Dio Chrysostom, *Dio Chrysostom*, 35–39.

110. Bruce, *Acts*, 1954, 368.

111. Bock, *Acts*, 566.

his plan.[112] God had largely ignored the pagans in the past (17:30) and did not judge their culpable idolatry and ignorance as harshly as he could have (Rom 3:25, Acts 14:16). But now he has acted as savior, not judge. There is now an urgency, as the return of Christ as judge was assured and repentance was the only response in the face of this. And to understand this it must be through God's revelation (17:30–31). Despite pointing out their foolishness and accusing those who thought they were the most learned as ignorant (17:30), Paul remained respectful throughout.

When Paul stood "before the most revered tribunal in the ancient world,"[113] he addressed the beliefs of both groups. His knowledge of them and Greek poets suggest his education was not limited to the study of the Law and Prophets. Paul's address begins and finishes with mention of the resurrection (17:18, 31–32) as big a stumbling block for the Pagans as the Jews. He did have an attentive audience until he mentioned the resurrection, not a new "god" but a concept diametrically opposed to their philosophical beliefs (refer to Table 9 below). This "unknown god" had control over human affairs when the others made of wood and stone did not. But knowing of this God was not sufficient.

Christianity	Epicureans	Stoics
God is involved with human affairs	Rejected, God is aloof	Accepted
God does not need man-made shrines	Accepted, their gods were remote	Accepted, God is Reason and it pervades the universe
Believed in the resurrection	Rejected, life completely ceases at death	Rejected, something continues but it is not a consciousness
Believed in judgment	Rejected.	Rejected
Totally rejected the pagan gods	Paid them lip service	Paid them lip service

Table 10. The views of the philosophers addressed in Paul's sermon

The philosophers started by standing in judgment of Paul, but he finished by standing in judgment of them. While God had overlooked their ignorance in the past, the pagans had sufficient knowledge to reject idols. Now he had designated "a man," Jesus, to carry out judgment and

112. Bock, *Acts*, 567.

113. Jipp, "Paul's Areopagus Speech," 574.

justice. Just as humanity came from one man, one man was resurrected, which carries implications for all people of all time because they also are human.[114] He is not called "God's son," likely because they would then only have considered him as a deity among other gods.

Aeschylus, in his tragic play *Eumenides*, portrays the founding of the Areopagus where a trial was held before Athena and leading citizens. There, Apollo said, "But when the dust has drawn up the blood of a man, once he is dead, there is no return to life."[115] It was beyond even his great power. The philosophers' belief that the soul effectively perished at death removed any fear of judgment but also the hope of justice for the wronged. God, who created the world (17:24), directed history (17:26–7), made mankind seek him (17:27–9), and has the authority to call them to repent.[116] His resurrection was the proof that Jesus had this authority (17:32). At this point, both groups would have strongly disagreed, yet some, including a high standing official, Dionysius, and a woman, Damaris, of whom nothing but speculation exists, believed. Paul has demonstrated that he can adapt his message to address Jews and God fearers in the synagogue, the common person in the Agora, and the sophisticated intellectuals at Areopagus.[117] His message had the full range of reactions: derision, wanting to know more, and belief. It shows how Paul could be all things to all people (1 Cor 9:20–22)

Despite having minimal success in Athens, Luke may have included this address as an example of Paul's approach to pagans much like the Pisidian Antioch address likely being an example of the message to Jews and God fearers. Possibly without permission to continue speaking, Paul moved on to Corinth, a byword for immorality and which was the polar opposite to Athens, yet God would have him stay there as he had many people in that city (18:11).

Paul, the New Socrates?

It is very possible that Luke presented Paul as the new Socrates. Similarities include the following:

- Arguing in the Agora every day

114. Gooding, *True to the Faith*, 302.

115. Aeschylus, *Eum.* 647.

116. Jipp, "Paul's Areopagus Speech," 576.

117. Stott, *Message of Acts*, 281.

- Accused of introducing foreign gods to Athens[118]
- The philosophers were arguing with him
- The philosophers "grasped"[119] him (17:19)
- Appearing before an Athenian tribunal
- Their request "to know" can be interpreted as the "right to know"[120]

While Paul will present Christianity as containing "the best features of Greco-Roman philosophical sensibilities and therefore a superior philosophy,"[121] it was not just a philosophy. He argued beyond philosophy to show that paganism and Christianity are completely incompatible.

PAUL MINISTERS IN CORINTH (18:1–11)

Corinth, roughly sixty-four kilometers southwest of Athens, was renowned for its luxury, immorality, and ornate architecture.[122] It was also an important seaport, or strictly a city with two seaports, as ships and/or cargo could be hauled over the 6.4-kilometer isthmus of Corinth connecting the Ionian Sea (to Italy from Lechaeum) and the Aegean Sea (to Asia from Cenchrea).[123] Likewise, the isthmus meant that it controlled the north–south land route, so like a hub with radiating spokes along with commerce; the new faith could spread through the empire. Until it was destroyed by the Romans in 146 BC after the battle of Corinth with Roman general Lucius Mummius, the city was one of the major cities of ancient Greece. The destruction was total and Mummius also killed most of the men and sold the women and children into slavery.[124] However, Julius Caesar founded a Roman colony there in 44 BC and started to rebuild the city. Like Philippi, it was a little Rome. It quickly became a

118. Xenophon, *Mem.* 1.1.1.

119. The verb is used in the latter part of Acts for the forceful seizure of the apostles (16:19; 18:17; 21:30, 33).

120. Jipp, "Paul's Areopagus Speech," 574.

121. Jipp, "Paul's Areopagus Speech," 568.

122. "Corinthian column" is the term used of slender columns with an ornate flowery top.

123. Pausanias, *Desc.* 2.1–5; Strabo, *Geogr.* 8.6.20–5. Strabo noted that the duties paid made the city rich but that mariners were glad to pay it because it avoided over 300 kilometers of treacherous seaways.

124. Pausanias, *Desc.* 7.16.8.

major city again,[125] with a mixed population but predominantly Romans, Greeks, and Jews. By Paul's time, it was still a new city and had risen to be the capital of the province of Achaea and was an important center for the imperial cult.

While Paul would experience fear during his ministry in Corinth (18:9), he later wrote to them saying that he came to the city "in weakness with great fear and trembling" (1 Cor 1:3). What was different about Corinth that caused him such concern before a word was said? He had been directed to Macedonia by a vision, but it had not gone smoothly, with a beating, being driven out violently, and treated contemptuously. Likely still in pain, he must have been wondering what further trouble lay ahead. Further, like Antioch, Corinth was not a city where Christianity could expect to make inroads. Along with its prosperity, it was a center of extreme vice, even for classical times. The new city could be described as the Las Vegas of its day.[126] When referring to classical times in Corinth, Strabo said of the city,

> The temple of Venus at Corinth was so rich, that it had more than a thousand women consecrated to the service of the goddess, courtesans, whom both men and women had dedicated as offerings to the goddess. The city was frequented and enriched by the multitudes who resorted thither on account of these women. Masters of ships freely squandered all their money, and hence the proverb, "It is not in every man's power to go to Corinth."[127]

But Strabo's reference was to the past and in his own time he would report that there was only a small temple of Venus in Corinth.[128] Still, when he wrote about Comana in Pontus,[129] an area that is outside the main Greek sphere of influence, he refers to the city as a little Corinth "on account of the multitude of harlots at Corinth, who are dedicated

125. Estimates of its population vary considerably, likely at least one hundred thousand. Winter, "Gallio's Ruling" 216. Longenecker puts it as probably over two hundred thousand. Longenecker, "Acts," 9:480.

126. Bock, *Acts*, 576. Another attraction to Corinth was the biannual Isthmian games.

127. Strabo, *Geogr.* 8.6.20.

128. Pausanias briefly describes this temple. Pausanias, *Descr.* 2.4.1. See also Strabo, *Geogr.* 8.6.21.

129. Strabo, *Geogr.* 12.3.36. Aquilla was from Pontus (18:2).

[possibly followers of] to Venus."[130] Horace described it as a city where only the tough survive.[131] So proverbial was the immorality that *korinthiazomai* meant "to practice immorality" and *korinthiastēs* was a synonym for a harlot.[132] Paul's Letters to the Corinthian church show how this Christian community had difficulty in resisting the corrupting influence of this city (1 Cor 5:1; 6:15–20).

Paul heard about another Christian Jew, Aquilla and his wife Priscilla[133] (18:2), who, along with all the other possibly fifty thousand Jews,[134] had been expelled from Rome by Claudius in AD 49.[135] This was because of the riots instigated by "Chrestus,"[136] probably about whether Jesus was the Christ. Rabbis were expected not to profit from their Torah studies, so Paul had a trade: tentmaking.[137] When he visited the pair (18:2), Paul found that Aquila practiced the same trade. The pair invited him into their home, and they joined forces (18:3) in commerce and the gospel. Again, like Luke, the Spirit was able to grow and develop strong and sound believers without the help of the apostles. Paul did as he always did, each week he reasoned in the synagogue trying to persuade the Jews and God fearers that Jesus was the Messiah (18:4–5). When Silas and Timothy arrived from Macedonia, likely with an offering from the church (2 Cor 11:7–9), he was able to stop working and devote his time exclusively to the mission work (18:5). Very intentionally, he was not a burden upon the Corinthian church.

130. Strabo, *Geogr.* 12.3.36.

131. Horace, *Ep.* 1.17.36. Horace (65–8 BC) was a leading Roman lyric poet.

132. Stott, *Message of Acts*, 296.

133. Paul generally uses the more formal Prisca in his letters (Rom 16:3; 2 Tim 4:19) and Luke the informal Priscilla. She is sometimes mentioned before her husband, possibly because she was connected to the prominent Roman family, Prisca. Longenecker, "Acts," 9:481. She could also just have had a very strong character.

134. Polhill, *Acts*, 383,

135. This decision would have seemed disastrous for Roman Christians but proved to advance the gospel through the empire, not quell it.

136. Suetonius, *Twelve Caesars*, 176–77. Whether this was Christ is hotly debated but some commentators rate this as "likely"; e.g. Bruce, *Acts*, 1954, 368. Notice how mobile people could be: Aquilla started in Pontus, went to Rome, then Corinth, then Ephesus, and depending on how you read the final chapter of Romans, back to Rome.

137. More likely a leatherworker in general rather than only making tents. Paul's teacher, Gamaliel, taught that working on the Torah and also at a trade left no time for sin. M. *'Avot* 2.12. While Paul personally renounced the privilege, he defended the right of other workers to be supported by their pupils.

Despite the immorality of Corinth, the Jews faithfulness had attracted God fearers and as Paul ministered in the synagogue, he experienced strong opposition to the point that he was fearful (18:9). He left the synagogue and went next door to the private home of a God fearer, Titius Justus, and there he was joined by the synagogue leader Crispus and his whole household. It is sad that two groups that worshiped the same God and revered the same Scriptures were forced to advertise their differences in this way.[138] Despite the difficulty this caused, they were joined by many Corinthians who believed in the Lord, i.e., Jesus, and were baptized (18:7–8). Crispus, along with Gaius and the household of Stephanas, were the only ones Paul baptized (1 Cor 1:14–16). Before moving next door, Paul symbolically shook the dust of the synagogue from his clothes and warned them of their guilt, using the Old Testament words "Your blood be on your own heads" (Josh 2:19; Judg 9:24; 2 Sam 1:16; 1 Kgs 2:33, 37; Ezek 33:4–6). With that, he concentrated on the gentiles while in Corinth. He had done all that he could for them and the responsibility God had given him for the Jews had been discharged. He also had a responsibility to the gentiles.

Luke's account reads as if Paul did not intend to spend long in Corinth due to Jewish opposition (18:9–11). At Paul's conversion, the Lord had promised to protect him (26:17), but that protection was largely by knowing through visions (22:17–18) or circumstances when to flee. In Corinth, the Lord used, not flight but an honest magistrate and Roman law. The "Lord" (18:9) promised to be with Paul (18:10), but this is the "Lord Jesus." His words reflect what God said to Joshua as they entered the promised land: "As I was with Moses, so I will be with you; I will never leave you nor forsake you" (Josh 1:5). Protection is not the same as a trouble-free existence. One commentator said of this promise, "So now Jesus, whose earthly ministry, death, and resurrection have accomplished the supreme exodus from slavery for his people, assures the messengers through whom he carries out his conquest of the Gentiles, I am with you."[139] The extraordinary nature of the assurance of Christ's abiding and saving presence was not, however, unique among the apostles. Matthew concludes his Gospel with Jesus' assurance that he will be with all his believers until he returns (Matt 28:20). As for the future believers, "The Lord said that they already, according to his purpose, belonged to him."[140]

138. Gooding, *True to the Faith*, 315.

139. Johnson, *Message of Acts*, 24.

140. Stott, *Message of Acts*, 298.

PAUL BEFORE GALLIO (16:12–17)

Paul appeared before a nameless Roman magistrate for the first time in Philippi where he was accused of breaching the peace and preaching a cult that had not been approved by Rome (16:20). The application of Roman law was shameful. At Thessalonica, his host, Jason, had to stand bail for Paul when he was accused before the again nameless municipal council for preaching contrary to the decrees of Caesar and saying there was another king (17:6). In neither case was the accusation settled. In Corinth, Paul stood before a named magistrate, the proconsul[141] Gallio, accused of persuading men to worship contrary to the "law" (18:13), a very vague charge. However, in the Lord's providence, Paul was standing before a person of entirely different caliber and with the skill and integrity needed to accurately determine the legal situation. At the very least, Theophilus would have known of Gallio as he was a very prominent magistrate and administrator in Rome at the time. So his ruling carried much weight. His decision in Corinth would enable the new faith to spread without legal impediment until the persecutions under Nero ten to twelve years later.

We know more about Gallio (5 BC—AD 65) than most of the people mentioned in Acts. He was born Lucius Annaeus Novatus, the oldest son of Seneca the Elder and brother of Seneca the Younger, both Stoic philosophers and prolific writers who mentioned him. When he was adopted[142] by an eminent rhetorician and senator, L. Junius Gallio, as the beneficiary of his estate, he changed his name to Lucius Junius Gallio. His birth father wrote about how zealous he was to train his sons in philosophy and rhetoric to set them up as senators and fit for a legal career in the Roman administration.[143] His brother wrote at length on Gallio's character, praising his gentle disposition and hatred for flattery, and concluding of him that he was neither willing to be or capable of being deceived.[144] Gallio became a senator in AD 37 and also served as a

141. Luke's accuracy with titles commends the accuracy of his history. Macedonia was an imperial province, and the magistrates were called *preators*; in Thessalonica they are *politarchs*, and in Corinth, a senatorial province is a *proconsul*. These provinces changed status over time and with that the titles. Longenecker, "Acts," 9:485.

142. This example of "testamentary adoption" casts light on our adoption as sons (Gal 4:4–7).

143. Winter, "Rehabilitating Gallio," 294.

144. Seneca the Younger, *Natural Questions* 4.pref.9.

praetor, i.e., a senior magistrate. Did he and Paul cross paths again during the appeal to Caesar?

Claudius had said Achaea was dear to him because of the exchange of shared cultures.[145] So whoever he appointed as proconsul of Achaea would have received careful thought. He was already a respected jurist with close imperial connections, and, on an inscription at Delphi, Claudius described him as "my friend and proconsul."[146] Gallio was made proconsul in Claudius's twelfth year (AD 51/52). This is one of the few fixed dating points in Acts. He was made a consul of Rome[147] in AD 59 and later a herald of Nero. His second brother, Annaeus Mela, committed suicide after being accused of a conspiracy against Nero in AD 65,[148] and Gallio appears to have also committed suicide, likely under instruction.[149]

When Paul's Jewish accusers brought him before the *bema*[150] they did not specify what law was being broken. Was it Mosaic or Roman, and if Roman, which law? Possibly they were saying that Christianity was not a faith recognized by Rome, a *religio illicita*.[151] Gallio was sufficiently versed in the law that he did not have to withdraw to consider his verdict but ruled against them immediately without Paul having to make his defense (18:14). Perhaps the Jews and Gallio were talking at cross purposes (18:15).[152] He refused to collaborate with the Jews as Pilate had done and Felix would do,[153] perhaps because he was an anti-Semite.[154] He ruled that the Jews' complaint only concerned Mosaic law, not Roman, against which there was no case to answer (18:14). He refused to intervene in a matter concerning "words," "names," and their "Law." "Names" may be a reference to Jesus as the Christ.

145. Suetonius, *Twelve Caesars*, 184.

146. Winter, "Gallio's Ruling," 213.

147. There were two consuls who served for a year. These elected officials were responsible for running Rome and its provinces. In peace they were the highest magistrates.

148. Tacitus, *Ann.* 16.17.

149. Tacitus, *Ann.* 15.73.

150. In Corinth, this was a raised platform in the northwest market in front of the proconsul's residence. It still exists.

151. Bock, *Acts*, 581.

152. Stott, *Message of Acts*, 299.

153. Winter, "Rehabilitating Gallio," 304.

154. Gallio's brother called the Jews "a detestable race." Augustine, *Civ.* 6.11.

Sosthenes,[155] the synagogue ruler, was driven[156] from the court and beaten by the mob, and Gallio chose to ignore it. Gallio would not have been indifferent to an urban uprising, especially a Jewish one (18:13), which could have very serious repercussions, and Sosthenes's beating would have fitted in well with his friend Claudius's anti-Semitism. As a clone of Rome there may have been an expectation that the Roman citizens would demonstrate their loyalty to the emperor's policy, especially in light of the civil unrest and public violence.[157]

If Christianity was ruled to be a sect outside of Judaism, it would have brought the faith under the laws governing associations, which meant that believers could gather no more than once a month. Augustus had introduced this to curb political dissent within societies, but Jews had an exemption allowing weekly meetings.[158] Also, if Christianity stood outside of Judaism, it would also have lost its legal immunity from offering sacrifices to the emperor as a god, which had occurred in Corinth since its founding as a colony.[159] While the decision was only legally binding in Achaia, Gallio's legal standing meant it would have been given serious credence elsewhere[160] and Festus later made the same judgment (25:19). Even when under constant guard in Rome, Paul was allowed to preach and teach without it being considered a breach of Roman law (28:16).

The content of Paul's two Letters to Corinth are driven by pastoral concern and contain many allusions to his time in Corinth. Luke, whose concern is apologetic, says very little.[161] Still, there are considerable overlaps with 1 Corinthians, being the following:

1. Working with Aquilla and Priscilla (Acts 18:2; 1 Cor 16:19)
2. Practicing his trade (Acts 18:8; 1 Cor 9:12, 15–18)
3. Converting and baptizing Crispus (Acts 18:8; 1 Cor 1:14)
4. His association with Sosthenes (Acts 18:8; 1 Cor 1:1)
5. Paul experiencing fear (Acts 18:9; 1 Cor 2:3)

155. Paul mentions a Sosthenes in 1 Cor 1:1. It is impossible to know if one of Paul's accusers became a coworker.

156. Likely he saw this as a vexatious matter. Winter, "Rehabilitating Gallio," 302.

157. Winter, "Rehabilitating Gallio," 304.

158. Winter, "Gallio's Ruling," 217.

159. Winter, "Gallio's Ruling," 219, 222.

160. Bruce, *Acts*, 1954, 373.

161. Longenecker, "Acts," 9:479.

6. The role of Timothy (Acts 18:5; 1 Cor 4:17; 16:10–11)

PAUL LEAVES CORINTH FOR EPHESUS AND ANTIOCH (18:18–22)

A considerable period elapsed after Gallio's judgment before Paul left Corinth for his home base in Antioch, travelling from the eastern port Cenchreae via Ephesus, Caesarea, and Jerusalem before returning home. The journey is told very briefly. The text does not mention Jerusalem but to "go up" and "go down" implies it. Paul shaved his head at Cenchreae in response to a vow (18:18), but we are not told of its significance. Luke was writing as a gentile to a gentile so there was no need to elaborate on Jewish practices.[162] It could have been at the beginning of a Nazirite vow[163] (Num 6:1–21) or at the end, as with a vow of thanksgiving for a personal matter such as his safety in Corinth. As this was not a matter related to salvation, his conscience was free to make this vow and would help with the Jerusalem church leaders.[164]

Paul only had a brief stop in Ephesus, which viewed itself as the "first and greatest metropolis of Asia,"[165] one of the largest cities in the empire. Ephesus is discussed in more detail in chapter 19. Alone, he spoke at the synagogue (18:19) and was well received; his shaved head is likely to have helped give a good impression. Paul could not stay despite being asked to do so but promised to return if it was God's will (18:20–21). If Paul was aiming to have Passover in Jerusalem, there was a rush as the seas closed to navigation over winter and only opened on March 10; Passover was in early April.[166] Alternatively, he may simply have wanted to promptly fulfill his vow at the temple.[167]

Paul left Priscilla and Aquilla (note the change of order) in Ephesus to watch over and extend the new work (18:24–26). The church met in their home (1 Cor 16:19). They may well have paid Paul's passage as they

162. Longenecker, "Acts," 9:488.

163. M. *Naz.* 3.6; Josephus, *J. W.* 2.15.1.

164. Stott, *Message of Acts*, 301.

165. The expression is found in numerous inscriptions and on coins. White, "Urban Development," 34.

166. Bock, *Acts*, 587.

167. If a Nazirite vow, this would have involved thirty days of purification in Judea, presenting his hair as a burnt offering and making the necessary sacrifices.

appeared to be relatively well off.[168] We do not know what happened to Silas and Timothy at this stage other than assuming they were gainfully employed in gospel work. With the loss of Paul, Aquilla, and Priscilla, someone was needed in Corinth.

168. They could afford a home large enough for the Ephesian church to meet.

13

Paul's Third Missionary Journey (Acts 18:23—21:26)

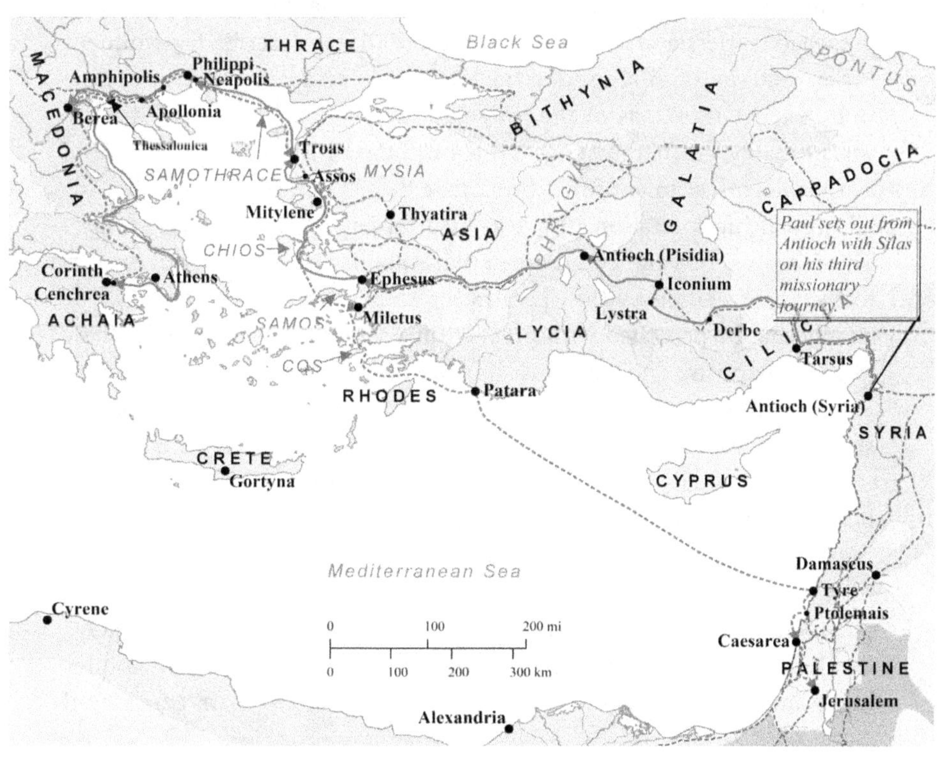

Figure 5. Paul's third missionary journey

THE TRIP COMMENCES (18:23)

Paul likely stayed in Antioch from the summer of AD 52 through to the spring of AD 53[1] before he set out on his third journey. A subsequent journey of twenty-four hundred kilometers is told very briefly. No motivation is given for this journey, but he had pastoral concern for the churches he established and perhaps the promise to return to Ephesus was further motivating him. First the Spirit and then circumstances had prevented him from ministering there.

INTERLUDE WHERE APOLLOS IS INTRODUCED (18:24–28)

In this interlude, Apollos, a Jew from Alexandria, visited Ephesus and preached fearlessly in the synagogue (18:26). He is described as eloquent (or learned) and well-versed in the Scriptures (18:24). Luke stresses how well instructed he was in the Way and taught this "accurately." Luther was probably the first to suggest that he could be the author of Hebrews as the allegorical tone of that book matches Alexandria's reputation for allegorical interpretation.[2] He was also fervent in Spirit/spirit (18:25). This is ambiguous and could mean that Apollos was fervent with respect to the Spirit, "gifted by the Spirit in his ability to preach effectively,"[3] or simply that he preached with great enthusiasm. However, he only knew of John's baptism, and this must imply a lack of awareness of the Spirit. How was this possible? Yet the account of the twelve believers (19:1–7) shows that not everybody had a basic understanding of the faith.

Providentially, Priscilla and Aquilla (note the reverse order again) heard Apollos before he went to Corinth where the difference in his message would have caused confusion. This scholar would have known less than the members.[4] They took Apollos to their home and privately corrected his understanding of the gospel, so he knew it "more accurately." Unlike the twelve disciples Paul found, there is no mention of Apollos being baptized,[5] which would have happened if the pair considered

1. Longenecker, "Acts," 9:489.

2. Stott, *Message of Acts*, 302. Philo was the most famous Alexandrian practitioner of this method.

3. Bock, *Acts*, 591–92.

4. Gooding, *True to the Faith*, 325.

5. It is possible that John's baptism of repentance that pointed to Jesus did not need

Aquilla not to be a Christian. The believers enabled Aquilla to fulfill his desire to move to Greece along with a letter of introduction (18:27). There his ministry was characterized by God's grace (18:27). It is not clear whether Luke was referring to those who believe through grace or whether Apollos helped through God's grace. Both are necessary. In Ephesus he "spoke with great fervor" (18:25), but after receiving further instruction he was able to vigorously refute his Jewish opponents (18:28). Was the Spirit given after learning of Jesus' baptism? Paul saw Aquilla as a colleague and fellow worker (1 Cor 1–4, especially 3:9), and they will meet in Ephesus (1 Cor 16:12) where he urged him to go to Corinth.

TWELVE GENTILES RECEIVE THE SPIRIT (19:1–7)

Paul reached Ephesus using the interior route, likely following the Cayster River valley and so avoided Colossae and Laodicea, which were on the main trade route. Ephesus was likely the third largest city in the empire's east behind Alexandria and Syrian Antioch and was the capital of the Roman province of Asia.[6] Ephesus, which faced the Greek world to the west, was ideally situated for commerce. Strabo,[7] the Greek geographer, wrote that Ephesus's location with an accessible harbor[8] and being effectively the start of the Persian royal road were the main reasons for its economic growth and rise to prominence.[9] Further, being sited on the north–south coastal road and with links by mountain passes to the Hermos River valley (modern Gediz River) strengthened its economic situation. Along with trade went the gospel. The temple of Artemis and religious tourism is mentioned during discussion of the riot (19:23–41).

to be "redone every time there was a growth in understanding." Longenecker, "Acts," 9:491.

6. McDonald, "Ephesus," 319. Estimated population figures vary from as low as 51,000 up to 250,000. There were known to be 40,000 citizens in the third century; to that had to be added women, children, and slaves. White, "Urban Development," 42.

7. Strabo (c. 54 BC–AD 24), a native of Pontus, was an eyewitness of much of his geographical information making it invaluable for people in the higher departments of administration and international politics. He was well acquainted with history and the mythological traditions of his nation, was a devout admirer of Homer, and acquainted with the other great poets.

8. While its harbor was silting and needed constant dredging, it could take ships up to thirty meters long and between four and five hundred gross register tons. Zabehlicky, "Preliminary Views," 209. There is 2.8 cubic meters to a gross register ton.

9. Strabo, *Geogr.* 14.1.24. The road was likely not paved till Roman times.

On arriving, he found some disciples (19:1). What was it about them that prompted Paul to ask if they received the Holy Spirit when they became believers (19:2)? They replied that they didn't even know there was a Holy Spirit and only knew John's baptism (19:2–3). Jews knew there was a Holy Spirit and its coming in a new way was foretold by John, but they had not heard that the promise had been fulfilled. Like Apollos, they were not just disciples of John as their belief included Jesus, but it was incomplete and needed "finishing."[10] Building on what they knew from John about Jesus, Paul explained the gospel to them, which they embraced and, unlike Apollos and the apostles, were baptized in his name. Paul, paralleling Peter (8:17), then placed his hands on them and the Spirit descended (19:5), and, like Acts 2, they spoke in tongues and prophesied. This is the only account of rebaptism and is the last mention of tongues.

This story raises many questions. How could they be Christians without the Spirit or were they at best nominal Christians or just followers of John?[11] Still again, is this evidence in support of the Pentecostal understanding of the baptism in the Holy Spirit? The brevity of the story causes the commentators to be very divided and makes dogmatic statements impossible. However, the twelve are not called disciples of John. The Spirit is always a gift from Jesus, but Acts gives no absolute pattern to how it is given. There is a clear similarity between effectively commissioning this twelve through baptism and the receipt of the Spirit and to Jesus' calling of the twelve apostles (Luke 6:13)[12] How much, if anything, we should read into the similarity is unclear, but this "mini-Pentecost"[13] was a reminder that the mission of the twelve extended to gentiles (Luke 9:1–6).

PAUL IS OPPOSED BUT GOD BLESSES (19:8–12)

Paul spent three months in the synagogue fearlessly trying to convince the Jews about the kingdom, an inseparable part of the gospel. This was a long time for Paul. The favorable reception from his first visit has

10. Bock, Acts, 599,

11. Larkin, *Acts*, 273.

12. Edwards, "Similarities," 491–92.

13. Stott, *Message of Acts*, 305. He points out that the modern church will not encounter Samaritans and disciples of John.

disappeared. The vitriol of this rejection led to severe testing from plots while in the city (20:19) and almost saw Paul killed in Jerusalem (21:27). They refused to believe, slandering the message before others. They completely rejected their Messiah as they hardened their hearts like Pharaoh (Exod 8:15; 9:35) and the children of Israel in the wilderness (Ps 95:7–8). However, some did believe, and Paul took them to the lecture hall (or school) of Tyrannus[14] where he spoke daily. Perhaps public lecturing avoided Roman restrictions on meetings. Paul's stamina and commitment must have been phenomenal to earn a living and lecture daily.[15] His ministry in Ephesus ran into its third year (20:31),[16] though during this time Paul made his "painful visit" to Corinth (2 Cor 2:1; 12:14; 13:1), but Luke does not record it.

Paul's ministry has been accompanied by miracles but what happened in Ephesus, the home of the occult and Artemis, took things to a different level (19:11), and Paul commented on them in his letters (2 Cor 12:12; Rom 15:18–19). Healings are distinguished from exorcisms (19:12). Like the woman with the hemorrhage, healing only required touching the sweatbands and aprons[17] that Paul used in his tentmaking (Luke 8:44). Likely, God was "meeting the needs of those people at the level of their understanding" rather than a model for all times. (The use of sweatbands could have been part of the extraordinary nature of the miracles.)[18] Ephesians adorned Artemis's image with expensive clothes and displayed them in her processions. They were considered holy and carried her power and virtue. By contrast, the "apostle's poor textiles in the face of the splendor of the patroness of Ephesus constitutes a profound theological statement. This statement not only offers an implicit critique

14. Was this his birth name or the name given to him by his students? Bruce, *Acts*, 1954, 388n18.

15. The Western text says that Paul preached from 11 a.m. to 4 p.m., i.e., the siesta time. Though not part of the original text, it is probably correct. It has been said that more people would be asleep at 1 p.m. than 1 a.m., so Paul's message must have had an impact for people to give up their siesta. Bruce, *Acts*, 1954, 389.

16. Churches were established at Colossae, Hierapolis and Laodicea at this time, but no information is given.

17. The "sweatband" was a common part of a speaker's attire and the context is of Paul being an orator. The word for "apron" could also be a belt. Strelan, "Paul's Aprons," 157. The "apron" is called a "semi-girdle," and the girdle had cultic significance especially to speed up childbirth and given as thanks to Artemis after the first intercourse. Strelan, "Paul's Aprons," 157; Stubbersfield, *Ephesus*, 51.

18. Longenecker, "Acts," 9:496.

of pagan worship, but also firmly establishes in the apostle's hands a humble and unobtrusive, yet highly effective, means of salvation."[19]

THE JEWISH EXORCISTS ARE HUMILIATED AND ITS AFTERMATH (19:13–20)

The fourth and fifth recorded encounter of the gospel with the occult along with the final summary of the progress of the gospel (19:20) are found in this passage. Ephesus was renowned for the temple of Artemis, one of the seven wonders of the ancient world, and as a center for magic and the occult. Magical formulas written on papyri were known as "Ephesian letters." In this city, the gospel came face to face with popular, personal religious practice of magic (19:11–19) and institutional religion through the famous temple of Artemus (19:23–41).

The power of God is prominent in this passage. It was preceded by miracles or acts of power and verse 20 closes with "become strong" after saying that the word of the Lord was growing mightily. Paul working alone through faith would cast out demons, his success demonstrating God's favor. But when seven Jewish exorcists fraudulently tried to use the names of Jesus and Paul, they were "overpowered" (19:16). Jewish practitioners of magic were especially valued as they knew the unspoken name of God, so giving their spells more power.[20] It is not surprising that the sons of Sceva, who claimed connection with a chief priest,[21] would use the names of Jesus and Paul given the powerful deeds that were being performed by him. Magical texts revealed that the names of the various gods could be heaped up with an attempt to make their spells and incantations more powerful.[22] There was power in the name of Jesus but only when it is used by faithful servants and received in faith, but the exorcists had no connection with Jesus.[23] Jesus they knew. Paul they knew about. But who were these imposters (19:15)? Luke describes the nakedness and bleeding of the sons of Sceva in a similar way to the demoniac Legion who rushed to meet Jesus in the region of the Gadarenes (Luke 8:27).

19. Marcello, "Artemis' Garments," 321.

20. Bruce, *Acts*, 1954, 390.

21. Likely a bogus advertising claim.

22. Arnold, *Ephesian Power*, 18.

23. In Luke 9:49–50 exorcists not associated with the disciples were using the name of Jesus, and he allowed that presumably because it was done with faith.

"Who but 'Jesus whom Paul preaches' had the power to use even hostile spirits to punish people he tried to manipulate and exploit his name in a magical incantation."[24]

The disgrace of Sceva's sons when they tried to use the name of Jesus without any allegiance to him, or the authority to do so, would have helped convince the Ephesian believers that they could not maintain dual loyalties. Believers were prepared to publicly burn their secret, expensive[25] magical books, which shows how deeply and powerfully the word of the Lord had impacted that pagan city and the growing maturity of the believers (19:19).[26] Despite the demonstrations of power, Luke emphasizes that it was the word of the Lord that transformed hearts and liberated from the counterfeits for which Ephesus was renowned (19:20). From verse 19 through to the end of Acts, Paul is not so much engaged in preaching the gospel but in publicly defending it.

PAUL SENSES GOD'S LEADING TO LEAVE EPHESUS (19:21–22)

Paul's three-year ministry (20:31) did not go unnoticed. It was resisted and slandered by the Jews (19:9), attempted to be imitated by the exorcists (19:13–16), embraced by gentiles formally engaged in the occult (19:18–19), and honored by Jew and Greek (19:17). This was only possible because Paul, whenever possible, immersed himself in a community for a long time and engaged with it using reasoned arguments. Stott compares this to modern gorilla-like evangelism based on an emotional response with minimal follow up.[27] But Paul sensed his time was concluding as his role in the areas he evangelized was completed (Rom 15:23), so he became "resolved in the Spirit" (19:21) to travel to Rome via Jerusalem after a brief detour through Greece and Macedonia (19:21). Paul would not build on another's foundations (Rom 15:20), so Rome with an established church was only intended as a visit; Spain was the destination (Rom 15:24, 28). The near riot, a precursor of the suffering that awaits

24. Johnson, *Message of Act*, 181.

25. Fifty thousand denarii, which were more common in Ephesus over drachmas, represented fifty thousand days wages. Bock, *Acts*, 605.

26. Johnson, *Message of Act*, 181.

27. Stott, *Message of Acts*, 311–14. He also notes that the churches now replace the synagogue as a haven for the religious but unconverted that must be evangelized.

Paul in Palestine and in Rome, may well have confirmed the Spirit's leading that his time in the city had ended.[28]

Though not mentioned in Acts, a major consideration for Paul was an offering for the Jerusalem church, so he sent Timothy and Erastus to Macedonia (1 Cor 16:1–4; 2 Cor 8–9) in part to prepare for this. As Acts concludes, Luke focused on Paul but there is no reason to believe he worked alone, especially as he had a team-ministry approach. After Paul's brief time in Macedonia and Greece the emphasis will be on Paul's determination to return to Jerusalem and subsequent imprisonment.

THE RIOT IN EPHESUS (19:23–41)

The temple of Artemis in Ephesus was three times the size of the Parthenon. Antipater of Sidon, (second century BC), who compiled the famous seven wonders of the ancient world, said of the temple of Artemis,

> I have set eyes on the wall of lofty Babylon on which is a road for chariots, and the statue of Zeus by the Alpheus, and the hanging gardens, and the colossus of the Sun, and the huge labor of the high pyramids, and the vast tomb of Mausolus; but when I saw the house of Artemis that mounted to the clouds, those other marvels lost their brilliancy, and I said, "Lo, apart from Olympus, the sun never looked on aught (anything) so grand."[29]

Ephesian Artemis had two faces. In her traditional Greek form, she skirts over the mountains in a light tunic; in the other she stands rigidly imprisoned in a ponderously embroidered pillar like garment. She seems to struggle to lift her arms, heavily weighed down by what the fathers of the church identified as breasts, and unable to take a step. Whatever the body language involved, both forms apparently belonged to the same person, at least in the late Hellenistic and Roman period.[30]

It was inevitable that the authority of Jesus would clash with that of Artemis.[31] The city's devotion to Artemis cannot be underestimated. It had been bypassed in 29 BC when a temple to Augustus was built in the smaller city of Pergamum and again in AD 26 for smaller Smyrna.

28. Johnson, *Message*, 201.
29. Antipater of Sidon, *Anth. Pal.* 3.9.58.
30. Brenk, "Artemis," 157.
31. Stott, *Message of Acts*, 308.

The whole city considered itself as the "temple warden," the protector of Artemis.[32] As an itinerant tentmaker and rabbi, Paul was completely powerless to directly confront one of the most powerful, famous, and entrenched pagan centers of the ancient world. As an evangelist for the resurrected Christ, sent and empowered by the Spirit, "with only the 'foolish' and 'weak' proclamation of his cross,"[33] Paul won over many people. When the archaeologist found the great temple, the remains were six meters under the surface of the swamp on which it was built.

The silversmith Demetrius's motive was greed following the declining sales of silver shrines of Artemis (19:24). Once again, finances come before promoting the gospel. Greed was transformed into concern for the honor of Artemis and her temple (19:27), so he had no problem finding supporters among his trade and the populace. They dragged Paul's Macedonian companions Gaius and Aristarchus to the theater[34] (19:29). However, most did not even know why they had gathered there (19:32). When they heard the accusations against Artemis, they were furious and began shouting, using words similar to the response to Jesus in the synagogue in Nazareth.[35] The response of Jews to Jesus's inaugural sermon becomes a pattern for the response to the proclamation of the gospel in both Palestine and the diaspora. (There was also a similar reaction in Antioch of Pisidia [14:5]).

Paul was friends with the Asiarchs (19:31) and followed their pleadings not to go to the theater. The exact role of the Asiarchs is not known but they were very senior and well-connected public officials. Part of their role was to organize games, at their own expense, in honor of the gods and Rome.[36] The Asiarchs had inadvertently became the best defense possible for Paul and Christians as they would not befriend those that could be a threat to Rome.[37] Paul's faith did not restrict him to an exclusive band of believers but allowed him friendships across faith and status. Aquilla and Priscilla likely remained for four or five years in Ephesus, meaning they would have been in the city for the riot. This may be the time when Paul feared for his life (2 Cor 1:8–10), and they risked

32. This is explained in my book *Ephesus: The Nursery of Christianity.*

33. Johnson, *Message of Acts*, 207.

34. The stadium is in a remarkable state of preservation. It had a seating capacity of twenty-five thousand.

35. Edwards, "Parallels," 491–92.

36. Friesen, "Asiarchs," 286–87.

37. Haenchen, *Acts*, 578.

their life for him (Rom 16:4). The Jews pushed forward Alexander,[38] but it is not certain who he was (19:33). Perhaps he was wanting to make a distinction between Jew and Christian, so the riot did not spill over to them. The uneasy peace between Greek and Jew and their religious views had been disturbed by Paul's presence. Yet, as the commentator Haenchen noted, "In final analysis the only thing heathenism can do against Paul is to shout itself hoarse."[39]

What the town clerk, the elected and highest official,[40] meant by the image of Artemis that fell from heaven[41] is conjecture, but he was likely saying that whatever Paul may have said about other gods did not apply to Artemis. (Paul is likely to have said something similar about Artemis as he did in Athens about God not living in temples made by human hands [17:24]). Unlike Demetrius, the city clerk had underestimated the movement afoot, but amid all the confusion (19:32), he did understand it was the opponents of Paul that were causing disruption and breaking the law. Luke was showing that Rome had no case against Paul. If the silversmiths had an argument, it could have been taken before the proconsuls.[42] Alternatively, they could take the matter to the assembly, the second legal system in a free Greek city. Rome's response to a riot could be severe. However, it would be doomed to fail as they had not robbed the temple or blasphemed Artemis.

PAUL TRAVELS THROUGH GREECE BACK TO ASIA (20:1–16)

After the commotion had subsided, Paul, perhaps in hiding,[43] called the disciples and bade them farewell, leaving for Macedonia where he encouraged the believers by speaking God's word to them (20:2), and moving onto Greece (likely Achaea) where he spent the winter months

38. Alexander was a common name so there is no way of knowing if this is the same person/s that shipwrecked his faith and caused Paul harm (1 Tim 1:19–20; 2 Tim 4:14).

39. Haenchen, *Acts*, 578.

40. He was the interface between the Roman and civic administration and any repercussions would be upon his head. Bruce, *Acts*, 1954, 401.

41. Ancient writers make similar references to images not made by hand in other cities, but none mention Ephesus.

42. There was only one proconsul. Bruce suggests that the "generalizing plural" may refer to the time between the murder of the sitting proconsul ordered by Nero's mother in AD 54 and his replacement, so giving a possible fixed date. Bruce, *Spreading Flame*, 133–34.

43. Stott, *Message of Acts*, 315.

(20:2) when navigation was not permitted. This is either AD 55–56 or AD 56–57 and during this time Paul wrote Romans. Titus had made an earlier trip to Greece and Corinth (2 Cor 1–9), possibly with the lost "Epistle of Tears," to confront the church (2 Cor 2:4). He had hoped to meet with Titus at Troas, but his delay caused Paul so much disquiet that he had to leave, despite the Lord opening a door for him (2 Cor 2:12–13). Paul moved on but met Titus in Macedonia where he had good news about the Corinthian church (2 Cor 2:13; 7:5–16). As Paul travelled, he continued the collection for the Jerusalem church (Rom 15:25–26; 2 Cor 8:16–24). The offering was intended to acknowledge the spiritual support of Jerusalem by returning physical support. Perhaps Luke did not mention the offering because his focus has become the "journey to divine destiny in Jerusalem and on to Rome."[44] Paul's trip to Jerusalem appears to roughly parallel that of Jesus and so reminiscent of the suffering servant.[45] The similarities include the following:

- Travelling with a group of disciples (Acts 20:4–5; Luke 10:38)
- Hostile Jews opposed and plotted to kill him (Acts 20:3; Luke 11:53–4)
- Made three predictions of his suffering (Acts 20:22–23; 21:4, 11; Luke 9:22, 44, 18:31–32)
- To be handed over to gentiles (Acts 21:11; Luke 18:32)
- Willing to lay down his life (Acts 20:24; 21:13; Luke 12:50; 22:19; 23:46)
- Determined not to be deflected (Acts 20:24; 21:13; Luke 9:51)
- Abandonment to God's will (Acts 21:14; Luke 22:42)[46]
- Jesus and Paul have a farewell discourse (Acts 29:17–38; Luke 22:14–38)

As we have seen a number of times in Acts, as the master, so the servant and his way of suffering continues in the church.

A plot against Paul caused him to abandon a sea journey[47] back to Syria so he took the overland route to Macedonia (20:3), sending his

44. Bock, *Acts*, 617.

45. Longenecker, "Acts," 9:515.

46. Stott, *Message of Acts*, 315.

47. Bruce suggests that this may have been a pilgrim ship, which explains the risk. Bruce *Acts*, 1954, 405.

seven gentile companions ahead of him to Troas. They were from the areas Paul evangelized and likely represented the churches that donated towards the offering:

- Macedonia (Sopater son of Pyrrhus from Berea, Aristarchus and Secundus from Thessalonica)
- Galatia (Gaius from Derbe, Timothy from Lystra)
- The Province of Asia (Tychicus and Trophimus) (20:4)

Corinth may have been represented by Titus who, with two trusted brothers, collected their offering (2 Cor 8:18) and Philippi by Paul or Luke. The "we" sections start where they left off, in Philippi (20:6). Luke joined Paul along with other unnamed companions. Surprisingly, Titus is not mentioned, though Ramsay suggested that Titus was the brother of Luke and is represented in the "we" sections.[48] Though told briefly, this trip may have taken one to two years and his journey taken him as far as Illyricum (Rom 15:19). Before sailing from Philippi to Troas, Paul, who is still observing the Jewish feasts, observed Passover (20:6) and was rushing to be in Jerusalem for Pentecost (20:16) fifty days later.

Paul spent a week in Troas (20:9), and on the first day of the week the church gathered to break bread, the first mention of a church meeting on a Sunday and suggests the early importance of both word and sacrament and this day. Paul spoke, likely intermixed with discussion,[49] until midnight[50] in a third story room with many lights (probably torches). This would have affected the air quality and is possibly why a young boy (20:12),[51] Eutychus, was seated in a window (20:9). Many, and quite likely Eutychus included, would not have been masters of their time, so a night meeting was appropriate, even though many would have already worked from dawn to sunset.[52] Falling asleep, he fell to the ground. Physician Luke's trained eye assessed he was dead (20:9), hardly the "lucky one,"[53] which his name means. After putting his arms around him, Paul told

48. Ramsay, *St. Paul*, 390. He based this on a comment by Eusebius and suggests that as Luke did not give his own name, he also excluded his relatives also.

49. Stott, *Message of Acts*, 321.

50. By Jewish reckoning, this would be Saturday evening, but by Roman it would be Sunday evening. While Roman is more likely, there is no certainty.

51. Likely between eight and fourteen. Philo, *Creation*, 36.

52. Bruce *Acts*, 1954, 408.

53. Fitzmyer, *Acts*, 667.

them not to be alarmed as he was alive; "soul" here refers to his whole being. It may still have been some time till he regained consciousness.[54] Luke uses ironic understatement to express the believers' joy: "They were not a little comforted" (20:12). Paul then broke bread and continued talking till daybreak.

This resuscitation recalls Jesus with the widow of Nain, Jairus's daughter, Lazarus (Luke 7:11–15; 8:49–56; John 11:38–44), and Peter (Acts 9:36–41), but the similarity is stronger with Elijah and Elisha (1 Kgs 17:19–22; 2 Kgs 4:34–35). This is the last miracle in Acts. The Ephesians fixated on a meteorite (likely) that fell from the sky, but when a boy fell and is restored to life it is only a "brief, temporary interruption in the main business of the church."[55] However, as Paul's becomes aware of the troubles facing him as he traveled to Jerusalem he does not expect or pray for a miraculous deliverance for himself.

Paul's coworkers sailed for Assos, thirty-two kilometers distant, but he stayed on in Troas, then traveled overland to meet them (20:13). Luke does not give a reason, but perhaps it was to confirm Eutychus's health, for his own safety (20:3), or even to contemplate the warnings he received. They all then sailed seventy kilometers to Mitylene, the main city of Lesbos, and over succeeding days they were off to Chios (opposite Smyrna), then Samos, intentionally avoiding Ephesus, which was roughly fifty kilometers north, and then to Miletus. Short one day trips were typical of ancient navigation and extra care was needed here as the winds were difficult and the coasts rocky.[56] There was probably a month left to travel one thousand kilometers.

PAUL'S FAREWELL TO THE EPHESIAN ELDERS (20:17–38)

On landing at Miletus, God's providence around the availability of ships[57] allowed Paul at least three days' delay in his rushed timetable (20:38) to send for the Ephesian elders. Paul had labored in Ephesus longer than in any other missionary church but had been away from there for one to two years. Luke recorded three public speeches of Paul: first to the

54. Bruce, *Acts*, 1954, 408.

55. Gooding, *True to the Faith*, 356.

56. They could die off to a dead calm in the evening. Ramsey, *St. Paul*, 293.

57. The turnaround, using the same ship, could involve unloading and carefully stowing perhaps two to three hundred tons of cargo and all by hand.

Jews in Antioch (13:16–41), then to the gentiles in Athens (17:22–31), and finally to Christian leaders in Miletus.[58] While there are at least four more years of Paul's life remaining in the Acts record, the farewell to the elders marks the closing of his missionary career and pointed to his death. The emotion and difficulty behind the words can be seen in Paul's many repetitions.

Luke had previously recorded the Last Supper as the end of Jesus' ministry and the shift of leadership to the apostles and now Paul's address points to "the establishment of order and authority for the approaching postapostolic age."[59] Paul's address is strongly trinitarian and urged them to rely on God's plans for them (20:27), which turned the elders away from himself. The Ephesian church they served was not like the costly pagan temples built in marble by enslaved artisans to contain lifeless idols and whose ministers had prestige. The church was of infinite value as it was purchased with God's blood. Paul reminded the elders that their God was alive and active, having equipped his church with the word of grace (20:32), and provided the Spirit (20:28) and the presence of Jesus who abided with them no matter how difficult things become. The direct guidance of an apostle was no longer needed to lead God's flock as they had been prepared as shepherds by Paul's example and sound teaching.

God	Spirit	Jesus
Repentance toward God (20:21)	Bound by the Spirit (20:22)	Faith in our Lord Jesus (20:21)
The good news of God's grace (20:24)	The Holy Spirit keeps testifying to me (20:23)	The ministry I received from the Lord Jesus (20:24)
The whole plan of God (20:27)		
The church of God (20:28)	The Holy Spirit has placed you as overseers (20:28)	Obtained by his own blood (20:28)
I entrust you to God (20:32)		Remember the words of the Lord Jesus (20:35)

Table 11. References to God, Spirit, and Jesus in Paul's farewell address to the Ephesians[60]

58. His farewell has content similar to his Letters, which is hardly surprising as the audiences are similar.

59. McGee, "Transitioning Authority," 212.

60. Petersen, "Saying Farewell," 56.

Paul's farewell started and closed by reminding the elders what they knew (20:18–21, 31, 33). They knew how Paul lived (20:18) and saw his example of faithful servant ministry in Ephesus. They knew his ministry was characterized by humility and sorrow in the face of great opposition (20:19). Yet, despite this opposition, Paul did not "shrink back" (20:20, 27) from preaching publicly and door-to-door what would be of benefit to them (20:20). This preparation was critical for the elders as they, in turn, could expect tribulation for the faith also.[61] Thirteen verses are given to how to defend the church and only four are given to the command to do so.[62] This was very different to the defense of Artemis by Demetrius (19:21–41). Despite the opposition, Paul had not hesitated (20:20) and had been thorough in his teaching, coverage, and methods[63] he used to preach a message that benefited Jew and Greek alike. It was summarized in the call to turn to God in repentance and to also have faith in the Lord Jesus (20:21; 1 Thess 1:9–19; 1 Cor 9:20–23). Repentance, a change in direction in a person's relationship with God, requires faith in Jesus; the two cannot be separated.

In verses 22–26, Paul moved to what he knew. The Spirit had warned him in all the cities he passed through that imprisonment and trouble await in Jerusalem (20:23), yet that same Spirit had taken him captive (20:22) and was leading him onward (20:23). While he requested prayer for his future (Rom 15:30–31), he did not consider the his "soul" (again the whole person) had any value other than what it did in completion of the service allotted to him by the Lord Jesus: to declare the gospel of the grace of God (20:24). He likened his life to an athlete completing a race (20:24; 2 Tim 4:7). He knew that the ordeal would be so severe that he would never see them again (20:25), but it would appear he read too much into the prophecies. The travels as indicated by Paul's fourth missionary journey, the subject of my final chapter, meant that he must have gone out of his way not to reach Ephesus again. However, he had told the elders all they needed to know to walk with God. He has been a successful watchman (Ezek 3:15–21; 33:4), fulfilling his task as "a pure offering or an act of worship done in cultic purity" (20:26).[64] His conscience is clean (20:26), which he will again declare before the Sanhedrin and Felix.

61. Attempts may already be underway to undermine Paul, which would explain why he was reminding them of the way he ministered.

62. Gooding, *True to the Faith*, 356–57.

63. Stott, *Message of Acts*, 328.

64. Bock, *Acts*, 629.

Like his master who sent out his disciples as sheep among wolves (Luke 10:3), Paul also warned about wolves who would savage the flock and spare no one (20:29). Attacks so far have been from outside the church, but these attacks will come from within by the trusted leadership. These fears were borne out and Paul later gave Timothy directions in the Pastoral Epistles on how to repair the damage. John also experienced issues in Ephesus, and God warned that church in Revelation because they left their first love (Rev 2:1–7). Despite being appointed to that role by the Spirit (20:28), from among those elders would emerge men who would "twist" the straight and true way of the gospel to attract their own disciples (20:30). These were men known to Paul throughout his three years in Ephesus (20:31) and were likely appointed by him, yet even he could not discern who among the shepherds were in fact "wolves." (This may be a reflection of Judas among the twelve.) The elders were to be on guard (20:28, 31), for themselves first and as guardians of the teachings they received from Paul and then for the flock. He reminded them of his constant example, warning them day and night with tears (20:31), a pattern they were expected to follow.

Luke did not portray "any kind of Apostolic succession from the past, nor does he lie down what is to be done in the future."[65] Outside of Acts 20:17–38, he has shown very little interest in the way the church was organized and its leadership. What this passage does show is the need for a team of "shepherds" (20:28) that act as guardians and protectors[66] (Phil 1:1; 1 Tim 3:2; Titus 1:7), not a single bishop[67] caring for God's flock purchased with his own blood. Paul emphasized the death of Jesus as foundational to the elders' task because it established the immense value of the church which was bought with blood. Whose blood it was is not stated. It could be his own son's, i.e., Jesus',[68] or God's own blood[69] where the two are not distinguished. Either way, it is the price God had paid to redeem it (20:28). The psalmist had also used this metaphor of purchasing to describe the exodus (Ps 74:1–2).[70] Verse 28 is the only place in Acts where the death of Jesus for the sins of believers is mentioned. However

65. Marshall, *Fresh Look*, 51.

66. BAGD, "ἐπισκόπους," 299.2.

67. I expand on this in Stubbersfield, *Pastoral Epistles*, 84–118.

68. Bock, *Acts*, 630.

69. Lenski, *Acts*, 849. He said, "When those who accept the deity of Jesus shrink from the expression 'the blood of God,' they are moved by an unnecessary timidity."

70. Johnson, *Message of Acts*, 149.

Paul could sum up salvation, the restoration of a broken relationship initiated by God through substitution, without referring to the cross.[71]

Like Samuel (1 Sam 12:1–3), Paul reminded the elders that he did not covet anything of theirs (20:33). An "inheritance," something that transcends this world, was promised to those who were sanctified (20:32; 26:18; 1 Cor 1:2; 5:11; 1 Thess 5:11), which was of more value than the wealth of those he, and they, serve. His companions likewise were supported by Paul and showed a similar spirit (20:34).[72] With a rare quotation of Jesus outside of the Gospels,[73] Paul reminded them that "it was more blessed to give than receive" (20:35) and that labors in serving the weak were an example of how to fulfill the Lord's command. Reflecting how solemn this departure was, they kneeled to pray,[74] and then all wept and embraced, heartbroken by the thought of not seeing each other again. With that they escorted him to the ship. If he escaped his trials, the western Mediterranean was to be the intended focus as his work in the east was complete (Rom 15:23–4).

As his journey to Jerusalem mirrors that of Jesus, so Paul's farewell speech also mirrors that of Jesus prior to his arrest (refer to Table 11 below). The linguistic parallels are even stronger in his defense before Agrippa in chapter 26.

Parallel	Acts	Luke
Common words: "take heed," "watch"	20:28, 31	21:34, 36
Belief that the end is near	20:25	22:15–16
Predictions of impending suffering	20:23	22:15
Reminders that they have been servants	20:19, 24	22:27
Recollections of past trials	20:19	22:28
Anticipation of blessings in the kingdom of God	20:32	22:29–30
Realization of the fulfillment of God's plan	20:24	22:37
Traitor(s) in their midst[75]	20:30	22:4–6

Table 12. Parallels to the pre-arrest addresses of Jesus and Paul

71. Marshall, *Fresh Look*, 62.

72. Elsewhere Paul defends the right of an evangelist to be supported (1 Cor 9:1–14; 1 Tim 5:17–18); he voluntarily gave up that right himself.

73. Luke noted in the introduction to his Gospel that many people had written accounts of the life of Jesus.

74. Jews normally stood to pray, e.g. Matt 5:5–6.

75. Edwards, "Parallels and Patterns," 494. Reference to Judas by author.

PAUL TRAVELS FROM MILETUS TO CAESAREA (21:1–14)

After a separation that tore at the emotions of the elders and Paul's group, Luke described how their ship hugged the coast as they sailed with the wind. His itinerary and brief travel notes describe how, after travelling about 64 kilometers, they sailed past the island of Cos, on the second day past Rhodes (another 134 kilometers distant), and then on to Patara (a further 97 kilometers). Patara was a major Lycian port on the southwest cost of Asia Minor that serviced the Eastern and Western Mediterranean, and it is likely that Paul took a larger ocean-going ship from there to Tyre in Phoenicia (about 645 kilometers). Without having to use smaller coastal traders or putting into Cyprus saved considerable time, which then allowed extended stays when they reached Phoenicia. Tyre, the first stopover, had become a Roman colony in 64 BC and was famous for its purple production. It was described by Josephus as being "notoriously our most bitter enemy,"[76] yet Jesus still ministered there (Matt 15: 21–28: Mark 7:24–37). Possibly hundreds of tons of cargo had to be unloaded then safely stowed by hand, which allowed Paul a full week to be with the believers. They still had roughly 160 kilometers to travel before reaching Jerusalem. His extended stays with the Christians in Tyre and Caesarea would have helped refresh and fortify him for the trials ahead.[77]

There would have been many Christians, as roughly twenty years earlier (11:19) the Hellenists fleeing persecution first evangelized that area where there were many Jews. The Spirit influenced the disciples (not a designated prophet as in 21:10) to warn Paul not to set foot in Jerusalem. But Paul was on a journey, which he likely felt was prompted by the Spirit (19:21), and as he progressed on his way he became captured by the same Spirit not to change his plans. Paul did not reject the prophetic utterances as such; the disciples had correctly discerned what would happen, but the inference they drew was incorrect. Reminiscent of the departure in Miletus, after Paul and the believers along with their families went to the shore, they again kneeled to pray, said their goodbyes, and took a ship to Ptolemais (Old Testament Acco and modern Acre, forty kilometers south). There they stayed a day, greeting the believers (21:7). On the following day they sailed (or perhaps walked) to the Roman provincial

76. Josephus, *Ag. Ap.* 1.13.

77. Stott, *Message of Acts*, 333.

capital and port for Jerusalem—Caesarea[78]—a further sixty-four kilometers south and stayed for perhaps as long as two weeks with Philip, one of the seven (6:5; 8:5). Being within striking distance of Jerusalem, he could control his own itinerary so he could be in Jerusalem for Pentecost (20:16).

Philip, known as "the evangelist" (21:8) to distinguish him from the apostle,[79] had four unmarried daughters who all prophesied but are not called "prophetesses." Prophecy was the greatest of all the gifts (1 Cor 14:1) and given without distinction to men and women, and their piety is implied by saying they were virgins.[80] However, it was Agabus, who is called a "prophet," that warned Paul after he came down from Judea (21:10; i.e., the ancient designation, not the Roman province). He had earlier warned about the famine (11:28). Like an Old Testament prophet (1 Kgs 11:29–33; Isa 20:2–6; Ezek 4:1–8), he predicted and acted out Paul's binding by the religious authorities before being given over to the gentiles (21:10–11). Like master, like servant; Agabus's warning used words reminiscent of Jesus' prediction of his imprisonment (Mark 10:33) and Paul's response was very close to Peter's failed claim to be willing to die with Jesus (Luke 22:33). However, showing discernment, Agabus did not urge Paul not to go to Jerusalem, but the believers did, including his companions (21:12). They appear silent on the matter up to now and this is the last chance to dissuade Paul. Their pleadings pounded Paul's emotions as he was fully aware that trials, so severe that it could cost his life, were ahead (20:22–4), and he was ready to face them for the name of Jesus (21:13). This name, which had proven powerful and brought deliverance for the suffering (3:6) and sin (4:12) and whose use the Sanhedrin tried to stop being used (4:14), could also lead through a path of suffering. This isn't human bravery, but a spirituality empowered by the knowledge of what death would bring (2 Tim 4:8) and a confidence that God can only do good to those that love him (Rom 8:28).[81] Like Jesus who set the example in the Garden of Gethsemane and submitted to his Father's will

78. The city is significant for Luke. The references in his Gospel are 8:40; 9:30; 10:1, 24; 11:11; 12:19; 18:22; 21:16; 23:23; 25:1, 4, 6, 13.

79. The two did get confused in later church history. See, e.g., Eusebius, *Eccl. Hist.* 3:31.2–5 (*NPNF*² 1:162–63).

80. Eusebius said that Philip and his daughters moved to Hierapolis in the province of Asia. Some of the daughters lived to a great age and became a source for Papias's five lost books on "Our Lord's Sayings." Eusebius, *Eccl. Hist.* 3:39 (*NPNF*² 1:170–73). Likewise, they and Philip would have been a source for Luke.

81. Lenski, *Acts*, 871–72.

(Luke 22:42), when they saw that Paul would not be diverted, they then committed him to the Lord's will (21:14). Paul was being driven willingly to his destiny in Jerusalem (refer to , Table 12, and Table 13). For Paul, it was vitally important that the offering be delivered personally.

PAUL IS URGED TO TAKE A VOW TO SHOW LOYALTY TO THE LAW (21:15–26)

Some of the disciples from Caesarea accompanied Paul and his eight companions (20:4) on the roughly one hundred kilometers to Jerusalem where they stayed with Mnason, a Jewish believer from Cyprus and one of the original disciples. With that, the third missionary journey that mentioned fifteen administrative districts ended. The following day, with Peter and John presumably no longer in Jerusalem, the group went to see James and the elders[82] where Paul told them everything that God had done through his ministry to the gentiles, backed up by the evidence of his companions. Despite Paul's tireless efforts, it was always God who acted (14:27; 15:12; 20:24). The leaders praised God for the gentile ministry (21:20), and, despite the Lord's followers earlier giving Paul and his gentile companions a warm welcome[83] (21:17), likely the old prejudices were not too far from the surface. Presumably Mnason, a Cypriot, was a Hellenist, so the presence of gentiles in his home may have been less of a concern.[84]. As the story progresses, names become far more prominent, even to incidental characters like Mnason and the accusing solicitor. While there was no certainty Acts was part of Paul's defense, the extra information would have been helpful in defending Christianity among the public in Rome. The "we" sections end in verse 18, but Luke must have stayed nearby as he accompanied Paul on the voyage to Rome. He may have been gathering material for his Gospel.

On an earlier visit, the only thing James had asked of Paul was that he remember the poor (Gal 2:10), which was in his nature to do. The offering was more than that though; the gentiles recognized the debt they owed the Jewish believers (Rom 15:27). They gave out of their

82. There had to be many of them given the believers numbered in the thousands (21:20).

83. Likely this welcome was from his host and a delegation from the church. The thousands of zealous Jewish believers had not heard that Paul had arrived and were very concerned about him (21:22).

84. Bock. *Acts*, 639.

transformed nature and were prepared to do so sacrificially. Paul had expressed concerns that this offering would not be received well (Rom 15:31), so he considered it extremely important that the motivation behind it be clearly understood. To that end, he delivered it personally, even postponing a planned visit to Rome on his way to evangelize Spain. Those concerns were well founded as James told Paul that there were thousands of believing Jews, in a city of likely thirty to fifty thousand, who were zealous for the Law[85] and who believed slanderous accounts about Paul. The murderous reaction of the mob in chapter 22 when Paul told them he was sent to the gentiles by God suggests a dangerous undercurrent among these believers against the gentile ministry.

They were told that Paul was teaching the diaspora Jews to turn away from the Law, not to have their children circumcised, and so live like God fearing gentiles (21:21). In this, they preferred not to trust their leaders—no light matter considering the reputation of James the Just. As well, they disapproved of Paul on grounds very similar to the accusation against Stephen, the first martyr (6:13). Yet there was a kernel of truth in the accusation as Jews of the dispersion, after becoming Christians, would have been forced to join predominantly gentile churches and so "lose the support base for their Jewish identity. . . . There would be a natural inclination to adapt to the ways of the Gentile majority in the Christian churches."[86] Paul's arrival was around AD 57 at a time of growing nationalism and mixed loyalties, at least for Christian Jews, in the buildup to the catastrophic revolt of AD 66–70. It was important that this accusation of disloyalty be addressed. Loyalty to a gentile mission and acceptance of an offering from them could have driven the wedge between the believing and unbelieving Jews even deeper.[87] For James, the elders, and Paul at least, this was not a salvation issue as there were no dissenting voices among them when Peter said at the Council of Jerusalem that both Jew and gentile are saved by grace (15:11).

Perhaps these concerns overshadowed any goodwill the offering may have engendered,[88] and the offering itself, which is not mentioned

85. An expression rich in nationalism as it was used in 1 Maccabees of the zealous Jews who stood against the impact of Hellenism on Judaism (1 Macc 2:42; 2 Macc 4:2).

86. Polhill, *Acts*, 448.

87. Longenecker, "Acts," 9:519. He suggests that the politics surrounding the offering may have been too difficult to explain to a gentile reader, so he omitted it. He also suggests that paying for the vow of the four men was the condition of accepting the offering. Longenecker, "Acts," 9:520.

88. Polhill, *Acts*, 446.

till 24:17, may have even been considered suspect by them. The moral code by which a gentile should live had been laid down by the Council some years earlier and James reminded Paul that the official position had not changed (21:25). What they were discussing was how a Jew should live in a Jewish community. James probably went too far when he said that he expected Paul to prove he always lived in obedience to the Law (21:24). Paul had shown that he was out of step with Judaism of the time and saw circumcision as of little value (Gal 6:15). But he was also concerned about Jewish matters and how the two covenants interacted with each other. He was also willing to compromise on matters that did not relate to salvation. He could make a vow (18:18), circumcise a travelling companion (16:3), and was anxious to be in Jerusalem for feasts. It is very likely that he was an observant Jew in Jewish communities, yet lived with more freedom outside (1 Cor 9:19–23). As Bruce observed, he was "not in bondage to his own emancipation."[89]

Given that Paul completed a vow on his last visit to Jerusalem, the solution put forward by the leadership was that Paul should make a public demonstration of his obedience to the Law by making a vow and also paying for that of four men who have also made a vow (21:23). The wisdom of agreeing to this is debated,[90] but when the Lord appeared to Paul in prison there was no rebuke, only encouragement as his actions had been met with approval (23:11). The vow of the four is likely associated with a Nazirite vow[91] because they needed to shave their heads, but the thirty-day minimum[92] precludes this for Paul. He may have had the option of sharing their vow for a week (21:27)[93] or, as he was approaching the temple, he may have chosen to cleanse himself after travelling in gentile territory (Num 19:11–3).[94] However, it remains a guess. Paying the vows of the poor was a recognized act of piety and Jewish identification,[95]

89. Bruce, *Acts*, 1954, 432n39.

90. See, e.g., Bruce, *Acts*, 1954, 432.

91. Bock, *Acts*, 648. The vow involved the person, and it could be a woman, abstaining from anything made from grapes, cutting their hair, and touching a dead body. This, in effect, made them priest-like for the period of the vow. When completed, the person's head was shaven. It was usually done to give thanks for healing, answered prayer, or as a sin offering. Barton and Blau, *Nazarite*, 9:195–97.

92. *M. Naz*, 6.3, 6.5—8.2.

93. Haenchen, *Acts*, 610n3.

94. *M. 'Ohal.* 2.3. Ceremonial purity would have been necessary to be at the completion ceremony of the four.

95. On returning from Rome, Agrippa 1 paid the expenses of Nazarites to gain

something which those that had doubted Paul had apparently not offered to do. The cost involved would have been staggering for an itinerant evangelist and required a strong commitment to Judaism.[96] Paul had to purchase a male and female lamb and a ram for each of the four at the highly inflated price of the "den of thieves" who sold approved animals in the temple, as well as a cereal and drink offering (Num 6:14–15). Luke did not record any controversy on day one.

favor with the Jews. Josephus, *Ant.* 19.6.1.

96. Polhill, *Acts*, 448–9.

14

Paul's Arrest and Imprisonment in Jerusalem (Acts 21:27—23:22)

THE RIOT IN THE TEMPLE (21:27–36)

A week later, Paul returned to the temple to complete the rites when Jews from Asia seized him, claiming first that he was doing just what the zealous believers were told: speaking against the Law and the temple. This is also similar to the charge against Stephen (6:11–14). They then added that he desecrated the temple by bringing a gentile into the main area (21:28).[1] They had seen him in the city with Trophimus, an Ephesian gentile, and wrongly assumed that he had brought him into the temple (21:29). Without evidence, the crowd reacted in a manner no better than that of the mob at Ephesus who tried to defend the sanctity of Artemis. Rather, any desecration was because a faithful worshiping Jew who was attempting to affirm that Jewishness was accused of denying it.[2] The city was in an uproar and quickly gathered and dragged Paul out of the temple to the court of the gentiles, and the gates were locked behind them (21:30).[3] They were intent on killing Paul and would have done so

1. Gentiles were permitted in an area outside the court of the women, but if they entered the main temple area they were subject to death, even if they were Roman citizens. Josephus, *J. W.* 6.2.4; 5.5.2. There were 1.4-meter-high stone warnings at the barrier, two of which have been found, which read, "No foreigner may enter within the barricade which surrounds the temple and enclosure. Anyone who is caught doing so will have himself to blame for his ensuing death." Bruce, *Acts*, 1954, 434. This is almost certainly what Paul was referring to in Eph 2:14 when he spoke of God breaking down the hostile dividing wall between Jew and gentile.

2. Larkin, *Acts*, 312.

3. Stott sees in the slamming of the gates the final Jewish rejection of the gospel and the vindication of turning to the gentiles. Stott, *Message of Acts*, 336.

had the Roman tribune, an officer in charge of one thousand men, not been alerted. He was later identified as Claudius Lysias (23:26; 24:22), and Luke portrays him as "an honest, open-minded Roman soldier,"[4] the very opposite of the mob. The fortress of Anatolia overlooked the temple (without violating its sanctity) and was connected to it by porticos, allowing the Romans to quickly quell any disturbance in the temple. He took at least two centurions and many soldiers with him and quickly stopped the beating (21:32).

The tribune's intent was to stop a riot, not rescue Paul who he assumed was a criminal, and on arresting the "culprit" had him secured with two chains for extra security, likely to a soldier on each side. There, in the middle of the mob, he started to question Paul (21:33). The crowd gave conflicting reports, and the uproar was such that the tribune could not make any decision, so he decided to take Paul back to the barracks (21:34). He could only do this by the soldiers physically carrying the prisoner through the still violent mob who were crying out for his death (21:36). The commentator Darrell Bock noted, "The bulk of Jerusalem has reacted now against Jesus, Peter, John, Steven, and Paul. For Acts this is the final key rejection of the gospel."[5] The city is left behind in God's salvation history despite a Christian community remaining there.[6] The Jewish mob had "seized" Paul and Luke uses the same word to describe how Rome "seized" Paul from them.[7] Romans had again been the protector of an innocent man against Jewish injustice and Paul would work within their legal system to secure his freedom. Nothing Paul has done has been a threat to Rome.

Paul had hitherto been on the offensive, being led to take bold moves at the leading of the Holy Spirit to evangelize much of Asia Minor and Greece. With his arrest, Paul moved to being the defender of the faith with five defenses ahead of him:

1. The Jewish crowd at the temple (22:1–22)
2. Before the Sanhedrin (23:1–10)
3. Before Festus (24:10–21)
4. Before Felix (25:1–12)

4. Stott, *Message of Acts*, 346.
5. Bock, *Acts*, 653.
6. Roloff, *Die Apostelgeschichte*, 318.
7. Stott, *Message of Acts*, 346.

5. Before Herod Agrippa (26:2–29)

A theme was developing in earlier chapters whereby the unbelieving Jews became increasingly hostile to Christianity, and Rome became as its inadvertent defender, even vindicating it in their courts. God had blessed the interaction between Christians and Rome—the first gentile convert was a centurion and Paul's first gentile convert was a Roman proconsul. In these remaining chapters, this theme will be expanded upon. The amount of space Luke devoted to Paul's defense speeches is more than his missionary addresses, which likely makes this the most important part of the book for him.[8] Ramsey called Paul's acquittal a formal charter of religious liberty for Christians.[9] Stott wisely observed that the only offense a devout Christian, operating within his conscience, should give the state is the offense of the cross.[10]

PAUL ADDRESSES THE MOB (21:37—22:22)

Using Greek, Paul courteously asked for permission to address the tribune. The officer was surprised that he could speak Greek as Aramaic was the common language in Judea. He may also have been impressed by his composure after what he had endured. This caused him to ask (and was probably expecting a positive answer) whether Paul was the Egyptian rebel that led four thousand assassins[11] into the desert (21:38). Josephus wrote about this unnamed insurrectionist who possibly only three years before Paul's arrest[12] claimed to be a prophet as well as a king.[13] He led his followers from the wilderness to the Mount of Olives and planned to take Jerusalem from there with the prediction that the walls would fall as with Jericho. Felix the governor (AD 52–60), who would later preside

8. Stott, *Message of Acts*, 338.

9. Ramsay, *St. Paul*, 308.

10. Stott, *Message of Acts*, 329.

11. The tribune uses the word *sikariōn*, from the Lattin for a "curved dagger." Josephus describes how, when the "dagger-men" appeared during Felix's rule, it was a time of great fear as many were killed. They would mingle with the crowds at festivals, etc., where they could strike with stealth using daggers hidden in their cloaks. The former high priest Jonathan was the first killed by them at the instigation of Felix. Josephus: *J. W.* 2.13.3; *Ant.* 20.8.5. This may be the group that intended to kill Paul in chapter 23.

12. Bruce, *Acts*, 1954, 436. The tribune would have had a physical description of the insurrectionist, and he or some of his men may have seen him.

13. Barnett, "Jewish Sign Prophets," 683.

over Paul, attacked them and those that were not killed or captured, scattered, but the Egyptian escaped, never to be heard of again.[14] The presence of this charlatan would definitely inflame the mob. Through this misidentification, Luke differentiated Christianity from the violent political movements that were afoot, showing it was no threat to Rome.

Instead of being an Egyptian, Paul told him with a note of pride that he was a citizen of Tarsus. He did not mention that he was a citizen of an even greater city, Rome, possibly as this would inflame the mob even further. The city was a major Cilician port with an economy based on agriculture and linen, and Paul's pride is hardly surprising as Strabo wrote of Tarsus being a flourishing and powerful city, ahead of Athens and Alexandria for its schools of philosophy and with many schools of rhetoric. While many left the city never to return, they always regarded it as their mother city.[15] Paul has shown himself as a cultured man, able to quote Greek poets and have high officials as friends. This may, in part, be due to his early upbringing in Tarsus with its love of learning.

Paul asked to address the crowd, and, perhaps hoping to calm the situation through them realizing that they also misidentified the man or seeking to gain more information, he allowed it. He motioned to the mob and possibly with help from the soldiers, there was relative silence. When they heard him start his defense in Aramaic (more likely than Hebrew, which would have been less understood) with "brothers and fathers" (22:1), they became very quiet (22:2). It was an affectionate way to describe those who were trying to tear him apart. Likely, Paul's motive was his love for his Jewish brothers who, "in their raw unredeemed human nature,"[16] were no harder to reach than he was. The first part of Paul's speech (22:3–5) showed how he was where they are by stressing his zeal for Judaism before becoming a follower of the Way. It was so impressive that "Paul could sum up the measure of his devotion simply by stating his affiliation with [the Pharisee] sect"[17] and his education in Jerusalem under Gamaliel (22:3). He still considered himself a "Hebrew of Hebrews" (Phil 3:5).

14. Josephus: *J. W.* 2.13.5; *Ant.* 20.8.6. In *J. W.*, Josephus puts the force at thirty thousand, but in *Ant.* four hundred were killed and two hundred taken captives, making the tribune's numbers more likely.

15. Strabo, *Geogr.* 14.5.13.

16. Gooding, *True to the Faith*, 377.

17. Johnson, *Message of Acts*, 108.

He had considered himself faultless (Phil 3:5) and extremely jealous for the traditions of his fathers (Gal 1:14). He was as "zealous"[18] as they were (22:3) and understands their motivation. God had approved, even declaring righteous, the zealous believers of the past, such as Phinehas who killed an Israelite man having relationships with a Midianite woman (Num 25:11–13; Ps 106:31). His actions stopped a plague, which resulted from Israel associating with Moabite religious practices and immorality. The high priest and the Sanhedrin could testify (22:5) how he emulated the zeal of Phinehas when doing their bidding. The mob merely acted with a soul-damning, spontaneous eruption of emotion,[19] but Paul had been deliberate and methodical in persecuting Christians to their death (22:4), not even showing compassion on the women. There is no superiority in his address; they, too, could find pardon.

In the second part of his defense Paul explains how he, like Moses and some of the prophets, was called directly by God (22:6–14) on the Damascus road on his way to arrest believers and bring them to Jerusalem for punishment. This is discussed in my notes on chapter 9 where the differences in the three accounts are noted. For brevity here I will only note the additional information found in this chapter. These are as follows:

- The Sanhedrin also gave authority to Paul.
- The time of day is mentioned.
- Light was brighter than the midday sun.
- Jesus the Nazarene spoke to him.
- The companions saw the light as well but no comprehendible voice.
- Paul asks what he should do.
- Ananias is described as a devout man, well-spoken of.
- There is no mention of a vision to Ananias.
- The God of our fathers sent him, not the Lord.
- Saul will know God's will, see the just one, and hear from him.
- He will be a witness to all of what he has heard.
- He is told to wash his sins away through baptism (reflecting Peter's Pentecost sermon [2:38]).

18. For more information about the group called the Zealots, refer to the note "An Apparent Historical Error" in my comments on Acts 5:40–42.

19. Gooding, *True to the Faith*, 378.

- He is told to call upon the name of the Lord who is Jesus.

The third section (22:17–21) was Paul's call to be a witness to the nations. He returned to Jerusalem from Damascus and went to the temple, so demonstrating that he was still following the practices of Judaism after his conversion (22:17). There, Paul fell into a trance in which the Lord warned that he must quickly leave the city because his testimony about him will not be accepted, with the implication that his life was in peril (22:18). In chapter 9, this danger came from the Hellenistic Jews and the warning came from the believers (9:29–30), which is likely a double confirmation rather than a contradiction. There are good arguments both ways as to whether the Lord here is Jesus or the Father, and the ambiguity may be intentional.[20]

Paul did not share God's poor opinion of the residents of Jerusalem. They all knew that he went from synagogue to synagogue beating those who believed in Jesus and approved of the stoning of Stephen (22:19–20). Jerusalem was Paul's intended area of ministry,[21] but because of their rejection of the former persecutor's testimony to Jesus, the Lord told him a second time to go and specifically to go to the gentiles (22:21). Luke uses "those far away"; this was used in Peter's Pentecost sermon (2:39) when he quoted Isa 57:19, which suggests that Paul was the person by which God's peace would reach the far away gentiles. However, despite the Lord's command to go to those far off, it could have been thirteen years before the first missionary journey.[22]

Like Stephen, Peter with Cornelius, and Paul himself at Athens, he did not get to finish his speech and what he said did not directly address the charges. The crowd, "protecting their own selfish privileges,"[23] reacted violently to this, throwing their cloaks and dust in the air[24] (22:23), and demanded that Paul be killed (22:22). They understood that Paul was saying that Jew and gentile were equal, and both needed to come on

20. Bock, *Acts*, 662. Elsewhere in Acts, the Father does not lead, but that is done through either Jesus or the Spirit, and the person speaking seems to be the same one speaking through Ananias (22:13–6), i.e., the God of our ancestors and Lord in verse 10 is Jesus. However, in verse 15, Paul was called to be God's witness, as was Stephen (22:20).

21. Longenecker, "Acts," 9:526.

22. Lenski, *Acts*, 914.

23. Gooding, *True to the Faith*, 380.

24. It is not certain what the reference to the cloaks means, but throwing dust is a sign of distress at what they heard (2 Sam 16:13; Job 2:12) and was probably used as stones were not at hand.

equal terms to God through Christ.[25] Their suspicions about Paul's pro-gentile leanings and his blasphemy had been confirmed. Paul's argument was that if they had an objection, there was no point blaming him. They should take the matter up with God as he instigated all this.[26] The tribune and his men were left with a clear understanding of the Jewish hatred of them. It is unlikely that none of them understood Aramaic as an occupying army needed at least some who spoke the local language.

PAUL IS SAVED FROM SCOURGING BY HIS ROMAN CITIZENSHIP (22:23–29)

The mob turned violent again, demanding Paul be killed. It was clear that the tribune was not going to get to the truth of the matter in front of them, so he ordered him taken to the fortress and scourged to extract the truth (22:24). Paul had received the thirty-nine lashes from the Jews five times and beaten with rods three times (2 Cor 11:24–5),[27] but scourging was at an entirely different level of brutality. The scourge comprised leather thongs with bits of metal and bone tied to one end and attached to a wooden handle at the other. If it did not kill, it crippled for life. Paul was likely tied up in the Gabbatha, the same spot where equally innocent Jesus was scourged.[28]

Paul, stretched out for the lash, asked the supervising centurion whether what he was about to do was lawful (22:25), knowing full well that scourging a Roman was an abomination with severe consequences for all involved, including the tribune. Augustus, building on earlier laws, required that charges first had to be laid, the penalty stipulated, and then the matter must be heard before a Roman magistrate. Only if found guilty could a citizen be punished.[29] This, along with the consequence of falsely claiming Roman citizenship, is discussed in my notes on 16:36–40. Likely there was a discussion about this with the centurion as he was convinced enough to say he "was" not "claimed to be" a citizen. The matter was referred to the tribune (25:26). Paul, beaten as he was by

25. Stott, *Message of Acts*, 348.

26. Bock, *Acts*, 663.

27. This points to how much Luke has omitted from Paul's story; we only know of one beating.

28. Williams, *Acts*, 381.

29. Building on the much earlier Valerian and Porcian laws.

the crowd, would not have looked anything like a Roman citizen, unlike the tribune who purchased his at great cost, i.e., likely a bribe. Claudius's wife Messalina and her associates frequently sold citizenships and military commands at a high price. It was expected that the person granted citizenship would adopt Claudius's name, as is the case with Claudius Lysias.[30] Paul, perhaps almost boastful, said he was born a Roman citizen. There was a realization among all parties at how close they came to committing a very serious crime by even just putting Paul in chains (22:29).[31] In the tribune's report to Felix, he presented his involvement more favorably and did not mention almost scourging Paul (23:27), and he never corrected it.

Nothing of certainty is known of Paul's family or how they gained citizenship, but the providence of God in this matter should be noted. This citizenship would have meant that his family was among the elite in Tarsus and bestowed on Paul advantages over others in almost all circumstances.[32] While Paul unjustly remained a prisoner, he was protected. The legal system of Rome had nothing to fear from Christianity, nor has any modern system that seeks justice from a Christian who lives with integrity.[33]

PAUL BEFORE THE SANHEDRIN (22:30—23:11)

Paul could neither be charged nor freed until the tribune had determined why the mob reacted so violently against him. On the following day, the chief priests along with the Sanhedrin were summonsed, likely to the fortress, for what could be described as a pretrial hearing. Before taking Paul to them, his chains, likely lighter than those first used, were removed (22:30). Paul's freedom before his accusers was recognition that he was a Roman citizen with no charges yet laid against him. He looked at them intently, not having seen the council since he was its emissary in persecution (23:1). His opponents had murdered, used a traitor, perjured witnesses, etc., and had done it with a seared conscience.[34] Yet, he ad-

30. Cassius Dio, *Hist. rom.* 7:60.17.

31. It is not entirely certain what the reference to chains is as he was in chains up to addressing the Sanhedrin (22:30) and in chains when he spoke to Agrippa (26:29). It may refer to the type and weight of chain, which in themselves could be a torture.

32. Cassius Dio, *Hist. rom.* 7:60.17.

33. Bock, *Acts*, 665.

34. Lenski, *Acts*, 927–28.

dressed these men as "brothers," and, perhaps being "recklessly defiant" immediately declares that he has had a clear conscience all his life, putting himself on the same footing the council would claim for themselves.[35]

Paul also stressed actions that spoke of a clear conscience to the Ephesian elders (20:18–20; 33–35) as something to emulate and repeated it before Felix (24:16). "Conscience" is a thoroughly Pauline word (Rom 2:15; 9:1; 13:5; 1 Cor 8:7, 10, 12; 10:25–29; 2 Cor 1:12; 4:2; 5:11). However, what should be a warning is that his vile persecution was done with a clear conscience at the time. As Bruce points out, "The purest conscience was an unsafe object of trust before God."[36] Before God, he relied on his justification when his sins were washed away (22:16; 2:38). In a show of authority, the high priest Ananias,[37] who had predetermined Paul's guilt in a system that presumed innocence until convicted, ordered him be struck on the mouth for what was considered an offensive remark. How could he be a good Jew and a good Christian at the same time?

When Jesus had been in the same situation, he was silent and made no threats (1 Pet 2:23) as Paul himself had done previously (1 Cor 4:12), but this time Paul stood his ground. Quite possibly, Paul lost his temper, even uttering what might be a curse (Deut 28:22) that God will strike the person who ordered him struck against the Law. Paul likened him to a "whitewashed wall" (23:3). The exact meaning is uncertain as the association is different to when Jesus referred to people as "whitewashed tombs" (Matt 23:27; Ezek 13:10–16). Perhaps it means hiding a tottering wall with a good coat of whitewash,[38] however, all knew it was an insult. Ananias, because of his extreme avarice and his pro-Roman position when in office that caused him to handle tensions badly, was hunted like a wild animal and eventually struck down in AD 66 by the zealot Menahem.[39] For Paul, it was obvious that someone like Ananias would come under God's judgment.[40] Instead of defending due process, those near him (and perhaps it was said a little under his breath and they were the only ones to hear him) were appalled that he had insulted the high priest.

35. Barclay, *Ambassador for Christ*, 120.

36. Bruce, *Acts*, 1954, 449.

37. Different from the Ananias that Jesus appeared before and in Acts 4:7.

38. Bruce, *Acts*, 1954, 451.

39. Josephus, *Ant.* 20.9.2–3; *J. W.* 2.17.6, 9.

40. Longenecker, "Acts," 9:530.

Again, associating with them as "brothers," he quoted Exod 22:28 where the Law forbade reviling the high priest (23:6). Some see this as backing down and suggest that he has been out of Jerusalem for too long to know who the high priest was, his eyesight failed him (Gal 4:13–14), or the situation simply required a response because it was wrong and he was defending the Law.[41] It is unlikely Paul knew what the high priest looked like and in a special meeting of the council the high priest may not have been in his robes or presiding. Luke simply does not say why he replied this way, however, rather than backing down, Barclay saw Paul's reply as going on the offensive. Ananias was the most hated man in Jerusalem whom everyone reviled,[42] including the Pharisees.[43] Barclay saw Paul's answer as, "This man the High Priest? I never knew a man like this could be the High Priest of God."[44] Either way Paul was apologizing to the office, not the office holder.[45]

Understanding that there was no chance of a fair hearing, Paul threw a "grenade" into the proceedings, playing on the hatred between the Pharisees and the Sadducees. He called out to his true brothers that he was on trial because of his hope of the resurrection of the dead (23:6).[46] (That Luke needed to describe what these people believed [23:8] means that he intended gentiles to read his book.) The Pharisees defended Paul, calling him innocent; coming to the same conclusion that Paul made the day before (23:9), it was very possible that a spirit or angel spoke to him but without going as far as accepting the authority or resurrection of Jesus. The dispute became so violent that the tribune feared that his prisoner would be torn apart, and yet again Rome rescued Paul and returned him to the fortress. The council's virtual riot was far more disrespectful to the office of high priest than Paul's outburst. Instead of allowing himself to be silently "railroaded," Paul was able to clearly show the tribune that this

41. Bock, *Acts*, 670.

42. Ananias was high priest between c. AD 47–58 or 59. His greed was without measure, even going to the threshing floor and taking the tithes that were intended for the priests. This caused such hardship that old priests even died of hunger. He was also responsible for the death of James. Josephus, *Ant.* 20.9.2–3.

43. Josephus, *Ant.* 13.10.5.

44. Barclay, *Ambassador for Christ*, 121.

45. Longenecker, "Acts," 9:531.

46. For similarities between Pharisees and Christians, refer to the note "Who Were the Pharisees?" in my comments on 5:32. See also the note "Who Were the Sadducees?" under 4:1–4.

was a religious matter outside of Roman law, a matter that they were not all agreed on, and that there was no chance of receiving a fair hearing.[47]

Understandably, Paul was discouraged with little chance of leaving Jerusalem alive. His fears of what would happen in Jerusalem were realized and his hopes to evangelize the west of the empire were dashed. That night the Lord appeared to him, as he had done before at crucial times (20:22; Rom 15:31), and encouraged him by telling him that he would be his witness in Rome as he was in Jerusalem at the steps in the temple court (23:11). The Lord said nothing about the frustrating two years of imprisonment ahead, but Paul was able to bear it with dignity.[48] Paul had only planned a fleeting visit to Rome on his way to Spain to encourage the church. God's plan was that he testified to Jesus at the highest level of pagan Roman society.[49]

THE PLOT AGAINST PAUL IS EXPOSED (23:12–22)

The following morning, more than forty men (*sicarii*?) took a vow not to eat or drink anything until they had murdered Paul (23:12–13). They were placing themselves under a curse if they did not fulfill the vow.[50] They then went to the high priest and asked for his assistance in making the murder possible by asking the tribune to have Paul returned to the council for further examination; on his way they would kill him (23:15). Attacking a heavily guarded prisoner would have resulted in many of them being killed,[51] a price they were willing to pay to rid the earth of Paul. In trying to uphold the Law they would violate God's revealed standard, and his secret will.[52] That the high priest would agree to this is not surprising and vindicates Paul's opinion of him (22:3). Fortunately for the conspirators, there was an out when it became impossible to fulfill a vow.[53] Given the location of the Sanhedrin, Paul would only have to have

47. Gooding, *True to the Faith*, 383–4.
48. Longenecker, "Acts," 9:532.
49. Bock, *Acts*, 679.
50. BAGD, "Ἀναθεμα," 54.1.
51. Bruce, *Acts*, 1954, 457.
52. Bock, *Acts*, 677.
53. M. *Ned.* 3.1, 3.

been escorted across the temple court,[54] so his murder there would have been a greater crime than what they were accusing the apostle of.

With so many conspirators, it is not too surprising that Paul's young nephew[55] somehow learned of the plan (23:16). He went to the fort, and, after gaining admission, told Paul about it. In Phil 3:8, Paul spoke of the loss of all things, likely being disinherited, and he wrote of the hardships he experienced in 2 Cor 11:23–27, which may have been the result. Whatever happened, there was a reconciliation with at least part of the family. Access to his uncle did not appear to be a problem as he was a Roman citizen without charge that the tribune thought was innocent. Paul in turn called one of the centurions (23:17) and asked that his nephew be taken to the tribune as he had something to tell him. The tenderness of the officer taking the young man by the hand and talking to him privately (23:19) and advising him to remain silent for his safety (23:22) is in marked contrast to the scourging he was prepared to inflict on Paul without finding even the basic facts.[56] Meeting members of Paul's family would have confirmed his citizenship and social standing. Paul's possible wealth is discussed under Felix's hope for a bribe.

54. Lenski, *Acts*, 944.

55. This is the only clear reference to a direct family member. He may have come to Jerusalem to study, or his mother may have lived in the city.

56. Paul's nephew may have also saved the tribune's life by avoiding the melee.

15

Paul's Imprisonment and Trials in Caesarea (Acts 23:23—26:32)

PAUL IS SENT TO CAESAREA FOR SAFETY (23:23–35)

The seriousness with which the tribune took the threat to a Roman citizen in his charge shows his low opinion of the high priest, Ananias,[1] that he would so quickly abandon the principles he represented. The tribune called two of his centurions and ordered 470 soldiers to be assembled and to leave for Caesarea at the third hour, i.e., 9:00 p.m., to escort Paul to the governor for his safety. The force of 200 soldiers, 70 horsemen, and 200 lancers[2] (23:23), likely about half the garrison, was probably more than was needed for the prisoner's safety, but a display of power when trouble was brewing may have been deemed necessary. Paul was given additional mobility in case of an attack by mounting him on a horse as well. The full complement only went on a forced march as far as Antipatris (22:31), roughly halfway between Jerusalem and Caesarea, roughly one hundred kilometers distance, but they were in mostly gentile territory and areas where they could be ambushed were behind them.[3] The horsemen took Paul the remaining distance (22:32).

Claudius Lysias sent an accompanying letter to Felix the governor (23:25–30) outlining the circumstances that led to Paul being sent to Caesarea and that he was not, in his opinion, guilty of any crime against Rome. The matter was purely related to Jewish Law. The original letter

1. Longenecker, "Acts," 9:534.

2. "Spearmen" is a guess for the term "right-handed." Suggestions range from "light-armed troops" to "led horses." Longenecker, "Acts," 9:535.

3. Bock, *Acts*, 683.

would have been in Latin but it is not certain if Luke is recording a paraphrase or verbatim quotation of the letter.[4] The tribune wrote the letter in such a way as to ingratiate himself with Felix[5] by exaggerating his role, saying that he rescued Paul because he was a Roman citizen (23:27) and omits that he had almost scourged a citizen. The horsemen delivered Paul to the governor along with the letter, and Felix asked what province Paul was from. As Cilicia was a Roman province, he had the option of ordering the case heard in Paul's home province or hearing the matter where the offence occurred.[6] He chose to hear the matter himself when his accusers arrived as it was not a major crime and there would have been extreme inconvenience for the already-agitated litigants. Paul was kept under guard and protection in what was Herod's government house (23:35), though not likely mistreated. So far, the Romans have just done their assigned duty and will make it possible, after a two-year hiatus, for Paul to go to Rome on God's terms.

Antonius Felix, a freed slave of Claudius's mother Antonia, became one of the favorite freedmen of Claudius, to whom he was distantly related by marriage through his first wife. With influence from his brother Pallas, Claudius's secretary of the treasury, the emperor appointed him first to senior military commands and then, at the request of the high priest Jonathan,[7] as governor to Judea[8] in AD 52. For his trouble, Felix later had Jonathan murdered.[9] He proved to be brutal[10] and corrupt (24:26) and a poor administrator, even allowing the high priest Ananias to rob the tithes of the poor priests.[11] To have risen from a slave to marry three princesses[12] and be appointed governor he must have been seen as having great ability.[13] He was, however, one of the worst Roman governors, and Tacitus wrote that "he practiced every kind of cruelty"

4. For paraphrase, see Bruce, *Acts*, 1954, 449 who later changed to literal in Bruce, *Acts*, 1990, 471.

5. Bock, *Acts*, 682.

6. If the offense had occurred in a client kingdom in Syria or Asia Minor, Felix would likely have had to consult the ruler there.

7. Josephus: *Ant.* 20.8.5; *J. W.* 2.12.8.

8. Suetonius, *Twelve Caesars*, 178–79.

9. Josephus, *Ant.* 20.8.5.

10. Josephus, *J. W.* 2.13.7.

11. Josephus, *Ant.* 20.8.8.

12. Suetonius, *Twelve Caesars*, 178–79.

13. Brenk and De Rossi, "Notorious Felix," 413, 417.

as he "exercised the power of a king in the spirit of a slave."[14] His third wife, Drusilla (24:24), was the sister of Agrippa II and Bernice.[15] Drusilla had to illegally divorce her husband to marry Felix. Such actions almost seemed design to drive priest and citizen to revolt and gave rise to the *sicarii* who killed many of the Jewish aristocracy who collaborated with the Romans. In AD 58 or 59 he was recalled by Nero after complaints by the Jews against the harsh measures he used to suppress riots against them in Caesarea and the associated pillaging.[16] However, his powerfully connected brother ensured he was not convicted. This only further stoked anti-Roman sentiment.[17] Paul's abuse by the governor strengthened his case as, by the time that Paul's two-year Roman imprisonment ended, Felix was discredited, and his once powerful brother/protector had been executed by Nero (AD 62).

Similarities between Luke 23 and Acts 23–26, 28

There are two blocks of material in Acts, most of which center on Jerusalem and all before the Sanhedrin and Roman prefects, which have parallels or similarities to Luke's account of Jesus. The first is the four trial appearances of both Jesus and Paul. This models and fulfills Jesus' prediction, "But before all this, they will seize you and persecute you. They will hand you over to synagogues and put you in prison, and you will be brought before kings and governors, and all on account of my name. And so you will bear testimony to me" (Luke 21:12–13). These similarities are listed in Table 12 below.

Jesus before the Sanhedrin (Luke 22:54–71)	Paul before the Sanhedrin (Acts 22:30—23:10)
Jesus before Pilate (Luke 23:1–5)	Paul before Felix (Acts 24:1–27)
Jesus before Herod Antipas (Luke 23:6–12)	Paul before Festus (Acts 25:1–12)
Jesus before Pilate (Luke 23:13–25)	Paul before Herod Agrippa II (Acts 25:13—26:32)

Table 13. The trial appearances of Jesus and Paul[18]

14. Tacitus, *Hist.* 5.9.
15. Josephus, *Ant.* 20.7.2.
16. Josephus, *J. W.* 2.13.7.
17. Josephus, *Ant.* 20.8.9.
18. Edwards, "Parallels and Patterns," 496.

There are also similarities in the charges and conduct of the trials that Jesus and Paul were subjected to—a further example of like master, like servant. These are found in Table 13 below.

"And they began to accuse him, saying" (Luke 23:2)	"presented his case" (Acts 24:2)
Found to stir up people (Luke 23:5)	Found to stir up people (Acts 24:5)
Caused sedition (Luke 23:5)	Caused sedition (Acts 24:5)
Pilate asks Jesus' origins with reference to Herodian dynasty (Luke 23:6–7)	Felix asks Paul's origins with reference to Herodian dynasty (Acts 23:34–35)
Jesus is remanded (Luke 23:7)	Paul is remanded (Acts 25:21)
Pilate orders Jesus to appear before Herod Antipas (Luke 23:7)	Festus orders Paul to appear before Herod Agrippa II (25:22)
Herod had desired to hear Jesus (Luke 23:8)	Herod had desired to hear Paul (Acts 25:22)
Jewish leaders vehemently accuse Jesus (Luke 23:10)	Jewish leaders vehemently accuse Paul (Acts 25:7)
Cry out "away with him" (Luke 23:18)	Cry out "away with him" (21:36)
Crowds shout for death of Jesus (Luke 23:21)	Crowds shout for death of Paul (Acts 21:36; 22:22)
Jesus is struck by attendants of the high priest (Luke 23:36)	Paul is struck by attendants of the high priest (Acts 23:2)
Jesus is accompanied by prisoners after his trial (Luke 22:37; 23:32)	Paul is accompanied by prisoners after his trial (Acts 27:1)
Jesus' innocence is declared four times (23:4, 14, 22, 41)	Paul is declared innocent seven times and on a broader sphere (Claudius Lysias—Acts 23:29; Festus—Acts 25:5, 25; 26:31; the last is corroborated by Agrippa II, residents of Malta (28:6) and the Jews of Rome (28:18–22)
Pilate would have released Jesus (Luke 23:16, 20)	Agrippa would have released Paul (Acts 26:32)

Table 14. Similarities of the trials of Jesus and Paul[19]

19. Edwards, "Parallels and Patterns," 496.

THE JEWISH LEADERS MAKE THEIR CASE TO FELIX (24:1–9)

Given that two of the five days were needed to travel to Caesarea, the leaders were quick to act against Paul. Through the advocacy of Tertullus (of whom nothing is known), the high priest Ananias and some elders stood before Felix claiming, in part, to be protecting the sanctity of the temple and the Law. Yet the high priest and his retinue only had to travel to Caesarea because they had intended to grievously break that same Law by murdering Paul, something the governor knew full well. Luke's abbreviated report gave almost equal space to the accusation, defense, and aftermath. However, a large proportion of Tertullus's words were simply flattering the governor. His promise of brevity (24:4) was not likely to have been met. Felix's rule was characterized by "ferocity, cruelty and greed"[20] for which very few felt "profound gratitude." As for any accountability for his misrule, when the former high priest Jonathan pressed him to govern better, he organized through the priest's best friends to have the *sicarii* murder him.[21] Despite all this, the lawyer described his administration as a time of peace, reforms, and improvements brought about by a man of vision (24:3). He did suppress the Zealots for a period,[22] so surely a man whose primary role was to ensure peace[23] in Judea would simply hand Paul over to them, or so they thought.

Without presenting any hard evidence, he laid out the charges against Paul which were as follows:

1. He was a public pest.
2. He was a ringleader of the sect[24] known as the Nazarenes.
3. He stirred up the Jews throughout the world (24:5).
4. He attempted to desecrate the temple (24:6).

Charges one to three put front and center Felix's responsibility to keep the peace, and charge four reinforced these as they knew how seriously Romans considered the sanctity of the Jerusalem temple. Paul's

20. Longenecker, "Acts," 9:539.

21. Josephus, *Ant.* 20.8.5.

22. Josephus: *J. W.* 2.13.2; *Ant.* 20.8.5.

23. Bock. *Acts*, 690.

24. The Pharisees and Sadducees were also called "sects," so this suggests a recognized body within Judaism.

Roman citizenship would not protect him from that.[25] There is no mention of Trophimus the gentile who was supposed to have entered the temple, nor is he recorded as a witness (21:29), but he would not be needed as the charge had changed. No longer was Paul accused of actually desecrating the temple but of only attempting to do so. Christians were painted as a similar risk as the Zealots and *sicarii* who hated Rome and who Felix had crucified by the hundreds, but the origin of the charge was that Paul was sympathetic to gentiles. How could Paul pose any threat to Rome?[26] However, Tertullus urged Felix to examine the matter (24:8) as he would find it true, and the others joined in agreement (24:9). (The last clause in verse 6, verse 7, and the start of verse 8, where Tertullus misrepresents Paul's arrest, are not in the best manuscripts, so no comment is made.)

PAUL MAKES HIS DEFENSE (24:10–23)

Felix then motioned to Paul to make his defense, and he opened with some flattery also. He acknowledged Felix's long[27] rule (24:10), which gave enough time to be well-acquainted with Jewish and Christian matters. The events surrounding the Way should be well-known as they were not a secret society, and their deeds were not done secretly in some obscure corner (25:26). Luke assesses Felix as having a relatively accurate knowledge of the Way (24:22), which should have meant that he knew that Christianity was not responsible for any disorder.[28] Paul is categorical in his defense and welcomed the governor investigating the vague generalities Tertullus had raised (24:11) as this would easily establish his innocence.[29] He addressed the lawyers' four points as follows:

1. *He was a public pest.* Paul had only arrived twelve days earlier,[30] which meant that there was insufficient time to foment a disturbance.
2. *He was a ringleader of the sect known as the Nazarenes.* Paul could not be a ringleader planning to cause trouble as, remarkably for

25. Josephus, *J. W.* 6.2.4, 5.5.2.

26. Bock, *Acts*, 691.

27. Before becoming governor, Felix was the aid to the previous governor, Ventidius Cumanus, and had been governor for approximately five years at this point.

28. Gooding, *True to the Faith*, 387.

29. Bruce, *Acts*, 1954, 469.

30. There is uncertainty how the seven days of purification, the next day of 22:30, the five days of 24:1, and the twelve days of 24:11 relate to each other.

Paul, he had not been engaged in any discussions in either the temple or the synagogues (24:12).

3. *He stirred up the Jews throughout the world.* Paul had only been in Judea for twelve days, so these matters were outside Felix's jurisdiction.

4. *He attempted to desecrate the temple.* Paul was simply engaged in genuine worship at the temple, alone (24:12) and in a state of ritual purity (24:11, 18).

Perhaps Paul had gone out of the way not to provoke trouble considering the prophecies of what awaited him. But Paul readily admitted his "guilt" of being a good Jew and at the same time a member of the Way. Tertullus referred to them as Nazarenes, not Christians or the Way, to avoid recognition of any claim Jesus may have made. However, rather than being a heresy (24:14), Paul says his faith is the fullest representation of Judaism as he holds to not only all that is written in the Law and prophets (24:14) but also to the hope of Israel, the resurrection of the good and the bad (24:15).[31] Perhaps Paul should have said, "Which they also *should* cherish," as the Sadducees were very opposed to a belief in an end-time judgment that a universal resurrection implied. Likely there were some Pharisees present who did share this hope, but, if so, their silence showed that the earlier goodwill has dissipated.[32] Paul did not mention the resurrection of Jesus or that Jesus would be the judge, but it would not be lost on the Jewish rulers. Before the religious court, Paul declared his clear conscience before God because he had discharged his duty (23:1). But before Rome, it is the hope of the resurrection that led him to maintain a clear conscience before God and man (24:16). He had faithfully discharged his duty to the laws of God and Rome.[33]

The context of his "crime" was that after about a five-year break, he made an act of charity towards the nation[34] and to quietly worship God as prescribed by the Law (24:17–18). In his Letters, Paul gave great importance to the collection of money from the gentile churches for the Jerusalem believers, yet 24:17 is the only mention of it in Acts, and then

31. This is the only place where Paul talks about the resurrection of the bad. His Letters refer to the resurrection of the righteous and its likeness to that of Jesus.

32. Bruce, *Acts*, 1954, 469.

33. Gooding, *True to the Faith*, 390.

34. While strictly intended for the Jerusalem Christians, "the conversion of the whole nation was the ultimate aim of all his exertions." Harnack, *Date of Acts*, 75.

it is only mentioned in passing. It may well have been that the offering did not have the desired effect of helping bring about unity between the two branches of the church[35] and so quickly passes over it. Worshiping correctly and bringing offerings to the poor of Jerusalem were not the actions of a temple desecrator.[36] The Jews from Asia that caused the trouble should have been bought as eyewitnesses (24:19), and their absence declared that Paul was innocent of the accusations that led to his arrest. In reality, they should be charged for bringing a false charge against Paul; indeed in any trial without witnesses the charges should be dropped.[37] The real reason for him being imprisoned was his belief in the resurrection, which he shouted at the council meeting (24:20–21). If not, let the leaders come up with some specific charges (24:20), not the general accusation made by Tertullus. His religious beliefs were not illegal for a Roman citizen.

Felix seems to have summed up the conflicting statements correctly as simply being a religious matter outside of Roman law, as had the tribune, so he advised all parties that he would reserve his judgment till the tribune came to Caesarea (24:22). In the interim (which stretched for a further two years), Paul's captivity was eased, and he was allowed to be attended on by his friends (24:23) such as Philip and his daughters who lived in Caesarea. While Paul could have been freed (25:31–32), he remained captive as a favor to the leaders (24:27), which is ironic considering Felix was recalled due to his insensitivity to them. Roman justice was shown to be lacking, but this was by a discredited governor of whom little else would be expected.

AFTERMATH OF THE TRIAL (24:24–27)

A few days later, Felix, with his Jewish wife Drusilla, called for Paul. Felix was described as having a fairly accurate knowledge of the Way (24:22), and as governor there would be no excuse for not having this. As Paul would remind Agrippa, the work of Jesus and the church were public and lawful. Drusilla's presence may have helped give Felix a Jewish understanding, or she may have been interested. Perhaps the governor

35. Bruce, *Acts*, 1954, 470.

36. Gooding, *True to the Faith*, 391.

37. Longenecker, "Acts," 9:541. Under Roman law, withdrawing charges could lead to heavy penalties being imposed against the accusers.

wanted to know more accurately about a movement that was sweeping Judea with potential, as Paul's case had shown, to cause civil disruption. Paul spoke, not as a servile prisoner but as an evangelist doing what Jesus had promised (23:11). Even before being a witness in Rome he was proclaiming him to a Roman governor and a princess. And why not? He had already seen a proconsul come to faith (13:12). Paul spoke to the pair about "righteousness, self-control and the judgment to come,"[38] which terrified Felix (24:25) but only likely offended Drusilla as she would not join Felix for later talks with Paul. John the Baptist likely declared publicly that it was wrong for Herod Antipas to have his brother's wife (Luke 3:19), but here the rebuke is private and before Bernice a different approach will be taken.

Drusilla was born in AD 38, so was about twenty years old at the time. She was the daughter of Agrippa I, sister to Agrippa II and Bernice, and "like a typical Herodian lady defiled Jewish law."[39] Josephus described in very graphic detail the contempt soldiers of Caesarea had for her and her sisters.[40] She was married at fourteen to Azizus, King of Emesa,[41] but because of her extraordinary beauty, Felix fell in love with (more likely lusted after)[42] her. He persuaded a Cypriot magician to convince her, at the age of sixteen, to leave her unhappy marriage and marry Felix instead, something that would cause her to avoid intense jealousy from her sister Bernice.[43] God's requirements for personal ethics were opposed to that of the prevailing Greek culture, which had no concept of a final judgment. This may have been new territory for Felix but not Drusilla.[44] However, while their irregular marriage is alluded to, and these were "three subjects which that couple specifically needed to learn about,"[45] this was about morality in the context of faith in Christ (24:24).

Paul was sent away, yet Felix would call for him frequently but with mixed motives. He was looking for a bribe (24:26), yet he was curious

38. Stott refers to this as "the three tenses of salvation": the past through forgiveness, the present through self-mastery, and the future through avoiding the judgment to come. Stott, *Message of Acts*, 364.

39. Brenk and De Rossi, "Notorious Felix," 412.

40. Josephus, *Ant.* 19.9.1.

41. Centered around Homs in Syria.

42. Stott, *Message of Acts*, 364.

43. Josephus, *Ant.* 20.7.1–2.

44. Bock, *Acts*, 695.

45. Bruce, *Acts*, 1954, 473.

about the Way. Perhaps the integrity of one of its ringleaders compared to the corruption of the leaders of Judaism puzzled him. Ramsay makes the fairly obvious case that at least from the time of Paul's final arrival in Jerusalem to the close of Acts, he needed access to considerable wealth.[46] The costs involved with the vows and then with the next four years of imprisonment, including supporting his attendants along with the legal costs, would have been enormous. He surmises that Paul "wore the outward appearance of a man of means, like one in a position to bribe a Roman procurator."[47] He believed the likelihood of a poor itinerant evangelist being given leave to appeal to Caesar would be remote.

After two years, Felix was eventually replaced by Porcius Festus, who was regarded as a better administrator than his predecessor.[48] Nothing is known about him other than what is written in Acts and Josephus, nor is the date of his arrival certain. He worked hard to prevent disturbances in the land from the *sicarii* and Zealots,[49] but given that Judea was a tinderbox from successive governors' misrule, Felix considered it better to have Paul in custody where he could do no harm (24:27).[50] Reopening the case with an inexperienced governor would have been very unfavorable to Paul.[51] But what Felix intended and what God planned were different. While the two years must have been very frustrating for Paul, this is likely the time when Luke researched and perhaps wrote drafts of his Gospel and the early portions of Acts.

PAUL BEFORE FESTUS (25:1–12)

On arriving in Caesarea, Governor Festus wasted no time before leaving the capital and travelling to Jerusalem to meet with the Jewish leaders, an indication of how volatile the situation was in Judea. The chief priests[52] and leaders also wasted no time in bringing up the matter of Paul. They

46. Ramsay, *St. Paul*, 177–78.

47. Ramsay, *St. Paul*, 178. The suggestion is that any family rift is healed, and he came into his inheritance. While the source of the funds is speculation, its need is not.

48. Josephus, *J. W.* 2.14.1.

49. Josephus, *Ant.* 20.8.9–10. The term Josephus used was "robbers," which likely covered both groups.

50. Bock, *Acts*, 696.

51. Bruce, *Acts*, 1954, 474.

52. High Priest Annanias had been replaced by Ishmael, however the previous priest still played a prominent role in Jerusalem affairs up to his death.

were hoping to take advantage of the new governor's inexperience and his desire to lower tensions by asking a favor: that Paul be brought from Caesarea to Jerusalem for trial (25:2). They would have stressed how Paul was kept in prison in the capital as a favor to them (24:27). All along they were simply planning to murder Paul on the journey, and if that failed, then try him for the capital offence of bringing a gentile into the temple (25:3). Unaware of their duplicity, Festus, likely following protocol, simply said that Paul is in Caesarea and that his accusers should travel back with him instead. It appears that Paul has spent two years in protective custody without a formal charge recognized by Rome (25:5), let alone a verdict. To his credit, Festus will not commit to anything without a trial, reflecting the view of Josephus that he was a better governor than his predecessors. Paul's defense before Festus is the shortest of the five appearances.

Likely Festus intended to conduct as much business as possible on his first stay in Jerusalem, which was about eight to ten days' duration (25:6), and an extended trial would cut into that time.[53] The day after the governor returned to the capital accompanied by Paul's accusers, he was brought to trial. Again, serious charges are made (25:7) that cannot be substantiated against Jewish or Roman law nor of desecrating the temple (25:8). Likely, new charges of treason were made, as at Thessalonica (17:7), since he had to defend his loyalty to Caesar (25:8). Notably, this charge is coming from the Jews, not the Romans. However, Festus was keen to curry favor with the Jewish leaders, but without acceding to their demands, asked if Paul would be willing to travel to Jerusalem to stand trial there if he is the judge (25:9). The request probably seemed reasonable to Festus.[54] There is indignation in Paul's reply as he shouldn't be tried at all as the governor knows that he is innocent (25:10). Festus could not know more about it in Jerusalem than in Caesarea. It would have allowed the Sadducees to publish a damming verdict on Paul and the gospel, which masqueraded as Roman justice.[55]

Rome was meticulous in keeping court records,[56] so presumably the governor was made aware of the facts by his officials. While he could not understand the case, Festus knew enough to realize that this was about religion and not Roman law (25:18–20). It is likely that Paul, his Roman

53. Longenecker, "Acts," 9:545.

54. Bruce, *Acts*, 1954, 477.

55. Gooding, *True to the Faith*, 395.

56. Bock, *Acts*, 701.

citizenship already having been established, sensed that all is not well in the request, and as a Roman citizen loyal to the emperor, demanded to be tried in a Roman court against Roman law and let the verdict fall where it may. Rome could hand an innocent man over to the mob just to maintain peace as the trial of Jesus showed. His Jewish accusers may have overplayed their hand by including treason as this was a matter for a Roman court. Fearing that Rome would be complicit with the Jewish leadership in their pursuit of him, Paul maneuvered around the trap by appealing to Caesar, i.e., Nero[57] (25:11), where a verdict of innocence could be delivered to the empire. After consulting with his officers,[58] Festus determined that Paul will indeed go to Rome fulfilling the Lord's prophecy (23:11). In the interim, Roman protection was better than being in the hands of the Jewish leadership. There is no hint that justice will actually be achieved but delivering the gospel to Rome is the main consideration, and the appeal is simply the means of doing it.[59] An appeal to Caesar, which was originally an appeal to the citizens of Rome, was one of their oldest rights, dating back to 509 BC. The similarity to the expression "calling on the name of the Lord" should be noted. Strictly, Paul could have been released by Festus simply acquitting him. Gallio had acquitted Paul and driven the accusing Jews from his court. But a political decision was made to not antagonize the leaders, and if he was in Rome it was someone else's problem.[60]

AGRIPPA AND BERNICE VISIT FESTUS (25:13–27)

Some days later, Agrippa II and his sister Bernice came to Caesarea where he had residence to congratulate Festus on his appointment (25:13). These two were very important, not only for Paul's future but

57. Nero's practice during a trial is given in Suetonius, *Twelve Caesars*, 193–94. In the early part of his reign, Nero lacked his later infamy. Suetonius, *Twelve Caesars*, 191–92. At that stage, he was under the influence of the Stoic philosopher Seneca and the Praetorian guard leader Afranius Burrus. Suetonius, *Twelve Caesars*, 190–91, 205–6, 216. It was considered a short golden age with little indication of the persecutions of AD 64.

58. The appeal is called the *provocatio*, and at this stage in Rome it was likely only available for cases classed as *extra ordinem*, i.e., cases for which there was no statute law, meaning governors could deal with ordinary cases. The discussion was likely to determine where this case sat. Sherwin-White, *Roman Society*, 57–70.

59. Bock, *Acts*, 704.

60. Longenecker, "Acts," 9:546.

for the history of the Jews. Agrippa II, brother to Drusilla and Bernice, whose full name was Marcus Julius Agrippa, was the last of the Herodian rulers. Agrippa was born in Rome in AD 27 or 28 after his father Agrippa I had to flee there to escape his creditors. On his father's eventual return, he stayed in Rome and was educated in the court of Claudius. Its moral depravity was likely to have a bad influence on him.[61] However, he did use his position to advance the petitions of the Jews.[62] On his father's death he was considered too inexperienced to rule his turbulent territories so they were then ruled by Rome instead. In AD 48 he was given the small and insignificant kingdom of Chalcis[63] as a client king. While Chalcis was outside of Judea, he was very significant to the Jews as he was given the right to superintend the temple in Jerusalem and appoint the high priest, which he did arbitrarily.[64] This role required him to be knowledgeable of Jewish affairs. Claudius and then Nero added to his territories in AD 55.[65] He finally completed the temple during his reign in AD 63 and spent lavishly, beautifying Jerusalem[66] and Berytus (modern Beirut).

When it became obvious that nothing could stop the revolt of AD 66, he addressed the Jews with "one of the most impressive and outstanding rhetorical statements from classical antiquity to have survived."[67] It is a very clear argument of the futility of their cause. He fled with his sister in AD 66 and on the Vespasian's arrival provided two thousand troops to his army. He was with Titus, Vespasian's son, at the destruction of Jerusalem and the temple in AD 70. He returned to Rome, and, for his loyalty, was proclaimed a praetor[68] and given more land. The date of his death is uncertain but is likely to be sometime between AD 93 or 94 and 100. Josephus was a close friend of Agrippa II who provided information for his *Antiquities of the Jews*. He called Agrippa a person who deserved the greatest admiration, and despite his reputation as being

61. Brann, "Agrippa II," 1:271. This was the time of Messalina and Agrippina.

62. Josephus: *Ant.* 15.11.4; *J. W.* 2.12.7.

63. Josephus, *J. W.* 2.12.1. Chalcis was the center of the small client kingdom of Iturea in the Levant, north of Galilee.

64. Brann, "Agrippa II," 1:272.

65. Josephus, *J. W.* 2.12.8; 2.13.2.

66. This avoided unrest as the artisans working on the temple would have been otherwise unemployed on its completion.

67. Rocca, *Human Freedom*, 130; Josephus, *J. W.* 2.16.3–5.

68. Cassius Dio, *Hist. rom.* 66.15.3–4. A praetor is a magistrate with the rank below consul.

knowledgeable on Jewish matters, there is little that is praiseworthy in his religious and personal life.[69]

Julia Bernice, the sister of Agrippa II and Drusilla, was a year younger than her brother. At thirteen years old, she was betrothed to the head of the Jewish community in Alexandria, but he died in AD 44. At sixteen years old, Agrippa I arranged her marriage to his older brother, Herod, king of Chalcis, and thus she became a queen. In AD 48, at the age of twenty years old, Bernice was widowed for a second time though she retained the title of queen. Her husband's land was given to Agrippa II, so brother and sister came back into close quarters, and were apparently joint rulers, and often appeared in public together.[70] To quell rumors about the incestuous relationship with her brother, Bernice sought a third marriage with Polemo, king of Cilicia. It ended quickly when he renounced his Jewish conversion, at which time she returned to Agrippa.[71] At the start of the Jewish revolt, she was in Jerusalem to fulfil a Nazirite vow, surprisingly for woman of her reputation as in part it meant shaving her hair. She walked barefoot and shaven, at considerable peril to the governor Florus, and totally disheveled, unsuccessfully begging for mercy for the Jews[72] who had revolted because of his outrages.[73] This vow and ending her marriage to Polemo showed her to be an independent woman who took her Jewish faith seriously, which makes her an enigma given her personal morals.

Josephus says no more about Bernice in his *Jewish Wars*, possibly because of his close friendship with Titus, and his account of her incest in *Antiquities of the Jews* was written after the death of his patron. When Vespasian and his son Titus (both later emperors) fought the local forces, Bernice sided with the Romans and provided local forces. Despite being eleven years older she also became a lover to Titus,[74] one of the most reviled people in Jewish memory. After the destruction of Jerusalem, she moved to Rome where she had citizenship, and, after AD 75, at the age of forty-seven years old lived openly as his consort. A rumored offer of marriage was withdrawn after public pressure forced him to cut his ties

69. Josephus, *Ag. Ap.* 1.9. Brann, "Agrippa II," 1:272.

70. Cassius Dio, *Hist. rom.* 66.18.1.

71. Juvenal, *Sat.* 6.155–8; Josephus, *Ant.* 20.7.3.

72. Josephus, *J. W.* 2.15.1.

73. Josephus, *J. W.* 2.16.7.

74. Tacitus, *Hist.* 2.2.1.

with her.[75] Their relationship was likened to the disastrous relationship between the Hellenist queen Cleopatra and Julius Caesar and Mark Antony who likewise had also previously "married" her brother. She was seen as threatening the core values of Roman society.[76] Bernice came to Rome again after Titus was made emperor but was rebuffed.[77] Such were the people determining Paul's future, and such were the people he would evangelize.

The prompt action by Festus with Paul stands in contrast to the delaying tactics of Felix, and the timing of the pair's visit could not be better as the governor was struggling to understand the case and did not know what to write in his report that was to accompany Paul. He understood the absurdity (25:27) of sending someone to Caesar for trial when you know that person to be innocent and against whom no charges have been made that a Roman judge would recognize (25:18). Festus explained that there was extreme pressure on him to pass judgment on Paul, but, to the credit of Festus, he refused as this went against Roman justice (25:16) as the accused must first face his accusers and have the right to defend himself.[78] This is different to the picture in verses 1–12 where he was considering doing just that, but perhaps the inexperienced governor was quickly learning his role. He did understand that this was a Jewish religious matter, which is where Agrippa's assistance was invaluable and gratefully received.

The charge of profaning the temple was gone, and if that was still a charge that would have been front and center with Agrippa as he was responsible for the temple. Festus understood the accusations to revolve around Jesus who was dead but Paul claimed to be alive (25:19). The Romans had no concept of resurrection, so this was far outside their law. Festus did want to be sensitive to the Jewish leaders and explained how he had suggested a trial in Jerusalem (25:20), but Paul refused and instead appealed to Caesar. On telling Agrippa about it, the king was very interested in hearing Paul (25:22). The following day, with full pomp and ceremony, the governor, Agrippa, and Bernice enter the audience hall, along with his tribunes and leading citizens of the city who were ordered to attend (25:23). Paul must have been a prisoner of some note to warrant this scrutiny. Perhaps Luke was in attendance.

75. Suetonius, *Twelve Caesars*, 265–66; Cassius Dio, *Hist. rom.* 66.15.3–4.

76. Anagnostou-Laoutides and Charles, "Titus and Bernice," 17–18, 25.

77. Cassius Dio, *Hist. rom.* 66.18.1.

78. Justinian, *Digest*, 14.17.1.

Bruce believes Luke is being quietly humorous as true greatness was with the handcuffed Paul, not in the pomp of the rulers, a judgment confirmed by history.[79] He certainly was not intimidated by it. The setting was not a trial as Paul's innocence has already been determined but was an examination to determine what needs to be written to accompany the prisoner to Rome (25:26–7). An absurd situation indeed. However, charges were not the problem as there had been plenty; what was lacking was the evidence to back them and make the charges credible. How can a report be written that did not show Festus was weak in the administration of Roman law against a citizen?[80] Festus called Nero his "lord," something initially rejected by early Caesars because of its association with kingship but would become directly linked with their claim to divinity.[81] Many Christians would die rather than ascribe this title to a worldly ruler.

PAUL'S DEFENSE BEFORE AGRIPPA AND BERNICE (26:1–23)

As with the Paul's master, Jesus, who had stood before the Roman governor, and Herod, he in turn stood before the governor and a Herod. However, while Jesus was silent before Herod Antipas, the great uncle of Agrippa II, Paul was not. Before Agrippa and Bernice, Paul delivered his detailed *apologia pro vita sua*,[82] or "the defence of one's life." This is the most important defense because it is the longest and most carefully constructed of the five, especially as it is focused on Paul and his gospel.[83] His address showed that he was neither a Jewish lawbreaker nor a threat to the Roman state or the emperor, and the report from Festus to Nero should reflect that. While Paul largely covered the same matters as when he spoke at the fortress steps, the hostility is absent, which allowed for a "joyful testimony to a Jewish believer."[84]

When given leave to speak, Paul motioned with his manacled hands and started by giving a genuine complement to Agrippa about his knowledge of Jewish affairs and how fortunate he considered himself to

79. Bruce, *Acts*, 1954, 434.

80. Stott, *Message of Acts*, 369.

81. Deissmann, *Ancient East*, 350–63.

82. Rackham, *Acts*, 458.

83. Longenecker, "Acts," 9:550.

84. Lenski, *Acts*, 1029.

appear before him (26:2–3). He could not fulfill his responsibility for the temple and appointing the high priest without this. As Agrippa believed the prophets (26:27), he was not identified as a Sadducee, and, like most Jews, he would not have been a member of any group. His extensive knowledge should allow him to see more clearly Paul's innocence relating to Jewish Law. Having been raised in Claudius's household, he would also have been familiar with Roman law, which he was expected to administer correctly. On that charge also Paul was innocent. Agrippa would have been a better judge than the Sanhedrin with their hostility, though at this stage he had no authority.

Unlike the lawyer Tertullus (24:1), Paul did not promise to be brief as he intended to explain clearly the motivation behind his life and ministry,[85] meaning we have a very abbreviated account. While Agrippa is addressed, Paul spoke to both he and Bernice and to all who were present. Paul had been called to be a witness in Rome, and these dignitaries represented Rome, but he was also called to testify to those of no importance (26:22). Likely from the dignitaries through to the slaves who had only experienced Jewish contempt, it was the first time they heard this inclusive offer of salvation. His evangelistic appeal towards the end of this chapter was extended to all present and those whom he had addressed in the "you" comment in verse 8.

26:4–8. The zealous young Pharisee. Paul outlined his early life growing up in Jerusalem, not just as a pious Jew but living by the requirements of the strictest group, the Pharisees (26:4). The charge of bringing a gentile into the temple was preposterous as his faithful observance to this sect was well-known by all his accusers (26:5). He is not in chains because of that false charge but because of the Jewish hope of the resurrection. Christianity was not some new innovation but grounded in the promise given to the patriarchs and the twelve tribes (26:6–7). The Way is so rooted in the old that "the true Jew must become a Christian, in order to remain a Jew."[86] To be on trial by the Jews before a Roman governor for the hope they strived for night and day is incomprehensible (26:7). Paul respected Agrippa's status and his claim to Jewish orthodoxy when he included Agrippa and Bernice in the promise given to "our" fathers and "our" twelve tribes.[87] The two would reply in the affirmative

85. Bock, *Acts*, 713.

86. Conzelmann, *Acts*, 210.

87. The ten tribes who practiced idolatry in the Northern Kingdom were largely "lost." This was either through intermarriage and becoming the Samaritans, being part

to Paul's rhetorical question about whether God can raise the dead (26:8) if they were truly Jewish. Resurrection, at the core of Jewish hope, was incredible for the gentile audience with their petty and immoral gods, so the question was directed to them, and this ultimately is what pagan Nero will be asked to rule on. The resurrection of Jesus is not specifically mentioned till verse 23.

26:9–11. Zeal turns to persecution. The question was also directed to the Jews to whom the very idea of the raising of Jesus was worse than impossible. His resurrection, the very proof of the Jewish hope, was considered blasphemy and Paul thought no differently (26:9). He fulfilled his duty as an "apostle of the Law" by actively tracking down the followers of Jesus the Nazarene, acting on the chief priest's authority (26:9). He imprisoned and punished them (26:10) in Jerusalem and foreign cities and all the time did it with a clear conscience (23:1). Paul admitted his enormous guilt by calling them "saints."

This "punishment" was done openly in the synagogues for maximum deterrent,[88] something not mentioned in the other two accounts of Paul's conversion. The faith of the persecuted was so earnest that it appeared his attempts were largely unsuccessful,[89] and so he voted with those that passed the death sentence.[90] Paul speaks repeatedly of "them" (26:10–11), pointing to many being killed, but only the Romans could impose the death penalty. This suggests their deaths were illegal acts in which Paul was complicit.[91] Peter declared in his Pentecost sermon that on Jesus' resurrection he went to God's side where he offered salvation and judgment, and that everyone was accountable to him (Acts 2:30–6). Paul would come to understand that attempts to make the saints renounce Jesus was attempting to make them blaspheme (26:11), and that his eager blasphemy was greater than any he extracted under torture.

26:12–18. Called to be a servant and witness. Paul was authorized by the high priests to continue the mission of cleansing Judaism in Damascus. Instead of resting during the midday heat he pressed onwards,

of the dispersion, or being absorbed into paganism. The two remaining were representative of the twelve.

88. The process of flogging is described in detail in M. *Mak* 3:10–15.

89. Pliny the Younger, in his Letter to Emperor Trajan (c. 112), reported that people who are really Christians cannot be made to blaspheme Jesus. Pliny the Younger, *Ep.* 96.

90. This opens the question of whether Paul was a member of the Sanhedrin, but he makes no mention of this in his Letters. Suggestions are that he was voicing his support for their actions or was given special voting rights as an agent of the Sanhedrin.

91. Bock, *Acts*, 715.

driven by his task, but he encountered the risen Jesus. What happened on the road was impossible for an honest heart to dismiss as it was not an internal private vision but an encounter experienced by the whole party. The account before Agrippa is the third time Paul's commissioning is told, and Luke told it slightly differently each time. For brevity, refer to my comments on 9:1–9 where the three accounts are examined together. The new information introduced here is that:

- the light was brighter than the sun;
- Paul and his companions saw the light;
- all fell to the ground;
- Jesus spoke in Aramaic (or Hebrew);
- Paul received his commission on the road; and
- Paul was kicking against the goads.

It took a theophany for Paul to understand that Jesus was risen and that in murdering his followers the Lord was saying he was pursuing God himself. What Paul knew of the teaching of the apostles and Stephen had turned his heart to murder, but he immediately understood that it was true with yet more to come through revelation (Gal 1:11).[92] Refer to my notes on Acts 9:5 for the significance of the goad.

Luke minimized any human aid in his third telling of the events on the road by omitting Paul's blindness, being led by others, and his healing by Ananias with his reassuring confirmation of the commission. All the emphasis is on the commission direct from Jesus.[93] The one he called "lord" from respect (26:13) revealed himself as the "Lord" he was to serve and be a witness to the things he had seen and to what Paul would yet see from him (26:16). The similarity of the call here to that of the apostles in 1:8 suggests Paul was elevated to a rank equal to that of the twelve.[94] Further, the similarity of the calling of Paul to Ezekiel (Ezek 2:1, 3) and Jeremiah (1:7–8) points to his elevation as a prophet.[95] Beyond that, as a "servant" (26:16) his gentile mission is told in a way that echoes the work of the servant of the Lord (Isa 42:7, 16, Acts 13:47) by bringing light to the oppressed. The servant's role in Isaiah was "to open their eyes and

92. Bock, *Acts*, 717.

93. Longenecker, "Acts," 9:553.

94. Bock, *Acts*, 717.

95. Longenecker, "Acts," 9:553.

turn them from darkness to light."[96] As a "witness" he stood before rulers in a court second only to that of Caesar and pleaded with high and low to be as he was but without the chains (26:29).

Jesus did not guarantee that Paul would not suffer. It was the vocation of a prophet to suffer,[97] but he did promise to deliver him (26:17) from Jew and gentile alike. All his suffering was put in perspective by the overwhelming appearance of Jesus in the light. Some of this suffering and deliverance has been recorded in Acts but is not the full story. Paul was shipwrecked three times prior to chapter 27 and beaten with rods at least three times. Jesus had also promised Paul that he would testify in Rome and that meant navigating many risks while imprisoned. His ministry of light, while primarily directed to the gentiles, was to both groups and always started with the Jews. The powers that are at work in the world and personal affairs transcends human malevolence and cannot be solved by personal effort. Both Jew and gentile needed their eyes opened as both are blind, they both need to be turned from darkness to light, and both needed deliverance from the dark power of Satan (26:18).[98] The sun shining on the silver clothing of Agrippa's father, another persecutor of Jesus, gave the illusion of glory and the gentiles declared him a god. Such was the darkness that the one who shone brighter than the sun came to dispel. The offer to share in this light was extended to the king for the first time in this address.

Jesus first described the gospel to Paul using images drawn from the Old Testament of the work of the servant such as bringing light and opening blind eyes, but he then stated very clearly what it was. It comprised two main parts:

- the forgiveness of sins; and
- receiving a place (or inheritance) among those sanctified by faith in him (26:18).

The person that has an inheritance from God must have fellowship with him. This inheritance is linked to sanctification which in turn is

96. Johnson, *Message of Acts*, 116.

97. Stott, *Message of Acts*, 373.

98. The commission from Ananias and at the Jerusalem temple so closely resemble the words of the commission given on the road that some suggest they are rolled into one for simplicity. Bruce, *Acts*, 1954, 491.

linked to the justification that comes through faith in Jesus, all three are distinguishable but not separate.[99]

26:18–21. Paul almost killed by Jews. Paul then demonstrated his complete obedience to that call (26:19) by preaching to Jew and gentile in Damascus, Jerusalem, and Judea[100] how they can receive forgiveness through faith in the resurrected Jesus. True turning to God through repentance and faith was demonstrated by a corresponding life, something that was very pointed to Agrippa and Bernice. Christianity was not just a moral code enhanced by a few ceremonies,[101] but was firmly founded on the hope of Israel. Works were not the basis of acceptance, but its evidence. People who live this way did not threaten Caesar as they were not looking for a military leader.[102] For many Jews, the hope of the resurrection had in effect been replaced with the hope of a military deliverer who would only triumph. The offer was extended to Agrippa for the second time.

Paul insisted that he was imprisoned because he preached the same message to Jew and gentile alike (26:21). Anything else the chief priests raised was simply a pretext used to justify his imprisonment and had nothing to do with breaching actual Roman law. Paul's preaching about Jesus was irritant enough, but for many Jews and some Christians, too, there was no possibility that the gentiles could share in the messianic blessings. For Paul to preach otherwise and to claim that it represented true Judaism was outrageous but when civil disturbance followed that message, Paul was not responsible for it.

26:22–23. Paul has constantly witnessed to that day. That Paul remained alive despite the murderous intent of the Jews over many years declared the divine nature of his call and of God's protection of his messenger (26:22). Despite their murderous intent and years of imprisonment, there is no hint of reproach from Paul against the Jews. The message of a

99. Bock, *Acts*, 718. He believes this summarizes the mission of Luke–Acts.

100. The Acts 9 account and Gal 1:22 does not allow for Paul evangelizing in Judea. Various explanations are suggested from Luke exaggerating, a compression of events including possibly some not being recorded, to some words being missing. It is of little importance.

101. Gooding, *True to the Faith*, 399.

102. Pliny the Younger describes how Christians "sang in alternate verses a hymn to Christ, as to a god, and bound themselves by a solemn oath, not to any wicked deeds, but never to commit any fraud, theft or adultery, never to falsify their word, nor deny a trust when they should be called upon to deliver it up." Pliny the Younger, *Ep.* 96. Such people were no threat to Caesar.

suffering messiah and of his resurrection may have appeared new but it was founded on old promises (26:22). The promises that blessings would flow to the gentiles dated back to Abraham's covenant (Gen 12:1–3) and the prophets (e.g., Isa 2:1–4, Rom 15:7–12). By rejecting Paul's use of the Old Testament, his accusers effectively denounced Moses, the giver of the Law, and all the Lord's prophets. Luke chose not to mention any of the verses Paul would have used to make his case. In verse 23, Paul returned to his opening remarks about being on trial for his belief in the resurrection (26:6–8) and looked to the resurrection of Jesus that confirmed Israel's hope and was the precursor of our own (26:23). Paul's gentile mission as a messenger of light echoes the servant's role in Isaiah, which was to "open their eyes and turn them from darkness to light."[103] When a light shone brighter than the sun on the road to Damascus it exposed his own darkness when he persecuted the saints; it was a light that led the church into its universal proclamation. The offer was extended to Agrippa for the third time.

When commenting on chapter 20 we saw that Luke drew similarities between the farewell message of Jesus and that to the Ephesian elders. There's an even closer link and similar wording between the farewell discourse of Jesus in Luke 24:44–48 and at the end of Paul's defense before Festus and Agrippa. Also, the charge to be witnesses, the opening theme of Acts, is continued. Here in verses 22 and 23 we see the following:

- the promise of the gospel is foretold in the Law and Prophets (Luke 24:44; Acts 26:22);
- the Messiah must suffer (Luke 24:46; Acts 26:23);
- he must be resurrected from the dead (Luke 24:46; Acts 26:23);
- the gospel must be proclaimed (Luke 24:47; Acts 26:23); and
- it must go to the gentiles (Luke 24:47; Acts 26:23).[104]

THE RESPONSE TO PAUL'S WITNESSING (26:24–32)

The Lord's chosen witness who was speaking at the height of his work must have gripped everyone present as only at this point was Paul

103. Johnson, *Message of Acts*, 116.

104. Edwards, "Parallels and Patterns," 495.

interrupted loudly by Festus (26:24).[105] If the governor was seeking clarity, he was likely more confused than before and, through his own ignorance, thought Paul's great learning had driven him to embrace insane things.[106] Likely he wondered how such fantasies could have enraged a whole nation.[107] The gospel, especially when adding its reconciliation of the races to the resurrection, was foolishness to the gentiles (1 Cor 1:23) and no sane Roman could believe it. Paul replied very respectfully that he was sane (26:25) and brushed aside the comment and looked to the king for support. This was reasonable because this was "not done in a corner" (26:26). Had the king ever been addressed this way, and especially by a prisoner? The expression "not done in a corner" meant to do philosophical reflection disconnected from the public.[108] Agrippa understood (26:2–3), even if he did not agree with Paul, that the claims were too public to be denied by anyone paying attention.

Paul was attempting publicly to make Agrippa a Christian, and in his rhetorical question—"Do you believe the prophets?"—was feeling his way towards a commitment. But Agrippa was not persuaded. The exact meaning of his reply to Paul (26:28) is debated, but as Paul uses a similar expression in verse 29 about "short time or long," the two are connected. However, the intent is clear. Agrippa was first reminded that the ministry, death, and resurrection of Jesus, along with the birth of the church with its signs and wonders, were public knowledge. Agrippa could not say that he disbelieved the prophets as his claim to orthodoxy would be destroyed, but if he said he believed then why was he not a Christian as they testify to Jesus? Agrippa chose to protect his reputation by deflecting the question with the claim that Paul's argument was too brief. The prisoner is unapologetic; he wanted and prayed that all who heard him, not just the king, would be Christians but without the chains.

From Herod the Great trying to murder the infant Jesus through to killing James, the son of Zebedee, the family had set themselves up in opposition to God over generations. John the Baptist had publicly denounced Herod Antipas for having his brother's wife. Drusilla was

105. Lenski, *Acts*, 1023–4.

106. Bock, *Acts*, 722. Gooding questions the sanity of anyone who could watch gladiatorial combat for pleasure. Gooding, *True to the Faith*, 405.

107. Bruce, *Acts*, 1954, 495.

108. Epictetus, *Diatr.* 2.12.17; Plutarch, *Mor.* 777b. The references to Greek plays and philosophers in this chapter and similarly in Athens, suggests Paul's knowledge was broad.

another Herodian woman who had divorced her husband to marry Felix and Paul spoke to them about righteousness, self-control and the judgment to come. The Herod that stood before Paul was believed to have been in an incestuous relationship with his sister. But instead of telling them how they should live, Paul told them how Christians lived (26:20). The commentator Richard Rackhan observed, "It is true that Agrippa somewhat cynically warded off S. Paul's advances, but had he been as morally worthless as the other Herods, we feel sure that the apostle would have adopted a different tone."[109]

At this the governor, Agrippa and Bernice arose (26:30), and they and the other dignitaries discussed the case. Paul is declared innocent for the third time by Festus (26:31; 25:19–20, 25), as was Jesus (Luke 23:4, 14, 22). Even a madman does not deserve death or even imprisonment. They conclude that Paul could have been set free if he had not appealed to the emperor (26:32). The matter was out of their hands and presumably Agrippa told Festus what to write. For his part, "Paul had demonstrated that he was a faithful Jew, a faithful Roman, and a faithful Christian."[110]

109. Rackham, *Acts*, 458.

110. Stott, *Message of Acts*, 178.

16

Paul's Journey to Rome (Acts 27:1—28:16)

FROM CAESAREA TO FAIR HAVENS (27:1–7)

Figure 6. Paul's voyage to Rome

Luke's retelling of the voyage to Rome may be the best piece of descriptive writing in the Bible and is also one of the great sources on ancient sea travel.[1] A direct sea journey to Rome was likely to take five weeks, about the same as travelling by land.[2] If choosing a sea voyage,

1. My comments on this chapter draw heavily on James Smith's *The Voyage and Shipwreck of St. Paul*, which is described by Bruce as "one of the completest services that has ever been rendered to New Testament scholarship." Bruce, *Acts*, 1954, 518.

2. Bruce, *Acts*, 1990, 511. Casson gives the time from Caesarea to Rhodes at five days and Rhodes to Rome at forty-five to sixty-three days. Casson, *Speed Under Sail*, 145–46.

the convenience of passenger ships did not exist in the ancient world. Travelers would simply board any ship heading in the general direction of the destination, "hopping from port to port if he could find none that would take him all the way."[3] However it was not always smooth sailing, and Greek culture had portrayed destruction during a storm as a sign of wickedness[4] and, conversely, surviving an ordeal at sea as a sign of a person's righteousness.[5] Paul's righteousness will be displayed through the three-fold deliverance from storm, shipwreck, and snake bite. However, the first part of the journey, presumably on a smaller, coastal trading ship, gave no indication of what would befall the group on the second stage.

The account starts with the final "we" section and is told in much more detail than earlier voyages. His readers would understand how far away Rome was and how God was determined to ensure Paul arrived there safely.[6] He and the other prisoners[7] were put under the charge of Julius, a centurion of the Augustine (or Imperial) regiment (27:1), and again a centurion is portrayed favorably. His regiment is known from inscriptions, but there is little certainty of its status. It is thought to be an auxiliary regiment made up mainly of Syrians, meaning they would be more likely to handle prisoners.[8] The ship was from Adramyttium (26:2) and may have been returning home. Adramyttium was a port in Mysia about 175 kilometers north of Ephesus and opposite Lesbos. Their journey was anything but direct, travelling along the ports of Asia,[9] but at any of these Asian ports the centurion could have expected a direct ship to Rome.

Paul had unusual freedom for a prisoner of Rome, but he was a citizen who had been declared innocent. However, we cannot minimize the effect of what was clearly a person with a very strong presence. He also had two attendants, marking him out as a gentleman.[10] Luke may

3. Casson, *Ancient Mariner*, 209.

4. Williams, *Acts*, 426.

5. See, e.g., Homer's *Odyssey*.

6. Bock, *Acts*, 728.

7. Ramsay says of the other prisoners that they "had been in all probability already condemned to death, and were going to supply the perpetual demand which Rome made on the provinces for human victims to amuse the populace by their death in the arena." Ramsay, *St. Paul*, 314.

8. Bruce, *Acts*, 1954, 500.

9. Over two years earlier the journey to Jerusalem was on the southern side of Cyprus to catch favorable winds.

10. Longenecker, "Acts," 9:558.

have been classed as his personal doctor and the second, Aristarchus, a Macedonian from Thessalonica (Col 4:10; Phlm 24), as his servant or perhaps even thought to be his slave.[11] From the pomp of his last hearing, Paul's jailor would have understood he was not the usual prisoner, so it is hardly surprising allowances were made. The following day they reached Sidon, their first stop, about 110 kilometers north. There, Julius graciously allowed Paul to visit his friends and provide for his needs, no doubt with a soldier in attendance. After years of uncertainty fighting for his life against his countrymen, Paul will only know unusual kindness for the remainder of Luke's account.

The ship then hugged the coast sailing between Asia and Cyprus. This route protected the ship from the westerly and northwesterly winds that blew in summer and autumn but required tacking all the way (27:4) and likely anchoring in protected inlets when needed. While the journey was very slow, a steady westward current helped. After leaving the protection of Cyprus, they passed Cilicia and Pamphylia and, in what may have been fifteen days'[12] sailing, reached Myra in Lycia (27:5), about a further eight hundred kilometers on. There, Julius found an Alexandrian grain ship (27:38) that was sailing directly to Rome (27:6), so he put his charges onboard. Myra was directly north of Alexandria and was an important stop on the grain ships' run to Rome because poor navigation at the time and prevailing winds made it an easy port to reach. It had a protected harbor and provided a safer run onto Rome.[13]

As this was dangerously late in the season, it is possible the captain was trying to cram in a second trip for the year.[14] Lucian gave us a description of the *Isis*, one of these Alexandrian grain ships, when it arrived in the port for Athens after being driven off course in a storm. It measured 55 meters long, 14.5 meters wide, and 13.5 meters from the deck to the bottom of the hold at its deepest.[15] This ship could carry between twelve hundred and thirteen hundred tons of grain. Ships as large as that

11. Ramsay, *St. Paul*, 316,

12. Bock, *Acts*, 732.

13. Smith, *Voyage*, 72–73.

14. Casson, *Ancient Mariner*, 238.

15. Lucian, "Ship," 4:36. Lucian's account also includes the captain's retelling of the ship being driven by a severe storm. The wreck of the *Isis* was discovered by Richard Ballard off Sicily in 1989. To compare sizes, the *Cutty Sark*, built in 1869, was 64.5 meters long, 11 meters wide, and carried 920 tons.

were not found on the transatlantic run until the nineteenth century.[16] Sailing continued to be slow, taking several days to be off Cnidus on the southwestern coast of Asia Minor, a journey of about 210 kilometers (27:7). They then sailed under the lee of Crete, hugging the coast till they reached Fair Havens, or "Good Harbor," a small bay near the town of Lasea (now only a ruin) on the central southwest coast.

FROM FAIR HAVENS TO SHIPWRECKED ON MALTA (27:9–44)

Fair Havens was open to the sea but well protected by islands. While not equal to ports such as Lutro further along the coast, James Smith believed it was still "a very fair winter harbor"[17] for the three stormy months ahead. Given the suddenness with which the storms arose and the risks involved in leaving a passable port, the decision to leave was very questionable on nautical grounds.[18] Slow progress had taken them into the "Dangerous Season," which started in mid-September. This was the date from which voyages should not start and sailing should cease from November 11.[19] Sailing did not normally start again till mid-February[20] or even mid-March. They arrived at Fair Havens after the Day of Atonement (27:9) (and presumably before the Feast of Tabernacles), a date that changed every year as it is based on a lunar calendar.[21] In AD 59 it fell on October 5, and for the other years either side from AD 57 to 62 it was earlier, strongly suggesting that AD 59 was the year the ships arrived at Fair Havens.

Paul, who had already been shipwrecked three times, knew how dangerous it was to proceed to a better harbor. He obviously had extraordinary freedom to be in a position to advise the centurion, ship owner,

16. Casson, *Ancient Mariner*, 209. He says that the "creation and maintenance of this [Alexandrian grain] fleet was Rome's single greatest maritime achievement, at once a great passenger and a great freight service." Casson, *Ancient Mariner*, 238.

17. Smith, *Voyage*, 85.

18. Smith, *Voyage*, 85.

19. Vegetius, *Epitome*, 4.39. In times of famine there could be big bonuses and insurance for any ships risking a winter crossing from Egypt. Suetonius, *Twelve Caesars*, 172.

20. Pliny, *Nat.* 2.47.

21. The Day of Atonement was on the tenth day of the lunar month Tishri while the Feast of Tabernacles started on the fifteenth day.

and pilot. Perhaps, in the face of danger they were willing to hear out a "religious" man,[22] especially one so experienced.[23] He sensed great danger and loss of life (27;10), but was he only speaking from experience[24] or as a prophet?[25] Contrary to almost all the commentators, I feel it was more likely as a prophet. The Spirit had driven him to Jerusalem with warnings all along the way of the impending imprisonment. Paul thought his task was to deliver the offering and knit the hearts of Jew and gentile believers, but God's plan saw further as he wanted Paul to stand before Nero. Now that plan is in grave jeopardy, and there is no tribune to rescue or Roman law to protect, so should we believe the Spirit is silent when he has led Paul on all his journeys? I think not. But to say his advice was Spirit-led imposes difficulties that are discussed in my comments on verses 24 and 31, difficulties that any prayerful person should embrace.

However, the views of the shipowner and the pilot sway Julius (27:11), who ultimately had no say as he was only a passenger, and the ship set out for the better Cretan harbor of Phoenix (27:12)[26] about eighty kilometers further along the coast. Setting off into a favorable light wind and sailing close offshore for safety (27:13), what could possibly go wrong as the harbor was only a few hours away? But once they rounded Cape Matala, a strong "typhonic" wind called the "Northeaster" came down from the 2,440-meter-high Mt. Ida (27:14) and drove the ship southwards away from the island's protection (27:15). Pliny described typhoons as being "very much dreaded by sailors, as it not only breaks their sail-yards, but the vessels themselves, bending them about in various ways."[27] These violent winds were a common occurrence in this region,[28] and it was so sudden that there wasn't even time to bring the dinghy onboard.

22. Bock, *Acts*, 734.

23. Eleven journeys amounting to fifty-six hundred kilometers are recorded in Acts. Stott, *Message of Acts*, 390.

24. Bruce, *Acts*, 1954, 508.

25. Or at least being portrayed that way by Luke. Haenchen, *Acts*, 700.

26. Ramsay and Smith identify Phoenix with Lutro, which is described as the only secure harbor in all winds in the south of Crete. But the harbor is not open to the northeast and southeast. Smith, *Voyage*, 91–92n3. Ramsay suggests this was the direction from which inbound ships approached the harbor. Ramsay, *St. Paul*, 326. Modern Phineka, a short distance away, is open to westerly winds but may have had a good harbor in the past. Bruce, *Acts*, 1954, 508. The topography has changed since then due to earthquakes and silting so we can't know what the harbors were like when Luke wrote.

27. Pliny, *Nat.* 2.48.

28. Smith, *Voyage*, 102.

With the crew unable to turn the bow into the wind, effective control of the ship was lost (27:15). This was not entirely uncommon,[29] but when they reached the protection of the small island of Cauda (modern Gavdos, thirty-seven kilometers distant), the sailors were able, with difficulty, to pull the water filled dinghy on board (27:16). They were also able to take emergency measures, running ropes under or along the ship to strengthen it and also lowered the spar. They were concerned that they might run aground on the Syrtis, a combination of sandbars and shoals in the Gulf of Sidra in Cyrene off North Africa, about 650 kilometers from where they started. They also lowered "their gear," sometimes called a sea anchor to create drag (27:17) but more likely lowering their fair-weather sails and spars.[30] The lull in the storm was only temporary and on the following day "they," likely every able-bodied person, threw some of the cargo overboard (17:18). Obviously from verse 38 and 40, not all the cargo and tackle were thrown overboard, the remainder may have been retained as ballast. On the following day they also threw overboard the "tackle" (27:19), so the ship was not so deep in the water. As everybody seemed to be involved with this it is likely that the massive main-yard, possibly as long as the ship, was jettisoned.[31] All the time the ship was being driven at the mercy of the storm (27:15), but not totally as doing nothing would have seen them driven to the Syrtis.

Smith's investigation with Royal Navy captains experienced in the region suggests the practice would have been to hoist the storm sail and set the ship on the starboard tack, i.e., with the right side to the wind and then drift in the storm at about 2.4 kilometers per hour, which would give a course of 8 degrees north of west.[32] After several days without sight of either sun or stars by which they could determine their location, even Paul had given up any hope of surviving the storm (27:20). During this time there was no chance of preparing food, let alone keeping it down, and, presumably, with this level of despair, the ship was in a poor state. The sailors for their part would have invoked the many foreign gods to no avail.

29. Lucian, "Ship," 4:7; Homer, *Od.* 9.82.

30. Smith, *Voyage*, 111. However, the sea anchor would have been part of normal procedure.

31. Smith, *Voyage*, 116. The main sail would have been the means of avoiding the Syrtis if they were driven that way.

32. Smith, *Voyage*, 107, 126. His drift rate was the average of all the suggested rates provided by experiences Royal Navy officers.

Paul had warned them that by leaving Fair Havens all they would "gain" was injury and loss (27:21), and while they awaited their inevitable destruction, he reminded them again that he was right. It is hard to imagine that with renewed hope Paul was totally free of the desire to say "I told you so," but he had proven that he deserved to be listened to. Now with a message of deliverance, the point of the reminder was that they must start to listen to God working through him (27:21). Paul had been visited by an angel of the God he served who reminded him about the promise Jesus gave that he must stand before Caesar (27:24). Now he alone has the best grasp of the situation[33] and listen to him they must as on three occasions he would tell them what needed to be done to be saved. His first advice was to take courage (27:22 and again in 27:25) as they would survive the storm and that only the ship would be lost when they ran aground on some island (27:26). People who had thrown in the towel were no use with the hard work ahead.

If speaking as a prophet in verse 10 as I suggest, the decision to leave Fair Havens was not something set in God's determinative will where no argument, however sound, could stop the departure. Two options were presented, both of which the owner and pilot were free to take, but the consequence of one was that there would be loss of life as well as the ship. Now, again speaking as a prophet, there will only be the loss of the ship and cargo. The implication is that God can change his mind as a gift to Paul, a person he has favored (27:24). What was determined was that Paul "must" stand before Caesar. Even as a prisoner of Rome, Paul can influence things, and his deliverance gave further evidence of his innocence and the impotence of pagan religion. As Bruce noted, "The world has no idea how much it owes, in the mercy of God, to the presence of righteous men."[34]

The remainder of the trip would not be easy, but it was survivable, and after fourteen days (27:27) being driven across the Adria or Hadria Sea (not our Adriatic), they neared Malta, about 725 kilometers from where the storm hit. Finding this small island, which was only 27 kilometers long and 14.5 kilometers wide was like finding a needle in a haystack.[35] At about midnight on that final night the sailors sensed they

33. Bock, *Acts*, 738,

34. Bruce, *Acts*, 1954, 512.

35. Bock, *Acts*, 738. Or perhaps not. The bearing suggested by Smith to avoid the Syrtis and the drift rate takes the ship to within five kilometers of St. Paul's Bay in roughly thirteen days. He admits that this is to a "certain extent accidental but could

were near land (27:27). Likely the wind had died down and they could hear breaking waves. On taking soundings, they found the depth to be thirty-six meters and shortly after only twenty-seven meters[36] (27:28). To avoid the ship smashing on rocks, four anchors were laid at the stern (normally done at the bow), and they prayed for daylight (27:29). Given their treachery the next morning, unlike the sailors in Jonah's storm (Jonah 1:16), they had not taken to heart their deliverance by the God that Paul served.

Paul's second piece of advice to ensure deliverance was to make sure that everyone stayed together. When morning arrived, the sailors lowered the boat claiming they were going to let anchors out from the bow but intended to save themselves and leave the others to the mercy of the sea. Paul, now the trusted source of advice, recognized their treachery and told Julius that without the sailors they cannot be saved, and he in turn cut the dinghy loose (27:31–2). Under stress to preserve his life, the centurion may have looked to Paul who was prophet-like. God had decreed that all would be saved (27:24), but then Paul saw a situation where they cannot be saved. Deliverance is partly a miracle in that they made it across 725 kilometers and fourteen days of extreme storm to come upon Malta, and partly human for the last few hundred meters the one depended on the other.

Thirdly, recognizing that everyone was weak as they had eaten very little over the preceding fourteen days, Paul urged all to eat as they would need their strength to survive (27:33–4). Again, safety was not automatic just because God had determined it. There was a Jewish proverb: "Not a hair of his head will fall to the ground" (1 Sam 14:45; 2 Sam 14:11; 1 Kgs 1:52). When speaking of the troubles and persecutions to come, Jesus used this proverb, but he instead said "perish" instead of "fall to the ground" (Luke 21:18). Paul repeated Jesus' version of the proverb, assuring the sailors and passengers that not a hair of their heads will perish. The meal on the ship is not the Lord's Supper, though very similar wording is used of Luke's account of the Last Supper and of the meal at

not have happened had there been any inaccuracy on the part of the author." Smith, *Voyage*, 126–28.

36. These are the soundings that would be expected passing Koura on the east coast of Malta on the way into St. Paul's Bay. The sound of the breaking waves on the rocks can be first heard at a sounding of thirty-six meters. Smith, *Voyage*, 130–31. He quotes from the court martial following the founding of the frigate *Lively* in 1810 at the same location where the person on watch said that "at the distance of a mile the land could not be seen but that he saw the surf on the shore."

Emmaus. Both took the bread, gave thanks, and broke it (Luke 22:19; Acts 27:35). It has been observed that "the core wording of the meal aboard ship . . . agrees verbatim with Jesus's eucharistic words in Luke 22:19, which in turn agrees with the earliest eucharistic wording in 1 Cor 11:23–24."[37] Notwithstanding, the meal was a sacred moment as they had passed through what should have been certain death for 276 people[38] (27:37), so he unashamedly blessed the lifesaving food in view of the pagans. Once strengthened, they threw the remainder of the grain overboard, so the ship rode still higher in the water (27:38).

Daylight eventually came, and the sailors did not recognize the land but saw a bay with a sandy beach where they aimed to run the boat ashore (27:39). The soundings, the creek, and the rocks nearby all match St. Paul's Bay, but the sand is now gone. They cut away the anchors, loosened the ropes on the rudders, hoisted a foresail, and made for the shore (27:40) In the process the ship ran aground on a sandbank where the bow stuck fast, allowing the already weakened stern to break up (27:41). The soldiers wanted to kill the prisoners as, should they escape, they would be likely to suffer the same punishment as the prisoner would have received (27:42). Normally the centurion would have had no issues with this, but he was successful in stopping it this time. He wanted to save Paul (27:43), likely not because he liked him but because the God his prisoner served had favored all with deliverance, something lost on those under him. It should have left a strong impression. Julius instructed those who could swim to make for land first and then those who could not swim were to make for the shore on broken up planks. It may have taken a while for there to be sufficient debris to make it possible for all 276 to be able to do this (27:44). All reached shore safely. In a reversal of the book of Jonah, deliverance came because of the presence of a prophet marked out by God and who was obedient to his call, which further reinforced the judgment made in Caesarea: Paul was innocent.

THREE MONTHS IN MALTA (28:1–10)

On reaching land safely they found that they had arrived on the island of Malta, about ninety-five kilometers south of Sicily. Malta was colonized

37. Edwards, "Parallels and Patterns," 498.

38. Josephus records being on a ship with six hundred others, which sank and only eighty were saved, so this number is not unrealistic. Josephus, *Life* 3.

by the Phoenicians at about 1000 BC but fell to Rome during the second Punic war in 218 BC. The population spoke Punic (Carthaginian) as their first language, not Greek or Latin,[39] and did not have the benefit of the strong influence of those cultures. So Luke called them "barbarians" (28:2). But they were far from our understanding of a barbarian as they showed "unconditional kindness, a love of humanity"[40] beyond what Luke expected to those who were shipwrecked. Culture and humanity are not always handmaidens. The island's name in Punic meant "place of refuge,"[41] which it had become. They lit a fire, or more likely a series of fires, to warm all 276 people. Paul continued to be useful by gathering sticks, picking up a poisonous snake in the process,[42] which bit him on the hand (28:3).[43]

The locals considered that even if he had escaped the shipwreck unharmed, "justice" had not allowed a murderer to go unpunished (28:4). He must surely swell up and die. To them justice was not a concept, but the god Dike, the daughter of Zeus and Themis, a role she shared with her mother. As for Paul, he simply shook the snake into the fire (28:5) and showed no ill effects. God had ordained that he will reach Rome. After watching in unbelief for some time, the locals changed their mind and considered that Paul must be a god (28:6), something that he would not allow to go uncorrected, and there is no mention of trying to worship him. No doubt he would have tried to explain that he was a "heaven-directed man with a God-given message but also a heaven-protected man";[44] but a man, nonetheless.

Luke has allocated a considerable amount of space to a relatively few days, traumatic though they were, in a book that was carefully constructed for its length. Some may see the story's value as out of proportion

39. Bruce, *Acts*, 1954, 521.

40. Bock, *Acts*, 742.

41. Longenecker, "Acts," 9:563. Paul would have understood the significance of this as Hebrew and Punic were closely related.

42. The snake is described as a viper. There are now no non-introduced snakes that are dangerous to humans in Malta, but there may have been venomous vipers then. Bruce uses the analogy of Ireland that once had poisonous snakes but does not now. Bruce, *Acts*, 1990, 531. A small island that has been populated for a long time must experience changes. Ramsay, *St. Paul*, 343.

43. A similar story of a viper biting a shipwreck victim, with the same irony, is found in *Anth. Pal.* 7.290.

44. Longenecker, "Acts," 9:564. This is the opposite of the response in Lystra where Paul is first thought a god and then stoned (14:11–19).

to its length, but this only means the reader has failed to understand how Luke was in awe of God's providence. Paul had a desire, implanted by God to visit Rome (19:21), but God had a plan for him to witness there (23:11), which he later revealed would include witnessing before Nero (27:24). Rome would even organize this themselves. Every danger was designed to prevent Paul from reaching his "God-planned, God-promised destination."[45] Paul has been rescued from the Jerusalem mob, years in prison, assassination attempts, the storm, a shipwreck, soldiers that wanted to kill him, and finally a poisonous snake bite. Yet it was not the forces of nature nor the machinations of men that were at play, but demonic forces working through them.[46] Understandably then, Luke constantly used vocabulary of salvation in his storm account (27:20, 31, 34, 43, 44; 28:1, 4),

The generosity of the rescuers was matched by Publius, the chief man of the island (either a governor[47] or simply the biggest landowner), who welcomed them into his nearby estate for three days (28:7). The island had its own unpleasant disease still known as Malta Fever. Publius's father was in bed suffering from fevers, which was likely this, along with dysentery.[48] Paul went to him, and, after praying, he placed his hands on the man who was then healed (28:8). This is the only place where healing through the laying on of hands is recorded in Acts and was for someone who was not a follower of the Way. The laying on of hands to heal is not found in the Old Testament nor in the Rabbinic literature[49] but is a distinctive Christian ministry that follows the example of Jesus (Luke 4:40). Nothing is known of Publius other than church tradition that says he was the first bishop of Malta and went on to be the second bishop of Athens. He is said to have been martyred there in either AD 112 or 125 under Trajan's persecutions. He is venerated as a saint by both the Roman[50] and Orthodox branch of Christianity. As Luke only uses his

45. Stott, *Message of Acts*, 402.

46. Stott, *Message of Acts*, 402.

47. This was a title given to the governor of the island by Augustus.

48. Malta Fever, otherwise known as brucellosis, is associated with infected goat's milk. Its effects last on average for four months but it could even be years. It is characterized by intermittent fevers. Longenecker, "Acts," 9:565.

49. Fitzmyer, *Acts*, 784. It is found in the Dead Sea Scrolls where Abraham prays and lays his hands on Pharaoh to heal him from a plague caused by stealing Sarah. *Genesis Apocryphon* 20:21–9.

50. Baltimore, *Roman Martyrology*, 21–22.

first name it may indicate that Paul, Publius, and he became friends over the three months there.

The residents did understand that Paul had a close connection with God, a connection that was reinforced when he healed the father of the leading man of the island, and so they come to him to heal their sick also (28:9). The image of a likely manacled Paul laying hands on the sick pagans without first requiring belief and baptism should not be minimized. Bruce suggests that as the honors were poured on all of them that Luke used his medical skills along with Paul's prayers.[51] He was returning the unconditional kindness and a love of humanity that he had received. To receive from and be able to return such kindness to "barbarians" after years of oppression where his own people wanted to kill him must have been very refreshing.[52] That God was hearing him further strengthened Paul's claim to innocence.

FROM MALTA TO ITALY (28:11–15)

Julius found another Alexandrian ship presumably carrying grain and set sail after three months (28:11), making this most likely sometime in February AD 60. This is early in the year for an ocean voyage though possibly acceptable for coastal sailing. However, the first part of the voyage was over one hundred kilometers of open sea to Sicily.[53] This early start likely had the unforeseen advantage of allowing Paul to reach Rome before a bad report was received from the Jewish leaders. The ship had the figurehead of Castor and Pollux (28:11), the twin gods who were said to be sons of Zeus and Leda, a queen of Sparta. They were especially popular in Egypt where the ship was from[54] and were the saviors of shipwrecked sailors.[55] Further, they were also seen as guarding truth and punishing perjurers.[56] Perhaps these attributes were not lost on the travelers.

51. Bruce, *Acts*, 1954, 524.

52. Longenecker, "Acts," 9:565.

53. The different starting date of Vegetius and Pliny the Elder may possibly be put down to open sea and coastal sailing. Ultimately it will be driven by the weather and favorable winds.

54. Haenchen, *Acts*, 717.

55. Lucian, "Ship," 4:9; Graves, *Greek Myths*, 196, 234, 525. They were said to be the brothers of Helen of Troy and had sailed with Jason and the Argonauts.

56. Euripides, *Electra*, 1342–55.

Their first stop was Syracuse (28:12) on the eastern coast of Sicily where, possibly waiting for favorable winds, they stayed three days. The port was the capital of the island and, being founded by the Corinthians in 734 BC, was a center of Greek culture. It had been under Roman control since 212 BC. Syracuse was a natural stop through the Straights of Messina, especially as it had two ports and was described as rich and beautiful.[57] The next stop was Rhegium (28:13) on the toe of Italy, a further 120 kilometers on and this likely required tacking all the way. From there to Puteoli (modern Pozzuoli) (28:13) was a further 320 kilometers northwest in the most sheltered part of the Bay of Naples.[58] The port was roughly 13 kilometers northwest of Neapolis (Naples) and a further 210 kilometers south of Rome. At the time, it was the main grain port. Jews were known to live in Puteoli,[59] so with a church already established in Rome it is not surprising that Paul and his companions were able to find Christians in the city. They urged Paul to stay a week with them (28:14) and circumstances allowed this to happen. Perhaps Julius needed to gather provisions, rest after the journey, or obtain fresh orders. As with Sidon (27:3), the extent of Paul's freedom is remarkable but presumably he was always accompanied by a guard.

Luke says at that point, after what had been a journey of over four months duration, that they reached Rome. However, it was still a five-day walk and Longenecker suggests that it "reflects Luke's eagerness to get to the climax of his story and that eagerness led him to anticipate their arrival in Rome."[60] Luke's account becomes much more concise from his arrival in Italy. News of Paul's presence in Italy had reached the Roman Christians and they came to the Forum of Appius (about seventy kilometers from Rome on the Appian Way) to meet him. Paul was facing an uncertain and testing future in an unfamiliar environment and his meeting with the Christians encouraged him, for which he thanked God. More greeted him at Three Taverns, about thirty-four kilometers from Rome. Both these communities were Roman "halting stations," built every twenty-five kilometers along the Roman road system. He had earlier written his masterpiece, the Book of Romans, to them and their presence greatly encouraged him. The final "we" section ends here.

57. Cicero, *Tusc.* 5.20.

58. Smith, *Voyage*, 157. He includes Cicero's account of the arrival of the grain fleet and shows how important it was.

59. Josephus, *Ant.* 17.12.1.

60. Longenecker, "Acts," 9:567.

17

Paul in Rome (Acts 28:17–31)

Diplomatic relations between the Jews and Roman go back as far as the Maccabees,[1] and Jews are first mentioned as living in Rome in 139 BC.[2] The population of the city itself could have been as large as one million, and it is suggested that Jews could be anywhere from twenty to fifty thousand at the time.[3] Given the difficult past Jews had experienced in Rome, it is likely that they were intentionally not well organized so as to keep a low profile and simply worshiped in independent synagogues.[4] Into this situation came Paul who was allowed to live alone (28:16) in a rented house (28:30) with only a single guard. How could he afford this? Perhaps an inheritance (see my notes on 24:26) or through the support of the Roman Christians. Some suggest that he may have worked at his trade,[5] but this would have been difficult even if lightly chained to a guard. There was also an offering from Philippi (Phil 4:10–9), which was helpful. What harm could Paul do penned up like this?

1. 1 Macc 14:16–18; 15:15–24.

2. Fitzmyer, *Acts*, 792.

3. Larkin, *Acts*, 386. Josephus said that Tiberius banished four thousand Jews from Rome, likely in AD 19 and from the context possibly those engaged in proselytizing or of poor character. Josephus, *Ant.* 18.3.5. Philo, in AD 38, described the respect given to Jews with Roman citizenship and the respect given to their places of worship. Philo, *Embassy* 23. Jews were also expelled during the reign of Claudius; see the notes on 18:2.

4. Polhill, *Acts*, 539. Their influence would increase substantially after AD 62 when Nero married Poppea who Josephus called a God fearer. Josephus: *Ant.* 20.8.11; *Life* 3. So Paul arrived at the "sweet spot," i.e., while Nero was relatively sane and not potentially overly influenced by Jewish leaders.

5. E.g., see Stott, *Message of Acts*, 400.

After settling in for three days, Paul called for the Jewish leaders who he called "brothers" (28:17). His practice of taking the message to the Jews first had not changed, but perhaps also he was trying to learn their attitude towards him as their influence and money could adversely impact his trial.[6] Paul's four points to them were as follows:

- he has done nothing against his people or customs (28:17);
- the Romans wanted to free him (28:18);
- Jewish opposition caused him to appeal to Caesar (28:19); and
- he was a prisoner for believing in the hope of Israel (28:20).

Luke did not elaborate on these points as he assumed the reader was already very familiar with them, but he does stress Paul's innocence just as Jesus was innocent in Luke 23 (refer to Table 14). Though in Roman chains, Rome was not Paul's enemy but protected him against his own nation "who are supposed to pursue justice and honor God."[7] Still, he had no animosity towards his persecutors (28:19). Paul was given a hearing as they said they have not heard anything official from Jerusalem about him (28:21), but any news would have had the same problems reaching Rome as Paul did and the more so as his journey from Malta started early.[8] The leaders' comments about only knowing of Christianity through hearsay must be disingenuous. The disruptive influence of Christianity in Judaism was so well-known that during the late AD 40s Claudius exiled the Jews from Rome because of riots over the preaching of Christ (see my comments on 18:2).

So, despite being well aware of Christianity, they said they only know that people everywhere are speaking against it (28:22). This may have been a diplomatic answer amounting to saying, "We do not want to get involved."[9] Their comment shows that at least they have made enquiries from Jews over a broad range of localities, and that they are not hostile to Paul. Paul's first encounter with a Jewish audience in Rome suggests they were more neutral than he had experienced beforehand, which may have elevated hopes for a positive response (28:17–22). A

6. Longenecker, "Acts," 9:569.

7. Bock, *Acts*, 752.

8. Witherington, *Acts*, 799. He notes that if Paul is in chains because of his Jewish belief, that should have caused them great concern.

9. Longenecker, "Acts," 9:571. The more so as he was a Roman citizen that had already been cleared three times of any wrongdoing.

disinterested one was possibly more problematic. Perhaps they thought that if two governors and one king would not convict Paul in the partisan environment of Caesarea, what chance would they have in Rome?

Paul summarized his trial experiences (28:17b–20) with words that recall Jesus' experiences in Luke's Gospel.

"Jesus in his forewarnings spoke of being 'handed over'" (Luke 9:44; 24:7; 18:32)	"Paul says he was given over into the hands of the Romans" (Acts 28:17; cf. 21:11)
Pilate judged Jesus and found no capital offence (Luke 23:14–15, 22; cf. Acts 13:28–29)	"Paul said in Acts 28:18–19 that the Romans judged him . . . finding no capital offense"
Pilate desired to release him (Luke 23:16, 20, 22)	Further, "they desired to release him" (cf. Acts 24:27; 26:32)
Jesus did "not respond to his accusers" (Luke 23:9–10)	Paul had no "counteraccusation . . . against his people" (Acts 28:19)

Table 15. Luke summarizes Paul's trial experiences with words recalling Jesus' in Luke's Gospel[10]

They agreed to meet at his home on a later date (28:23), and many more people arrived. He spoke to them from all the Scriptures from morning to evening, making the following points:

- He is a witness to the Roman Jews about the kingdom of God that comes through Jesus (28:23).
- Their rejection of Jesus is a fulfilment of Isaiah's prophecy (28:25–27).
- The message will go to the gentiles (28:28).

Presumably, the content of Paul's message included what was in his sermon at the synagogue in Pisidian Antioch (13:13–42) and the Book of Romans and was not a monologue but involved lively discussion. The prophecy of Simeon that Jesus would bring division (Luke 2:34) once again proved true as the experience with the Roman Jews is no different to Jews elsewhere: some believe but most do not. Paul quoted Isa 6:9–10 and attributed it the Holy Spirit (28:25). Isaiah had warned his generation, and Jesus is recorded in all gospels using this passage to warn the Jews in his generation (Matt 13:14–17; Mark 4:10–13; Luke 8:1; John 12:36–41). Like a prophet, Paul also warned his hearers that they also were falling

10. Taken, with adaptations, from Troftgruben, "Ending," 343n52.

into the national pattern of unbelief.[11] They are so hard-hearted that no sensory part is left unaffected. Because of their calloused hearts they cannot hear, see, or understand so they cannot turn to their God who wanted to heal them (28:27). Paul's testimony to the Jews makes it clear that there can be no peace with any alternative to faith in Jesus.[12] Stott, in his commentary, stresses that hardheartedness is only part of the story. The evangelists' preaching, God's judgment, and the suicidal obstinacy of the people are all in play and "all three are true and must be held with equal tenacity."[13] Verse 29 is not considered to be part of the original text, so no comment is made though we can expect it is what happened.

Luke's Gospel gave an end to the earthly ministry of Jesus, which is appropriate as it is a book about fulfilment, but Acts 28 leaves Paul's fate hanging. It "draws attention to unresolved tensions around salvation for Israel in ways Luke 24 does not."[14] This is also appropriate as it is a book about the beginnings, and with Paul in prison the command to witness is an unfinished task. Luke concluded his second book with the statement that Paul lived in rented accommodation for two years (28:30). Is that time significant? His litigants had eighteen months to bring an accusation, which brought speculation that they simply did not appear and that the case lapsed.[15] There were very serious consequences for people that brought vexatious cases. But this goes contrary to the assurance that Paul must stand before Caesar, so it is safer to assume that Luke's readers did expect that this did/would happen. His imprisonment did not stop the free flow of visitors, which shows Rome's remarkable toleration of Christianity at that time. Paul was able to speak freely to them about the Lord Jesus Christ, so nothing must have been deemed seditious even under this close scrutiny. What impact did this have on his succession of guards who would have heard things so foreign to their understanding?

While Paul would much rather have been free and evangelizing, Stott argues that his witness was "expanded, enriched and authenticated" by his two years of Roman custody. His sufferings authenticated his ministry, which was expanded, of course, by witnessing to the highest authority in the highest court. He was enriched, and we in turn shared in

11. Bock, *Acts*, 755.

12. Johnson, *Message of Acts*, 49.

13. Stott, *Message of Acts*, 399.

14. Troftgruben, "Ending," 325.

15. Longenecker, "Acts," 9:572.

this through the three main prison Epistles—Ephesians, Philippians, and Colossians—of which Stott says,

> They set forth more powerfully than anywhere else the supreme, sovereign, undisputed and unrivalled lordship of Jesus Christ. . . . Paul's perspective was adjusted, his horizons extended, his vision clarified, and his witness enriched by his prison experience.[16]

As mentioned, Acts came to a halt, not a conclusion. While it appears evident that Luke knows more about Paul's fate, nothing is said. Acts opened with Jesus' *teaching* and closes with Paul *teaching* about Jesus; it also opens with the commission to take the gospel to the whole world and closes on the same note. It is on the journey to the ends of the earth. Some regard Paul's arrival in Rome as fulfilling Jesus' command to witness "to the end of the earth" (1:8), thereby enhancing closure. But Rome was far more the center of the Mediterranean world than its distant border. Further, Christianity came to Rome before Paul's arrival, making his arrival not as climactic as it may seem. Paul did bear witness in Rome, which served as an initial sign of worldwide witness, but this movement is far from over at the end of Acts. My good friend, evangelist Fred Kornis, calls himself an Acts-29 Christian, a small cog in an ongoing chapter of the expansion of Christianity with the message of "the hope of Israel" (28:20). I said in the introduction that reading this book—and congratulations for getting this far—means nothing if you have not become, in effect, an Acts-29 Christian. What is your role in this unfolding story? God forbid it is the apparent disinterest of the Roman Jewish leaders.

16. Stott, *Message of Acts*, 404.

18

"Chapter 29": The Aftermath of Acts

Luke has completed his account. Did he intend to write a third book? We have no way of knowing. But the story is obviously not finished as the Pastoral Epistles do not fit with Paul's travels as we read in Acts, though it is a record we know to be very incomplete (2 Cor 11). Attempts have been made to fit these journeys into this period with suggestions that 1 Timothy was written between 1 and 2 Corinthians and Titus being written on the last journey back to Jerusalem. The Caesarean imprisonment was then the occasion for 2 Timothy. This suggestion has never received much support.[1] The journeys appear to have occurred beyond the time covered in Acts so this requires a second Roman imprisonment. The only independent reference to Paul being released from prison in Rome is found in 1 Clement 5: "After preaching both in the east and west, he gained the illustrious reputation due to his faith, having taught righteousness to the whole world, and come to the extreme limit of the west,[2] and suffered martyrdom under the prefects."[3]

A possible but not the only reconstruction[4] of the events and travels referred to the Pastorals is given below:

1. On Paul's release from his first Roman imprisonment, he sent Timothy to Philippi with the good news (Phil 2:19–23).

1. Guthrie, *Pastoral Epistles*, 613.
2. Some think Rome, others Spain, and others even Britain, to be here referred to.
3. *ANF* 9:231.
4. Refer to Elwell, *Encountering the New Testament*, 334 for an alternative map.

2. Paul headed for Asia Minor via Crete where he left Titus behind to complete the organization of the churches.
3. Paul travelled to Ephesus, on to Colossae, (Phlm 22), and returned to Ephesus.
4. Timothy joined Paul in Ephesus. Paul asked him to remain there.
5. Paul journeyed to Macedonia (Phil 2:24). He wanted to return to Ephesus, but, as he expects to be delayed, he wrote 1 Timothy and Titus. Titus was asked to meet him at Nicopolis (Titus 3:12).
6. Paul travelled to Nicopolis, wintered there (Titus 3:12), and was joined there by Titus.
7. Paul and possibly Titus visited Spain (Rom 15:28; 1 Clement 5).[5]
8. Paul returned. Trophimus was left sick at Miletus near Ephesus (2 Tim 4:20). He may have met Timothy again (2 Tim 1:4).
9. Paul visited Carpus in Troas and left his cloak behind (2 Tim 4:13). He went on to Rome via Corinth where Erastus remained (2 Tim 4:20). It was probably in one of these cities that he was arrested.
10. His Roman imprisonment was severe and brief. He wrote 2 Timothy asking Timothy to come to Rome.[6]

This possible reconstruction is shown in the map below.

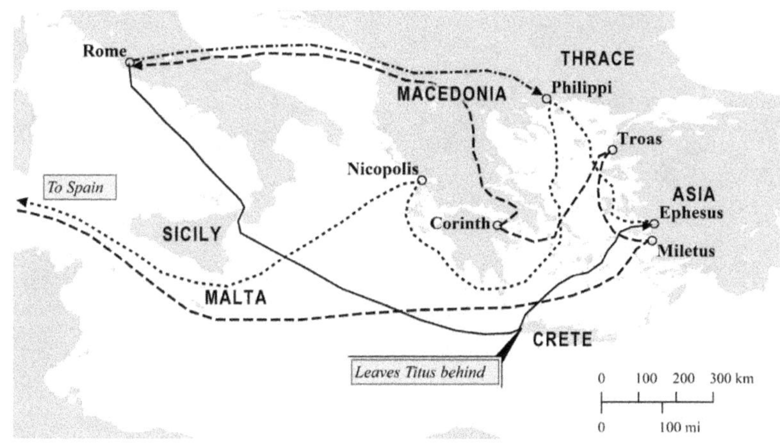

Figure 7. The proposed fourth missionary journey

5. Mounce, *Pastoral Epistles*, lix. See also *ANF* 9:231 for the remark from 1 Clement.
6. Hendriksen, *1 Thessalonians*, 39–40.

This reconstruction sees that Paul, contrary to expectation, arrived in or near Ephesus again c. AD 62. He left Timothy behind to sort out matters in the church. At the time of Timothy's ministry, the Jewish foundation (Acts 18:24–26; 19:1–7) has been replaced with a church that was heavily if not predominantly gentile (Acts 20:21; Eph. 2:11–13, 19; 3:1; 4:17–24). The church in Ephesus was in trouble with "savage wolves" doing great damage to the church (20:20), but not in the full-blown form that Paul had predicted in Acts 20 and 1 Tim 4:1. Tradition records that John lived to an old age and eventually died in Ephesus, perhaps another 20 years on from Timothy's ministry. This long-predicted falling-away would happen during the time John was there, during which he wrote 1 John. The name of the heretic is known: Cerinthus. But the church and Paul's legacy would survive. Cerinthus and his followers departed from among them (1 John 2:18–19).

19

Technical Matters

The liberal scholar Rudolf Bultmann described the modern mindset's rejection of supernaturalism this way:

> It is impossible to use electric light and the wireless and avail ourselves of modern medical and surgical discoveries, and at the same time to believe in the New Testament world of spirits and miracles. We might think we can manage it in our own lives but to expect others to do so is to make the Christian faith unintelligible and unacceptable to the modern world.[1]

Yet this is exactly what the Book of Acts demands of us! It declares that God became a man, that he was murdered, was resurrected, and that he is coming again. It also speaks of a church so empowered by God's Spirit that the dead were raised and the lame walked. Acts asks that we accept all this as historical fact and not a philosophical theory. This can be a big ask given the powerless state of much of the Christian church now. Because you are reading this book, most likely you have concluded that the one who spoke the universe into existence has indeed done remarkable things in the past. Should you be asking why these miracles don't occur today, Augustine,[2] the saint of old, saw the danger in this

1. Bultmann, *New Testament and Mythology*, 5. It assumes that ancient Greece at least was completely different to us. A bodily resurrection was inconceivable and for the Epicureans and Stoics even the existence of the soul after death was impossible.

2. Augustine, bishop of Hippo in North Africa (AD 352–430), is considered one of the most important church fathers. His writings were very influential in the Catholic, Lutheran, and Anglican churches.

question. He believed that "the purpose of the question is to discourage belief in the occurrence of those miracles in the past."[3] God forbid that the church should cease to be asking big things from a big and loving Savior. The cost to allow us to enter boldly before almighty God was too great to only ask for trivial matters.

One writer said of Acts that it is "meant to recall the memory of foundations and thus to shape the audience's identity in their own time, to construct an image of the past that is meaningful and helpful for the present."[4] But that was the present of Luke and Theophilus. I am a baby boomer, born in 1950, a time of peace and prosperity in Australia. My father was born in 1911 and knew two world wars and the Great Depression. Though I know the history, it is true: "The past is a foreign country." How then do we bridge two thousand years when only one hundred is difficult? Acts will challenge us with its historical distance. It will also challenge us about how much we should use this history as a template for our expectation for church life and practice. For example, we see an apostle chosen by lot, deacons chosen by the church on the basis of being full of the Spirit, elders appointed by church founders, and the foundation set in chapter 20 for church officers to be appointed mainly on an examination of their character. We will see a church so powerful that the dead are raised, yet for many of us our prayers often seem to be unheard.

Seldom are we told if the examples recounted are good or bad or even if they are meant for all ages of the church, and we are left to make up our own minds. The antagonism between the traditional church and the Pentecostal branch testifies to that. Many Christians are more comfortable with a God who acted in the past and will do so in the future but not one who is still working in the here and now. Yet, we will see in the Book of Acts the unambiguous fundamentals of what a church should be: gathered, prayerfully seeking God's will in unity, and with the intention to carry out God's mission. Our reality can be fractures, prayerlessness, powerlessness, and a resultant indifference, if not actually resistance to mission. In this, Acts should bring us to repentance. We will also see, starting with Judas, Satan's attempts to destroy the effectiveness of that mission. These are constants, whatever your church tradition.

3. Augustine, *Civ.* 1033.

4. Witetschek, "Artemis and Asiarchs," 336.

From at least the second century, "Acts of the Apostles" was the title given to this second part[5] of a history of Christian origins. Others have called it the "Acts of the Holy Spirit." Neither of these titles describe our book adequately. The traditional title does not acknowledge that there were other faithful witnesses for Jesus who share in the spreading of the gospel to the ends of the earth regardless of opposition. God is the main actor. The second overemphasizes the Spirit when Jesus is also acting with the Father guiding it all. One commentator suggests that a "more appropriate [title] would be *The Acts of the Sovereign God Through the Lord Messiah Jesus by his Spirit on Behalf of the Way.*[6]

Someone who heard Luke's book being read in the first century would have recognized that it followed the conventions of a Greek history. Hellenistic writing had an established genre that retold the deeds of a single great man, or sometimes a group, that was intended to show that person/group as someone sent from and used by God. But here the great one is God himself working through people in different localities as Jesus directs.[7] The need for courageous truthfulness was also well established in secular histories, and Luke has been proven reliable.[8] The Greeks also valued personal observation, the variety of races,[9] and the use of actual, not invented speeches to summarize events.[10] It is not surprising then that a third of Acts is made up of speeches, though obviously shortened. As for the content of this history, Luke's scope is global,[11] and his concern is the "Who" of salvation. The cross and justification are a given. In contrast, Paul was a theologian with a rabbinic foundation and in his Letters, he was generally writing to Christians on local issues and was concerned with the "how."

When Josephus concluded book 1 of *Against Apion*, he wrote, "Since this book is arisen to a competent length, I will make another beginning, and endeavor to add what still remains to perfect my design in the

5. Some think that Luke–Acts was originally one work but became separated soon after the writing of John's Gospel, which is when the four gospels started to circulate as a separate collection. Bruce, *English*, 13.

6. Bock, *Acts*, 50.

7. Bock, *Acts*, 1–2. Examples are those of Alexander the Great and Augustus.

8. As in Lucian of Samosata, "How to Write History," 49–53, 63. Lucian lived from AD 125 to after 180.

9. Bock, *Acts*, 11.

10. Polybius, *Hist.* 12.25A–B; 2.56.11. Polybius lived c. 200–c. 118 BC.

11. Bock, *Acts*, 119.

following book."[12] By contrast, Luke and Acts, the longest books in the New Testament, both fit a standard Roman scroll. When Luke drew from the first thirty or so years of the church, he had no shortage of material, so he must have given considerable thought and planning to its content with what he included and excluded, e.g., ignoring Paul's missionary trip to Illyricum (Rom 15:19) and the second offering. Rather than chronicle history he interpreted it and used it to edify. But it is theology and history without a disservice to the other.

With his obvious care about the length of the work, we should see the repetitions (Paul's conversion, his resolve to turn to the gentiles, Peter with Cornelius) and long sections such as Stephen's sermon as pointing us to pivotal events in the church's history. We should also take note of the parallels with his gospel and of God's suffering servant. This likeness was described "as the master, so shall the servant be."[13] Again, selecting his material to suit his own purposes does not mean that the book is historically dubious. Rather, it is written with a "strong sense of sacredness of the concrete facts it narrates,"[14] so strong, in fact, that most Christians hold that it was God-breathed (2 Tim 3:16).

ACTS' PLACE IN THE NEW TESTAMENT

From at least the second century, "Acts of the Apostles" was the title given to this second part of a history of Christian origins composed by a first-century Christian and dedicated to a man called Theophilus (Luke 1:1–4; Acts 1:1). The two books, Luke–Acts, written for an unknown man by an "insignificant" person make up about 30 percent of the New Testament. At about the same time that the collection of the four Gospels was circulating, the first collections of Paul's Writings were taking shape. While Luke's Gospel acknowledges the existence of other gospels, there is no mention of works similar to Acts. Our book stands alone, and, without it, the two collections would be hard to relate to each other. This history provided clear evidence that a very definite act of God turned Saul into Paul and so support the claims in his Letters that he was an apostle.[15] This was not universally accepted during his lifetime. The book also provided

12. Josephus, *Ag. Ap.* 1.35.
13. Rackham, *Acts*, 404.
14. Dix, *Jew and Greek*, 39.
15. Wood, *Acts*, 16.

an answer to the ancient heretic Marcion (AD 144)[16] who, among other things, would not accept Peter, John, James, etc., as apostles and held them as false apostles and corruptors of the truth.

Acts parallels Paul's words in Romans 1:16—"first to the Jew, then to the Gentile"—and shows that the inclusion of gentiles was not an afterthought but was a promise of Scripture (13:47; 15:16–18). The turbulent history between Jew and gentile needs to be understood to fully appreciate the reconciliation that was bought by the gospel to these two groups. Luke goes to great pains to shows that the gospel was for all people. As one commentator noted, "All types of people benefit: the powerful and the weak, the rich and the poor, male and female, old and young, (2:17–18), poor widows (9:36–41), provincials (14:15–8), merchants (16:14), jailers (16:30–32), sailors (27:25), centurions in the military (10:34–48), proconsuls (13:7), governors (24:10), kings (26:2), and philosophers (17:18)."[17]

The ancient origins of Christianity were important for both Jew and gentile. It is quite possible that Luke was "reassuring a God-fearer who has come to faith that being a Gentile in an originally Jewish movement was by God's design."[18] Someone immersed in polytheism believed that harmony in all relationships of life and with the gods came through the practice of *eusebia*, described by Isocrates as

> not [destroying] any institution of their fathers and to introduce nothing which was not approved by custom, believing that reverence consists, not in extravagant expenditures, but in disturbing none of the rites which their ancestors had handed on to them. And so also the gifts of the gods were visited upon them, not fitfully or capriciously, but seasonably both for the ploughing of the land and for the ingathering of its fruits.[19]

16. Marcion of Sinope in Pontus (Asia Minor) came to Rome in AD 139 and was expelled from the church in 144 because of his gnostic beliefs. He rejected the Old Testament God (and with it the Old Testament) as an inferior God to Jesus. He accepted only ten Pauline Epistles and a purged Luke. This was the first known attempt to form a New Testament canon.

17. Bock, *Acts*, 34.

18. Bock, *Acts*, 24.

19. Isocrates, *Areop.* 2.33—41:123. This was a long-lived belief. Isocrates lived between 436 and 338 BC, and the same belief in *eusebia* is found in Aelius Aristides (AD 117–181). See Aristides, *Orat.* 24.42.

While Christianity might at first appear new to them it was based on old promises and what was tested by time was respected.[20]

There are some foil characters in Acts: those who are not believers, yet treat Christians with a greater sense of fairness then do most Jews who do not believe. The Romans are the neutral evaluators of the new message. Yet for all the many actors in Luke's history, God is the key character of the book, and its major concern is the activity of God from heaven. It is also Jesus, now vindicated and in an exalted position and ministering from God's side in heaven as Savior Jesus. He mediates the Father's will and distributes his blessings. The commentator Bock notes about how Jesus is presented in speeches:

> In Acts 2 he is the promised Lord and Christ who mediates the long promised Spirit from the right hand of God. In Acts 3 he fulfills the promise to Abraham and is the Holy One killed but now raised as he waits in heaven to return as judge, just as the prophets promised. In Acts 10, he is appointed the judge of the living and the dead in fulfillment of the prophets. . . . Jesus is the sent Messiah (Acts 2:36; 3:20; 5:42; 8:5; 17:3b; 18:5), son of David (2:30; 13:23), Lord (2:36; 10:36), Son of God (9:20; 13:33), prophet like Moses (3:22–23; 7:37), servant of the Lord (3:13, 26; 4:30; 8:32–33), and Son of Man (7:56). He is the righteous one (3:14; 7:52; 22:14), the author of life (3:15), leader and savior (5:31), and the one destined to suffer (3:18; 17:3a; 26:23) and be rejected (2:23–24; 3:13–15; 8:32–33; 13:28). Jesus shares the name of Lord, and a variety of acts are performed in his name from exorcism to baptism (2:21 read with 2:36, 38; 3:6; 4:12, 30; 5:28, 40–41; 8:16; 9:14–16, 21, 27–28; 10:48; 15:14, 17; 16:18; 19:5, 13, 17; 22:16; 26:9). He is the agent for miracles (3:6; 4:10; 9:34). Jesus is an active, exalted figure in Acts. He is not passive as he sits at God's right hand but is at work for his people.[21]

It was this active proclamation of an active Jesus and through God's guidance that saw the expansion of the gospel as it penetrates the world from Jerusalem to the hub of the world, Rome, despite intense opposition.

20. Bock, *Acts*, 24.

21. Bock, *Acts*, 35–36.

THE HOLY SPIRIT IN ACTS

Luke's book, as noted, has been called the "Acts of the Holy Spirit." Here we read of the promise (1:4, 8) and fulfilment of the Spirit poured out on Jew (chapter 2), Samaritan (chapter 8), and gentile (chapter 10) alike. As Christianity spreads throughout the empire, we see the Spirit directing (13:2) and guiding its messengers (8:29, 39; 10:19). His coming can be felt and seen, and his guidance is clear and definite (16:6–9) and is the authority for their actions (15:28). As in the Old Testament, he speaks through prophets (11:28; 21:11), telling of future events and bears witness to the truth (5:32). Yet the Spirit does not act alone but under the direction of God and Jesus who gave him.

Though there is not one aspect of the advancement of the church not directly related to the Spirit's power, the church's response is not always correct. In Acts we see him as a person of the Godhead who is lied to (5:3), tempted (5:9), and resisted (7:51).

DATE OF WRITING

The date of writing as presented by Acts can be fixed reasonably closely. The earliest date is AD 61 or 62 after Paul had spent two years under house arrest awaiting his appeal. Paul is still putting trust in the impartiality of the Roman legal system, and this reflects Paul's position in Rom 13:1–7 where he urges submission to the governing authorities. There is no hint of the changed political atmosphere after Nero's persecution of AD 64, and there is no hint of the destruction of the temple in AD 70 or of the changed relationship of the Jews to Rome. It would be best to think of Christianity as a suspect cult but not actually proscribed at the time Luke wrote.

There are possible references to Acts in the early church writings, which would require it to be written before the end of the first century.[22] Clear references are found after AD 150 but the proliferation of apocryphal Acts suggests that our book existed as a model. However, many scholars insist on a later date as they see the model of church government with elders as an un-Pauline invention. It is thought that in degenerate times the apostolic tradition had to be protected by qualified guardians.[23]

22. E.g., 1 Clement 2.2 (Acts 2:17); 1 Clement 5.4.7 (Acts 1:25). Bock, *Acts*, 25. See Conzelmann, *Acts*, xxvii–iii for examples.

23. Campenhausen, *Spiritual Authority*, 80.

An objection to an early date for Acts is that it requires a very early date for the Gospel. Notwithstanding, a very large study by C. J. Hemer of the archeological evidence with much fresh evidence that the Acts record is completely consistent with life in the middle of the first century with much of its background information corroborated through secular sources.[24]

WHO WROTE ACTS?

The author of Luke–Acts is not named but Luke has been credited with this as far back as the early part of the second century, preceding the anti-Marcionite prologues[25] and the Muratorian fragment.[26] Despite the author never naming himself, he can be identified on four different occasions when he uses the term "we." These are the following:

- 16:10–17 Philippi in Macedonia
- 20:5–15 Troas
- 21:1–18 Journey from Ephesus to Jerusalem
- 27:1—28:6 Journey from Jerusalem to Rome

By comparing who *is* mentioned in the Prison Epistles written from Rome and *not* mentioned in the above passages, the author would need to be either Mark, Jesus Justus, Demas, Luke, or Epaphroditus. Combining this with the church's tradition and Luke's authorship is very reasonable. He was not prominent in the New Testament, so there was no reason to pick him.[27] Luke's authorship is further supported by looking at the fifty-seven words and expressions found in Luke and Acts that are not found elsewhere in the New Testament.[28] Many of these are medical terms, which is what we would expect "the beloved physician" to use. Tradition says Luke was from Syrian Antioch, but Philippi is also a possibility. He has an interest in both cities. There is nothing in Luke–Acts

24. Hemer, *Book of Acts*, 411–14.

25. Three short prologues to Mark, Luke, and John, which were added to exclude Marcion's interpretation.

26. Believed to have originated from c. AD 170 and gives the books accepted by the church as inspired.

27. Bock, *Acts*, 16.

28. Carter and Earle, *Acts*, i.

that can provide a compelling argument to determine if he was a Jew or gentile.[29]

CRITICAL OPINION

As mentioned earlier, the author was writing in a recognized historical style. Further, it is claimed to be anchored in geography and history. Much "biblical study operates on the basis of a 'hermeneutics of suspicion' . . . that tends to be based on finding problems."[30] Without a signed and dated original manuscript, countless theories about who wrote Acts, why, and when he did it have abounded, changing with the winds of theological debate over time. In the 1830s, under the driving force of liberal German scholars, it became accepted that Acts was a very unreliable second-century work written in part to answer Marcion's claims. Accounts of the miraculous simply had to be rejected.

German liberalism was driven by a framework of Hegelian dialectic, which advocated that Christianity developed from a conflict between Peter, who more closely represented Jesus, and Paul, who represented a later Christian understanding free of the Law. The scholars could not understand how the Paul of Acts could compromise to accommodate Jewish scruples as they saw this contrary to the Christian freedom of Romans, 1 and 2 Corinthians, and Galatians. They also believed the book was full of historical inaccuracies, which only a second-century author could make. In effect, this turned Acts into a book of fiction written somewhere between AD 110 and 130 and was intended to paint a conciliatory vision of the two adversaries.

By 1865, scholars[31] were beginning to question the conflict premise understanding of Acts, claiming that the hostility between Peter and Paul was a figment of the scholar's imagination. Clearly there is a conciliatory approach whereby Paul does concede authority to Peter and the twelve. But Peter and the Jerusalem church also acknowledge Paul's authority is of a different nature and to a different audience. The contents of Acts

29. Mitchell, *Fresh Look*, 38.

30. Mitchell, *Fresh Look*, 83. An example is Luke recording the revolt of Theudas before that of Judas (5:36–37), but a revolt by a Theudas occurred ten years after Gamaliel's speech. The expectation is that Luke must be a perfect historian, not a good one. Hermer, *Book of Acts*, 162–63. That perfection requires conformity with our sketchy understanding.

31. Notably, Lightfoot and Harnack. See, e.g., Harnack, *Date of Acts*, 67–89.

could just as easily have been written about two men who were lockstep in purpose. The book was also in the process of being found to be historically reliable, bringing a broader understanding of Paul's actions. The First World War brought an end to the nineteenth-century worldview and with that, some of the extreme interpretations.

Many scholars now put the writings of Luke–Acts later in the first century,[32] with most placing it between AD 80 and 85.[33] As Acts is written after Luke's Gospel, which predicts the destruction of the temple in AD 70[34] (Luke 19:43–44; 21:20–24), and as there can be no predictive prophecy, these dates cannot be avoided. It means that Luke–Acts represents the theology rather than the history of Christ and his church. Either way, it is claimed to be written for second or even third generation believers with a later theology than the early church.[35] In other words, it has been said to represent early Catholicism, and not the early church.

The first half of Acts is seen as being made up of multiple Semitic sources, which led to duplications and Luke's own travel documents. This approach that looked for sources has been described as saying that "so called historical writings tell us more about the authors who wrote them then they do about the events they purport to relate."[36] By focusing on the theological concerns of the author, there often came a rejection of the historical facts of the book. Acts had become seen as a piece of religious propaganda, which attempted to counter the rising disillusionment following the delay in the second coming[37] and the rise of Gnosticism.[38] The vibrant church expecting the immediate return of Jesus would have no interest in writing a history for future generations. All we are left with is a few names that have been preserved.[39] One of the scholars put the value of Acts very bluntly: "to him who knows how to read between the lines

32. Dates of authorship ranging from the early sixties to the nineties are suggested with "the majority of scholars favoring a later rather than an earlier point." Marshall, *Fresh Look*, 17.

33. Longenecker, Acts," 9:237.

34. E.g., Conzelmann, *Acts*, xxxiii.

35. Conzelmann, *Luke's Place*, 305–7.

36. Longenecker, "Acts," 9:211.

37. Conzelmann, *Theology of St. Luke*, 12–15, 210–11.

38. Longenecker, "Acts," 9:211.

39. Haenchen, *Book of Acts*, 262.

and to hear what is left unsaid, the Book of Acts gives rich information about what is commonly called 'the post Apostolic age.'"[40]

Another theory suggests that the author was writing a historical novel[41] that allows someone to believe that he was a brilliant author, which he undoubtedly was, but a poor historian. The miracles could not possibly have occurred, so the work is obviously fiction but something that was still spiritually profitable to read. This of course must then apply to his Gospel. However, the "wholesale invention of stories about the early apostles and evangelists belongs to a later generation that was out of touch with Christian beginnings."[42]

Conservative scholars still hold to traditional dating with good reason. An earlier archaeologist, Sir William Ramsay, said, "In fact beginning with a fixed idea that the work was essentially a second century composition and never relying on its evidence as trustworthy for first century conditions I gradually came to find it a useful ally in some obscure and difficult investigations."[43] It is now agreed that Luke's descriptions of public titles, official names, and territories are so precise that a second-century author could not have written Acts. An example of its historical precision can be seen in Acts 14:6. There, Luke implies that Iconium was not in Lycaonia while contemporary Romans such as Cicero said it was. Archaeologists claimed Acts to be unreliable until 1910 when Ramsay found evidence that Iconium was in Phrygia. This was further confirmed in later discoveries. The author of a very large study into the historical setting of Acts assesses the critics refusal to consider it was "unfortunate in that the vacuum seems to have been caused not by a lack of relevant evidence for consideration or the fruitful consummation of debate, but rather by exegetical and theological taste and fashion."[44]

This commentary is written from the conservative understanding and will only mention critical opinions when necessary.

40. Haenchen, *Book of Acts*, 261.

41. The similarities of Acts to ancient novels have long been recognized. Barrett, *Luke the Historian*, 15, 53.

42. Marshall, *Fresh Look*, 20.

43. Ramsay, *St. Paul*, 8. Sir William Ramsay (1851–1939) was a Scottish archaeologist and leading New Testament scholar. He was regarded as the leading authority on the history of Asia Minor.

44. Hermer, *Book of Acts*, 411.

PURPOSE OF WRITING

Tacitus wrote c. AD 112 of Christians, "The Christians get their name from one Christus, who was executed by the sentence of the Procurator Pontius Pilate when Tiberius was emperor; and the pernicious superstition was checked for a short time, only to break out afresh—not only in Judea, the home of the plague, but in Rome itself, where all the horrible and shameful things in the world collect and find a home."[45] While Acts gave the answer to such an attitude, being precise about its purpose is not easy. However, the former sceptic Ramsay came to see it very simply as a mere uncolored recital of the important facts, going on to say,

> It would be difficult in the whole range of literature to find a work where there is less attempt at pointing a moral or drawing a lesson from the facts. The narrator who's persuaded that the facts themselves in their barest form are a perfect lesson and a complete instruction and he feels it would be an impertinence and even an impiety to intrude his individual views into the narrative.[46]

Most commenters would see its purpose more nuanced than that of only a historian seeking to inform. For a modern reader, Acts has many loose ends, such as leaving the careers of Peter and Paul in obscurity and giving us little information about the nature of leadership in the early church. We can also be left pondering how the Ethiopian eunuch fared as well as the converts in the gentile churches.[47] We know only of the spread of the gospel north and west of Jerusalem but nothing of the south and east. These "omissions" cannot be separated from what Luke's purpose was in writing, but what he wanted to say is disputed. The omissions point to his work being more than a simple church history. Even saying it is a history of the missionary expansion of the church fails to explain why a quarter of the book is given over to Paul's trial.[48] Whatever biases Luke had, his work is a history nonetheless, warts and all. He could easily have written an idealized version that only showed worthy patterns to follow.

There are likely to be many facets to Luke's motivation for writing Acts. However, it cannot be considered in isolation from the purpose of

45. Tacitus, *Ann.* 15.44.
46. Ramsay, *St. Paul*, 20–21.
47. Mitchell, *Fresh Look*, 29–30.
48. Mitchell, *Fresh Look*, 32.

the former treatise. We don't need to speculate as to its purpose as Luke stated it explicitly:

> Many have undertaken to draw up an account of the things that have been fulfilled among us, just as they were handed down to us by those who from the first were eyewitnesses and servants of the word. With this in mind, since I myself have carefully investigated everything from the beginning, I too decided to write an orderly account for you, most excellent Theophilus, so that you may know the certainty of the things you have been taught. (Luke 1:1–4)

With Acts, Luke has had the opportunity to discuss the events with the main players. However, for the most part, his Gospel is not the report of an eyewitness but rests upon thoroughly accurate research. What is not immediately clear is why Luke believed a new Gospel was needed when others already existed. Answer that highly debated question satisfactorily and you will have gone a long way to answering the purpose of Acts. In part, he must have seen that Gospels like that of Mark that starts with John the Baptist did not give a full account of Christian beginnings and the Gospels "had not shown sufficiently clearly how the ministry and teaching of Jesus linked up with the history of the early church."[49] Perhaps also the implications of the death and resurrection of Jesus were not yet fully clear to him.

The stated purpose of Luke is to strengthen the faith of believers through being a true witness to Jesus, the same as the command to the new church to the risen Jesus. However, both volumes, but especially the second, do have a strong apologetic emphasis, which also would have an evangelistic role as any witness to Jesus has. Perhaps we can be more specific. The title given to Theophilus indicates at the very least that he was Roman. Paul was proud of his citizenship and Roman believers in the church would have had an ongoing loyalty to the state. With Jesus being executed by Rome, and the empire having attacked his followers, it was important to show that Christianity had not violated Roman law,[50] nor had any of its magistrates ruled against them. This theme is expanded in the section "The Church's Relation to Rome" and Table 18.

Some thought that Acts was a trial document sent to a Roman magistrate named Theophilus and perhaps even intended for the eyes of Nero.

49. Marshall, "Luke and His Gospel," 283.

50. Mitchell, *Fresh Look*, 80.

The objection raised against this is that "no Roman official would ever have filtered out so much of what to him would be theological and ecclesiastical rubbish in order to reach so tiny a grain of relevant apology."[51] However, that is not totally correct. On one hand, when Ephesus had to defend before the emperor Tiberius why the temple of Artemis should keep its sanctuary rites, they simply recited their myths to him.[52] On the other hand, the actions of the apostles and the miracles were not done in a corner (26:26) but were verifiable even by king Agrippa. However, the primary purpose for writing must remain conjecture as Luke's work goes beyond what is required for a legal document.

Notwithstanding the primary role, there are several themes running through his book. Another theme is the growth of the church as God's salvation spreads through the world. Implicit with this is the transition from Jewish to gentile Christianity under God's direction and, along with that, the church's ongoing relation to the Jews and Jewish Christians. With official Judaism having rejected Jesus as the Messiah, were Jews who had believed correct in doing so or were they apostates? Further complicating matters would be their relationship with uncircumcised gentiles. Luke's retelling of their origins reminded them that Jesus met the prophesied requirements of the messiah and that, likewise, his well-attested resurrection was also prophesied. Further, God himself had sanctioned the inclusion of uncircumcised gentiles.[53] His work reassures "the Christians of his day that their faith in Jesus is no aberration, the authentic goal towards which God's ancient dealings with Israel were driving."[54] The book sets guidelines for fellowship between two previously antagonistic groups.

The Romans held great store in law and order, and, as Christianity's founder was crucified by a Roman governor and its chief proponent was under house arrest in Rome, it was handicapped. But, in successive trial scenes, Christians are seen as law-abiding. Luke shows that "Christian faith and witness are not contrary to the laws and true interest of Judaism or of the Roman state."[55] The blame for the strife rests on the Jewish authorities and local Jewish communities. Yet Acts contains much that is concerned with other matters, which speaks against it being specifically a defense of Paul, though much of the second half points to it. That defense

51. Barrett, *Luke the Historian*, 63.

52. Tacitus, *Ann.* 3.61.1.

53. Mitchell, *Fresh Look*, 39.

54. Maddox, *Purpose of Luke–Acts*, 187.

55. Mitchell, *Fresh Look*, 46.

could equally be to Christians who disagreed with Paul's theology.[56] However, there are eleven chapters without Paul.

While Rome features prominently, Acts is more concerned with the relationship with the Jews. Luke's Gospel tells how, despite promises being given to the Jews, they were largely unresponsive. Acts continues this theme but recording how many still believed. It shows how a seemingly new movement was "actually rooted in ancient promises associated with Judaism and yet includes Gentiles."[57]

Acts shows a generally healthy church that "serves, preaches, teaches, heals, and prays. As it preached, the message is vindicated through the power and activity of the Holy Spirit. The community values peace, promotes unity, settles disputes, is good, and exemplifies grace. In this way it shows its health as it grows."[58] Luke's history shows that a healthy church is also one where there is the legitimate possession of wealth alongside "a powerful call to the rich to care for the poor."[59] The need for a healthy church was vitally important as the *parousia*, the return of Jesus in glory, which many expected in a short time, had not eventuated. While the church was coming to terms with the long-term absence of Jesus, this was compensated for by the active presence of the Spirit.[60] If this was not a purpose as such, it certainly helped shape its contents, showing a waiting church serving, being a witness, and being reminded of its origins.

OUTLINE OF ACTS

Knowing a book's outline can be an important help in understanding its message, but Acts "does not have a clear logical division."[61] Clearly though, the emphasis is on the mission to the gentiles (chapters 11–28). Many attempts have been made to divide the book, and I will only mention three. One outline is to see it as constructed logically around the Great Commission given to the apostles in 1:8: "[You] will be witnesses for me not only in Jerusalem, but throughout Judea and Samaria, and to the ends of the earth." This would give an outline as follows:

56. Mitchell, *Fresh Look*, 34.
57. Bock, *Acts*, 6.
58. Bock, *Acts*, 41.
59. Mitchell, *Fresh Look*, 42.
60. Mitchell, *Fresh Look*, 35.
61. Marshall, *Fresh Look*, 27.

1. Introduction 1:1–11
2. The origin of the church—Jerusalem 1:12—8:3
3. The period of transition 8:4—11:8
4. The expansion to the gentiles through the Pauline mission from Antioch to the empire 11:19—21:16
5. The imprisonment and defense of Paul in Caesarea and Rome 21:17—28:31

The book can also be divided by personalities as follows:

1. Peter 1–5
2. Stephen 6–7
3. Various (including Philip, Barnabas, and Saul) 8–12
4. Paul 13—28

Another division is as follows:

Introduction: The preparation for world mission 1:1—2:41
Part 1: Christian mission to the Jewish world 2:42—12:24
Section 1. The earliest days of the church at Jerusalem (2:42—6:7). Summary statement: *So the word of God spread. The number of disciples in Jerusalem increased rapidly, and a large number of priests became obedient to the faith (6:7).*
Section 2. Critical events restatement in the lives of three pivotal figures (6:8—9:31). Summary statement: *Then the church throughout Judea, Galilee, and Samaria enjoyed a time of peace and was strengthened. Living in the fear of the Lord and encouraged by the Holy Spirit, it increased in numbers (9:31).*
Section 3. Advance of the gospel in Palestine–Syria (9:32—12:24). Summary statement: *But the word of God continued to spread and flourish (12:24).*
Part 2: The Christian mission to the gentile world 12:25—28:31
Section 1. The first missionary journey and the Jerusalem Council (12:25—16:5). Summary statement: *So the churches were strengthened in the faith and grew daily in numbers (16:5).*
Section 2. Wide outreach through two missionary journeys (16:6—19:20). Summary statement: *In this way the word of the Lord spread widely and grew in power (19:20).*
Section 3. To Jerusalem and Rome (19:21—28:31). Summary statement: *He proclaimed the kingdom of God and taught about the Lord Jesus Christ—with all boldness and without hindrance (28:31)!*

Table 16. Division of Acts[62]

62. Adapted from Longenecker, "Acts," 9:232–35 with emphasis added.

Despite the difficulty in finding a formal structure, there is "vast scope for detecting 'resonances' as we read the story of Acts, with different parts calling others to mind and thus imposing a remarkable unity upon the whole."[63] This is explored in Tables 4, 6 and 16. The literary connections to Luke are noted in the commentary as they arise.

A COMPARISON BETWEEN PETER AND PAUL

At the time of Paul's captivity, his apostleship had been denied by many and had been forsaken by most except the church in Philippi. Despite this, Acts places Paul on the same footing as Peter and makes a definite comparison between the two as equals (Table 16). While their work was not confined to one class of hearers, Peter would be the champion of the early Jerusalem church while Paul would be the founder of the first gentile churches.

Event	Peter	Paul
Both leaders	To the Jews	To the gentiles
Separate area of work	Jerusalem	gentile world
Sermon recorded in full	2:14–40 Pentecost	13:16–42 Antioch of Pisidia
Healed a lame man	3:1–10	14:8–10
Brought swift judgment	5:1–11 Ananias and Sapphira	13:6–11 Elymas
Healed at a distance	5:15 Peter's shadow healed	19:12 Paul healed with his sweatbands
Freed from prison	5:19–21, 12:1–11	16:19–30
Stressed work of Holy Spirit	2:38	19:2–6
Resurrection primary part of preaching	2:24–36; 3:15, 26; 4:2	13:30–37; 17:3, 18, 31; 24:15
Both converted a Roman official	10:1–48	16:25–34
Both appeared before the Sanhedrin	4:1–4, 5:17–21	22:30—23:10

Table 17. Peter and Paul contrasted in Acts

There is no indication of antagonism between the two in Acts, though a strong disagreement is recorded in Galatians (2:11–21).

63. Marshall, *Fresh Look*, 27.

CHRONOLOGY

Luke is the only New Testament writer that places his story fully in its historical setting, referring to events that can be verified by outside writers such as the famine under Claudius[64] and his expulsion of the Jews from Rome.[65] His work covers thirty years and Table 17 has a suggested chronology. The dates are far from agreed upon.

Time	Date (AD)	Event
April/May	30	Resurrection, ascension, Pentecost
	c. 33	Conversion of Paul
	35	Paul's first post-conversion visit to Jerusalem
	44	Execution of James, son of Zebedee; imprisonment of Peter; death of Herod Agrippa
	46	Famine in Judea, Barnabas and Paul visit Jerusalem
	47–48	Barnabas and Paul evangelize Cyprus and Asia Minor
	49	Council of Jerusalem
	49–50	Barnabas and Paul visit Philippi, Thessalonica, Berea, Athens
Fall–Spring	50–52	Paul in Corinth
July–June	51–52	Gallio proconsul in Achaia
Fall–Summer	52–55	Paul in Ephesus
Summer	55–57	Paul in Macedonia and Greece
April	57	Paul and his company set off for Jerusalem
	57–59	Paul in custody in Caesarea
February	60	Paul's two years in custody in Rome begin

Table 18. Chronology of Acts[66]

THE CHURCH'S RELATION TO ROME

Overall, Rome was protective of other religions. The emperor, as god of the Roman state, took an intermediary position between the multitude of gods, protecting their ancient rites,[67] and they in turn protected the

64. E.g., Josephus, *Ant.* 20.2.5; Pliny, *Nat.* 5:38; 18:168.
65. Suetonius, *Twelve Caesars*, 176–77.
66. Taken from Bruce, *Acts*, 1979, 43.
67. White, "Urban Development," 38.

emperor.[68] All this contributed to maintaining the *pax deorum*, the gods' peace.[69] This toleration ended when it led to civil disorder, and then the repercussions could be severe, as when Claudius expelled the Jews from Rome.[70]

The church could not escape the fact that its founder had been crucified by the Romans, but Luke's Gospel shows that his trial did not meet the standard of Roman justice. Three times Pilate declared Jesus innocent (Luke 23:4, 14, 22). The Jews of the diaspora insisted that Christianity did not have the same rights of imperial protection as their own faith. The charges against them, if carried, would have seen Christianity considered a *religio licita*. However, when accusations were bought against them by their opponents, Roman officials recognized that Christianity was not a lawless organization. Rome did not always show goodwill towards Paul and the other missionaries. However, it would admit there was no basis for the claims.

Place	Accusation	Reaction
Cyprus	None	Proconsul impressed by evangelists and their message
Philippi	"These men are Jews, and are throwing our city into an uproar by advocating customs unlawful for us Romans to accept or practice" (16:20–21).	Magistrates apologize to Paul and Silas for beating them.
Thessalonica	"They are all defying Caesar's decrees, saying that there is another king, one called Jesus" (17:7).	City officials make them post bond and leave the city.
Corinth	"'This man,' they charged, 'is persuading the people to worship God in ways contrary to the law'" (18:13).	Proconsul Gallio pronounces them innocent of any offence against Roman law.

68. Friesen, *Twice Neokoros*, 152.

69. Magyar, "Imperial Cult," 386.

70. Suetonius, *Twelve Caesars*, 176–77.

Place	Accusation	Reaction
Ephesus	"Paul has convinced and led astray large numbers of people here in Ephesus . . . also that the temple of the great goddess Artemis will be discredited; and . . . robbed of her divine majesty" (19:26–27).	Leading officials are friends of Paul. He was absolved of the charge of sacrilege.
Palestine	"We have found this man to be a troublemaker, stirring up riots among the Jews all over the world" (24:5).	Procurators Felix and Festus find him innocent of crime. King Herod finds him innocent, not deserving imprisonment.
Rome	"For two whole years Paul stayed there in his own rented house and welcomed all who came to see him" (28:30).	Paul is allowed to carry on his missionary role while under charge of the imperial guard.

Table 19. Rome's reaction to Christian mission

Worship of the emperor is not encountered directly in Acts, though we do see God's judgment on Herod when he accepted divine honors. In case the church should be tempted to be too friendly with the world, this same Rome, at times friendly and at other times neutral, would a few years later be described by John as a harlot drunk with the blood of the saints (Rev 17:6). It has been argued that Paul's later Epistles to Timothy speak of this in veiled terms.

Contacts with the East brought the idea of a divine ruler into favor with Rome. Through it, Rome was able to merge political subservience and entrenched religious practices in the areas it controlled throughout the empire. In the areas Paul travelled, the process of change had started. By the time the provincial cult where the emperors were worshiped was established in Ephesus by Domitian (emperor between AD 81 and 96), there were known to be fifty statues to the emperors in the city, many hailing them as "lord" and "savior." Caesar was starting to usurp the accepted role of Artemis.[71] Those ruled by Rome must surely have seen the inconsistency in saying that Caesar, prone to illnesses and death, was god, and the fact that he would have sacrifices made to the other gods. Yet most of the evidence links the emperor with the gods.[72]

71. Gill, *Jesus as Mediator*, 52.

72. An example is a letter to the Roman proconsul L. Mestrius Florus saying that

THE CHURCH'S RELATION TO PAGANISM

The ancient Greek Stoic philosopher Panaetius[73] suggested that "there were three kinds of gods: those of the philosophers (the natural gods), which are true; those of the poets (the mythical gods), which are false; and those of the state (the political gods), which are somewhat in the middle for they tie the others together and are to be worshiped for their value to society."[74] Olympian religion, which is the one encountered by Paul in Acts, was concerned with the preservation of the ancient ways and relationships under a proper hierarchy. Temples, games, priesthoods, sacrifices, and reverence were more important than "emotional sincerity, assent to doctrines, or divine essence."[75]

The traditional Olympian gods were finding increased competition from the gods of Persia and Egypt, sometimes fusing with existing gods and sometimes replacing them. Into the plethora of gods came the missionaries declaring that their God alone created the whole universe, challenging the accepted role of images and local gods and gods who only dealt with certain areas of life. Instead of gods who were incredibly immoral and petty, they witnessed to a single and ethical God who cared how his creation lived and who would give an account to him. Luke records three encounters:

1. *Zeus and Hermes at Lystra* (14:8–18). Paul emphasized control of nature and agriculture as a testimony to God's dominion.
2. *The unknown god of Athens* (17:16–34). Paul emphasized God's control of human affairs.[76]
3. ARTEMIS AT EPHESUS (19:23–41). Salvation is brought to the ends of the earth, not by violence but by preaching.

mysteries and sacrifices "were made to Demeter Karpophoros and Thesmophoros, and to the gods Sebastoi by the initiates in Ephesus every year." Friesen, *Twice Neokoros*, 149.

73. Panaetius (c. 185–c. 110 BC) His views mentioned here were developed by Varro (116–27 BC) in his *Divine Antiquities.* Augustine answers Varro in books 6 and 7 of his *City of God.*

74. Ferguson, *Backgrounds*, 287–88.

75. Friesen, *Twice Neokoros*, 166.

76. Johnson, *Message of Acts*, 197.

THE CHURCH'S RELATION TO THE OCCULT

The spirit world was seen to exercise influence over all aspects of life. The magician's role was to know which spirits were helpful and which were harmful and to know the operation, strengths, and authority of the spirits.[77] By knowing the right formula, power could be exerted for good, such as enhancing sexual passion or for ill through uttering a curse. Magic focuses on the manipulation of supernatural forces for the benefit of individuals or for harm. At a time when people were crushed by oppressive, grinding fate, the promise magic offered of gaining control of the unseen forces that impinged on one's life was very attractive. Yet a person seeking refuge in magic has been described as having the hunger to control their own destinies free from the need for and dependence on God's grace.[78]

In Acts, Luke provides a sampling of the gospel's confrontation with the religious and philosophical options of the Hellenistic world: magic and the occult, institutional polytheism, and worship of rulers as divine. Through his witnesses, the risen Christ extended "his arms to fugitives who have sought refuge from life's assaults in idols of wood or images of the mind."[79] In Acts we see the following:

1. *Simon, the spokesman for ancient magic.* His attempts to enfold the power of Christ into his own syncretistic system were rebuffed. He confessed that the word of Jesus was superior.
2. *Elymas, the Jewish "prophet."* He used his spoken words to manipulate the forces surrounding Sergius Paulus, "but the words of God's messengers address the conscience of the hearers, bending their will to the lordship of Jesus."[80]
3. *The slave girl who foretold the future.* The servants of Jesus rejected convenient alliances with religious systems that are lies.
4. *The Jewish exorcists.* They learned that Jesus' name brings no benefit to those who do not serve him.

77. Arnold, *Ephesian Power*, 18. For more on this subject, refer to the section "Magic in Ephesus" in Stubbersfield, *Ephesus*, 93–96.

78. Johnson, *Message of Acts*, 184.

79. Johnson, *Message of Acts*, 169.

80. Johnson, *Message of Acts*, 175.

5. *Burning of the magic scrolls.* The Ephesian believers understood that they could not maintain dual loyalties.

Every clash between the gospel and magic had to do with money, which is the opposite of Luke's attention to the free gift of the words of Jesus and its impact on people's minds and hearts (8:5, 12, 25; 13:5, 7, 12; 19:10, 20). Only they have the power to give eternal life as salvation is found in no other.

THE CHURCH'S RELATION TO DIVINE RULERS

Acts does not directly address the issue of worshiping Caesar as a god other than the principle that those who confess Jesus cannot accept any rival lord as legitimate. This was happening but had not reached its full extent in the cities Paul visited even though the mingling of religion and politics was a major factor in the ancient world. Also, the horrors of the persecution under Nero are just outside of the events that Luke recounts. Before the Roman emperors there was Nebuchadnezzar who had boasted of his glory and power, but the Lord had brought him low (Dan 4; 5:20–1), and Isaiah compared his former glory to his body covered with worms (Isa 14:11). However, Herod Agrippa did not correct the people of Tyre and Sidon when they addressed him as a god: "The Lord struck him down, and he was eaten by worms and died" (12:23). His extremely repulsive death "where God initiated the wormy decomposition . . . even before the king had expired"[81] is told in similar terms to that of two other blasphemers: Herod the Great and Antiochus Epiphanes.[82]

THE CHURCH'S RELATION TO SUFFERING

The Gospel of Luke tells of the humiliation, suffering, and execution of the author of life while his followers are spared the same fate. The Book of Acts starts with his resurrection, glorification, and ascension but the suffering continues with his followers. Luke told how Jesus foretold that his disciples would need to carry their own cross (Luke 14:27). Likewise, Paul and Barnabas told the young Christians in Asia Minor that "we must go through many hardships to enter the kingdom of God" (14:22). This

81. Johnson, *Message of Acts*, 206.

82. 2 Macc 9; Josephus, *Ant.* 17:6.5.

can be the hard truth of Christianity and a very unwelcome message, especially to our modern generation, yet for many of the first believers this did not dissuade them from following Jesus.

Suffering is presented, not as an unfortunate and unforeseen consequence but an ordained necessity and at the center of Christian life. It was necessary for the Christ to suffer as these things were written about him in the Law and the Prophets (Luke 24:26–27). His humiliation and exultation we saw as we progressed through Acts was at the very core of the Father's redemption plan. However, we also saw that, as with the master, so the servant. This same necessity continued and became a path to glory and a sign of their Father's blessing (9:16). They could endure it as it was accompanied by hope (Luke 6:22–23) and a clear conscience, knowing they are following "the pattern laid down long ago."[83] Those that suffer for Christ can expect the same welcome (7:54–60).

THE IMMEDIATE AFTERMATH OF ACTS

In a world of multiple gods, each with their own areas of responsibility, that of the emperor was the very important role of god of the Roman state and so was important in maintaining the *pax deorum*, the gods' peace.[84] If the gods were angry, it resulted in civil wars, natural disasters, and disease. Augustus was the first emperor with the title *pontifex maximus* and through this role could restore and maintain the "gods' peace" and along with that the peace and stability of the state.[85] The title given to the emperors, *divi*, represents the lowest rank of the gods, meaning the earthly rulers were not considered their equal but through their wealth, power, and status were rather viewed as alongside the gods.[86]

Christians refused to acknowledge any spiritual role to the emperor, which was considered reprehensible as this upset the fragile peace of the gods. This was seen as atheism.[87] In July of AD 64, likely only two years after the end of Acts, a great fire destroyed much of Rome, affecting ten of its fourteen areas. Nero was blamed for this even by contemporary historians (Suetonius, Pliny the Elder, and Cassius Dio). To deflect the

83. Johnson, *Message of Acts*, 217.

84. Magyar, "Imperial Cult," 386.

85. Magyar, "Imperial Cult," 391.

86. Magyar, "Imperial Cult," 386.

87. Polycarp, bishop of Smyrna (69–155), was martyred, accused of the charge of atheism. Lake, "Martyrdom of Polycarp," 3.2, 9.2.

blame, Nero accused the Christians of this, and the first persecution began. Tacitus wrote about this in his *Annals*:

> Accordingly, an arrest was first made of all who confessed; then, upon their information, an immense multitude was convicted, not so much of the crime of arson, as of hatred of the human race. Mockery of every sort was added to their deaths. Covered with the skins of beasts, they were torn by dogs and perished, or were nailed to crosses, or were doomed to the flames. These served to illuminate the night when daylight failed. Nero had thrown open his gardens for the spectacle, and was exhibiting a show in the circus, while he mingled with the people in the dress of a charioteer. Hence even for criminals who deserved extreme and exemplary punishment, there arose a feeling of compassion; for it was not, as it seemed for the public good, but to glut one man's cruelty that they were being destroyed.[88]

Sulpicius Severus[89] in his *Sacred History* continued the story from Tacitus, saying,

> In this way, cruelty first began to be manifested against the Christians. Afterwards, too, their religion was prohibited by laws which were enacted; and by edicts openly set forth it was proclaimed unlawful to be a Christian. At that time Paul and Peter were condemned to death, the former being beheaded with a sword, while Peter suffered crucifixion.[90]

88. Tacitus. *Ann.* 15.44.

89. Sulpicius Severus (c. AD 363–c. 425) was a Christian writer from Aquitania in France.

90. Severus, *Chronica.* 2:29 (*NPNF*^{2} 11:111)

Appendix 1

When Jesus gave the Great Commission, fundamental to the work of the church, he drew on the mission of the servant of the Lord in Isaiah. The connections are given in Table 19 below.

Acts 1:8	Isaiah (LXX)
"When the Holy Spirit comes upon you"	"Until the Spirit shall come upon you from on high" (32:15).
"You shall be my witnesses"	"'Be ye my witnesses, and I too am a witness,' saith the Lord God, 'and my servant whom I have chosen'" (43:10). "Ye are my witnesses, and I am the Lord God" (43:12). "Ye are witnesses if there is a God beside me" (44:8).
"To the ends of the earth"	"It is a great thing for thee to be called my servant, to establish the tribes of Jacob, and to recover the dispersion of Israel: behold, I have given thee for the covenant of a race, for a light of the Gentiles, that thou shouldest be for salvation to the end of the earth" (49:6). "Turn ye to me, and ye shall be saved, ye that come from the end of the earth: I am God, and there is none other" (45:22).

Table 20. The Great Commission in Isaiah[1]

1. Johnson, *Message of Acts*, 35–36. Septuagint translations from Brenton, *Septuagint*.

Appendix 2

Because there are similarities in Galatians to Romans and 1 Corinthians, it was assumed that it must have a similar date that was well after the Council of Jerusalem.[2] But this means three visits to Jerusalem, not the two mentioned in Galatians. Scholars conclude that either:

1. Acts 15 represents Gal 2:1–10;
2. Acts 11:30 equates to Galatians 2:1–10;
3. the matter cannot be resolved; or
4. the Council is a fabrication.

It could well be that in Galatians. Paul only counted the important visits to Jerusalem that related to the matter of salvation. Also, Luke may not have noted all the issues discussed in chapter 11 and intentionally leaves the discussion of the gentile problem until the big meeting. Yet, for Paul to feel obliged to explain his Jerusalem visits and likely his authority, too, shows that they were being used against him. So why not mention his overwhelming vindication at the Council if it had already occurred?[3] Some commentators now opt for what was the less common view—option 2 above—that Galatians was written before the Council as the one with fewer issues. The issues for 1 and 2 are tabled below:

2. Lightfoot, *Galatians*, 49.

3. Longenecker, "Acts," 9:440.

Argument against Acts 15 representing Galatians 2:1–10[4]	Argument for Acts 11:30 equating to Gal 2[5]
1. Gal 2:2 is a private meeting. 2. Conditions of Acts 15 are not mentioned. 3. How could the situation in Gal 2:11–14 of refusing table fellowship occur after the decree? 4. Gal 2 is Paul's second post-conversion visit to Jerusalem and Acts 15 is his third.	1. Paul spoke of a second visit and Acts 11 is the second visit recorded. 2. It came as the result of a revelation. 3. Both mention the material needs in Judea. 4. Gentile mission is already mentioned in Acts 11:19–26. 5. There is no mention of Peter.
Strength	
1. It allows for Galatians to be written before the Council. 2. It allows for the problem to be fermenting but not fully surfaced.	It allows for some aspects of gentile ministry to be discussed but not circumcision.
Weakness	
It can involve a fusion of Acts 15 and Acts 11 and see Paul accepting a compromise.	1. The Apostles are mentioned in Gal 2 but not Acts 11. 2. Titus is not mentioned in Acts 11. 3. The Galatians issue concerns table fellowship, not circumcision. 4. Paul and Barnabas are commended before the first missionary journey. 5. The chronology does not fit as Galatians mentions a three- and a fourteen-year period (Gal 1:18, 2:1), and the Council can be no later than AD 46.[6]

Table 21. Connection of Acts 11, 15 and Galatians 2

While having less problems, it is acknowledged that the timeline is very difficult to fit.[7] However, the dating of the crucifixion, the events in Jerusalem, and Paul's conversion are very uncertain and the fourteen years may have been reckoned from Paul's conversion. There is just sufficient time allowing for the variables.

While the inclusion of gentiles seemed to be settled in Acts 11, equating Gal 2 with Acts 11 would allow for some in the Jerusalem

4. Marshall, *Acts*, 244–45.
5. Schnabel, *Early Christian Mission*, 2:988–89.
6. Others give a later date, which does help somewhat.
7. Bock, *Acts*, 490.

church wanting to revisit the matter. It would also allow for Luke being selective and only focusing on matters that led to a resolution.[8] It also allows for some flexibility in Paul after being dogmatic in Galatians.[9] It is difficult to come to a definitive answer, e.g., Paul does not mention the decree in Galatians but neither does he mention them elsewhere when it does seem relevant (Rom 14 and 1 Cor 8–10). Rather than labor the issue, I have followed option 2 with reservation. As far as harmonizing the two books, Bock put the issue this way:

> Paul's letters and Acts cover the topic with a selectivity that makes bringing all the details together difficult, not because either played fast and free with the facts but because they made different choices and had different concerns and emphases.[10]

8. Bock, *Acts*, 490–91.
9. Bock, *Acts*, 491.
10. Bock, *Acts*, 492.

Bibliography

Aeschylus. *Agamemnon*. Pages 5–154 in vol. 2 of *Aeschylus, with an English Translation*. Translated by Herbert Weir Smyth. Loeb Classical Library. London: William Heinemann, 1930.

———. *Eumenides*. Pages 269–373 in vol. 2 of *Aeschylus, with an English Translation*. Translated by Herbert Weir Smyth. Loeb Classical Library. London: William Heinemann, 1930.

Anagnostou-Laoutides, Eva, and Michael B. Charles. "Titus and Berenice: The Elegiac Aura of an Historical Affair." *Arethusa* 48 (2015) 17–46.

Anderson, Robert. *The Silence of God*. 9th ed. London: Pickering & Inglis, n.d.

The Ante-Nicene Fathers. Edited by Alexander Roberts and James Donaldson. 1885–1887. 10 vols. Repr., Peabody, MA: Hendrickson, 1994.

Antipater of Sidon. *The Greek Anthology*. Translated by W. R. Paton. 5 vols. Loeb Classical Library. London: William Heinemann, 1943.

Aratus. "Phaenomena." In *Callimachus, Hymns and Epigrams. Lycophron. Aratus*, translated by G. R. Mair, 206–301. Loeb Classical Library. London: William Heinemann, 1921.

Aristides, P. Aelius. *Orations I–XVI*. Vol. 1 of *P. Aelius Aristides: The Complete Works*. Translated by Charles A. Behr. Leiden: E. J. Brill, 1981.

Arnold, Clinton E. *Ephesians. Power and Magic: The Concept of Power in Ephesians in Light of Its Historical Setting*. Cambridge: Cambridge University Press, 1989.

Arthur, William. *The Tongue of Fire: or The True Power of Christianity*. London: Epworth, 1956.

Augustine. *City of God*. Harmondsworth: Pelican, 1972.

Augustus. *Res Gestae Divi Augusti: Text, Translation, and Commentary*. Cambridge: Cambridge University Press, 2009.

Barclay, William. *Ambassador for Christ*. Edinburgh: Saint Andrews, 1973.

———. *The Daily Study Bible. The Acts of the Apostles*. Edinburgh: St. Andrews, 1976.

Barnett, P. W. "The Jewish Sign Prophets." *New Testament Studies* 27 (1981) 679–92.

Barrett, C. K. *The Acts of the Apostles in Two Volumes*. Edinburgh: T&T Clark, 1994.

———. *Luke the Historian in Recent Study*. London: Epsworth, 1962.

Barton, George A., and Ludwig Blau. "Nazarite." In *The Jewish Encyclopedia*, edited by Isidore Singer, 9:195–97. New York: Funk and Wagnalls, 1912.

Bauer, Walter, et al. *English Lexicon of the New Testament and Other Early Christian Literature*. 2nd ed. Chicago: Chicago University Press, 1979.

Bibliography

Bava Batra. The William Davidson Edition. Sefaria. https://www.sefaria.org/Bava_Batra?lang=bi.

Bertram, Georg. "ὠδίν." In *Theological Dictionary of the New Testament*, edited by Gerhardt Friedrich, translated by Geoffrey W. Bromiley, 9:673–74. Grand Rapids: Eerdmans, 1981.

Blaiklock, E. M. *The Acts of the Apostles: An Historical Commentary*. London: Tindale, 1959.

Bock, Darrell L. *Acts*. Grand Rapids: Baker Academic, 2007.

Brann, M. "Agrippa II." In *Jewish Encyclopedia*, edited by Isidore Singer, 1:271–72. New York: Funk and Wagnalls, 1901.

Brenk, Frederick E. "Artemis of Ephesos: An Avant Garde Goddess." *Kernos Revue Internationale et Pluridisciplinaire de Religion Grecque Antique* 11 (1998) 157–71.

Brenk, Fredrick E, and Filippo Canali De Rossi. "The 'Notorious' Felix, Procurator of Judaea, and His Many Wives (Acts 23–24)." *Biblica* 82 (2001) 410–17.

Brenton, Lancelot. *The Septuagint Version of the Old Testament with an English Translation*. London: Samuel Bagster, 1844.

Brown, Raymond. *The Gospel According to John XIII–XXI*. New York: Doubleday, 1970.

Bruce, F. F. "Acts of the Apostles." In *The International Standard Bible Encyclopedia*, edited by Geoffrey W. Bromiley, 1:33–47. Grand Rapids: Eerdmans, 1979.

———. *The Book of Acts*. London: Marshall, Morgan and Scott, 1954.

———. *The Book of Acts*. Rev. ed. Grand Rapids: Eerdmans, 1990.

———. *The Epistle to the Galatians*. Exeter: Paternoster, 1982.

———. *The Spreading Flame*. Grand Rapids: Eerdmans, 1992.

Buckley, Theodore Alois, trans. *The Canons and Decrees of the Council of Trent*. London: George Routledge, 1851. https://en.wikisource.org/wiki/Canons_and_Decrees_of_the_Council_of_Trent.

Bultmann, Rudolf. "New Testament Mythology." In *Kerygma and Myth: A Theological Debate*, edited by Hans-Werner Bartsch, translated by Reginald H. Fuller, 1–44. London: SPCK, 1972.

Caird, G. B. *The Apostolic Age*. London: Duckworth, 1962.

Campenhausen, Hans von. *Ecclesiastical Authority and Spiritual Power in the Church of the First Three Centuries*. Translated by J. A. Baker. Stanford, CA: Stanford University Press, 1969.

Capitolinus, Julius. "Avidius Cassius." Pages 213–64 in vol. 1 of *Scriptores Historiae Augustae*. Translated by David Magie. Loeb Classical Library. Cambridge: Harvard University Press, 1921.

Carter, Charles W., and Ralph Earle. *The Acts of the Apostles*. Grand Rapids: Zondervan, 1959.

Cassius Dio. *Roman History*. Translated by Earnest Cary. 9 vols. Loeb Classical Library. Cambridge: William Heinemann, 1955.

Casson, Lionel. *The Ancient Mariners: Seafarers and Sea Fighters of the Mediterranean in Ancient Times*. 2nd ed. Princeton: Princeton University Press, 1991.

———. "Speed Under Sail of Ancient Ships." *Transactions and Proceedings of the American Philological Association* 82 (1951) 136–48.

Chagigah. The William Davidson Talmud Edition. Sefaria. https://www.sefaria.org/Chagigah?tab=contents.

Chrysippus. "Fragment 1169. On the Problem of Evil." In *The New Testament Background: Selected Documents*, rev. ed., by C. K. Barrett, 68–69. San Francisco: Harper and Row, 1989.

Chrysostom, John. *The Homilies of St. John Chrysostom, Archbishop of Constantinople, on the Acts of the Apostles*. In vol. 11 of *The Nicene and Post-Nicene Fathers*, Series 1. Translated by J. Walker. Edited by Philip Schaff. 1889. 14 vols. Repr., Peabody, MA: Hendrickson, 1999.

———. *The Homilies of St. John Chrysostom, Archbishop of Constantinople, on the Gospel of St. John*. In vol. 14 of *The Nicene and Post-Nicene Fathers*, Series 1. Translated and edited by Philip Schaff. 1889. 14 vols. Repr., Peabody, MA: Hendrickson, 1999.

Cicero, M. Tullius. *The Orations of Marcus Tullius Cicero*. Translated by C. D. Yonge. London: George Bell, 1903.

———. *Tusculan Disputations*. Boston: Little, Brown, 1886.

Cleanthes. "Fragment." In *The New Testament Background: Selected Documents*. Rev. ed., by C. K. Barrett, 67–68. San Francisco: Harper and Row, 1989.

Conybeare, F. C. "The Testament of Solomon." *The Jewish Quarterly Review* 11 (1898) 1–45.

Conzelmann, Hans. *Acts of the Apostles: A Commentary on the Acts of the Apostles*. Philadelphia: Fortress, 1987.

———. "Luke's Place in the Development of Early Christianity." In *Studies in Luke-Acts*, edited by Leander E. Keck and J. Louis Martyn, 298–315. Nashville: Abingdon, 1980.

———. *The Theology of St. Luke*. New York: Harper, 1961.

Cowley, A. Joseph Jacobs, and Henry Minor Huxley. "Samaritans." In *Jewish Encyclopedia*, edited by Isidore Singer, 10:669–81. New York: Funk & Wagnalls, 1912.

Deissmann, Adolf. *Light from the Ancient East: The New Testament Illustrated by Recently Discovered Texts of the Graeco-Roman World*. New York: Harper, 1922.

DeLacy, Phillip. "Cicero's Invective against Piso." *Transactions and Proceedings of the American Philological Association* 72 (1941) 48–58.

De Vos, Craig Stephen. "Finding a Charge That Fits: The Accusation Against Paul and Silas at Philippi (Acts 16.19–21)." *Journal for the Study of the New Testament* 21 (1999) 51–63.

Dibelius, Martin. *Studies in the Acts of the Apostles*. Mifflintown: Sigler, 1999.

Dick, John. *Lectures on the Acts of the Apostles*. 2nd ed. New York: Robert Carter and Brothers, 1850.

Dio Chrysostom. *Dio Chrysostom*. Translated by H. Lamar Crosby. 5 vols. Loeb Classical Library. Cambridge: Harvard University Press, 1946.

Dix, Gregory. *Jew and Greek: A Study in the Primitive Church*. Westminster: Dacre, 1953.

Dodd, C. H. *The Apostolic Preaching and its Developments*. New York: Harper and Brothers, 1944.

Donald, Guthrie. *The Pastoral Epistles*. Grand Rapids: Eerdmans, 1957.

Du Plessis, Johannes. *The Life of Andrew Murray of South Africa*. London: Marshall Brothers, 1930.

Durand Marion, et al. "Stoicism." Stanford Encyclopedia of Philosophy, Jan. 2023. https://plato.stanford.edu/entries/stoicism/.

Bibliography

Edersheim, Alfred. *Life and Times of Christ the Messiah*. Grand Rapids: Eerdmans, 1977.

Edwards, James R. "Parallels and Patterns Between Luke and Acts." *Bulletin for Biblical Research* 27 (2017) 485–501.

Elwell, Walter A. *Encountering the New Testament: A Historical and Theological Survey.* Grand Rapids: Baker, 1998.

Epictetus. *Discourses and Selected Writings*. Translated by Robert Dobbin. London: Penguin, 2008.

Eskenazi, Tamara Cohn, and Tikva Frymer-Kensky. *Ruth*. Philadelphia: Jewish Publication Society, 2011.

Euripides. *Bacchae of Euripides*. Cambridge: Cambridge University Press, 1892.

———. *The Electra*. Translated by Gilbert Murray. New York: Oxford University Press, 1907.

Eusebius. *Church History*. In vol. 1 of *The Nicene and Post-Nicene Fathers*, Series 2. Translated by Arthur Cushman McGiffert. Edited by Philip Schaff and Henry Wace. 1890. 14 vols. Repr., Peabody, MA: Hendrickson, 1999.

Fant, Clyde E., and Mitchell G. Reddish. *A Guide to Biblical Sites in Greece and Turkey.* Qxford: Oxford University Press, 2003.

Fee, Gordon D. *Corinthians, A Study Guide*. Brussels: International Correspondence Institute, 1979.

———. *God's Empowering Presence*. Peabody: Hendrickson, 1994.

Ferguson, Everett. *Backgrounds of Early Christianity.* Grand Rapids: Eerdmans, 1987.

Fernando, Ajith. *Acts*. Grand Rapids: Zondervan, 1998.

Fitzmyer, Joseph A. *The Acts of the Apostles: A New Translation with Introduction and Commentary.* New York: Doubleday, 1998.

Fleetwood, John. *The Life of Our Blessed Lord and Savior Jesus Christ: And the Lives and Sufferings of His Holy Apostles and Evangelists*. Galesburg: William Garretson, 1874.

Frank, Tenney. *Rome and Italy of the Empire*. Vol. 5 of *An Economic Survey of Ancient Rome*. Baltimore: Johns Hopkins University Press, 1940.

Freeman, D. "Pentecost." In *The New Bible Dictionary*, edited by J. D. Douglas, 936–37. London: Inter-Varsity, 1962.

Freisen, Steven J. "Asiarchs." *Zietschrift fur Papyrologie und Epigraphik* 126 (1999) 275–90.

———. *Twice Neokoros: Ephesus, Asia and the Cult of the Flavian Imperial Policy.* Leiden: Brill, 1993.

Gapp, Kenneth S. "The Universal Famine Under Claudius." *The Harvard Theological Review* 28 (1935) 258–65.

Gill, Malcolm. *Jesus as Mediator.* Oxford: Peter Lang, 2008.

Gooding, David. *True to the Faith*. London: Hodder and Stoughton, 1990.

Gibbon, Edward. *The History of the Decline and Fall of the Roman Empire*. Vol. 2. London: Strahan and Cadell, 1781.

Graves, Robert. *The Greek Myths*. London: Folio, 1998.

Griffith, M. *The Example of Jesus*. London: Hodder and Stoughton, 1985.

Haenchen, Ernst. *The Acts of the Apostles* . Oxford: Blackwell, 1971.

Harnack, Adolf von. *The Date of the Acts and the Synoptic Gospels*. New York: G. P. Putnam's Sons, 1911.

———. "The Sect of the Nicolaitans and Nicolaus the Deacon in Jerusalem." *The Journal of Religion* 3 (1923) 413–22.

Hawnchen, Ernst. "The Book of Acts as Source Material for the History of Early Christianity." In *Studies in Luke-Acts*, edited by Leander E. Keck, 258–78. Philadelphia: Fortress, 1980.

Hendrickson, William. *1 & 2 Thessalonians, 1 & 2 Timothy, and Titus*. New Testament Commentaries. Edinburgh: Banner of Truth, 1983.

Hermer, Colin J. *The Book of Acts in the Setting of Hellenistic History*. Winona Lake: Eisenbrauns, 2016.

Horace. *Horace: The Epistles*. Edited by F. G. Plaistowe. London: W. B. Clive, 1983.

Hunt, Stan. *The Assemblies of God, Queensland Conference*. Brisbane: Assembly, n.d.

Hunter, S. F. "Bar-Jesus." In *The International Standard Bible Encyclopedia*, edited by Geoffrey W. Bromiley, 1:431. Grand Rapids: Eerdmans 1979.

Isocrates. "Areopaguiticus." Pages 100–59 in vol. 2 of *Isocrates*. Translated by George Norlin. Loeb Classical Library. Cambridge: Harvard University Press, 1980.

Jacobs, Joseph, and Emil G. Hirsch. "Proselyte." In *Jewish Encyclopedia*, edited by Isidore Singer, 10:220–24. New York: Funk and Wagnalls, 1907.

Jastrow, Marcus, and Henry Malter. "Begging and Beggars." In *Jewish Encyclopedia*, edited by Isidore Singer, 2:639–40. New York: Funk and Wagnalls, 1902.

Jipp, Joshua W. "Paul's Aeropgus Speech of Acts 17:16–34 as Both Critique and Propaganda." *Journal of Biblical Literature* 131 (2012) 567–88.

Johnson, Dennis E. *The Message of Acts in the History of Redemption*. Phillipsburg: P&R, 1997.

Johnson, L. T. *The Acts of the Apostles*. Collegeville: Liturgical, 1992.

Josephus, Flavius. *Complete Works*. Translated by William Whiston. London: Pickering and Inglis, 1960.

———. *The Life of Flavius Josephus*. In *Complete Works*, translated by William Whiston, 1–27. London: Pickering and Inglis, 1960.

Juvenal. "Satires." In *Juvenal and Persius*, translated by Susanna M. Braune, 128–512. Loeb Classical Library. Cambridge: Harvard University Press, 2004.

Keil, Carl Friedrich, and Franz Delitzsch. "Joel." In *Biblical Commentary on the Old Testament*, 6:169–232. Edinburg: T&T Clark, 1884.

Kendall, R. T. *Once Saved Always Saved*. London: Hodder, 1983.

Kennedy, Daniel. "Sacraments." In *The Catholic Encyclopedia*. New York: Robert Appleton, 1912. http://www.newadvent.org/cathen/13295a.htm.

Kohler, Kaufmann. "Pharisees." In *Jewish Encyclopedia*, edited by Isidore Singer, 9:661–66. New York: Funk and Wagnalls, 1912.

———. "Sadducees." In *Jewish Encyclopedia*, edited by Isidore Singer, 10:630–33. London: Funk and Wagnalls, 1905.

Laertius, Diogenes. "Epimenides." In *Lives of Eminent Philosophers*, translated by R. D. Hicks, 109–11. London: W. Heinemann, 1925.

Lake, Kirsopp, trans. "The Martyrdom of Polycarp." Pages 307–45 in vol. 2 of *The Apostolic Fathers*. Loeb Classical Library. London: Heinemann, 1913.

Larkin, William J. *Acts*. Downers Grove, IL: InterVarsity, 1995.

Latham, Robert Gordon. "Daphne." In *Dictionary of Greek and Roman Geography*, 731–32. Boston: Little and Brown, 1854.

Lee, Edgar R. "Baptism in the Holy Spirit and the Book of Acts." *Enrichment* (2010). https://enrichmentjournal.ag.org/Issues/2010/Spring-2010/Baptism-in-the-Holy-Spirit-and-the-Book-of-Acts.

Lenski, R. C. H. *Acts.* Minneapolis: Arzburg, 1961.

Lightfoot, Joseph Barber. *St. Paul's Epistle to the Galatians.* Andover: W. F. Draper, 1870.

Lloyd-Jones, D. Martin. *Romans (The Sons of God).* Edinbrough: Banner of Truth, 1975.

Longenecker, Richard N. "The Acts of the Apostles." In *The Expositors Bible Commentary*, edited by Frank E. Gaebelein, 9:207–573. Grand Rapids: Zondervan, 1981.

Lucian. "Anacharsis." Pages 1–70 in vol. 4 of *Lucian of Samosata.* Translated by A. M. Harmon. Loeb Classical Library. London: Heinemann, 1961.

———. "How to Write History." Pages 1–74 in vol. 6 of *Lucian.* Translated by K. Kilburn. Loeb Classical Library. Cambridge: William Heinemann, 1959.

———. "The Ship: or The Wishes." In *The Works of Lucian of Samosata*, translated by H. W. Fowler and G. F. Fowler, 4:32–51. London: Clarendon, 1905.

Lucretius, Titus. *On the Nature of Things.* New York: Barnes & Noble, 2005.

Luther, Martin. "Instructions to the Perplexed and Doubting, to George Spenlein, April 8, 1516." In *Luther: Letters of Spiritual Counsel*, translated by Theodore G. Tappert, 109–38. Vancouver: Regent College, 2003.

Maddox, Robert. *The Purpose of Luke–Acts.* Edinburgh: T&T Clark, 1985.

Magar, Z. "Imperial Cult and Christianity: How and to What Extent Were the Imperial Cult and Emperor Worship Thought to Preserve Stability in The Roman World." *Acta Archaeologica Academiae Scientiarum Hung* 60 (2009) 385–95.

Marcello, Fabrizio. "Artemis' Garments and Paul's Aprons (Acts 19:11–12)." *Novum Testamentum* 66 (2024) 321–36.

Marshall, I. Howard. *Acts.* Leicester: Inter-Varsity, 1980.

———. *The Acts of the Apostles, An Introduction and Commentary.* Leicester: Inter-varsity, 1987.

———. *A Fresh Look at the Acts of the Apostles.* Homebush West: Lancer, 1992.

———. "Luke and His 'Gospel.'" In *The Gospel and the Gospels*, edited by Peter Stuhlmacher, 273–92. Grand Rapids: Eerdmans, 1991.

McDonald, L. M. "Ephesus." In *Dictionary of New Testament Background*, edited by Craig A. Evans and Stanley E. Porter, 318–21. Downers Grove, IL: Intervarsity. 2000.

McGee, Zane B. "Transitioning Authority and Paul's Farewell Address: Examining the Narrative Function of Acts 20." *Stone-Campbell Journal* 20 (2017) 203–14.

Megillah. The William Davidson Edition. Sefaria. https://www.sefaria.org/Megillah?tab=contents.

Merrill, Eugene H. "Paul's Use of 'About 450 Years' in Acts 13:20." *Bibliotheca Sacra* 138 (1981) 246–57.

Midrash Tehillim. Sefaria. https://www.sefaria.org/Midrash_Tehillim.146.3?lang=bi.

Miralles, Antonio. "A New Response of the Congregation for the Doctrine of the Faith on the Validity of Baptism." https://www.vatican.va/roman_curia/congregations/cfaith/documents/rc_con_cfaith_doc_20080201_validity-baptism-miralles_en.html.

Mishna Ketubot. Sefaria. https://www.sefaria.org/Mishnah_Ketubot?tab=contents.

Mishnah Makkot. Sefaria. https://www.sefaria.org/Mishnah_Makkot?tab=contents.

Mishnah Nazir. Sefaria. https://www.sefaria.org/Mishnah_Nazir?tab=contents.

Mishnah Nedarim. Sefaria. https://www.sefaria.org/Mishnah_Nedarim?tab=contents.

Mishnah Ohalot. Sefaria. https://www.sefaria.org/English_Explanation_of_Mishnah_Oholot?tab=contents.

Mishnah Pirkei Avot. Sefaria. https://www.sefaria.org/Pirkei_Avot?tab=contents.

Mishnah Sanhedrin. Sefaria. https://www.sefaria.org/Mishnah_Sanhedrin?tab=contents.

Mishnah Torah. Sefaria. https://www.sefaria.org/texts/Halakhah/Mishneh%20Torah.

Monier, Mina. "Reading Luke in Rome: The Temple and Pietas." *Studia Patristica* 99 (2018) 115–38.

Moulton, James H., and George Milligan. *The Vocabulary of the Greek Testament Illustrated from the Papyri and Other Non-Literary Sources*. London: Hodder and Stoughton, 1929.

Mounce, William D. *Pastoral Epistles*. Nashville: Thomas Nelson, 2000.

Oakes, Peter. *Reading Romans in Pompei*. Minneapolis: Fortress, 2013.

Oliver, Isaac W. "Simon Peter Meets Simon the Tanner: The Ritual Insignificance of Tanning in Ancient Judaism." *New Testament Studies* 59 (2013) 50–60.

Ovid. *Metamorphoses*. Translated by Brookes More. Boston: Cornhill, 1922.

Pausanias. *Description of Greece*. Translated by J. G. Frazer. 6 vols. New York: Biblo and Tannen, 1965.

Pesachim. The William Davidson Edition. Sefaria. https://www.sefaria.org/Pesachim?tab=contents.

Petersen, Paul B. "Saying Farewell: Paul's Last Word to the Elders in Acts 20:18-35." *Spes Christiana* 33 (2022) 47–66.

Petronius. "Satyricon." In *Petronius, Seneca, Satyricon, Apocolocyntosis*, translated by Michael Heseltine and W. H. D. Rouse, 1–384. Loeb Classical Library. London: William Heinemann, 1913.

Philo. *On the Account of the World's Creation Given by Moses*. Vol. 1 of *Philo*. Translated by G. H. Whitaker et al. Loeb Classical Library. Cambridge: Harvard University Press, 1929.

———. *On the Decalogue (De Decalogo)*. Pages 3–97 in vol. 7 of *Philo*. Translated by F. H. Colson. Loeb Classical Library. Bury St. Edmond: St. Edmondsbury, 1937.

———. *On the Embassy to Gaius*. Vol. 10 of *Philo*. Translated by F. H. Colson. Loeb Classical Library. Cambridge: Harvard University Press, 1962.

———. "Flaccus." Pages 295–406 in vol. 9 of *Philo*. Translated by F. H. Colson. Loeb Classical Library. Cambridge: Harvard University Press, 1985.

———. "The Special Laws." Pages 7–157 in vol. 8 of *Philo*. Translated by F. H. Colson. Loeb Classical Library. Cambridge: Harvard University Press, 1999.

Plato. "Apology." Pages 17–42 in vol. 1 of *Plato*. Translated by Harold North Fowler. Loeb Classical Library. Cambridge: Harvard University Press, 1966.

Pliny the Elder. *The Elder Pliny on the Human Animal*. Natural History Book 7. Oxford: Oxford University Press, 2005.

———. *The Natural History*. Translated by John Bostock and H. T. Riley. London: Bell, 1893.

Pliny the Younger. *Letters*. London: Heinemann, 1915.

Plumber, W. S. *Psalms*. Edinburgh: Banner of Truth, 1975.

Plutarch. *Plutarch's Moralia*. Translated by Harold North Fowler. Loeb Classical Library. Cambridge: Harvard University Press 1927.

Polhill, John P. *Acts: An Exegetical and Theological Exposition of Holy Scripture*. Nashville: Broadman, 1992.

Polybius. *The Histories*. Translated by W. R. Paton. Loeb Classical Library. Cambridge: Harvard University Press, 1922.

Rackham, Richard Belward. *The Acts of the Apostles: A Exposition*. London: Methuen, 1919.

Ramm, Bernard. *Protestant Biblical Interpretation: A Textbook of Hermeneutics*. Grand Rapids: Baker, 1982.

Ramsay, William M. *The Bearing of Recent Discovery on the Trustworthiness of the New Testament*. Aberdeen: Aberdeen University Press, 1900.

———. *The Cities of St. Paul*. New York: A. C. Armstrong and Son, 1908.

———. *St. Paul: The Traveler and Roman Citizen*. Grand Rapids: Kregel, 1939.

Razafiarivony, Davidson. "Exclusion of the Blind and Lame from the Temple and the Indignation of the Religious Leaders in Matt 21:12–15." *The Journal of Biblical Theology* 19 (2018) 93–113.

Rendal, Harris J. "The Cretians Always Liars." *The Expositor* 7 (1906) 305–17.

Rengstorf, Karl H. "ἀπόστελλω." In *Theological Dictionary of the New Testament*, edited by Gerhard Kittel, translated by Geoffrey W. Bromiley, 1:398–447. Grand Rapids: Eerdmans, 1981.

Renwick, A. M. "Roman Empire and Christianity." In *The International Standard Bible Encyclopedia*, edited by Geoffrey W. Bromiley, 4:207–221. Grand Rapids: Eerdmans, 1988.

Rocca, Samuele. "From Human Freedom to Divine Intervention: Agrippa II's Address on the Eve of the Jewish War." In *The Future of Rome: Roman, Greek, Jewish and Christian Visions*, edited by Jonathan Price and Katell Berthelot, 130–54. Cambridge: Cambridge University Press, 2020.

Roloff, Jurgen. *Die Apostelgeschichte*. Gottingen: Vandenhoeck and Ruprecht, 1981.

Roman Catholic Church. *The Roman Martyrology*. Baltimore: John Murphey, 1916.

Rosivach, Vincent J. "Autochthony and the Athenians." *The Classical Quarterly* 37 (1987) 294–306.

Rubarth, Scott. "Stoic Philosophy of Mind." Internet Encyclopedia of Philosophy. https://iep.utm.edu/stoicmind/#SH2c.

Schnabel, Eckhard J. *Paul and the Early Church*. Vol. 2 of *Early Christian Mission*. Downers Grove, IL: InterVarsity, 2004.

Schneider, Carl. "ῥαβδίζω." In *Theological Dictionary of the New Testament*, edited by Gerhard Kittel, translated by Geoffrey W. Bromily, 6:970–71. Grand Rapids: Eerdmans, 1968.

Scott, S. P. *The Civil Law, Including the Twelve Tables, the Institutes of Gaius, the Rules of Ulpian, the Opinions of Paulus, the Enactments of Justinian, and the Constitutions of Leo*. Cincinnati: Central Trust, 1932.

Seneca the Younger. *Letters from a Stoic*. London: Penguin, 1969.

———. *Natural Questions*. Translated by Harry M. Hine. Chicago: University of Chicago Press, 2010.

Severus, Sulpitius. *The Sacred History Of Sulpitius Severus*. In vol. 11 of *The Nicene and Post-Nicene Fathers*, Series 2. Translated by Alexander Roberts. Edited by Philip Schaff. 1894. 14 vols. Repr., Peabody, MA: Hendrickson, 1994.

Shaw, George Bernard. *Preface to Androcles and the Lion: On the Prospects of Christianity*. Project Gutenberg, Dec. 10, 2012. https://www.gutenberg.org/files/4004/4004-h/4004-h.htm.

Sherwin-White, A. N. *Roman Society and Roman Law in the New Testament.* Eugene, OR: Wipf and Stock, 2004.

Shulam, Joseph, with Hillary Le Cornu. *A Commentary on the Jewish Roots of Romans.* Baltimore: Messianic Jewish, 1997.

Smith, James. *The Voyage and Shipwreck of St. Paul.* 4th ed. London: Longmans, Green, 1880.

Sota. The William Davidson Edition. Sefaria. https://www.sefaria.org/Sotah?tab=contents.

Speidel, Michael P. "The Roman Army in Judaea Under The Procurators: The Italian and the Augustan Cohort in the Acts of the Apostles." *Ancient Society* 13/14 (1982/1983) 233–40.

Stott, John R. W. *The Message of Acts: To the Ends of the Earth.* Leicester: InterVarsity, 1991.

Strabo. *The Geography of Strabo. Literally Translated, with Notes, in Three Volumes.* London: George Bell and Sons, 1903.

Strelan, Richard. "Paul's 'Aprons' Again." *The Journal of Theological Studies* 54 (2003) 154–57.

———. "Recognizing the Gods." *New Testament Studies* 46 (2000) 488–503.

Stubbersfield, Edgar. *Introduction to the Pastoral Epistles.* Gatton: Rachel Stubbersfield, 2013.

———. *Ephesus: The Nursery of Christianity.* Eugene, OR: Wipf & Stock, 2022.

Suetonius, Gius. *The Twelve Caesars.* Translated by Robert Graves. London: Cassell, 1962.

Tacitus, Cornelius. "The Annals." In *The Complete Works of Tacitus,* translated by Alfred John Church and William Jackson Brodribb, 3–418. New York: Random House, 1942.

Thucydides. *The History of the Peloponnesian War.* Translated by M. L. Finley. Hammondsworth: Penguin, 1978.

Trebilco, Paul R. "Paul and Silas—'Servants of the Most High God' (Acts 16:16–18)." *Journal for the Study of the New Testament* 36 (1989) 51–73.

Troftgruben, Troy M. "The Ending of Luke Revisited." *Journal of Biblical Literature* 140 (2021) 235–346.

Vegetius, Flavius Renatus. *Epitome of Military Science.* Liverpool: Liverpool University Press, 1996.

Vermes, Geza. *The Complete Dead Sea Scrolls In English.* Rev. ed. London: Penguin, 2004.

———. "The Dead Sea Scrolls." In *Interpreters Dictionary of the Bible,* edited by Thomas K. Kepler and George Arthur Buttrick, S:210–19. Nashville: Abingdon, 1976.

White, L. Michael. "Urban Development and Social Change in Imperial Ephesos." In *Ephesos, Metropolis of Asia: An Interdisciplinary Approach to Its Archaeology, Religion, and Culture,* edited by Helmut Koester, 27–80. Harvard Theological Studies. Valley Forge, PA: Trinity, 1995.

Wilkins, Michael J. *Matthew.* NIV Life Application Commentary. Grand Rapids: Zondervan, 2004.

Williams, David John. *Acts.* Peabody: Hendrickson, 1990.

Wilson, R. McL., trans. "The Acts of Paul and Thecla." In *Anthology of Ancient Greek Popular Literature,* edited by William Hansen, 55–63. Bloomington: Indiana University Press, 1998.

Winter, Bruce W. "Gallio's Ruling on the Legal Status of Early Christianity (Acts 18:14–15)." *Tindale Bulletin* 50 (1999) 213–23.

———. "Rehabilitating Gallio and His Judgement in Acts 18:14–15." *Tindale Bulletin* 57 (2006) 291–308.

Witetschek, Stephan. "Artemis and Asiarchs." *Biblica* 90 (2009) 334–55.

Witherington, Ben, III. *The Acts of the Apostles: A Socio-Rhetorical Commentary.* Grand Rapids: Eerdmans, 1998.

Wood, G. O. *Acts, A Study Guide.* Brussels: International Correspondence Institute, 1980.

Yamauchi, Edwin M. *Pre-Christian Gnosticism.* 2nd ed. Grand Rapids: Baker, 1983.

Zabehlicky, Heinrich. "Preliminary Views of the Ephesian Harbor." In *Ephesos, Metropolis of Asia: An Interdisciplinary Approach to Its Archaeology, Religion, and Culture*, edited by Helmut Koester, 201–16. Harvard Theological Studies. Valley Forge, PA: Trinity, 1995.

www.ingramcontent.com/pod-product-compliance
Lightning Source LLC
LaVergne TN
LVHW020529100826
845148LV00010B/1395
9781666783889